Gaylord Watson

Handbook of the United States of America and guide to emigration

Gaylord Watson

Handbook of the United States of America and guide to emigration

ISBN/EAN: 9783337184940

Printed in Europe, USA, Canada, Australia, Japan

Cover: Foto ©Lupo / pixelio.de

More available books at **www.hansebooks.com**

HANDBOOK

OF THE

UNITED STATES OF AMERICA,

AND

GUIDE TO EMIGRATION;

GIVING THE LATEST AND MOST COMPLETE STATISTICS

OF

THE GOVERNMENT, ARMY, NAVY, DIPLOMATIC RELATIONS, FINANCE, REVENUE, TARIFF, LAND SALES, HOMESTEAD AND NATURALIZATION LAWS, DEBT, POPULATION OF THE UNITED STATES, AND EACH STATE AND CONSIDERABLE CITY, AGRICULTURAL CONDITION, AREA FOR CULTIVATION, FOREIGN COINS AND THEIR VALUE, FOREIGN AND DOMESTIC POSTAGES AND LABOR TABLES, EDUCATION AND RAILWAYS, ETC., ETC.,

FURNISHING ALL THE NECESSARY INFORMATION CONCERNING THE COUNTRY,

FOR

THE SETTLER, THE BUSINESS MAN,
THE MERCHANT, THE FARMER, THE IMPORTER & THE PROFESSIONAL MAN.

COPYRIGHTED, 1879.

NEW YORK:
GAYLORD WATSON, PUBLISHER, 61 BEEKMAN STREET.
1881.

CONTENTS.

THE GENERAL GOVERNMENT.

THE PRINCIPAL DEPARTMENTS, OFFICERS OF THE CABINET, THE ARMY AND NAVY, AND THEIR SUBORDINATES—DIPLOMATIC RELATIONS—OUR MINISTERS AND CONSULS TO FOREIGN COUNTRIES, AND THEIRS TO THIS COUNTRY.

UNITED STATES GOVERNMENT.

PRESIDENT.

RUTHERFORD B. HAYES, of Ohio. Term expires March 4, 1881.

The President is chosen by Electors, who are elected by the People, each State having as many as it has Senators and Representatives in Congress. He holds office four years; is Commander-in-Chief of the Army and Navy of the United States; has power to grant pardons and reprieves for offenses against the United States; makes treaties, by and with the advice and consent of the Senate; nominates, and, with the consent of the Senate, appoints, all Cabinet, Diplomatic, Judicial and Executive officers; has power to convene Congress, or the Senate only; communicates with Congress by message at every session; receives all Foreign Ministers; takes care that the laws are faithfully executed, and the public business transacted. Salary $50,000 a year.

VICE-PRESIDENT.

WILLIAM A. WHEELER, of New York. Term expires March 4, 1881.

Is chosen by the Electors at the same time, and in the same manner as the President; is President of the Senate, and has the casting vote therein. In case of the death, resignation, disability or removal of the President, his powers and duties devolve upon the Vice-President for the residue of his term. In cases of vacancy, where the Vice-President succeeds to the Presidential office, the President of the Senate becomes *ex-officio* Vice-President. Salary $10,000 a year.

THE STATE DEPARTMENT.

Preserves the public archives, records, laws, documents and treaties, and supervises their publication; conducts all business and correspondence arising out of Foreign Relations; makes out and records passports, commissions, etc.

Department Officers.

	Salary.
Secretary of State—WM. M. EVARTS, of New York	$8,000
Assistant Secretary—Fred. W. Seward, of New York	3,500
Second Assistant Secretary—Wm. Hunter, of Rhode Island	3,500
Third " " —Charles Payson, of Mass.	3,500

COUNTRY.	NAMES.	OFFICE.	FOREIGN RESID'NCE	SALARY
Great Britain	James Russell Lowell	Minister	London	$17,500
do	Wm. J. Hoppin	Secretary Legation	do	2,625
do	Ehrman S. Nadal	2d Sec. Legation	do	2,000
do	Adam Badeau	Consul General	do	6,000
do	Stephen B. Packard	Consul	Liverpool	6,000
do	S. F. Cooper	do	Glasgow	3,000
do	Lewis Richmond	do	Belfast	2,500
East Indies	A. C. Litchfield	Consul-General	Calcutta	5,000
Australia	Oliver M. Spencer	Consul	Melbourne	4,500
Canada	John Q. Smith	Consul-General	Montreal	4,000
Russia	John W. Foster	Minister	St. Petersburg	17,500
do		Secretary Legation	do	2,625
do	Wm. H. Edwards	Consul-General	do	2,000
do	S. P. Young	Consul	Moscow	3,000
do	L. E. Dyer	Consul	Odessa	2,000
do	A. Wilkins	Consul	Cronstadt	2,000
France	Edward F. Noyes	Minister	Paris	17,500
do	R. R. Hitt	Secretary Legation	do	2,625
do	Henry Vignaud	Asst. Secretary	do	2,000
do		Consul-General	do	6,000
do	John A. Bridgeland	Consul	Havre	3,000
do	John B. Gould	do	Marseilles	2,500
Spain	Lucius Fairchild	Minister	Madrid	12,000
do	Dwight T. Reed	Secretary Legation	do	1,800
do	Alfred N. Duffie	Consul	Cadiz	1,500
Cuba	Henry C. Hall	Consul-General	Havana	6,000
Portugal	Benjamin Moran	Charge d'Affairs	Lisbon	5,000
do	Henry W. Diman	Consul	do	2,000
do	William Stuve	Consular Agent	Oporto	2,000
Belgium	Wm. Cassius Goodloe	Minister Resident	Brussels	7,500
do	John Wilson	Consul	do	2,500
do	James R. Weaver	do	Antwerp	2,500
Netherlands	James Birney	Minister Resident	The Hague	7,500
do	John F. Winter	Consul	Rotterdam	2,000
do	David Eckstein	do	Amsterdam	1,500
Denmark	M. J. Cramer	Charge d'Affairs	Copenhagen	5,000
do	Henry B. Ryder	Consul	do	1,500
Sweden & Norway	John L. Stevens	Minister Resident	Stockholm	7,500
do do	E. L. Oppenheim	Consul	Gottenburg	1,500
Germany	Andrew D. White	Minister	Berlin	17,500
do	H. Sidney Everett	Secretary Legation	do	2,625
do	Chapman Coleman	Asst. Secretary	do	2,000
do	H. Kreismann	Consul General	do	4,000
do	Alfred E. Lee	Consul-General	Frankfort	3,000
Saxony	John H. Steuart	do	Leipsic	2,000
Bremen	Wilson King	do	Bremen	2,500
Hamburg	John M. Wilson	do	Hamburg	2,500
Bavaria	G. Henry Horstman	do	Munich	1,500
Wurtemburg	Jos. S. Potter	do	Stuttgart	1,500
Baden	Edward M. Smith	do	Manheim	1,500
Austria-Hungary	John A. Kasson	Minister	Vienna	12,000
do	John F. Delaplaine	Secretary Legation	do	1,800
do	James Riley Weaver	Consul-General	do	3,000
do	A. W. Thayer	do	Trieste	2,000
Switzerland	Nicholas Fish	Charge d'Affairs	Berne	5,000
do	John A. Campbell	Consul	Basle	2,000
do	J. E. Montgomery	do	Geneva	1,500
Italy	George P. Marsh	Minister	Rome	12,000
do	George W. Wurtz	Secretary Legation	do	1,800
do	Eugene Schuyler	Consul-General	do	3,000
do	John F. Hazleton	Consul	Genoa	1,500
do	B. Odell Duncan	do	Naples	1,500
Turkey	J. B. Longstreet	Minister Resident	Constantinople	7,500
do	G. Harris Heap	Sec. Leg. & C. Gen'l.	do	3,000
do	A. A. Gargullio	Interpreter	do	3,000
do	Frank S. DeHaas	Consul	Jerusalem	1,500
Egypt	John T. Edgar	Consul	Beirut	2,000
do	Elbert E. Farnam	Agent & Con.-Gen'l	Cairo	4,000
Greece	J. Meredith Read	Charge d'Affairs	Athens	5,000
Barbary States	F. A. Matthews	Consul	Tangier	3,000
Liberia	John H. Smyth	Min. & Consul-Gen.	Monrovia	4,000
Muscat	Wm. H. Hathorne	Consul	Zanzibar	1,200
Madagascar	William W. Robinson	Consul	Tamatave	2,000
Japan	John A. Bingham	Minister	Yeddo	12,000
do	Durham W. Stevens	Secretary Legation	do	2,500
do	David Thompson	Interpreter	do	2,500
do	I. H. Haws	Consul	Hakodadi	2,500
do	T. B. Van Buren	Consul-General	Kanagawa	4,000
do	W. P. Mangum	do	Nagasaki	3,000
do	N. J. Newitter	do	Osaka	3,000
Siam	David B. Sickles	do	Bangkok	3,000
China	George F. Seward	Minister Resident	Peking	12,000
do	Chester Holcombe	Secretary Legation	do	5,000
do	Owen N. Denny	Consul-General	Shanghai	5,000
do	Joseph J. Henderson	Consul	Amoy	3,500
do	Charles P. Lincoln	do	Canton	3,500
do	Wm. A. Conahe	do	Chi Foo	3,500
do	J. C. S. Colby	do	Chin Kieng	3,500
do	M. M. Delano	do	Foo Choo	3,500
do	R. M. Johnston	do	Han Kow	3,500
do	E. C. Lord	do	Ning Po	3,500
do	E. T. Sheppard	do	Tien Tsin	3,500
Hawaiian Islands	James M. Comly	Minister	Honolulu	7,500
do do	James Scott	Consul	do	4,000
Hayti	John M. Langston	Minister Res. & C. G.	Port au Prince	7,500
San Domingo	Paul Jones	Consul	St. Domingo	1,500
Mexico	Philip H. Morgan	Minister	Mexico	12,000
do	Daniel S. Richardson	Secretary Legation	do	1,800
do	Augustus J. Cassard	Consul	Tampico	1,500
do	David H. Strother	Consul-General	Mexico	2,000
do	Warner P. Sutton	Consul	Matamoras	2,000
do	S. T. Trowbridge	Consul	Vera Cruz	3,000
Cen. Am. States	Cornelius A. Logan	Minister	Guatemala	7,500

COUNTRY.	NAME.	OFFICE.	FOREIGN RESID'NCE	SALARY
Guatemala.........	T. Francis Medina..................	Consul	Guatemala.......	.....
Colombia...........	Ernest Dichman..................	Minister Resident...	Bogota	7,500
do	James Thorington................	Com. Agent...........	Aspinwall.........	3,000
Venezuela...........	John Baker.........................	Minister...............	Caracas..........	7,500
do	James C. Eckert..................	Consul	Laguayra.........	1,500
Ecuador..............	Phanor M. Eder..................	do	Guayaquil........	1,200
Brazil................	Henry W. Hilliard.................	Minister...............	Rio de Janeiro...	12,000
do	John C. White....................	Secretary Legation..	do do	1,800
do	Thomas Adamson..................	Consul General......	do do	6,000
do	Joseph W. Stryker................	....	Pernambuco......	2,000
Argentine Conf.....	Thomas O. Osborn...............	Minister...............	Buenos Ayres....	7,500
do do	Edward L. Baker..................	Consul..................	do do	3,000
Paraguay & Uru'y.	John C. Caldwell..................	Charge do Affaires..	Montevideo, Ur'y.	5,000
do	Frederick Crocker	Consul..................	do do	2,000
Chili..................	Thomas A. Osborn...............	Minister...............	Santiago..........	10,000
do	Vacant.............................	Consul..................	Valparaiso........	3,000
Peru..................	Isaac P. Christiancy.............	Minister...............	Lima...............	10,000
do	Robert T. Clayton.................	Consul..................	Callao............	3,000
Bolivia..............	S. Newton Pettis..................	Minister & Con. Gen.	La Paz............	5,000
Costa Rica..........	Arthur Morrell	Consul................	San Jose.........	3,000
Friendly Islands...	Thomas M. Dawson...............	do	Apia	3,000
Honduras....	George A. K. Morris.............	do	Amapala	3,000
Salvador	Clarence O. Ford.................	do	La Union.........	2,500
Society Islands	Dorrance Atwater.................	do	Tahiti	3,000

FOREIGN LEGATIONS IN THE UNITED STATES.

COUNTRY.	NAME.	RANK.
ARGENTINE REPUBLIC.	Senor Don Manuel R. Garcia	E. E. and M. P.
"	Senor Don Julio Perrie	Sec. of Leg., Ch. d'Aff. *ad int.*
"	Senor Don Episanio Portela..................	Attache.
AUSTRIA-HUNGARY.....	Vacant..................	E. E. and M. P.
"	Chevalier Ernest von Tavera..................	Sec. of Leg., Ch. d'Aff. *ad int.*
"	Mr. E. B uhdorn..................	2d Sec. of Legation.
BELGIUM	Mr. Maurice Delfosse..................	E. E. and M. P.
"	Mr. Leon Von den Bossche..................	Councillor of Legation.
BRAZIL..............	Councillor A. P. de Carvalho Borges..................	E. E. and M. P.
"	Mr. Benjamin Franklin Torreao de Barros..................	Secretary of Legation.
"	Mr. Joaquin Nabuco..................	Attache.
"	Captain Arthur Silveira da Motta..................	Naval Attache.
CHILI..............	Senor Don Ignacio Zenteno..................	E. E. and M. P.
"	Senor Don E. V. Zanartu..................	Attache.
CHINA	Chen Lan Pin..................	E. E. and M. P.
"	Mr. Yung Wing..................	Assistant E. E. and M. P.
"	Yung Tsang Siang..................	Secretary of Legation.
"	David W. Bartlett..................	Secretary of Legation.
COLOMBIA..............	Senor Doctor Santiago Perez..................	Minister Resident.
"	Senor Roberto R. de Narvaez..................	Secretary of Legation.
"	Don G. Espinosa..................	Attache.
COSTA RICA..............	Senor Don Manuel M. Peralta..................	Minister Resident.
DENMARK..............	Herr Bille..................	Minister Resident.
FRANCE..............	Mr. Max Outrey	E. E. and M. P.
"	Mr. Millon de la Vertville..................	Secretary of Legation.
"	Mr. François de Corcella..................	Secretary of Legation.
"	M. le Capitaine Anfrye..................	Military Attache.
"	Mr. Paul DeJardin..................	Consul Chancellor.
GERMANY..............	Mr. Kurt von Schlozer..................	E. E. and M. P.
"	Baron Max von Thielmann..................	Secretary of Legation.
"	Mr. P. W. Buddecke..................	Chancellor of Legation.
GREAT BRITAIN..............	The Right Hon. Sir Edward Thornton, K. C. B..................	E. E. and M. P.
"	Victor Arthur Wellington Drummond, Esq..................	Secretary of Legation.
"	Rear Admiral William Gore Jones, R. N..................	Naval Attache.
"	Hon. Power H. le Poer Trench	Second Secretary.
"	Mr. Frank C. Lascelles..................	Second Secretary.
"	Mr. Francis C. E. Denys..................	Third Secretary.
"	Charles Fox Frederick Adam, Esq..................	Attache.
GUATEMALA, SALVADOR & HONDURAS..	Senor Don Vicente Dardon..................	E. E. and M. P.
"	Senor Don J. Saborio..................	Secretary of Legation.
HAWAII..............	Mr. Elisha H. Allen..................	E. E. and M. P.
HAYTI..............	Mr. Stephen Preston..................	Minister Resident.
"	Mr. Charles A. Preston..................	Secretary of Legation.
ITALY..............	Baron Albert Blanc..................	E. E. and M. P.
"	Count B. Litta	Secretary of Legation.
JAPAN..............	Jushie Yoshida Kiyonari..................	E. E. and M. P.
"	Shorokiu Yoshida Djiro..................	Secretary of Legation.
"	Mr. Asada Yasunori..................	Attache.
"	Mr. Seinoske Tashiro..................	Attache.
MEXICO	Senor Don Manuel M. de Zamacona..................	E. E. and M. P.
"	Senor Don Jose Y. de Cuellar..................	Secretary of Legation.
"	Senor Don Cayetano Romero..................	Second Secretary.
NETHERLANDS..............	Mr. de Pestel..................	Minister Resident.
NICARAGUA..............	Senor Doctor Don Adam Cardenas..................	E. E. and M. P.
"	Senor Don Joaquin Elizondo..................	Secretary of Legation.
PARAGUAY..............	Dr. Benjamin Aceval	E. E. and M. P.
"	Senor Don Jose S. Decond..................	Secretary of Legation.

Foreign Legations in the United States—Continued.

COUNTRY.	NAME.	RANK.
PERU	Vacant	E. E. and M. P.
"	Senor Don Ernesto Aservi	Secretary of Legation.
"	Don Eduardo Villena	Secretary of Legation.
PORTUGAL	Viscount das Nogueiras	E. E. and M. P.
RUSSIA	Mr. Nicholas Shishkin	E. E. and M. P.
"	Mr. Gregoire de Willamov	First Secretary.
"	Mr. George Bakhmeteff	Second Secretary.
SPAIN	Vacant	E. E. and M. P.
"	Senor Don Jose Brunetti	1st Sec. & Ch. d'Aff. *ad int.*
"	Senor Don Francisco Soliveres	Second Secretary.
"	Senor Don Jose de Soto	Second Secretary.
"	Senor Don Luis Polo de Bernabe	Third Secretary.
"	Senor Don Carlos Erenchum	Attache.
"	Senor Don Tomas de Rueda	Attache.
"	Senor Col. Don Teodoro Bermudez	Military Attache.
"	Com. Senor Don Juan Montajo	Naval Attache.
SWEDEN AND NORWAY	Count Carl Leweuhaupt	E. E. and M. P.
"	Mr. C. de Bildt	Secretary of Legation.
TURKEY	Gregoire Aristarchi Bey	E. E. and M. P.
"	Baltazzi Effendi	Secretary of Legation.
VENEZUELA	Senor Don Juan B. Dalla Costa	E. E. and M. P.
"	Senor Don Andres S. Ibarra	Secretary of Legation.

THE TREASURY DEPARTMENT

Receives and has charge of all moneys paid into the United States Treasury, has general supervision of the fiscal transactions of the Government, the collection of revenue, the auditing and payment of accounts, and other disbursements; supervises the execution of the laws relating to Commerce and Navigation of the United States, the Revenues and Currency, the Coast Survey, the Mint and Coinage, the Light-House Establishment, the construction of Marine Hospitals, Custom-Houses, &c. The First Comptroller prescribes the mode of keeping and rendering accounts for the civil and diplomatic service, and the public land. To him the First, Fifth, and Sixth Auditors report. The Second Comptroller prescribes the mode of keeping and rendering accounts for the Army, Navy, and Indian Departments, and to him the Second, Third, and Fourth Auditors report. The First Auditor adjusts the accounts of the customs, revenue, civil service and private acts of Congress. The Second Auditor adjusts accounts relating to pay, clothing and recruiting of the army, the arsenals, armories and ordnance, and the Indian Department. The Third Auditor adjusts accounts for army subsistence, fortifications, military academy and roads, quartermaster's department and military claims. The Fourth Auditor adjusts the navy accounts, the Fifth diplomatic, and the Sixth postal affairs.

Department Officers.

	Salaries.
Secretary of the Treasury—JOHN SHERMAN, of Ohio	$8,000
Assistant Secretary—John B. Hawley, of Illinois	4,500
" —Henry F. French, of Massachusetts	4,500
Supervising Architect—James G. Hill, of Massachusetts	4,500
Treasurer of United States—James Gilfillan, of Connecticut	6,000

Department Officers—Continued.

	Salary.
Assistant Treasurer of United States—Albert U. Wynan, of Nebraska.......	3,600
Solicitor—Kenneth Rayner, of Mississippi..........................	3,000
Superintendent of Life Saving Station—Sumner I. Kimball, of Maine......	4,000
Superintendent Coast Survey—C. P. Patterson, of California..............	6,000
Cashier—J. W. Whelpley, of New York.........................	4,500
Director of the Mint—A. L. Snowden, of Pennsylvania..................	4,500
Register of the Treasury—Glenni W. Scofield, of Pennsylvania...........	4,000
Comptroller of the Currency—John J. Knox, of New York................	5,000
Commissioner of Internal Revenue—Green B. Raum, of Illinois..........	6,000
Bureau of Statistics—Joseph Nimmo, Jr., of New York................	2,400
Bureau of Engraving and Printing—O. H. Irish, of Nebraska...........	4,500
First Comptroller—Albert G. Porter, of Indiana..........................	5,000
Second Comptroller—William W. Upton, of New Hampshire..............	5,000
Commissioner of Customs—Henry C. Johnson, of Pennsylvania............	4,000
1st Auditor—Robert M. Reynolds, of Alabama.........................	3,600
2d Auditor—Ezra B. French, of Maine............................	3,600
3d Auditor—Horace Austin, of Maine............................	3,600
4th Auditor—Stephen J. W. Tabor, of Iowa.........................	3,600
5th Auditor—Jacob H. Ela, of New Hampshire.........................	3,600
6th Auditor—J. M. McGrew, of Ohio..............................	3,600

THE WAR DEPARTMENT

Has charge of business growing out of military affairs, keeps the records of the army, issues commissions, directs the movement of troops, superintends their payment, stores, clothing, arms and equipments and ordnance, constructs fortifications, and conducts works of military engineering, and river and harbor improvements.

Department Officers.

	Salary
Secretary of War—Alexander Ramsey, of Minnesota	$8,000
Chief Clerk--H. T. Crosby, of Pennsylvania........................	2,500
Inspector General—Brevet Major General Randolph B. Marcy, of Mass....	
Judge Advocate General—Colonel Joseph McKee Dunn, of Indiana........	
Adjutant General—Brevet Major General E. D. Townsend, of D. C.......	
Quarter Master General—Brevet Major General M. C. Meigs, of Penn......	
Commissary General—Brigadier General Robert Macfeely, of Penn........	
Surgeon General—Brevet Major General Joseph K. Barnes, of Penn........	
Paymaster General—Brevet Brigadier General Benjamin Alvord, of Vt....	
Chief of Bureau of Engineers—Brevet Major Gen. A. A. Humphreys, of D. C.	
Chief of Ordnance Bureau—Brigadier General S. V. Benet, of Florida......	
Signal Officer—Brevet-Major General Albert J. Myer, of New York.........	

General Officers of Regular Army.

NAME AND RANK.	ENTRY INTO SERVICE.	APPOINTED FROM.
General.		
Wm. T. Sherman.....	July 1, 1840	Ohio
Lieutenant-General.		
Philip H. Sheridan...	July 1, 1853	Ohio
Major-Generals.		
Winfield S. Hancock.	July 1, 1844	Penna.
John M. Schofield....	July 1, 1837	California.
Irwin McDowell.....	July 1, 1838	Ohio.
Brigadier-Generals.		
Oliver O. Howard.....	July 1, 1854	Maine.
Alfred H. Terry......	Jan. 15, 1865	Conn.
Edward O. C. Ord....	July 1, 1839	Maryland.
Christopher C. Augur	July 1, 1843	New York.
George Crook........	July 1, 185[illegible]	Ohio.
John Pope...........	July 1, 1842	Illinois.
Retired List.		
Major-Generals.		
Joseph Hooker.......	July 1, 1837	California.
S. P. Heintzelman....	July 1, 1826	Penna.
Thomas J. Wood.....	July 1, 1845	Kentucky.
John C. Robinson....	Oct. 27, 1839	New York.
Daniel E. Sickles.....	Nov. 29, 1862	New York.
Samuel S. Carroll....	July 1, 1856	Dist. Col.
Richard W. Johnson.	July 1, 1849	Kentucky.
James B. Ricketts...	July 1, 1839	New York
Eli Long.............	Jun. 27, 1856	Kentucky.

Military Geographical Divisions and Departments.

1. *Division of the Missouri.*—Departments of Dakota, of the Missouri, of the Platte, and of Texas; headquarters at Chicago, Illinois.
2. *Division of the Atlantic.*—The New England States, the States of New York, New Jersey, Pennsylvania, Delaware, Maryland, Virginia, West Virginia, Ohio, Michigan, Wisconsin, Indiana, and the District of Columbia; headquarters at New York City.
3. *Division of the Pacific.*—Departments of California, of the Columbia, and of Arizona; headquarters at San Francisco, California.
4. *Division of the South.*—Departments of the South and of the Gulf; headquarters at Louisville, Kentucky.
5. *Department of the Missouri.*—The States of Missouri, Kansas and Illinois, and the Territories of Colorado and New Mexico, and Camp Supply, Indian Territory; headquarters at Fort Leavenworth, Kansas.
6. *Department of the Platte.*—The States of Iowa and Nebraska, and the Territories of Utah and Wyoming; headquarters at Omaha, Nebraska.
7. *Department of Dakota.*—The State of Minnesota, and the Territories of Dakota and Montana; headquarters at St. Paul, Minnesota.
8. *Department of California.*—The State of Nevada, the post of Fort Hall, Idaho Territory, and so much of the State of California as lies north of a line from the north-west corner of Arizona Territory to Point Conception, California; headquarters at San Francisco, California.
9. *Department of the Columbia.*—The State of Oregon, and the Territories of Washington, Idaho, excepting Fort Hall, and Alaska; headquarters at Portland, Oregon.
10. *Department of Arizona.* —The Territory of Arizona, and so much of the State of California as lies south of a line from the north-west corner of Arizona Territory to Point Conception, California; headquarters at Prescott, Arizona Territory.
11. *Department of the South.*—The States of North Carolina, South Carolina, Georgia, Florida, (except the Gulf posts from Pensacola Harbor to Fort Jefferson and Key West, inclusive), Alabama, including the posts in Mobile Bay, Tennessee and Kentucky; headquarters at Louisville, Kentucky.
12. *Department of Texas.*—The State of Texas and the Indian Territory, excepting Camp Supply; headquarters at San Antonio, Texas.
13. *Department of the Gulf.*—The States of Louisiana, Arkansas and Mississippi, and the Gulf posts as far eastward as, and embracing, Fort Jefferson and Key West, Florida, excluding the posts in Mobile Bay; headquarters at New Orleans, Louisiana.

THE NAVY DEPARTMENT

Has charge of the Naval Establishment and all business connected therewith, issues Naval Commissions, instructions and orders, supervises the enlistment and discharge of seamen, the Marine Corps, the construction of Navy Yards and Docks, the construction and equipment of Vessels, the purchase of provisions, stores, clothing and ordnance, the conduct of surveys and hydrographical operations.

Department Officers.

	Salary.
Secretary of the Navy—RICHARD W. THOMPSON, of Indiana................	8,000
Chief Clerk—John W. Hogg, of District of Columbia....................	2,500
Superintendent of Naval Observatory—Rear-Admiral John Rodgers........	
Hydrographic Office—Captain S. R. Franklin...........................	
Superintendent National Almanac—Prof. Simon Newcomb.................	
Commander of Marine Corps—Colonel C. G. McCawley....................	
Chief Signal Officer—Commodore John C. Beaumont......................	
Chief of Bureau of Yards and Docks—Commodore R. L. Law.............	
Civil Engineer—W. P. S. Sanger	
Chief of Navy Bureau—Commodore W. D. Whiting.........................	
Chief of Bureau of Ordnance—Commodore Wm. M. Jeffers...............	
Chief of Bureau of Provisions and Clothing—P. M. General G. F. Cutter..	
Chief of Bureau of Medicine and Surgery—Surgeon-Gen. J. W. Taylor....	
Chief of Bureau of Construction and Repairs—Naval Constructor J. W. Easby	
Chief of Bureau of Equipment and Recruiting—Commodore Earl English..	
Chief of Bureau of Steam Engineering—Chief Engineer W. H. Shock.....	

Officers of the Navy.

NAME AND RANK.	STATE FROM.	ENTRY INTO SERVICE.
Admiral.		
David D. Porter......	Penn.....	Feb. 2, 1829
Vice-Admiral.		
Stephen C. Rowan....	Ohio......	Feb. 1, 1826
Rear-Admirals. Active List.		
John Rodgers.........	Maryland	April 18, 1828
Wm. E. Le Roy.......	New York	Jan. 11, 1832
J. R. M. Mullany.....	New York	Jan. 7, 1835
C. R. P. Rodgers.....	N. Jersey	Oct. 5, 1833
Stephen D. Trenchard	Penn.....	Oct. 23, 1834
Thos. H. Patterson...	Louisiana	April 5, 1836
John C. Howell......	Penn.....	June 5, 1836
Edward T. Nichols...	Georgia..	Dec. 14, 1836
Robert H. Wyman...	N. H.....	March 11, 1837
George B. Balch......	Alabama.	Dec. 30, 1837
Commodores. Active List.		
Thomas H. Stevens..	Conn.....	Dec. 14, 1836
Foxhall A. Parker....	Virginia..	March 11, 1837
John M. B. Clitz......	Michigan	April 12, 1837
Andrew Bryson......	New York	Dec. 1, 1837
Donald McN. Fairfax.	N. C......	Aug. 12, 1837
James H. Spotts.....	Kentucky	Aug. 2, 1837
J. W. A. Nicholson...	New York	Feb. 10, 1838
G. H. Cooper.........	New York	Aug. 4, 1837
J. C. Beaumont......	Penn.....	March 1, 1839
J. C. Febiger.........	Ohio.....	Sept. 4, 1838
Pierce Crosby........	Penn.....	June 5, 1838
J. B. Creighton......	New York	Feb. 10, 1838
A. K. Hughes........	New York	Oct. 20, 1838
C. R. Calhoun.......	Missouri.	April 1, 1839
Chas. H. Baldwin....	New York	April 24, 1839
R. W. Shufeldt.......	New York	May 11, 1839
A. C. Rhind..........	New York	Sept. 3, 1838
F. M. Ransom.......	New York	July 25, 1839
W. E. Hopkins.......	Vermont.	Nov. 13, 1839
Thomas Patterson...	New York	March 2, 1839
Wm. N. Jeffers......	N. Jersey	Sept. 25, 1840
Edward Simpson.....	New York	Feb. 11, 1840
Wm. G. Temple......	Vermont.	April 18, 1840
Samuel B Carter.....	Tenn	Feb. 14, 1840

THE DEPARTMENT OF THE INTERIOR

Has charge of the survey, management, sales and grants of Public Lands, the examination of Pension and Bounty Land claims, the management of Indian affairs, the examination of Inventions and award of Patents, the collection of Statistics, the distribution of Seeds, Plants, etc., the taking of Censuses, the management of Government mines, the erection of Public Buildings, and the construction of wagon roads to the Pacific.

Department Officers.

	Salary.
Secretary of the Interior—CARL SCHURZ, of Missouri......................	$8,000
Assistant Secretary—Charles F. Gorham, of Mich	3,500
General Land Office—James A. Williamson, of Iowa, Commissioner........	4,000
Indian Office—Ezra A. Hayt, of New York, Commissioner..................	4,500
Pension Office—John A. Bentley, of Wisconsin, "	3,600
Patent Office—Halbert E. Paine, " "	4,500
Bureau of Education—John Eaton, of Tenn., "	3,000
Census Office—Francis A. Walker, Conn., Superintendent	

THE POST OFFICE DEPARTMENT

Has charge of the Postal System, the establishment and discontinuance of Post Offices, appointment of Postmasters, the contracts for carrying the mails, the Dead Letter Office, maintains an inspection to prevent frauds, mail depredations, etc.

Department Officers.

	Salary.
Postmaster-General—HORACE MAYNARD, of Tennessee	$8,000
Appointment Office—1st Assistant P. M. General, Jas. M. Tyner, Ind	3,500
Contract Office—2d Assistant P. M. General, Thomas A. Brady, Indiana	3,500
Finance Office—3d Assistant P. M. General, Abraham D. Hazen, Penn	3,500
Superintendent of Money Order System—C. F. McDonald, of Mass	3,000
Superintendent of Foreign Mails—J. H. Blackfan, of New Jersey	3,000
Superintendent of Free Delivery—R. W. Gurley, of Louisiana	3,000
Superintendent of Dead Letter Office—E. J. Dallas, of Kansas	3,000
General Superintendent R. R. Mail Service—W. B. Thompson, of Ohio	3,000
Auditor Railroad Accounts—Theophilus French	2,000
Superintendent of Bank Agency—Dudley W. Rhodes, of Ohio	3,000
Topographer—W. F. Nicholson, of D. C	

DEPARTMENT OF JUSTICE.

The Attorney-General, who is the head of this department, is the legal adviser of the President and heads of departments, examines titles, applications for pardons, and judicial and legal appointments, conducts and argues suits in which Government is concerned, etc.

Department Officers.

	Salary.
Attorney-General—CHARLES DEVENS, of Mass	$8,000
Assistant Attorney-General—Edwin B. Smith, of Maine	5,000
do do Thomas Simons, of New York	5,000
Solicitor-General—Samuel F. Phillips, of North Carolina	7,000
Assistant Att'y-General for Department of Interior—E. M. Marble, of Mich	5,000
do do P. O. Department—Alfred A. Freeman, of Tenn	4,000
Solicitor of Internal Revenue—C. Chesley, of New Hampshire	4,500
Solicitor of the Treasury—Kenneth Raynor, of N. Carolina	4,500
Assistant Solicitor of Treasury—Joseph H. Robinson	3,000
Examiner of Claims for State Department—H. O'Connor, of Iowa	3,500
Law Clerk and Examiner of Titles—A. J. Bentley, of Ohio	2,700
Chief Clerk—George C. Wing, of Ohio	2,200

THE JUDICIARY.

Supreme Court of the United States.

Appointed.			Age.	Salary.
1874.	MORRISON R. WAITE, of Ohio	*Chief Justice.*	63	$10,500
1880.	Geo. F. Edmunds, of Vermont	*Asso. Jus.*	68	10,000
1858.	Nathan Clifford, Portland, Maine,	do	75	10,000
1862.	Noah H. Swayne, Columbus, Ohio,	do	74	10,000
1862.	Samuel F. Miller, Keokuk, Iowa,	do	63	10,000
1863.	Stephen J. Field, California,	do	62	10,000
1870.	Joseph P. Bradley, New Jersey,	do	66	10,000
1870.	William Strong, Pennsylvania,	do	70	10,000
1877.	John M. Harlan, Kentucky	do	64	10,000

The Court holds one general term, annually, at Washington, D. C., commencing on the first Monday in December.

	Salary.
D. Wesley Middleton, of Washington, Clerk	
William T. Otto, of Washington, D. C., Reporter	
John G. Nicolay, of Illinois, Marshal	

Circuit Judges of the United States.

	Salary.
FIRST CIRCUIT.—(Maine, New Hampshire, Massachusetts and Rhode Island)—John Lowell, of Boston, Mass	$6,000
SECOND CIRCUIT.—(Vermont, Connecticut, Northern New York, Southern New York, and Eastern New York)—Samuel Blatchford, New York	6,000
THIRD CIRCUIT.—(New Jersey, Eastern Pennsylvania, Western Pennsylvania, Delaware)—William McKennen, of Pennsylvania	6,000
FOURTH CIRCUIT.—(Maryland, West Virginia, Virginia, North Carolina and South Carolina)—Hugh L. Bond, Maryland	6,000
FIFTH CIRCUIT.—(Georgia, Florida, Alabama, Mississippi, Louisiana, Texas, Colorado, Missouri, and Nebraska)—Wm. B. Woods, of Alabama	6,000
SIXTH CIRCUIT.—(Ohio, Michigan, Kentucky and Tennesee)—John Baxter, of Tennessee	6,000
SEVENTH CIRCUIT.—(Indiana, Illinois and Wisconsin)—Thomas Drummond, of Illinois	6,000
EIGHTH CIRCUIT.—(Minnesota, Iowa, Missouri, Kansas and Arkansas)—Geo. W. McCrary, of Iowa	6,000
NINTH CIRCUIT.—(California, Oregon and Nevada)—Lorenzo Sawyer, of California	6,000

District Courts.—Judges. (States.)

ALABAMA, N. D., M. D. and S. D.—John Bruce, of Montgomery, Ala. ARKANSAS, W. D.—I. C. Parker, of Fort Smith, Ark.; E. D., H. C. Caldwell, of Little Rock, Ark. CALIFORNIA—Ogden Hoffman, of San Francisco. COLORADO—Moses Hallett of Denver. CONNECTICUT—Nathaniel Shipman, of Hartford. DELAWARE—Edward G. Bradford, of Wilmington. FLORIDA, N. D.—Thomas Settle, of Jacksonville; S. D., James W. Locke, of Key West. GEORGIA, N. D. and S. D.—John Erskine, of Atlanta. ILLINOIS, N. D.—Henry W. Blodgett; S. D., Samuel H. Treat, Jr. INDIANA—Walter Q. Gresham. IOWA—James M. Love. KANSAS—Cassius G. Foster. KENTUCKY—W. H. Hays. LOUISIANA—Edward C. Billings. MAINE—Edw. Fox. MARYLAND—Thos. J. Morris. MASSACHSUETTS—T. L. Nelson. MICHIGAN, E. D.—H. B. Brown; W. D., S. L. Withey. MINNESOTA—R. R. Nelson. MISSISSIPPI, N. D. and S. D.—Robert A. Hill. MISSOURI, E. D.—Samuel Treat; W. D., Arnold Krekel. NEBRASKA—Elmer S. Dundy. NEVADA—Edgar W. Hillyer. NEW HAMPSHIRE—Daniel Clark. NEW JERSEY—John T. Nixon. NEW YORK, N. D.—W. J. Wallace; S. D., W. G. Choate; E. D., Charles L. Benedict. NORTH CAROLINA, E D.—George W. Brooks; W. D., Robert P. Dick. OHIO, N. D.—Martin Welker; S. D., Philip B. Swing. OREGON—Matthew P. Deady. PENNSYLVANIA, E. D.—Wm. Butler; W. D., W. W. Ketcham. RHODE ISLAND—John P. Knowles. SOUTH CAROLINA—George S. Bryan. TENNESSEE, E. D. and M. D.—Conally F. Trigg; W. D., E. S. Hammond. TEXAS, E. D.—Amos Morrill; W. D., T. H. Duval. VERMONT—Hoyt H. Wheeler. VIRGINIA, E. D.—Robert W. Hughes; W. D., Alexander Rives. WEST VIRGINIA—John J. Jackson. WISCONSIN, E. D.—Charles E. Dyer; W. D., Romanza Bunn. Of these District Judges, two (Cal. and Col.) receive $5,000 each; one (La.), $4,500; nine (Md., Mass., N. J., N. Y. 3, Penn. 2, and W. D. Ohio), $4,000 each; all the remainder $3,500 each.

District Courts.—Judges. (Territories).

ARIZONA—C. G. W. French. DAKOTA—Peter C. Shannon. IDAHO—John T. Morgan. MONTANA—D. S. Wade. NEW MEXICO—L. Bradford Prince. UTAH—

John A. Hunter. WASHINGTON—Roger S. Green. WYOMING—James B. Sauer. DISTRICT OF COLUMBIA—David K. Cartter, Chief Justice, $4,500. Alexander B. Hagner, Walter S. Cox, Charles P. James, Andrew Wiley, Arthur B. McArthur, Associates, $4,000 each.

Court of Claims.

	Salary.
C. D. Drake, Missouri, Chief Justice	$4,500
J. C. Bancroft Davis, New York	4,500
Wm. H. Hunt, Louisiana	4,500
Charles C. Nott, New York	4,500
William A. Richardson	4,500
Archibald Hopkins, Clerk	3,000
John Randolph, Assistant Clerk	2,000

DEPARTMENT OF AGRICULTURE.

	Salary.
Commissioner of Agriculture—WM. G. LE DUC, of Minnesota	$3,000
Chief Clerk—E. A. Carman, of New Jersey	1,800
Statistician—C. Worthington, of Maryland	2,000
Entomologist—J. W. Potter	2,000
Chemist—Peter Cottier, of Vermont	2,000
Superintendent of Botanical Gardens—Wm. Saunders, of Pennsylvania	
Superintendent of Seed Room—A. Glass, of Dist. of Columbia	
Botanist—G. Vasey, of Illinois	
Librarian—E. H. Stevens, of Louisiana	
Disbursing Clerk—B. F. Fuller, of Illinois	

GOVERNMENT PRINTING OFFICE.

	Salary.
Congressional Printer—J. D. DEFREES, of Indiana	3,600
Chief Clerk—A. F. Childs, of Dist. Columbia	

DEPARTMENT OF EDUCATION.

	Salary.
Commissioner of Education—Gen. JOHN EATON, Jr., of Tenn	$3,000
Chief Clerk—Charles Warren	1,800
Translator—Herman Jacobson	

UNITED STATES MINT AND BRANCHES.

			Salary.
A. Landon Snowden,	Superintendent	Philadelphia	
Thomas C. Acton,	do	New York	
Henry L. Dodge,	do	San Francisco, Cal	
Henry S. Foote,	do	New Orleans, La	
James Crawford,	do	Carson City, Nev	
Calvin J. Cowles,	Assayer	Charlotte, N.C	
Herman Silver,	do	Denver, Col	
Wm. Penn Prescott,	do	Carson City, Nev	
Albert Walters,	do	Boise City, Idaho	
Charles Rumley,	do	Helena, Montana	
Benjamin F. Flanders,	Treasurer,	New Orleans, La	

THE LEGISLATIVE BRANCH OF THE GOVERNMENT.

THE National Legislature consists of a Senate of two members from each State, making the full Senate now consist of seventy-six members, and a House of Representatives, now having two hundred and ninety-three members. The Senators are chosen by the Legislatures of their several States, for a term of six years, either by concurrent vote or by joint ballot, as the State may prescribe. The members of the House of Representatives are usually elected by a plurality vote in districts of each State, whose bounds are prescribed by the Legislature, for the term of two years. In a few instances they have been elected at large: *i. e.*, by the plurality vote of the entire State.

The Constitution requires nine years' citizenship to qualify for admission to the Senate, and seven years to the House of Representatives. An act approved July 26, 1866, requires the Legislature of each State which shall be chosen next preceding the expiration of any Senatorial term, on the second Tuesday after its first meeting, to elect a successor, each House nominating *viva voce*, and then convening in Joint Assembly to compare nominations. In case of agreement, such person shall be declared duly elected; and if they do not agree, then balloting to continue from day to day at 12 M. during the session until choice has been made. Vacancies are to be filled in like manner. The members of each House receive a salary of $5,000 per annum, and actual mileage at twenty cents per mile. For each day's absence, except when caused by sickness, $8 per diem is deducted from the salary. The Speaker of the House of Representatives receives $10,000.

CONGRESSIONAL DISTRICTS.

The House of Representatives of the United States is composed of members elected by Districts. The number apportioned to the States has varied at each decennial census, as shown by the following Table:

Census.	When Apportioned.	Whole No. Rep.	Ratio, One to
	By Constitution	65	——
1790	April 14, 1792	105	33,000
1800	Jan. 14, 1803	141	33,000
1810	Dec. 21, 1811	181	35,000
1820	March 7, 1822	212	40,000
1830	May 22, 1832	240	46,700
1840	June 25, 1842	223	70,680
1850	July 30, 1852	233	93,423
1860	April —, 1861	242	127,000
1870	Dec. — 1871	281	142,000

By adding members for fractions of the ratio, and the admission of Colorado, the number of Representatives has been brought up to 293.

Presidents under the Federal Constitution.

Names.	Inaugurated.	Born.	Age at Inauguration.	Years in office.	Died.	Age at Death
1. George Washington, of Virginia	April 30, 1789	1732	57	8	Dec. 14, 1799	68
2. John Adams, of Massachusetts	Mar. 4—1797	1735	62	4	July 4—1826	91
3. Thomas Jefferson, of Virginia	Mar. 4—1801	1743	58	8	July 4—1826	83
4. James Madison, of Virginia	Mar. 4—1809	1751	58	8	June 28, 1836	85
5. James Monroe, of Virginia	Mar. 4—1817	1759	58	8	July 4—1831	73
6. John Quincy Adams, of Mass.	Mar. 4—1825	1767	58	4	Feb. 23, 1848	80
7. Andrew Jackson, of Tennessee	Mar. 4—1829	1767	62	8	June 8—1845	78
8. Martin Van Buren, of New York	Mar. 4—1837	1782	55	4	July 24, 1862	79
9. William Henry Harrison, of Ohio	Mar. 4—1841	1773	68	—	April 4, 1841	68
10. John Tyler, of Virginia, *Vice-President*, succeeded President Harrison, who died April 4, 1841	Apr. 4—1841	1790	57	4	Jan. 17, 1862	72
11. James K. Polk, of Tennessee	Mar. 4—1845	1795	49	4	June 15, 1849	54
12. Zachary Taylor, of Louisiana	Mar. 4—1849	1784	65	1	July 9—1850	66
13. Millard Fillmore, of N. Y., *Vice-President*, succeeded Pres. Taylor, who died July 9, 1850	July 9—1850	1800	50	3	Mar. 8—1874	74
14. Franklin Pierce, of N. Hampshire	Mar. 4—1853	1804	49	4	Oct. 8—1869	65
15. James Buchanan, of Pennsylvania	Mar. 4—1857	1791	65	4	June 1—1869	77
16. Abraham Lincoln, of Illinois	Mar. 4—1861	1809	52	4	April 15, 1865	56
17. Andrew Johnson, *Vice-President*, succeeded President Lincoln, who was assassinated April 14, 1865	Apr. 15-1865	1808	57	4	July 31, 1875	67
18. Ulysses S. Grant, of Illinois	Mar. 4—1869	1822	47	8		
19. Rutherford B. Hayes, of Ohio	Mar. 4—1877	1822	55			

Vice-Presidents.

Names.	Inaugurated.	Born.	Died.
1. John Adams, of Massachusetts	1789	1735	1826
2. Thomas Jefferson, of Virginia	1797	1743	1826
3. Aaron Burr, of New York	1801	1756	1836
4. George Clinton, of New York	1805	1739	1812
5. Elbridge Gerry, of Massachusetts	1813	1744	1814
6. Daniel D. Tompkins, of New York	1817	1744	1825
7. John C. Calhoun, of South Carolina	1825	1782	1850
8. Martin Van Buren, of New York	1833	1782	1862
9. Richard M. Johnson, of Kentucky	1837	1780	1850
10. John Tyler, of Virginia	1841	1790	1862
11. George M. Dallas, of Pennsylvania	1845	1792	1865
12. Millard Fillmore, of New York	1849	1800	1874
13. William R. King, of Alabama	1853	1786	1853
14. John C. Breckenridge, of Kentucky	1857	1821	1875
15. Hannibal Hamlin, of Maine	1861	1809	
16. Andrew Johnson, of Tennessee	1865	1808	1875
17. Schuyler Colfax, of Indiana	1869	1823	
18. Henry Wilson, of Massachusetts	1873	1812	1875
19. William A. Wheeler, of New York	1877		

Chief Justices of the Supreme Court of the United States.

Name.	State.	Term of Service.	Born.	Died.
John Jay	New York	1789—1795	1745	1829
John Rutledge	South Carolina	1795—1795	1739	1800
Oliver Ellsworth	Connecticut	1796—1801	1752	1807
John Marshall	Virginia	1801—1836	1755	1836
Roger B. Taney	Maryland	1836—1864	1777	1864
Salmon P. Chase	Ohio	1864—1873	1808	1873
Morrison R. Waite	Ohio	1874—....	1815	....

Associate Justices of the Supreme Court of the United States.

Name.	State.	Term of Service.	Born.	Died.
John Rutledge	South Carolina	1789—1791	1739	1800
William Cushing	Massachusetts	1789—1810	1733	1810
James Wilson	Pennsylvania	1789—1798	1742	1798
John Blair	Virginia	1789—1796	1732	1800
Robert H. Harrison	Maryland	1789—1789	1745	1790
James Iredell	North Carolina	1790—1799	1750	1799
Thomas Johnson	Maryland	1791—1793	1732	1819
William Patterson	New Jersey	1793—1806	1743	1806

Associate Justices of the Supreme Court of the U. S. (Continued.)

Name.	State.	Term of Service.	Born.	Died.
Samuel Chase	Maryland	1796—1811	1741	1811
Bushrod Washington	Virginia	1798—1829	1759	1829
Alfred Moore	North Carolina	1799—1804	1755	1810
William Johnston	South Carolina	1804—1834	1771	1834
Brockholst Livingston	New York	1806—1823	1757	1823
Thomas Todd	Kentucky	1807—1826	1765	1826
Joseph Story	Massachusetts	1811—1845	1779	1845
Gabriel Duval	Maryland	1811—1835	1751	1844
Smith Thompson	New York	1823—1845	1767	1845
Robert Trimble	Kentucky	1826—1829	1776	1829
John McLean	Ohio	1829—1861	1785	1861
Henry Baldwin	Pennsylvania	1830—1846	1779	1846
James M. Wayne	Georgia	1835—1867	1786	1867
Philip H. Barbour	Virginia	1836—1841	1779	1841
John Catron	Tennessee	1837—1865	1780	1865
John McKinley	Alabama	1837—1852	....	1852
Peter V. Daniel	Virginia	1841—1860	1785	1860
Samuel Nelson	New York	1845—1851	1792	1863
Levi Woodbury	New Hampshire	1845—1851	1790	1851
Robert C. Grier	Pennsylvania	1846—1870	1794	1870
Benjamin R. Curtis	Massachusetts	1851—1857	1809	....
James A. Campbell	Alabama	1853—1856	1802	....
Nathan Clifford	Maine	1858—....	1803	....
Noah H. Swayne	Ohio	1862—....	1805	....
Samuel F. Miller	Iowa	1862—....	1816	....
David Davis	Illinois	1862—1877	1815	....
Stephen J. Field	California	1863—....	1817	....
William Strong	Pennsylvania	1870—....	1809	....
Joseph P. Bradley	New Jersey	1870	1813	....
Ward Hunt	New York	1872—....	1811	....
John M. Harlan	Kentucky	1877—....	1814	....

APPORTIONMENT OF REPRESENTATIVES.

By Act Dec. **14, 1871,** *under census of* 1870.

State		State		State		State	
Alabama	8	Kansas	3	Nebraska	1	Rhode Island	2
Arkansas	4	Kentucky	10	Nevada	1	South Carolina	5
California	4	Louisiana	6	New Hampshire	3	Tennessee	10
Connecticut	4	Maine	5	New Jersey	7	Texas	6
Delaware	1	Maryland	6	New York	33	Virginia	9
Florida	2	Massachusetts	11	North Carolina	8	Vermont	3
Georgia	9	Michigan	9	Ohio	20	West Virginia	3
Illinois	19	Minnesota	3	Oregon	1	Wisconsin	8
Indiana	13	Mississippi	6	Pennsylvania	27	Colorado,	1
Iowa	9	Missouri	13			Total	293

The ratio of apportionment is about 142,000 inhabitants for a Member of Congress, though allowance is made for fractions in excess of one-half.

Expense of maintaining the government, not including the interest on the bonds, for each year from 1861 to 1878 :

June 30, 1862	$570,841,700 25		June 30, 1871	$292,177,188 25
" 1863	714,709,995 58		" 1872	270,559,695 91
" 1864	865,234,087 86		" 1873	262,254,216 97
" 1865	1,290,312,982 41		" 1874	302,633,873 76
" 1866	1,141,072,666 09		" 1875	268,447,543 76
" 1867	346,729,124 33		" 1876	258,459,797 10
" 1868	377,340,284 00		" 1877	238,660,0 8 93
" 1869	321,490,597 75		" 1878	236,964,326 80
" 1870	309,653,560 75		" 1879	161,619,933 53

ASSESSED AND TRUE VALUATION OF PROPERTY IN THE UNITED STATES IN 1870; TAXES OF EACH STATE AND TERRITORY; STATE DEBTS; CAPITAL INVESTED IN AND PRODUCT OF MANUFACTURES IN 1870; VALUE OF FARMS AND AMOUNT OF FARM PRODUCTS IN 1870.

No.	States and Territories.	Valuation of Property, 1870.				Taxes, not national, of each State.	State Debts.	Manufacturing Statistics, 1870.		Agricultural Wealth, 1870.	
		Assessed.			True.						
		Total.	Real Estate.	Personal.	Real & Pers'l. Est.	Total.	Totals.	Capital Invested.	Product in 1870.	Value of Farms.	Products in 1870.
1	Alabama	$155,582,595	$117,223,043	$38,359,552	$201,855,841	$2,982,029	$13,277,154	$5,714,032	$13,040,644	$67,739,036	$67,522,335
2	Arkansas	94,528,843	63,102,304	31,426,539	156,394,691	2,856,890	4,151,152	1,782,913	4,629,234	40,029,698	40,701,699
3	California	239,644,068	176,527,160	93,116,908	638,767,017	7,817,115	18,089,082	39,728,202	66,594,556	141,240,028	49,856,024
4	Connecticut	425,433,237	204,110,509	221,322,728	774,631,624	3,[illegible]64,643	17,088,906	95,281,278	161,065,474	124,241,382	26,482,150
5	Delaware	64,787,223	48,744,783	16,042,440	97,180,833	418,092	526,125	10,839,093	16,791,382	46,712,870	8,171,667
6	Florida	32,480,843	20,197,691	12,283,152	44,163,655	495,166	2,185,838	1,679,930	4,685,403	9,947,920	8,909,746
7	Georgia	227,219,519	143,948,216	83,271,303	268,169,207	2,627,020	21,753,712	13,930,125	31,196,115	94,559,468	80,390,228
8	Illinois	482,899,575	348,433,906	134,465,669	2,121,680,579	21,825,008	42,191,869	94,358,057	205,620,672	920,506,346	210,860,585
9	Indiana	663,455,044	460,120,974	203,334,070	1,268,180,543	10,791,121	7,818,710	52,052,425	108,617,278	634,804,189	122,914,302
10	Iowa	302,515,418	226,610,638	75,904,780	717,644,750	9,035,614	8,043,133	22,420,183	46,534,322	392,652,441	114,386,441
11	Kansas	92,125,861	65,499,365	26,626,496	188,892,014	2,673,992	6,442,282	4,319,060	11,775,833	90,327,040	27,630,651
12	Kentucky	409,544,294	311,479,694	98,064,600	604,318,552	5,730,118	18,953,484	29,277,809	54,625,809	311,238,916	87,477,374
13	Louisiana	253,371,890	191,343,376	62,028,514	323,125,666	7,060,722	53,087,441	18,313,974	24,161,905	66,215,421	52,006,622
14	Maine	204,253,780	134,580,157	[illegible]673,623	348,155,671	5,348,645	16,624,624	39,796,190	79,497,521	102,961,951	33,470,044
15	Maryland	423,834,918	286,910,332	1[illegible],924,586	643,748,976	6,632,842	29,032,577	36,[illegible]8,729	76,593,613	170,369,684	35,343,927
16	Massachusetts	1,591,983,112	901,037,841	690,945,271	2,132,148,741	24,922,900	69,211,538	231,67[illegible],862	553,912,568	116,432,784	32,192,378
17	Michigan	272,242,917	224,663,667	47,579,250	719,208,118	5,412,957	6,725,231	71,71[illegible],283	118,394,676	398,240,578	81,508,623
18	Minnesota	84,135,332	62,079,587	2[illegible],055,745	228,909,590	2,848,372	2,788,797	11,993,729	23,110,700	97,847,442	33,446,400
19	Mississippi	177,278,890	118,278,460	59,000,430	209,197,345	3,7[illegible],432	2,594,415	4,501,714	8,154,758	81,716,576	73,137,953
20	Missouri	526,129,969	418,527,535	137,602,434	1,284,922,897	13,908,498	46,909,865	80,257,244	206,213,429	392,908,047	103,035,759
21	Nebraska	54,584,616	38,365,909	16,218,617	69,277,483	1,027,327	2,089,264	2,169,963	5,738,512	30,242,186	8,604,742
22	Nevada	25,740,973	14,594,722	11,146,251	31,134,012	820,308	1,986,093	5,127,790	15,870,539	1,485,505	1,659,713
23	New Hampshire	149,065,290	85,231,288	63,834,002	252,624,112	3,255,793	11,153,373	36,023,743	71,038,249	80,589,313	22,473,547
24	New Jersey	624,868,971	448,832,127	176,036,844	940,976,064	7,416,724	22,854,304	79,606,719	169,237,732	257,523,376	42,125,198
25	New York	1,967,001,185	1,532,720,907	434,280,278	6,500,841,264	48,550,308	159,808,234	366,994,320	785,194,651	1,272,857,766	253,526,153
26	North Carolina	130,378,622	83,322,012	47,056,610	260,757,244	2,352,809	22,474,036	8,140,473	19,021,327	78,211,083	57,845,940
27	Ohio	1,167,731,697	707,846,836	459,884,861	2,235,430,300	23,526,548	22,241,988	141,923,964	269,713,610	1,054,465,226	198,256,907
28	Oregon	31,798,510	17,674,202	14,124,308	51,558,932	580,956	218,486	4,376,849	6,877,387	22,352,989	7,122,790
29	Pennsylvania	1,313,236,042	1,071,680,934	241,555,108	3,808,340,112	24,531,397	89,027,131	406,821,845	711,894,344	1,043,481,582	183,946,027
30	Rhode Island	244,278,854	132,876,581	111,402,273	296,965,646	2,170,152	6,938,642	66,557,322	111,418,354	21,574,368	4,761,163
31	South Carolina	183,913,337	119,494,675	64,418,662	208,146,989	2,767,675	13,075,229	5,400,418	9,858,981	44,808,763	41,909,402
32	Tennessee	253,782,161	223,035,375	30,746,786	498,237,724	3,381,579	48,827,191	15,595,295	34,362,636	218,743,747	86,472,887
33	Texas	149,732,929	97,186,568	52,546,361	159,052,542	1,129,577	1,613,907	5,284,110	11,517,302	60,149,950	49,185,170
34	Vermont	102,548,528	80,993,100	21,555,428	235,349,553	2,135,919	3,594,700	20,329,637	32,184,606	139,367,075	34,647,027
35	Virginia	365,439,917	279,116,017	86,323,900	409,588,133	4,613,798	45,921,255	18,455,400	38,364,322	213,020,845	51,774,800
36	West Virginia	140,538,273	95,924,774	44,613,499	190,651,491	1,722,158	561,767	11,084,320	24,102,201	101,604,381	23,379,692
37	Wisconsin	333,209,838	252,322,107	80,887,731	702,307,329	5,387,970	5,903,532	41,981,872	77,214,326	300,414,064	78,027,032
	Total States	14,021,297,071	9,804,637,462	4,216,659,609	29,822,535,140	278,391,286	864,785,067				
1	Arizona	1,410,295	538,355	871,940	3,440,791	31,323	10,500	150,700	185,400	161,340	277,998
2	Colorado	17,338,101	8,840,811	8,497,290	20,243,303	362,197	681,158	2,835,605	3,852,820	3,385,748	2,335,106
3	Dakota	2,924,489	1,695,723	1,228,766	5,599,752	13,867	5,761	79,200	178,570	2,085,265	495,667
4	District of Columbia	74,271,693	71,437,468	2,834,225	126,873,618	1,581,569	2,596,545	5,021,925	9,292,173	3,800,230	312,617
5	Idaho	[illegible],292,205	1,926,565	3,365,640	6,552,681	174,711	222,621	742,300	1,047,624	492,860	637,797
6	Montana	9,943,411	2,728,128	7,215,283	15,184,522	198,527	278,719	1,794,300	2,494,511	729,193	1,676,610
7	New Mexico	17,784,014	9,917,991	7,866,023	31,349,793	61,014	7,560	1,450,695	1,489,868	2,260,139	1,905,[illegible]
8	Utah	12,565,842	7,047,881	5,517,961	16,159,995	167,355	....	1,391,898	2,343,019	2,297,922	1,973,[illegible]
9	Washington	10,642,863	5,146,776	5,496,087	13,562,164	163,992	88,827	1,893,674	2,851,052	3,978,341	[illegible]111,902
10	Wyoming	5,516,748	883,665	4,633,083	7,016,748	34,471	....	889,400	765,424	18,187	42,[illegible]
	Total Territories	157,089,531	110,143,303	47,546,298	245,983,367	2,789,026	3,891,691				
	Aggregate, 1870	14,178,986,732	9,914,780,825	4,264,205,907	30,068,518,507	281,180,312	868,676,758				
	1860	12,084,560,005	6,111,553,966	6,973,006,049	16,159,616,068		Total U. S.	$2,118,208,769	$4,232,325,442	$9,262,803,861	$2,447,538,658

PUBLIC DEBT OF THE UNITED STATES.

OCTOBER 1, 1880.

Debt bearing Interest.

Bonds at 6 per cent	$222,819,050 00
Bonds at 5 per cent	474,531,550 00
Bonds at 4½ per cent	250,000,000 00
Bonds at 4 per cent	738,263,950 00
Refunding Certificates	1,083,850 00
Navy Pension Fund	14,000,000 00
Principal	$1,700,698,400 00
Interest	18,134,503 00

Debt on which Interest has ceased since Maturity.

Principal	$6,011,665 00
Interest	764,356 00

Debt bearing no Interest.

Old demand and Legal-Tender Notes	$346,741,841 00
Certificates of Deposit	9,965,000 00
Fractional Currency	7,181,940 00
Gold and Silver Certificates	26,033,660 00
Principal	$389,922,441 00
Unclaimed Interest	8,077 00

Total Debt.

Principal	$2,096,632,507 00
Interest	18,906,936 00
Total	$2,115,539,443 00

Cash in Treasury.

Total Cash in Treasury, at date	$199,945,260 00
Debt less Cash in the Treasury, December 1, 1875	$2,117,917,132 57
Debt less Cash in Treasury, December 1, 1876	2,089,336,099 42
Debt less Cash in Treasury, December 1, 1877	2,046,027,065 94
Debt less Cash in Treasury, December 1, 1878	2,027,414,325 79
Debt less Cash in Treasury, December 1, 1879	2,010,049,722 83
Debt less Cash in Treasury, October 1, 1880	1,915,594,183 00

Bonds to Pacific Railway Companies, Interest payable in Lawful Money.

Principal outstanding	$64,623,512 00
Interest accrued and not yet paid	969,352 00
Interest paid by the United States	47,589,861 00
Interest repaid by Transportation of Mails, etc.	13,824,655 00
By Cash Payments 5 per cent. net earnings	655,199 00
Balance of Interest paid by the United States	33,110,008 00

THE PUBLIC DEBT—MARCH 1, 1879.

THE LOANS MADE BY GOVERNMENT NOT YET REDEEMED.

1.—Debt bearing Interest on Coin.

TITLE OF LOAN.	Amo'nt Issued in Millions.	Per Cent Interest	When Redeemable.	Amount Outstanding.	Accrued Interest to Date.
Loan of June 14, 1858	20,000	5	After Jan. 1, 1874	260,000	3,250 00
Loan of Jan. 1, 1861 (Act of June 22, 1860	7,022	5	After Jan. 1, 1871 & before Jan. 1, 1881	....	....
Loan of Feb. 8, 1861 (1881's)	18,415	6	Payable Jan. 1, 1881	18,415,000	184,150 00
Oregon War Debt, July 1, 1861 (Act of March 2 1861)	1,091	6	Payable July 1, 1881	945,000	9,450 00
L'n July 17 & Aug. 5, '61 ('81's)	189,327	6	Payable Jan. & July, 1881	189,321,350	1,893,213 50
Loan of 1863, dated June 15, 1864 (1881's), 3d issue	75,000	6	Pay'ble after June 30, 1881	75,000,000	750,000 00
Ten-Forties of 1864	194,567	5	After March 1, 1874, & Payable M'ch 1, 1904.	194,566,300	4,864,157 50
Five-Twenties of 1867 *	379,506	6	After July 1, 1872	161,857,600	5,612,472 75
Five-Twenties of 1868	42,540	6	After July 1, 1873		
Fun'd L'n 1881, issued under Acts J'ly 14, '70 & Jan. 20, '71	508,440	5	After May 1, 1881	508,440,350	2,118,501 46
Fun'd L'n 1891, Acts '70 & '71	250,000	4½	After Sept. 1, 1891	250,000,000	937,500 00
Fund'd L'n of 1907, same Acts	......	4	After July 1, 1907	406,900,000	8,220,567 25
Aggregate of Debt	....	....	....	2,014,271,900	24,603,587 00

2.—Debt bearing Interest in Currency or lawful money.

TITLE OF LOAN.	Per Cent. Interest.	Principal Outstanding.	Interest Accrued & not yet Paid.	Balance of Int'st paid by Unit'd States.
Navy Pension Fund	3	$14,000,000	$210,000	
PACIFIC RAILWAY COMPANIES LOANS.				
Conditional—Half interest now and all the principal and interest eventually to be paid by Companies—				
Central Pacific	6	25,885,120	646,235	41,773,745 00
Kansas Pacific	6	6,303,000		
Union Pacific	6	27,236,512		
Central Branch of Union Pacific	6	1,600,000		
Western Pacific	6	1,970,560		
Sioux City and Pacific	6	1,628,320		
Totals	....	$64,623,512	$646,235	$41,773,745 00

There had been also to March 1, 1879, $10,658,076 of interest paid by transportation of mails, &c. These loans are to run 30 years from date of their issue.

3.—Debt on which the Interest has ceased since maturity.

	PrCt	Principal.	Interest.	Total.
Called Bonds not yet Surrendered May 1, 1979	6	67,429,110	1,203,641	68,629,755

4.—Debt bearing no Interest.

TITLE OF DEBT.	Principal.	Remarks.
Old Demand and Legal Tender Notes	$346,742,941	
Certificates of Deposit	46,100,000	
Fractional Currency	15,986,412	More than half of this is probably destroyed by fire or otherwise.
Coin and Silver Certificates	19,087,680	Am'nt diminished since redempt'n.

* Before May 1, 1879, all the Five-Twenties, amounting to $1,602,587,350, were funded into the 5, 4½ and 4 per cent. Loans, the Loan of June 14, 1858 and all the Ten-Forties of 1864, amounting together to $194,826,300, were called in, and by July 10, all would be refunded in Four per cents.

PUBLIC DEBT AT ITS MAXIMUM—CURRENCY AT ITS COIN VALUE.

The public debt reached its maximum on August 31, 1865, when it amounted to $2,845,907,626, composed as follows:

Funded debt	$1,109,568,192
Matured debt	1,503,020
Temporary loans	107,148,713
Certificates of debt	85,093,000
Five per cent. legal-tender notes	33,954,230
Compound-interest legal-tender notes	217,024,160
Seven-thirty notes	830,000,000
United States notes, (legal tenders)	433,160,569
Fractional Currency	26,344,742
Suspended requisitions uncalled for	2,111,000
Total	$2,845,907,626

Of these obligatioms $684,138,959 were a legal-tender in the payment of all debts, public and private, except customs, duties and interest on the public debt.

The amount of legal-tender notes, demand notes, fractional currency, and national currency, and national bank notes, outstanding on August 31, 1865, and annually thereafter, from January 1, 1866, to January 1, 1878, and the amounts outstanding November 1, 1878, are shown by the following table, together with the currency price of gold, and the gold price of currency, at each date:

Date.		United States Issue.			Notes of national banks including Gold Notes.	Aggregate.	Cur'ncy price of $100 Gold.	Gold price of $100 Currency
		Legal-tender Notes.	Old Demand Notes.	Fractional Currency.				
Aug.	31, 1865	$432,757,604	$402,965	$26,344,742	$176,213,955	$635,719,266	$144 25	$69 32
Jan.	1, 1866	425,839,319	392 070	26,000,420	298,588,419	750,820,228	144 50	69 20
Jan.	1, 1867	380,276,160	221,682	28,732,812	299,846,206	709,076,860	133 00	75 18
Jan.	1, 1868	356,000,000	159,127	31,597,583	299,747,569	687,504,279	133 25	75 04
Jan.	1, 1869	355,892,975	128,098	34,215,715	299,629,322	689,866,110	135 00	74 07
Jan.	1, 1870	356,000,000	113,098	39,762,664	299,904,029	695,779,791	120 00	83 33
Jan.	1, 1871	356,000,000	101,086	39,995,089	206,307,672	702,403,847	110 75	90 29
Jan.	1, 1872	357,500,000	92,801	40,767,877	328,465,431	726,826,109	109 50	91 32
Jan.	1, 1873	358,557,907	84,387	45,722,061	344,582,812	748,947,167	112 00	89 28
Jan.	1, 1874	378,401,702	79,637	48,544,792	350,848,236	777,874,367	110 25	90 70
Jan.	1, 1875	382,000,000	72,317	46,390,598	354,128,250	782,591,165	112 50	88 89
Jan.	1, 1876	371,827,220	69,642	44,147,072	346,479,756	762,523,690	112 75	88 69
Jan.	1, 1877	366,055,084	65,462	26,348,206	321,595,606	714,064,358	107 00	93 46
Jan.	1, 1878	349,943,776	63,532	17,764,109	321,672,505	689,443,922	102 87	97 21
Nov.	1, 1878	346,681,016	62,065	16,211,193	322,400,715	685,414,989	100 25	99 75

REDUCTION OF THE NATIONAL DEBT OF THE UNITED STATES,

from March 1, 1869, *to January* 1, 1881.

DATES.	Debt of the United States, less cash in the Treasury.	DATES.	Debt of the United States, less cash in the Treasury.	DATES.	Debt of the United States, less cash in the Treasury.
1869		1873		1877	
Mar. 1..	2,525,463,260	Mar. 1.	2,157,380,700	Mar. 1.	2,088,781,143
June 1..	2,505,412,613	June 1.	2,149,963,873	June 1.	2,063,377,342
Sept. 1..	2,475,962,501	Sept. 1.	2,140,695,365	Sept. 1.	2,055,469,779
Dec. 1..	2,453,559,735	Dec. 1.	2,150,862,053	Dec. 1.	2,046,027,066
1870		1874		1878	
Mar. 1..	2,438,328,477	Mar. 1.	2,154,880,066	Mar. 1.	2,042,037,129
June 1..	2,406,562,371	June 1.	2,145,268,438	June 1.	2,035,786,841
Sept. 1..	2,355,921,150	Sept. 1.	2,140,178,614	Sept. 1.	2,029,105,020
Dec. 1..	2,334,308,494	Dec. 1.	2,138,938,334	Dec. 1.	2,027,414,326
1871		1875		1879	
Mar. 1..	2,320,708,846	Mar. 1.	2,137,315,989	Mar. 1.	2,026,207,541
June 1..	2,299,134,184	June 1.	2,130,119,975	July 1.	2,027,207,256
Sept. 1..	2,274,122,560	Sept. 1.	2,125,808,789	Oct. 1.	2,027,202,452
Dec. 1..	2,248,251,367	Dec. 1.	2,117,917,132	Dec. 31.	2,011,798,505
1872		1876		1880	
Mar. 1..	2,225,813,497	Mar. 1.	2,114,960,306	April 1.	1,980,392,824
June 1..	2,193,517,378	July 1.	2,099,439,344	July 1.	1,942,172,296
Sept. 1..	2,177,322,020	Sept. 1.	2,095,181,941	Oct. 1.	1,915,594,183
Dec. 1..	2,160,568,030	Dec. 1.	2,089,336.099	Dec. 31.	

DEBT OF EACH ADMINISTRATION.

Washington's First Term	1793	$80,352,636
do Second Term	1797	82,064,479
John Adam's	1801	82,038,050
Jefferson's First Term	1805	82,312,150
do Second Term	1809	57,023,192
Madison's First Term	1813	59,962,827
do Second Term	1817	123,491,965
Monroe's First Term	1821	89,987,427
do Second Term	1825	83,788,432
John Quincy Adams	1829	59,421,413
Jackson's First Term	1833	7,001,022
Interest	1836	291,089
Jackson's Second Term	1837	1,895,312
Van Buren	1841	6,488,784
Tyler	1845	17,093,794
Polk	1849	64,704,693
Fillmore	1853	67,340,620
Pierce	1857	29,060,387
Buchanan	1861	90,867,828
Lincoln	1865	2,682,593,026
Johnson	January 1 1866	2,810,310,357
Johnson	March 4 1869	2,491,399.904
Grant	March 1 1871	2,320,708,846
do	March 1 1872	2,225,813,497
do	March 4 1873	2,157,380,700
do	March 1 1876	2,114,960,306
do	March 4 1877	2,088,781,143
Hayes	March 4 1878	2,042,037,129
do	March 1 1879	2,026,207,541
do	March 1 1880	1,995,112,221

PAPER MONEY OF THE UNITED STATES.

The amount of Legal Tender notes, Demand Notes, Fractional Currency, and National Bank Notes outstanding on August 31, 1865, and annually thereafter, from January 1, 1866, to January 1, 1879, and the amounts outstanding November 1, 1878, are shown by the following table, together with the currency price of gold and the gold price of currency at each date, prepared by the Comptroller of the Currency:

Date.	United States Issues.			Notes of National Banks, including Gold Notes.	Aggregate.	Cur'ncy price of $100 Gold.	Gold price of $100 Currency
	Legal-Tender Notes.	Old Demand Notes.	Fractional Currency.				
Aug 31, 1865	$432,757,604	$402,955	$26,344,742	$176,213,955	$635,719,266	$144 25	$69 32
Jan. 1, 1866	425,839,319	392,070	26,000,420	298,588,419	750,820,228	144 50	69 20
Jan. 1, 1867	380,276,160	221,682	28,732,812	299,846,206	709,076,860	133 00	75 18
Jan. 1, 1868	356,000,000	159,127	31,597,583	299,747,569	687,504,279	133 25	75 04
Jan. 1, 1869	355,892,975	128,098	34,215,715	299,629,322	689,866,110	135 00	74 07
Jan. 1, 1870	356,000,000	113,098	39,762,664	299,904,029	695,779,791	120 00	83 33
Jan. 1, 1871	356,000,000	101,086	39,995,089	306,307,672	702,403,847	110 75	90 29
Jan. 1, 1872	357,500,000	92,801	40,767,877	328,465,431	726,826,109	109 50	91 32
Jan. 1, 1873	358,557,907	84,387	45,722,061	344,582,812	748,947,167	112 00	89 28
Jan. 1, 1874	378,401,702	79,637	48,544,792	350,848,236	777,874 367	110 25	90 70
Jan. 1, 1875	382,000,000	72,317	46,390,598	354,128,250	782,591,165	112 50	88 89
Jan. 1, 1876	371,827,220	69,642	44,147,072	346,479,756	762,523,690	112 75	88 69
Jan. 1, 1877	366,055,084	65,462	26,348,206	321,595,606	714,064,358	107 00	93 46
Jan. 1, 1878	349,943,776	63,532	17,764,109	321,672,505	689,443,922	102 87	97 21
Nov. 1, 1878	346,681,016	62,065	16,211,193	322,460,715	685,414,989	100 25	99 75
Jan. 1, 1879	346,681,016	62,035	16,108,155	319,652,121	682,503,327	100 00	100 00
Nov. 1, 1879	346,681,016	61,365	15,710,960	337,181,418	699,634,759	100 00	100 00
April 1, 1880	346,681,016	61,195	15,625,297			100 00	100 00

From the organization of the U. S. Government to the 30th day of June, 1861, that day being the close of the fiscal year, the U. S. Government had called into its Treasury from the people the following sums from the following sources:

Customs Revenues	$1,575,152,579 92
Land Disposed of	175,817,961 00
Taxes and other Receipts	95,305,322 56
Total Ordinary Revenue from 1789 to 1861	1,846,275,863 48
Total Expenditure, same period	1,453,790,786 00
Excess Revenue	$392,485,077 48

The following sums have been paid out as interest on Bonds for the past 15 years for the fiscal years ending:

June 30, 1861	$6,112,296 18
" 1862	13,190,324 45
" 1863	24,729,846 61
" 1864	53,685,421 69
" 1865	132,987,350 25
" 1866	133,067,741 69
" 1867	135,034,011 04
" 1868	140,424,045 00
" 1869	130,694,242 80
June 30, 1870	129,235,498 00
" 1871	125,576,565 93
" 1872	117,357 839 72
" 1873	140,947,583 27
" 1874	107,119,815 21
" 1875	103,093,544 57
" 1876	100,243,271 23
" 1877	97,124,511 58
" 1878	*102,500,874 65
" 1879	*105,327,949 00

* This apparent increase is due to the payment of three months interest on the called bonds, interest being paid also on the 4½ and 4 per cent. bonds from the time of purchase. The next two years will show a large reduction.

GOLD AND SILVER COINS.

Country.	Monetary Unit.	Standard.	Value in U.S. Mon'y	Standard Coins.
Austria	Florin	....	......	8 Guldens or 20 f. Gold, $3.85.89.
Belgium	Franc	Gold&Silv'r	$.19.3	5, 10, and 20 Francs.
Bolivia	Dollar	Gold&Silv'r	0.96.5	Escudo, half Bolivar, and Bolivas.
Brazil	Milreis of 1,000 reis.	Gold	0.54.5	None.
Brit.Poss.N.Am	Dollar	Gold	1.00.0	None.
Bogota	Peso	Gold	0 96.5	None.
CentralAmerica	Dollar	Silver	0.93.5	Dollar.
Chili	Peso	Gold	0.91.2	Condor, Doubloon and Escudo.
Denmark	Crown	Gold	0.26 8	10 and 20 Crowns.
Ecuador	Dollar	Silver	0.93.5	Dollar.
Egypt	Pound, 100 Piasters.	Gold	4.97.4	5, 10, 25 and 50 Piasters.
France	Franc	Gold&Silv'r	0.19.3	5, 10 and 20 Francs.
Great Britain	Pound Sterling	Gold	4.86.65	Half Sovereign and Sovereign.
Greece	Drachma	Gold&Silv'r	0.19.3	5, 10, 20, 50 and 100 Drachmas.
German Empire	Mark	Gold	0.23.8	5, 10 and 20 Marks.
Japan	Yen	Gold	0.99.7	1, 2, 5, 10 and 20 Yen.
India	Rupee of 16 Annas.	Silver	0.44.4	
Italy	Lira	Gold&Silv'r	0.19.3	5, 10, 20, 50 and 100 Liro.
Liberia	Dollar	Gold	1.00.0	
Mexico	Dollar	Silver	1 01.5	Peso or Dollar, 5, 10, 25 & 50 Centaoo
Netherlands	Florin	Gold&Silv'r	0 38.5	Florin; Ten Guldens, Gold, $4.01.09.
Norway	Crown	Gold	0.26.8	10 and 20 Crowns.
Peru	Dollar	Silver	0 93.5	
Portugal	Milreis of 1,000 reis	Gold	1.08.0	2, 5, and 10 Milreis.
Russia	Rouble of 100 Copecs	Silver	0.74.8	Quarter, Half and One Rouble.
Sandwich Isl'ds.	Dollar	Gold	1.00.0	
Spain	Peseta of 100 Centm's	Gold&Silv'r	0.19.3	5, 10, 20, 50 and 100 Pesetas.
Sweden	Crown	Gold	0.26.8	10 and 20 Crowns.
Switzerland	Franc	Gold&Silv'r	0 19.3	5, 10 and 20 Francs.
Tripoli	Mahbub of 20 piast'rs	Silver	0.84.4	
Turkey	Piaster	Gold	0.04.3	25, 50, 100, 250 and 500 Piasters.
U.S. of Colombia	Peso	Silver	0.93.5	

PETROLEUM PRODUCTION.

PETROLEUM, crude and refined. Its production east of the Mississippi, and the amount exported in each of the last eight calendar years.

Years.	Production.	Exportation.		REMARKS.
	Gallons.	Quantities, Gallons.	Values.	
1871	208,581,600	*149,892,691	*$36,894,810	* Fiscal Years. After 1874, the Amounts and Values are for Calendar Years.
1872	250,243,200	*145,171,593	*34,058,390	
1873	394,850,400	*187,815,187	*42,050,756	
1874	432,104,400	*247,806,483	*41,245,815	1874 was a year of exceptionally large production, and the exports increased in proportion, but leaving out that year, and there has been a steady, and for the most part, rapid increase, both in the production and export of Petroleum.
1874	6 M. Je 30 to D. 31	130,106,065	17,072,677	
1875	350,320 920	238,548.312	31,734,093	
1876	366,683,400	263,453,296	49,045,040	
1877	602,459,200	361,887.225	57,539.873	
1878	619.007.004	349.346.253	41.022.007	
Totals.	3,224,250,124	2,074.027,097	$351,163,461	

TERRITORIAL GOVERNMENTS.

Territories.	Capitals.	GOVERNORS.	Territories.	Capitals.	GOVERNORS.
Arizona	Prescott	Gen. J. C. Frémont.	Montana	Helena	Benj. F. Potts.
Alaska	Sitka	....	New Mexico	Santa Fe	Gen. Lew Wallace.
Dakota	Yankton		Utah	Salt Lake City.	Eli H. Murray.
Dist. Col'bia	Washington.	Commissioners.	Washington	Olympia	Elisha P. Ferry.
Idaho	Boise City	Mason Brayman	Wyoming	Cheyenne	John H. Hoyt.
Indian	Tahlequah	Lewis Downing.	....	....	....

The Governors of the organized Territories receive a salary of $2,600 each.

BANKS AND BANKING IN THE U. S.

NATIONAL BANKS IN THE UNITED STATES.

Table, by States and geographical divisions, of the number of banks organized, closed and closing, and in operation, with their capital, bonds on deposit, and circulation issued, redeemed and outstanding on the 1st day of November, 1878.

STATES AND TERRITORIES.	BANKS.			CAPITAL.	BONDS.	CIRCULATION.		
	Organized.	In Liquidation.	In Operation.	Capital Paid in.	Bonds on Deposit	Issued.	Redeemed.	Outstanding.
Maine	74	2	72	$10,660,000	$9,626,250	$20,538,580	$11,738,656	$8,799 924
New Hampshire	47	1	46	5,740,000	5,769,000	12,118,075	6,923,328	5,194,747
Vermont	50	3	47	8,531,000	7,662,500	18,979,600	11,627,166	7,352,434
Massachusetts	242	5	237	95,407,000	72,221,950	166.473,645	102,777.080	63,696,565
Rhode Island	62	1	61	20,009.800	14 254.400	35,026,715	21,976,505	13,050,210
Connecticut	86	4	82	25,504,620	20,323,700	47,555,410	29,564.017	17,991,393
Totals, E. States	561	16	545	165,854,420	129,857,800	300,692,025	184,606,752	116,085,273
New York	340	60	280	90,689.691	55,766.300	169,862,715	118.900.888	50,871,827
New Jersey	71	2	69	13,858,350	12.626,350	29,531,520	18,172,195	11,359,325
Pennsylvania	257	22	235	55,909,840	46,677,650	109,208,135	66,960,830	42,247,305
Delaware	14	...	14	1,763.985	1,549,200	3.432,665	2,000,605	1,432,060
Maryland	34	2	32	12,865,010	7,821,000	22,314,450	14,614.276	7,700,174
Totals, M. States	716	86	630	175,086,876	124,440,500	334,349,485	220,738,794	113,610,691
Distr't of Columbia	11	4	7	1.507,000	1,155,000	3,549,600	2,450,001	1.090,599
Virginia	29	11	18	3,285.000	2,529,850	7.226,270	4.865.578	2,360,692
West Virginia	20	5	15	1,756,000	1.458,000	4,941,430	3,393.022	1,548,408
North Carolina	15	....	15	2,551,000	1,764,000	3,986,200	.2,272,720	1,713,480
South Carolina	12	....	12	2,851.100	1,490,000	3,580.325	2,230,960	.1,349,365
Georgia	17	5	12	2,041,000	1,925,000	4,817,790	2,891.381	1,926,409
Florida	2	1	1	50,000	50,000	59,500	15,700	43,800
Alabama	11	1	10	1,658,000	1,621,000	2,999.130	1,511,142	1,478,988
Mississippi	2	2	....	....	....	66,000	65,389	611
Louisiana	11	4	7	3,475,000	1,820,000	6,557,760	4.533,224	2,024,536
Texas	12	1	11	1,100,000	680.000	1,686,420	1,149,415	537,005
Arkansas	3	1	2	205,000	205,000	531,900	280,307	251,593
Kentucky	55	7	48	9,936,500	8,546.350	18,039,495	9,812.155	8,227,340
Tennessee	32	7	25	3,080.300	2.754,500	6,400,280	3,832.947	2,567,333
Missouri	43	21	22	7,175,000	2,000,000	10,947,335	8,602,943	2,344,432
Totals, So. States.	275	70	205	40,670,900	27,998,700	75,380,475	47,915,884	27,464,591
Ohio	196	34	162	26,986.900	23,157.250	56,231,270	34.845,147	21,386.123
Indiana	115	21	94	15,026.530	12,918,500	34,542,755	22,144,156	12,398,599
Illinois	165	26	139	17.194,000	9,988,500	33,574,905	24.659,677	9,915,228
Michigan	90	11	79	9,514.500	6,275,750	16,253,190	10,255,860	5,997,330
Wisconsin	56	18	38	3,315.000	2,094.500	7,165,660	4,878,370	2,287,290
Iowa	99	23	76	5,927,000	4.557,000	12.427,740	8,038,221	4,389.519
Minnesota	39	8	31	4,968.700	2,679,400	7,124.660	4,502,396	2,622 264
Kansas	27	16	11	800,000	740.000	2,813,680	1,891,161	922,519
Nebraska	12	2	10	1.000,000	844,000	1.853,340	1,112,106	741,234
Totals, W. States	799	159	640	81,733,230	63 254.900	171,987,200	111.327,094	60,660,106
Nevada	1	1	....	....	....	131,700	128,587	3.113
Oregon	1	....	1	250,000	250,000	487,000	263.100	223,900
Colorado	18	5	13	1,235,000	823,000	1,611,910	868,639	743.281
Utah	4	3	1	200,000	50,000	614,930	545,874	69,056
Idaho	1	....	1	100,000	100,000	197,740	115,739	82,001
Montana	6	3	3	350 000	280,000	544,420	297,871	246,549
Wyoming	2	....	2	125 000	60,000	116,360	62,360	54,000
New Mexico	2	....	2	300,000	300,000	591,070	325,510	265,560
Dakota	3	....	3	175.000	110,000	155,530	56,530	99,000
Washington	1	....	1	150,000	50,000	45,000	....	45,000
Totals, Pac. St. & T'rs	39	12	27	2,885,000	2,023,000	4,495,670	2,664,210	1,831,460
Mutilt'd Notes Retir	.....	....	....	....	....	....	....	1,339,674
Grand Totals	2,390	343	2,047	469,230.426	347,574,900	886,904,855	567,252,734	320,991,795
Add Gold Banks	10	1	9	4,300,000	1,834,000	3,051,220	1,582.300	1,468,920
Totals for all Banks	2,400	344	2,056	473,530,426	349 408,900	889,956,075	568,835,034	322,460,715

STATE BANKS AND SAVINGS BANKS IN THE UNITED STATES, June, 1878.

States and Territories.	No. of Banks	Capital.	Deposits.	Tax. On Capital.	Tax. On Deposits	Tax. Totals.
Maine	69	$92,108	$28,957,428	$188 98	$1,253 21	$1,442 19
New Hampshire	71	61,000	28,309,624	152 50	4,270 50	4,423 00
Vermont	21	344,167	8,140,383	829 33	4,096 57	4,925 90
Massachusetts	170	834,666	157,816,812	1,429 33	5,085 19	6,514 52
Boston	59	3,061,597	70,746,941	3,826 47	17,694 04	21,520 51
Rhode Island	58	3,883,267	50,028,328	8,188 16	39,301 63	47,489 79
Connecticut	107	2,840,000	78,858,210	5,604 82	31,271 53	36,876 35
New England States	555	11,116,605	422,857,726	20,219 59	102,972 67	123,192 26
New York	328	10,427,448	148,258,669	20,290 36	100,972 62	121,262 98
New York City	443	40,700,289	247,964,314	56,276 58	214,356 85	270,633 43
Albany	14	642,000	12,153,169	706 47	4,039 36	4,745 83
New Jersey	59	1,741,071	19,326,498	3,536 29	14,587 16	18,123 45
Pennsylvania	313	10,807,358	29,979,015	25,172 82	74,851 74	100,024 56
Philadelphia	59	2,113,756	42,552,729	4,648 68	61,604 26	66,252 94
Pittsburgh	37	4,657,547	13,727,252	10,284 93	22,599 96	32,884 89
Delaware	9	712,578	1,798,521	1,667 97	2,031 54	3,699 51
Maryland	13	627,513	559,703	962 01	913 51	1,875 52
Baltimore	41	4,162,516	34,604,030	8,795 49	15,740 49	24,535 98
Washington	10	496,742	3,151,613	513 18	6,469 94	6,983 12
Middle States	1,326	77,088,818	544,075,533	132,854 78	518,167 43	651,022 21
Virginia	77	3,281,667	6,499,580	7,753 69	15,421 29	23,174 98
West Virginia	22	1,497,782	3,927,737	3,668 37	9,819 28	13,487 65
North Carolina	13	588,290	978,018	1,470 72	2,445 93	3,915 75
South Carolina	18	911,523	1,004,868	2,278 77	2,428 28	4,707 05
Georgia	67	4,317,817	3,948,488	10,711 49	9,190 49	19,901 85
Florida	6	89,483	233,405	223 70	583 48	807 18
Alabama	22	993,276	1,813,605	2,420 69	4,533 93	6,954 62
Mississippi	32	1,289,573	1,732,397	2,535 64	4,331 42	6,867 06
Louisiana	3	116,000	48,110	177 50	120 28	297 78
New Orleans	21	4,473,905	7,994,123	10,726 42	15,184 95	25,911 37
Texas	102	3,707,057	4,626,420	8,744 54	11,565 63	20,310 17
Arkansas	15	225,576	298,605	514 24	746 48	1,260 72
Kentucky	74	7,010,103	6,287,262	16,656 29	15,718 26	32,374 55
Louisville	17	5,288,296	5,650,057	12,971 68	14,125 04	27,096 72
Tennessee	31	1,769,671	2,731,199	4,833 85	6,828 00	11,061 85
Southern States	520	35,559,029	47,774,074	85,087 50	113,041 84	198,129 34
Ohio	255	6,042,364	15,952,238	12,959 68	38,776 39	51,736 07
Cincinnati	21	2,022,369	7,361,629	3,388 23	17,295 38	20,683 61
Cleveland	9	898,623	12,244,967	1,590 98	17,403 31	18,994 29
Indiana	150	5,091,175	10,224,039	11,724 36	21,838 78	33,563 14
Illinois	319	4,509,738	12,472,557	10,153 55	29,981 71	40,135 26
Chicago	31	3,612,908	6,832,575	4,892 45	17,043 45	21,935 90
Michigan	153	2,636,707	4,737,722	6,454 25	11,844 11	18,298 36
Detroit	15	1,108,368	5,179,009	1,800 91	11,038 32	12,839 23
Wisconsin	89	1,386,425	3,714,069	3,026 20	9,284 96	12,311 16
Milwaukee	11	729,853	5,747,509	1,669 66	14,368 72	16,038 38
Iowa	287	5,255,013	8,224,785	12,711 94	20,377 82	33,089 76
Minnesota	77	1,510,502	3,233,693	3,662 47	7,950 50	11,612 97
Missouri	176	4 124,269	10,184,792	9,811 03	25,461 50	35,272 53
St. Louis	32	6,576,033	16,387,002	14,540 48	40,967 45	55,507 93
Kansas	109	1,472,344	2,508,746	3,441 85	6,496 55	9,938 40
Nebraska	48	503,595	1,189 250	1,203 76	2,972 96	4,176 71
Western States	1,782	47,470,286	126,284,766	103,031 80	293,101 91	396,133 71
Oregon	10	643,223	1,489,547	1,499 49	3,602 45	5,101 94
California	84	9,143,129	17,422,175	24,733 99	37,946 00	62,679 99
San Francisco	33	21,787,036	78,070,629	46,256 46	132,601 59	178,858 05
Colorado	28	526,190	934,915	1,315 46	2,336 38	3,651 84
Nevada	18	412,268	1,914,583	1,030 66	4,786 37	5,817 03
Utah	8	190,000	714,555	475 00	1,786 37	2,261 37
New Mexico	4	5,000	61,180	12 50	152 95	165 45
Wyoming	3	82,794	148,682	198 69	371 70	570 39
Idaho	2	54,000	16,358	135 00	40 88	175 88
Dakota	12	78,039	277,927	195 10	694 80	889 90
Montana	8	133,413	188,918	333 53	472 28	805 81
Washington	3	20[illegible],000	537,450	520 00	1,343 62	1,863 62
Arizona	4	85,000	25,885	212 50	64 70	277 20
Pacific St's & Teritor's	217	34,148,094	101,802,804	76,918 38	186,200 09	263,118 47
Totals	4,400	205,382,832	1,242,794,903	418,112 05	1,213,483 94	1,631,595 00

In the following table the number of State Banks & Trust Companies was, on the 1st of June, 1878, 853; their average capital was $124,347,262; the amount of their deposits, $229,482,625.
The number of private Bankers was 2856; their average capital for the previous six months was $77,798,228; the average amount of deposits, $183,832,995. The number of Savings Banks with capital was 23; amount of capital $3,237,342. The number of Savings Banks without capital was 668; the amount of their deposits $803,299,345.

STATE BANKS AND SAVINGS BANKS.

The laws of the United States require returns of capital and deposits to be made to the Commissioner of Internal Revenue, for purposes of taxation, by all State banks, savings-banks, and private bankers. The data of the following table were obtained from that Commissioner. This table exhibits, by geographical divisions, the number of State banks, and trust companies, private bankers, and savings-banks, and their average capital and deposits for the six months ending May 31, 1878:

Geographical Divisions.	No. of Banks.	Capital.	Deposits.
STATE BANKS AND TRUST COMPANIES.			
New England States	42	$8,189,517	$15,062,430
Middle States	217	42,446,037	122,098,847
Southern States	233	27,378,751	30,667,577
Western States	296	20,247,869	38,877,287
Pacific States and Territories	65	26,085,088	22,776,484
United States	853	124,347,162	229,482,625
PRIVATE BANKERS.			
New England States	71	2,858,688	3,228,297
Middle States	916	34,482,781	61,922,908
Southern States	280	7,298,396	13,683,874
Western States	1,450	26,917,565	75,107,656
Pacific States and Territories	139	6,240,798	29,830,230
United States	2,856	77,798,228	183,832,965
SAVINGS-BANKS WITH CAPITAL.			
New England States	1	68,400	1,139,916
Middle States	3	160,000	1,273,145
Southern States	4	881,882	1,278,900
Western States	11	304,852	1,931,700
Pacific States and Territories	4	1,822,208	20,456,307
United States	23	3,237,342	26,179,968
SAVINGS-BANKS WITHOUT CAPITAL.			
New England States	441	....	403,427,083
Middle States	190	....	358,680,633
Southern States	3	....	2,143,723
Western States	25	....	10,308,123
Pacific States and Territories	9	....	28,739,783
United States	668	....	803,299,345
SUMMARY.			
New England States	555	11,116,605	422,857,726
Middle States	1,326	77,088,818	544,075,533
Southern States	520	35,559,029	47,774,074
Western States	1,782	47,470,286	126,284,766
Pacific States and Territories	217	34,148,094	101,802,804
United States	4,400	205,362,832	1,242,794,903

LEGAL INTEREST.

Alabama.—Eight per cent. On usurious contracts the principal only can be recovered.

Arkansas.—Six per cent., but parties may contract for any rate not exceeding ten. Usury forfeits both principal and interest.

California.—Ten per cent. after a debt becomes due, but parties may agree upon any rate of interest whatever, simple or compound.

Colorado Territory.—Ten per cent. on money loaned.

Connecticut.—Six per cent. Usury forfeits interest taken in excess of legal rate.

Dakota.—Seven per cent. Parties may contract for a rate not exceeding twelve. Usury forfeits all the interest taken.

Delaware.—Six per cent. Penalty for usury forfeits a sum equal to the money lent.

District of Columbia.—Six per cent. Parties may stipulate in writing for ten. Usury forfeits all the interest.

Florida.—Eight per cent. Usury laws repealed. Money may be loaned at any rate.

Georgia.—Seven per cent. Parties may contract for twelve. A higher rate than twelve forfeits interest and excess.

Idaho Territory.—Ten per cent. Parties may agree in writing for any rate not exceeding two per cent. per month. Penalty for greater rate is three times the amount paid, fine of $300, or six months imprisonment, or both.

Illinois.—Six per cent., but parties may agree in writing for ten. Penalty for usury forfeits the entire interest.

Indiana.—Six per cent. Parties may agree in writing for any rate not exceeding ten. Beyond that rate is illegal as to excess only.

Iowa.—Six per cent. Parties may agree in writing for ten. A higher rate works a forfeiture of ten per cent.

Kansas.—Seven per cent. Parties may agree for twelve. Usury forfeits the excess.

Kentucky.—Six per cent., but contracts may be made in writing for ten. Usury forfeits the whole interest charged.

Louisiana.—Five per cent., eight per cent. may be stipulated for, if embodied in the face of the obligation, but no higher than eight per cent.

Maine.—Six per cent. Parties may agree in writing to any rate.

Maryland.—Six per cent. Usurious contracts cannot be enforced for the excess above the legal rate.

Michigan.—Seven per cent. Parties may contract for any rate not exceeding ten.

Minnesota.—Seven per cent. Parties may contract to pay as high as twelve, in writing, but contract for higher rate is void to the excess.

Mississippi.—Six per cent. Parties may contract in writing for ten. Where more than ten is taken the excess cannot be recovered.

Missouri.—Six per cent. Contract in writing may be made for ten. The penalty for usury is forfeiture of the interest at ten per cent.

Montana.—Parties may stipulate for any rate of interest.

Nebraska.—Ten per cent. or any rate on express contract not greater than twelve. Usury prohibits the recovery of any interest on the principal.

Nevada.—Ten per cent. Contracts in writing may be made for the payment of any other rate.

New Hampshire.—Six per cent. A higher rate forfeits three times the excess to the person aggrieved suing therefor.

New-Jersey.—Six per cent. Usury forfeits all interest and costs.

New-Mexico Territory.—Six per cent., but parties may agree upon any rate.

New-York.—Six per cent. Usury is a misdemeanor, punishable by a fine of $1,000 or six months imprisonment, or both, and forfeits the principal, even in the hands of third parties.

North Carolina.—Six per cent.; eight may be stipulated for when money is borrowed. Penalty for usury is double the amount lent and indictment for misdemeanor.

Ohio.—Six per cent. Contract in writing may be for eight. No penalty attached for violation of law. If contract is for a higher rate than eight it is void as to interest and recovery is limited to principal and six per cent.

Oregon.—Ten per cent. Parties may agree on twelve.

Pennsylvania.—Six per cent. Usurious interest cannot be collected. If paid it may be recovered by suit therefor within six months.

Rhode Island.—Six per cent. Any rate may be agreed upon.

South Carolina.—Seven per cent. Usury laws are abolished, and parties may contract without limit. Contracts must be in writing.

Tennessee.—Six per cent. Parties may contract in writing for any rate not exceeding ten per cent.

Texas.—Eight per cent. All usury laws abolished by the Constitution.

Utah Territory.—Ten per cent. No usury laws. Any rate may be agreed on.

Vermont.—Six per cent. Usury forfeits only the excess.

Virginia.—Six per cent. Lenders forfeit all interest in case of usury.

Washington Territory.—Ten per cent. Any rate agreed upon in writing is valid.

West Virginia.—Six per cent. Excess of interest cannot be recovered if usury is pleaded.

Wisconsin.—Seven per cent. Parties may contract in writing for ten. No interest can be computed on interest. Usury forfeits all the interest paid.

Wyoming Territory.—Twelve per cent., but any rate may be agreed upon in writing.

Upper Canada.—Six per cent., but parties may agree upon any rate.

Lower Canada.—Six per cent., but any rate may be stipulated for.

The Currency Act of Congress limits National Banks to a rate of six per cent. In the District of Columbia Congress allows a rate of ten per cent.

BUSINESS AND FAILURES IN THE UNITED STATES IN 1878.

From Dun, Barlow & Co.'s Report.

Number reported in Bus'ns	States and Cities.	Number of Failures.	Amount of Liabilities.
5,315	Alabama	51	$874,062
202	Arizona	6	81,307
4,211	Arkansas	41	407,653
17,058	California	310	6,899,539
	City of San Francisco	222	4,700,591
2,522	Colorado	58	541,542
12,587	Connecticut	281	4,680,588
840	Dakota	7	83,000
3,635	Delaware	23	281,500
2,713	District of Columbia	30	820,202
1,879	Florida	22	133,288
7,748	Georgia	119	3,738,134
299	Idaho	...	....
51,075	Illinois	470	7,672,931
	City of Chicago	362	12,926,800
25,402	Indiana	374	5,243,549
22,760	Iowa	400	3,428,100
8,863	Kansas	44	647,902
16,846	Kentucky	220	5,905,756
7,859	Louisiana	127	4,830,462
11,004	Maine	170	1,406,200
13,329	Maryland	119	2,568,986
36,713	Massachusetts	604	12,707,645
	City of Boston	325	11,279,523
23,336	Michigan	369	6,627,709
9,127	Minnesota	149	1,052,403
5,525	Mississippi	99	1,073,660
26,878	Missouri	101	1,036,416
	City of St. Louis	167	4,171,300
401	Montana	...	....
4,029	Nebraska	106	825,400
1,516	Nevada	37	419,797
7,587	New Hampshire	111	854,730
19,500	New Jersey	168	4,741,993
110,600	New York	969	15,791,084
	City of New York	863	42,501,731
6,635	North Carolina	89	11,059,200
49,158	Ohio	515	10,799,300
	City of Cincinnati	216	7,570,311
2,679	Oregon	13	173,500
79,608	Pennsylvania	770	15,714,270
	City of Philadelphia	257	101,373,700
5,123	Rhode Island	130	2,521,981
4,693	South Carolina	59	1,788,522
8,243	Tennessee	194	2,205,873
11,909	Texas	228	2,733,725
1,265	Utah	17	121,050
6,751	Vermont	113	1,843,350
15,534	Virginia and West Va	166	1,584,626
816	Washington Territory	3	16,900
20,305	Wisconsin	163	2,317,382
394	Wyoming	11	62,050
674,741	Total	10,478	$234,383,132

The great increase in the number of failures and the amount of liabilities in 1878, was due to several causes. Prominent among these were the culmination of five years of business depression; unfavorable weather in the winter and spring; attempts in Congress to defeat resumption; a general decline of prices all over the world; the yellow fever epidemic, and the repeal of the bankrupt law, which took effect Sept. 1, and hastened the bankruptcy of many who sought to take advantage of its provisions. The resumption of specie payments in 1879, the immense crops of 1878, and the cheering prospects for trade, give a much better outlook for the present year.

RATES OF POSTAGE

BETWEEN THE UNITED STATES AND GREAT BRITAIN AND OTHER FOREIGN COUNTRIES.

The standard single rate to Great Britain is ½ oz. avoirdupois; to France and the Continent (by French Mails), it is 15 grammes, or ½ oz. avoirdupois.

* Prepayment of Union Rates are optional. When not prepaid, double Rates are collected.

DESTINATION.	Letters ½ oz. or less	News-papers.	Samples of Mdze. per 2 oz. or less.
	CTS.	CTS.	CTS.
Africa, Spanish Possessions on Northern Coast	*5	2	2
Australia, except New South Wales and Queensland, via San Fran.	5	2	2
Austria	*5	2	2
Azores	*5	2	2
Balearic Isles	*5	2	2
Belgium	*5	2	2
Bermuda	5	2	2
Canary Islands	*5	2	2
Carthagena and U. S., of Colombia, direct Mail	5	2	–
Costa Rica, direct Mail, *via* Aspinwall	5	2	–
Cuba, direct Mail	5	2	2
Denmark	*5	2	2
Egypt	*5	2	2
Faroe Islands	*5	2	2
Fiji Islands, direct, *via* San Francisco	5	2	–
Finland	5	2	2
France	*5	2	2
Germany	*5	2	2
Gibraltar, British Mail	*5	2	2
Great Britain	*5	2	2
Greece	*5	2	2
Hayti, by direct Steamer	5	2	–
Honduras, Spanish, *via* Panama	5	2	2
Iceland	*5	2	2
Island of Malta	*5	2	2
Island of Madeira	*5	2	2
Italy	*5	2	2
Japan, direct, *via* San Francisco	5	2	2
Luxemburg	*5	2	2
Moldavia, Montenegro, Roumania and Servia	5	2	2
Morocco—Western Coast—Spanish Postal Stations	*5	2	2
Netherlands	*5	2	2
New Foundland	5	2	2
New Granada, direct Mail	5	2	2
Nicaragua, direct Mails, Western Ports only	5	2	2
Norway	*5	2	2
Panama, direct Mail	5	2	–
Pekin, Tien Tsin, Kalgan, and Ourga, *via* Germany and Russia	5	2	2
Persia, German Mail	5	2	2
Poland	5	2	2
Porto Rico, direct Mail	5	2	2
Portugal	*5	2	2
Roumania	*5	2	2
Russia	*5	2	2
Servia	*5	2	2
Shanghai, direct from San Francisco	5	2	2
Spain	*5	2	2
St. Domingo, direct Steamer	5	2	2
Sweden	*5	2	2
Switzerland	*5	2	2
Tangier, *via* Spain	*5	2	2
Tripolis, Italian Mail	5	2	2
Tunis, " "	5	2	2
Turkey	*5	2	2
West Indies, direct Mail	5	2	2

Postal Union Rates. Miscellaneous Mails on next page.

RATES OF POSTAGE.—Continued.

The standard single rate to Great Britain, is ½ oz. avoirdupois; to France and the Continent (by French Mails), it is 15 grammes, or ½ oz. avoirdupois, nearly.

* Prepayment of Union Rates are optional. When not pre-paid, double Rates are collected.

DESTINATION.	Letters ½ oz. or less.	News-papers.	Samples of Mdze. per 2 oz. or less
	CTS.	CTS.	CTS.
Africa, British Possessions on West Coast, by British Mail	*10	4	4
Argentine Confederation, U. S. Packet, *via* Brazil	10	4	4
Australia, New South Wales and Queensland, *via* Southampton	15	4	4
Bolivia, British Mail, *via* Aspinwall	17	4	5
Brazil, direct Mail	10	4	4
British Columbia	3	1	†10
Burmah, German Mail	*10	3	†4
Burmah, British Mail, *via* Brindisi	10	4	4
Buenos Ayres, U. S. Packet, *via* Brazil	10	4	4
Canada	3	1	†10
Carthagena, New Grenada, British Mail and U. S. of Colombia	13	4	‡6
Cape of Good Hope, British Mail	*15	4	4
Curaçoa, British Mail, *via* St. Thomas	10	4	‡8
Ceylon, British Mail, *via* Southampton	*10	4	4
Chili, British Mail, *via* Colon	17	4	‡10
Costa Rica, Eastern parts of British Mail, *via* Colon	13	4	‡10
Ecuador, British Mail *via* Colon	17	4	‡10
Gambia, British Mail, *via* Southampton	10	4	4
Gold Coast, British Mail	*10	4	4
Guadaloupe, British Mail, *via* St. Thomas	*10	4	4
Greytown, British Mail, *via* Aspinwall	13	4	‡10
Guiana, British, French and Dutch, *via* St. Thomas	10	4	4
Guatemala, direct Mail, *via* Aspinwall	10	2	–
Hawaiian Kingdom, direct Mail	6	1	–
Honduras, British	10	4	4
Honduras, other	13	6	3
Hayti, *via* St. Thomas	13	6	3
Hong Kong, Canton, Swatow, Amoy and Foo Chow, *via* San Fran.	10	2	4
India (Hindostan except Ceylon) British Mail	*10	4	4
Java, British Mail, *via* Southampton	10	2	4
Liberia, British Mail, *via* Southampton	*15	4	4
Martinique, " " " St. Thomas	10	4	4
Morocco, " " except Spanish Possessions on West Coast	15	4	4
Mexico, by sea	10	2	2
New Caledonia and all French Colonies	10	4	4
" overland	3	1	–
New South Wales, direct Mail	12	2	4
New Zealand, " "	12	2	4
Nicaragua, (Eastern ports of) British Mail, *via* Colon	13	4	10
Paraguay, British Mail	27	4	4
Persia, *via* Persian Gulf	10	4	4
Peru, British Mail, *via* Aspinwall	10	4	4
Queensland, British Mail, *via* Southampton	12	2	4
Salvador direct Mail	10	2	‡–
Siam, direct from San Francisco	10	2	8
Sierra Leone, British Mail, *via* Southampton	*10	4	4
St. Domingo, *via* St. Thomas	13	6	3
St. Helena, British Mail	*27	4	4
Straits Settlements, Singapore, &c.	10	4	‡4
Turks Island, British Mail, *via* St. Thomas	13	4	6
Uruguay, British Mail	27	4	4
Venezuela, British Mail, *via* St. Thomas	13	6	3
Victoria	12	2	4
West Indies, British Mail, *via* St. Thomas	13	4	6
" " French Colonies, *via* France	10	4	4
Zanzibar, British Mail, *via* Southampton	*10	4	4

† This rate for 8 oz. Samples—No Samples exceeding 8 oz. in weight can be forwarded. ‡ For 4 oz.

RATES OF DOMESTIC POSTAGE.

LETTERS.

The standard single-rate weight is ½ oz. avoirdupois.

Single-rate letter, throughout the United States....3 cts.
For each additional ½ oz. or fraction....3 "
Drop letters, for local delivery, single rate....2 "
Drop letters, where there is no local delivery, single rate....1 ct.
Postal card, throughout the United States....1 "
Advertised letters are charged extra....1 "

These postages must be prepaid by stamps. Letters are to be forwarded without additional charge, if the person to whom they are addressed has changed his residence, and has left proper directions to such effect. Letters uncalled for will be returned to the sender, if a request to that effect be written upon the envelope. Properly certified letters of soldiers and sailors will be forwarded without prepayment. No extra charge is made for the service of carriers taking letters to or from the Post-offices.

NEWSPAPERS.

1. On newspapers (excepting weeklies), whether regular or transient, and without regard to weight or frequency of issue, 1 cent each.
2. On periodicals (other than newspapers), whether regular or transient, not exceeding two ounces in weight, 1 cent each.
3. On periodicals (other than newspapers), whether regular or transient, exceeding two ounces in weight, 2 cents each.
4. Circulars, unsealed, 1 cent each. These rates to be prepaid by ordinary postage stamps affixed.
5. Weekly newspapers, excepted above, to regular subscribers, 2 cents per pound, to be weighed in bulk, and prepaid with "newspaper and periodical stamps" at the office of mailing.
6. Weekly newspapers to transient parties, 1 cent for each ounce or fraction thereof, to be prepaid by ordinary postage stamps affixed.

RATES OF POSTAGE ON THIRD-CLASS MATTER.

Mailable matter of the third class embraces all pamphlets, occasional publications, transient newspapers, magazines, handbills, posters, unsealed circulars, prospectuses, books, book manuscripts, proof-sheets, corrected proof-sheets, maps, prints, engravings, blanks, flexible patterns, articles of merchandise, sample cards, phonographic paper, letter envelopes, postal envelopes and wrappers, cards, plain and ornamental paper, photographic representations of different types, seeds, cuttings, bulbs, roots, scions, and all other matter which may be declared mailable by law, and all other articles not above the weight prescribed by law, which are not, from their form or nature, liable to destroy, deface, or otherwise injure the contents of the mail-bag or the person of any one engaged in the postal service. Weight of packages not to exceed four pounds.

By act of July 12, 1876, third-class matter is divided as follows:

One cent for two ounces.—Almanacs, books (printed), calendars, catalogues, corrected proofs, handbills, magazines, when not sent to regular subscribers, maps—lithographed or engraved—music (printed sheet), newspapers when not sent to regular subscribers, occasional publications, pamphlets, posters, proof-sheets, prospectuses, and regular publications designed primarily for advertising purposes, or for free circulation, or for circulation at nominal rates.

One cent for each ounce.—Blank books, blank cards, book manuscript passing between authors and publishers, card boards and other flexible material, chromo-lithographs, circulars, engravings, envelopes, flexible patterns, heliotypes, letter envelopes, letter paper, lithographs, merchandise, models, ornamented paper, postal cards, when sent in bulk and not addressed, photographic views, photographic paper, printed blanks, printed cards, sample cards, samples of ores, metals, minerals, and merchandise, seeds, cuttings, bulbs, roots, and scions, stereoscopic views.

Any article of mail-matter, subject to postage at the rate of one cent for each ounce or fraction thereof, which may be inclosed in the same package with items subject to the rate of one cent for each two ounces or fraction thereof, will subject the entire package to the highest rate, viz.: one cent for each ounce or fraction thereof.

All packages of matter of the third class must be so wrapped or enveloped, with open sides or ends, that their contents may be readily and thoroughly examined by postmasters without destroying the wrappers; but seeds, and other articles liable, from their form or nature, to loss or damage unless specially protected, may be inclosed in unsealed bags or boxes which can readily be opened for examination of the contents and reclosed; or sealed bags, made of material sufficiently transparent to show the contents clearly, without opening, may be used for such matter.

Matter of the third class inclosed in sealed envelopes notched at the ends or sides, or with the corners cut off, cannot be mailed except at letter postage rates.

Matter of the second and third classes containing any writing whatever will be charged with letter postage, except as follows:

The sender of any article of the third class of mail-matter may write his or her name or address therein, or on the outside thereof, with the word "from" above or preceding the same, or may write briefly or print on any package the number and names of the articles inclosed.

POSTAL CARDS.

The object of the postal card is to facilitate letter correspondence and provide for the transmission through the mails, at a reduced rate of postage, of short communications, either printed or written in pencil or ink. They may therefore be used for orders, invitations, notices, receipts, acknowledgments, price-lists, and other requirements of business and social life; and the matter desired to be conveyed may be either in writing or in print, or partially in both.

In their treatment as mail-matter they are to be regarded by postmasters the same as sealed letters, and not as printed matter, *except that in no case will unclaimed cards be returned to the writers or sent to the Dead Letter Office.* If not delivered within sixty days from the time of receipt they will be burned by postmasters.

The postage of one cent each is paid by the stamp impressed on these cards, and no further payment is required.

No card is a "postal card" except such as are issued by the Post Office Department. An ordinary *printed* business card may be sent through the mails when prepaid by a one-cent postage stamp attached; but such card must contain absolutely *no written matter except the address*; otherwise it will be treated as not fully prepaid, and refused admission into the mails.

In using postal cards, be careful not to write or have anything printed on the side to be used for the address, except the address; also be careful not to paste, gum, or attach anything to them. They are unmailable as postal cards when these suggestions are disregarded.

THE FOLLOWING ARTICLES ARE UNMAILABLE.

Packages containing liquids, poisons, glass, explosive chemicals, live animals, sharp-pointed instruments, flour, sugar, or any other matter liable to deface or destroy the contents of the mail, or injure the person of any one connected with the service. All letters upon the envelope of which, or postal card upon which, indecent, lewd, obscene, or lascivious delineations, epithets, terms, or language may be written or printed, or disloyal devices printed or engraved, and letters or circulars concerning illegal lotteries, so-called gift concerts, or other similar enterprises offering prizes, or concerning schemes devised and intended to deceive and defraud the public. Also, all obscene, lewd, or lascivious books, pamphlets, pictures, papers, prints, or other publications of an indecent character.

Registration.—Letters may be registered on payment of a fee of ten cents, but the Government takes no responsibility for safe carriage or compensation in case of loss.

Registration Fee on Packages.—Prepaid at letter rates, not over *four pounds* in weight, to any part of the United States, 10 cents for each package, in addition to the postage. The package must be endorsed on the back, with the name and address of the sender, and a receipt will be returned from the person to whom it is addressed.

Money Orders.—All principal post-offices now receive small sums of money, and issue drafts for the same upon other post-offices, subject to the following charges and regulations.

These Orders, payable at any Money Order Post Office in the country, are issued at the following rates:

On orders not exceeding $15	10 cts.
Over $15 and not exceeding $30	15 "
Over $30 and not exceeding $40	20 "
Over $40 and not exceeding $50	25 "

When more than $50 is required, additional orders must be obtained, but not more than three orders will be issued in one day to the same payee, at the same office.

If a money order is lost, a certificate should be obtained from both the paying and issuing Postmaster that it has not been paid, and will not be paid, and the Department at Washington will issue another on application.

If a money order is not collected within one year from date, it is invalid, and can only be paid by the Department at Washington on application through the issuing or paying Postmaster.

PRINTED MATTER TO THE BRITISH PROVINCES.

The regular United States rates must be prepaid, but these only pay for transportation to the boundary line; a second fee is charged on delivery by the Provincial post-office.

ACT OF JANUARY 27, 1873, ABOLISHING THE FRANKING PRIVILEGE.

Be it enacted, &c., That the franking privilege be, and the same is hereby abolished, from and after the first day of July, A. D. 1873, and that henceforth all official correspondence of whatever nature, and other mailable matter, sent from or addressed to any officer of the Government or person now authorized to frank such matter shall be chargeable with the same rates of postage as may be lawfully imposed upon like matter sent by or addressed to other persons.

RAILROAD STATISTICS.

MILEAGE OF RAILROADS IN OPERATION, AND ANNUAL INCREASE, 1830-1878.

[*From Poor's Manual of the Railroads of the United States.*]

Years.	Miles in Operati'n.	Annual Increase of Mileage.	Years.	Miles in Operati'n	Annual Increase of Mileage.	Years.	Miles in Operati'n.	Annual Increase of Mileage.
1830....	23	....	1847....	5,598	668	1864....	33,908	738
1831....	95	72	1848....	5,996	398	1865....	35,085	1,177
1832....	229	134	1849....	7,365	1,369	1866....	36,827	1,742
1833....	380	151	1850....	9,021	1,656	1867....	39,276	2,449
1834....	633	253	1851....	10,982	1,961	1868....	42,255	2,979
1835....	1 098	465	1852....	12,908	1,926	1869....	47,208	4,953
1836....	1,273	175	1853....	15,360	2,452	1870....	52,898	5,690
1837....	1,497	224	1854....	16,720	1,360	1871....	60,568	7,670
1838....	1,913	416	1855....	18,374	1,654	1872....	66,735	6,167
1839....	2,302	389	1856....	22,016	3,642	1873....	70,840	4,105
1840....	2,818	516	1857....	24,503	2,487	1874....	72,741	1,901
1841....	3,535	717	1858....	26,968	2,465	1875....	74,658	1,917
1842....	4,026	491	1859....	28,789	1,821	1876....	77,514	2,856
1843....	4,185	159	1860....	30,635	1,846	1877....	79,795	2,281
1844....	4,377	192	1861....	31,286	651	1878....	82,483	2,688
1845....	4,633	256	1862....	32,120	834			
1846....	4,930	297	1863....	33,170	1,050			

It is estimated that there are 1,900 miles of railroad track, in double, treble or quadruple tracks, sidings, etc., making the total length in single track, January 1, 1878, 98,203 miles, and January 1, 1879, about 101,000 miles. The mileage of 1878 is 2,688 against 2,281 in 1877.

MILEAGE OF NEW RAILROADS CONSTRUCTED IN EACH STATE AND TERRITORY FOR FIVE YEARS.

[*From the Railway Age.*]

States, &c.	1874.	1875.	1876.	1877.	1878.	States, &c.	1874.	1875.	1876.	1877.	1878.
Alabama.....	18	......	......	1½	22	Missouri.....	31	27	109½	36	209
Alaska	......	......	......	......	......	Montana.....	......	......	......	......	......
Arizona......	......	......	......	......	30	Nebraska....	......	22	52	69	55
Arkansas.....	18	38½	49	......	7	Nevada	40	64	......	......	......
California...	140½	195	344¾	235⅜	71½	N. Hampshire	45	15½	9¼	18	35
Colorado.....	23	111½	154½	123½	103¼	New Jersey .	39	72¼	64	81½	3
Connecticut..	......	21	7	3½	......	New Mexico.	......	......	......	......	......
Dakota.......	......	......	......	......	15	New York ...	125¼	206	69¾	151¾	129½
Delaware....	19	5	......	......	6	N. Carolina ..	68	13	43	27	16
Florida.......	18	......	......	13	......	Ohio	172½	26	275	209	97
Georgia......	5	4	42	......	62	Oregon.......	......	......	......	......	36
Idaho	......	......	......	......	126	Pennsylvania	191½	136¾	90½	119¾	188½
Illinois.......	231	200	53	55¼	103	Rhode Island.	14	......	9	9⅜	......
Indiana......	209½	109½	72¼	24	74	S. Carolina ..	......	15	17	48¾	16½
Indian Ter'ty	......	......	2	......	......	Tennessee ...	......	......	7½	21¾	10
Iowa.........	48	84½	96¾	165½	235½	Texas	75	34½	387¾	108½	118½
Kansas.......	61	......	76	86½	169¼	Utah	59	27	......	20	......
Kentucky....	31¼	......	138	28¼	20	Vermont.....	5	32	......	71	......
Louisiana....	......	......	......	2	......	Virginia.....	70¾	......	10	16¾	16½
Maine........	37½	10	20	......	......	Washington T	6	......	......	52½	15
Maryland....	12	17	15	......	5½	W. Virginia..	......	......	......	20½	16½
Massachus'ts	27¾	36	5	17¼	6	Wisconsin ...	102	23	123¾	62	83¾
Michigan	48	30	46	56	110½	Wyoming Ter	......	......	......	5	......
Minnesota ...	36	......	34	204	338¼						
Mississippi ..	27	......	10	......	26	Total.......	5,025	1,561	2,430	1,281	2,688

GENERAL RESULT OF RAILROAD OPERATIONS, 1871-1878.

Years.	Miles Operated.	Capital and Funded Debt	Earnings.		Dividends Paid.
			Gross.	Net.	
1871........................	44,614	$2,664,627,645	$403,329,208	$141,746,404	$56,456,681
1872........................	57,327	3,159,423,057	465,241,055	165,754,373	64,418,157
1873........................	66,233	3,784,543,034	526,419,935	183,810,562	67,120,709
1874........................	69,273	4,221,763,594	520,466,016	189,570,958	67,042,942
1875........................	71,757	4,415,631,630	503,065,505	185,506,438	74,294,208
1876........................	73,508	4,468,591,935	497,257,959	186,452,752	68,039,668
1877........................	74,112	4,568,597,248	472,909,272	170,976,697	58,556,312
1878........................	73,960	4,589,948,193	490,103,351	187,575,167	53,629,368

DIFFERENCE OF TIME.

WHEN it is 12 o'clock at noon at New York City, it will be morning at all places west of New York, and afternoon at all places east, as in the annexed table.

PLACES WEST.	MORN'G. H.	M.	S.	PLACES WEST.	MORN'G. H.	M.	S.	PLACES WEST.	MORNING H.	M.	S.
Acapulco, Mexico	10	16	48	Little Rock, Ark	10	47	16	Sacramento, Cal	8	56	44
Auburn, New York	11	50	12	Louisville, Ky	10	14	4	St. Augustine, Fla	11	29	4
Augusta, Ga	11	28	28	Mexico, Mex	10	19	44	St. Louis, Mo	10	55	44
Baltimore, Md	11	49	38	Milledgeville, Ga	11	22	45	St. Paul, Minn	10	43	45
Burlington, N. J	11	56	31	Milwaukee, Wis	11	4	16	San Antonio, Texas	10	22	8
Buffalo, N. Y	11	40	24	Mobile, Ala	11	0	2	San Diego, Cal	9	7	11
Charleston, S. C	11	36	22	Monterey, Mex	10	14	22	San Francisco, Cal	8	46	19
Chicago, Ill	11	6	2	Monterey, Cal	8	48	35	Santa Fe, N. Mex	9	51	59
Cincinnati, O	11	13	16	Nashville, Tenn	11	8	48	Santa Cruz, W. I	8	48	4
Columbus, O	11	24	52	Natchez, Miss	10	50	26	Savannah, Ga	11	31	32
Dayton, O	11	19	20	Newark, N. J	11	59	24	Scarboro Har., W. T	8	37	36
Detroit, Mich	11	21	54	Newbern, N. C	11	47	44	Springfield, Ill	10	57	53
Dover, Del	11	54	4	New Orleans, La	10	56	4	Tallahassee, Fla	11	17	40
Ewing Harbor, O. T	8	38	9	Norfolk, Va	11	50	49	Tampico, Mex	10	24	37
Ft. Leavenworth, Kan.	10	37	8	Pensacola, Fla	11	8	0	Toronto, C. W	11	32	38
Galveston, Texas	10	36	58	Petersburg, Va	11	46	44	Trenton, N. J	11	57	28
Geneva, N. Y	11	47	53	Philadelphia, Pa	11	55	25	Tuscaloosa, Ala	11	5	16
Harrisburg, Pa	11	48	44	Pittsburg, Pa	11	35	56	Utica, N. Y	11	55	12
Honolulu, S. I	6	24	8	Point Hudson, W. T	7	45	6	Vera Cruz, Mex	10	31	30
Huntsville, Ala	11	8	16	Princeton, N. J	11	57	26	Vincennes, Ind	11	6	24
Indianapolis, Ind	11	11	44	Racine, Wis	11	5	23	Washington, D. C	11	47	53
Jackson, Miss	10	55	32	Raleigh, N. C	11	40	52	Wheeling, W. Va	11	33	16
Jefferson, Mo	10	47	32	Richmond, Va	11	46	15	Wilmington, N. C	11	43	24
Key West, Fla	11	28	54	Rochester, N. Y	11	44	40	Wilmington, Del	11	54	12
Knoxville, Tenn	11	20	28	Sacketts Harbor, N.Y.	11	52	16	Yorktown, Va	11	49	48

PLACES EAST	AFTERNOON. H.	M.	S.	PLACES EAST.	AFTERNOON. H.	M.	S.	PLACES EAST.	AFTERNOON. H.	M.	S.
Albany, N. Y	0	1	6	Halifax, N. S	0	41	38	Paris, France	5	5	26
Augusta, Me	0	16	44	Hamburg, Germany	5	35	58	Portland, Maine	0	15	10
Bangor, Me	0	26	56	Hartford, Conn	0	5	21	Providence, R. I	0	10	25
Berlin, Prus	5	49	39	London, England	4	55	41	Quebec, Canada	0	11	0
Boston, Mass	0	11	30	Lowell, Mass	0	10	44	Rome, Italy	5	45	59
Constantinople, Tur	6	52	0	Middletown, Conn	0	5	23	St. Petersburg, Rus	6	57	18
Dublin, Ireland	4	30	43	Montreal, L. C	0	1	44	Stockholm, Sweden	6	8	18
Edinburgh, Scotland	4	43	21	New Haven, Conn	0	4	23	Vienna, Austria	6	1	37
Fredericton, N. B	0	29	4								

THE LARGE CITIES OF THE WORLD.

CITIES.	POPULATION.	CITIES.	POPULATION.	CITIES.	POPULATION.	CITIES.	POPULATION.
London	3,533,164	Chicago	503,298	Saikio	300,000	Buenos Ayres	95,000
Paris	1,988,748	Ningpo	500,000	Lucknow	284,779	Bristol	190,589
Peking	1,500,000	Naples	448,743	Sheffield	282,000	Prague	89,949
Canton	1,300,000	Hamburg	406,014	Rio de Janeiro	274,972	Bradford	80,000
New York	1,209,561	Manchester	403,000	Milan	261,976	Santiago	80,090
Constantinople	1,075,000	Birmingham	400,000	Rome	256,022	Benares	175,188
Berlin	1,045,000	Nanking	400,000	Bangkok	255,000	Belfast	174,394
Vienna	1,020,770	Amoy	400,000	Barcelona	252,017	Sydney, N.S.W.	174,249
Philadelphia	847,452	Madras	397,522	Warsaw	251,584	Florence	167,093
Tokio, l'te Yedo	800,000	Brussels	380,238	Melbourne	251,000	Stockholm	165,677
Foochow	800,000	St. Louis	377,000	Havana	250,000	Lille	162,975
Calcutta	794,615	Madrid	367,284	Cincinnati	246,153	Odessa	161,814
New Yedo	780,621	Boston	363 565	Breslau	239,050	Washington	160,000
St. Petersburg	670,000	Che Foo	350,000	San Francisco	227,350	Pittsburgh	159,065
Bombay	644,405	Cairo	349,883	Bucharest	221,805	Patna, India	158 900
Macao	625,000	Lyon	342,815	Palermo	219,988	Cleveland	157,946
Moscow	611,970	Baltimore	330,000	Edinburgh	218,740	Buffalo	154,766
Hankow	600,000	Shanghai	320,000	Bordeaux	215,140	Delhi	154,417
Kon Kiang	600,000	Marseilles	318,864	New Orleans	215,123	Salford	152 500
Brooklyn	566,930	Mexico	315,596	Alexandria	212,054	Seville	152,009
Kioto, Japan	560,200	Dublin	314,666	Turin	207,770	Monte Video	150,000
Glasgow	555,044	Buda-Pesth	313,401	Copenhagen	205,000	Dundee	149,720
Osaca, Japan	533 000	Amsterdam	302,266	Munich	198,829	Agra, India	149,008
Liverpool	527,000	Leeds	300,000	Dresden	197,295		

TABLE OF IMPORTS, FOREIGN EXPORTS, NET IMPORTS AND DOMESTIC EXPORTS, FROM 1844 TO 1880.

The following table exhibits the Imports, Exports of Foreign Goods, net Imports and Exports of goods, the production, growth or manufacture of the United States from the year 1821, when for the first time, the distinction was made between the imports and exports of merchandize and that of coin and bullion. The fiscal year closed September 30, till June 30, 1843, when it closed as now, June 30. An additional column gives the value of our domestic exports, since 1861, in mixed values—gold and currency, all the other columns being in gold values.

YEAR, ENDING:	Imports.	Foreign Exports	Net Imports.	DOMESTIC EXPORTS. Total Gold Value.	Mix'd Values Gold & C'rncy.
	$	$	$	$	
Sept. 30 ....1821....	62,585,724	21,302,488	41,283,236	43,671,894	
" " ....1822....	83,241,541	22,886,202	60.955,339	49,874,079	
" " ....1823....	77,579,267	27,543,622	50,035,645	47,155,408	
" " ....1824....	80,549,007	25,337,157	55,211,850	50,649,500	
" " ....1825....	96,310,075	32,590,643	63,749,432	66,944,745	
" " ....1826....	84,974,477	24,539,612	60,434,865	53,055,710	
" " ....1827....	79,484,068	23,403,136	56,080,932	58,921,691	
" " ....1828....	88,509,824	21,595 017	66,914,807	50,669,669	
" " ....1829....	74,492,527	16,658,478	57,834,049	55,700,193	
" " ....1830....	70,876,920	14,387,479	56,489,441	59,462,029	
" " ....1831....	103,191,124	20 033,526	83,157,598	61,277,057	
" " ....1832....	101,029,266	24,039,473	76,989,793	63,137,470	
" " ....1833....	108,118,311	19,822,735	88,295.576	70,317,698	
" " ....1834....	126,521,332	23,312,811	103,208,521	81,024,162	
" " ....1835....	149,895,742	20,504,495	129,391,247	101,189,082	
" " ....1836....	189,980,035	21,746,360	168,233,675	106,916,680	
" " ....1837....	140,989,217	21,854,962	119,134,255	95,564,414	
" " ....1838....	113,717,404	12,452,795	101,264,609	96,033,821	
" " ....1839....	162,092,132	17,494,525	144,597,607	103,533,891	
" " ....1840....	107,141,519	18,190,312	88,951,207	113,895.634	
" " ....1841....	127,946,177	15,469,081	112,477,096	106.382,722	
" " ....1842....	100,162,087	11,721,538	88,440,549	92,969,996	
June 30............1843*...	64,753,799	6,552,697	58,201,102	77,793,783	
June 30............1844....	108,435,035	11,484 867	96,950,168	99,715,179	
" " ....1845....	117,254,564	15,346,830	101,907,734	99,299,776	
" " ....1846....	121,691,797	11,346,623	110,345,174	102,141,893	
" " ....1847....	146,545,638	8,011,158	138,534,480	150,637.464	
" " ....1848....	154,998,928	21.128,010	133,870,918	132.904.121	
" " ....1849....	147,857,439	13,088,865	134.768,574	132,666,955	
" " ....1850....	178.138,318	14,951 808	163,186,510	136,946,912	
" " ....1851....	216,224,932	21,698,293	194,526,639	196,689,718	
" " ....1852....	212 945,442	17,289,382	195,656,060	192,368,984	
" " ....1853....	267,978,647	17,558,460	250,420,187	213,417,697	
" " ....1854....	304,562,381	21,850,194	279,712,187	252,047,806	
" " ....1855....	261,468,520	28,448,293	233,020,227	246,708,553	
" " ....1856....	314,639,942	16,378,578	298,261,364	310,586,330	
" " ....1857....	360,890,141	23,975 617	336,914,524	338,985,065	
" " ....1858....	282,613,150	30,886,142	251,727.008	293,758,279	
" " ....1859....	338,768,130	20,895,077	317,873,053	335,894,385	
" " ....1860....	362,166,254	26,933,022	335,233,232	373,189,274	
" " ....1861....	335.650,153	20,645,427	315,004,726	228,699,486	
" " ....1862....	205,771,729	16,869,466	188,902,263	210,688,675	$213,069,519
" " ....1863....	252.919.920	26,123,584	226,796,336	241,997.474	305,884,998
" " ....1864....	329,562,895	20,256,940	309,305,955	243,977,589	320,035,199
" " ....1865....	248.555,652	32,114,157	216,441,495	201,558,372	323,743,187
" " ....1866....	445,512,158	14,742,117	430,770,041	420,161,476	550,684,277
" " ....1867....	417,833,575	20 611,508	397,222,067	332,618,089	438,577,312
" " ....1868....	371,624,808	22,601,126	349,023,682	353,135,875	454.301,713
" " ....1869....	437,314.255	25,173,414	412.140.841	318,082,663	413,961,115
" " ....1870....	462,377,587	30,427,159	431,950,428	420,500,275	499,092,143
" " ....1871....	541,493,708	28,459,899	513,033,809	512,802.267	562,518,651
" " ....1872....	640,338,766	22,769,749	617,569,017	501,285,371	549,219,718
" " ....1873....	663,617,147	28,149 511	635,467,636	578,938,985	649,132,563
" " ....1874....	595,861,248	23,780,338	572,080,910	629,133,107	693,039,054
	....	....	....	§10,200,059	§11,424,066
" " ....1875....	553,906,153	22,433,624	531,472,529	583,141,229	643,094,767
	....	....	....	§15,596,524	§15 596,524
" " ....1876....	476,677,871	21,270,035	455,407,836	575,620,938	644,956,406
	....	....	....	§10,507,563	§10,507 563
" " ....1877....	492,097,540	25,832,495	466,265.045	632,804,962	676,115,592
" " ....1878....	466,872,846	20,834,738	446,038,108	707,771,153	722,811,815
					§10,535,857
" " ....1879....	466,078,775	12,098,651	446,532,718	717,093 777	717,093,777
" " ....1880....	743,481,765	11,692,805		845,990,528	845,990,528

* Nine months only.

§ Addition to Domestic Exports, Merchandise only, taken from Canadian reports.

SILK MANUFACTURE AND THE IMPORTATION OF SILK GOODS IN THE UNITED STATES IN THE YEARS 1875–'78.

American Silk Industry.—Value of Goods Manufactured each Year.

ARTICLES MANUFACTURED.	1875.	1876.	1877.	1878.
	$	$	$	$
Trams	2,976,551	768,490	2,368,485	
Organzine	1,819,000	614,901	1,353,488	
Spun Silk	850,000	805,000	850,000	
Fringe Silk	243,489	203,172	225,720	
Floss Silk	42,568	35,428	32,698	
Sewing Silk	885,079	951,460	349,490	
Machine Twist	5,535,754	5,301,059	4,136,463	
Dress Goods	1,412,500	1,350,535	1,712,081	
Foulards and Millinery Silks	2,544,191	2,679,166	1,319,080	
Women's and Men's Scarfs	134,523	119,946	109,955	
Handkerchiefs	905,115	927,000	1,324,166	
Ribbons	4,815,485	4,526,556	3,927,490	
Laces	164,000	220 000	156,580	
Coach Laces	35,652	24,500	18,040	
Veils and Veiling	65,264	16,518	11,860	
Silk Hose	6,000	2,200	4,500	
Braids and Bindings	383,100	315,000	220,400	
Military Trimmings	33,000	28,000	22,500	
Upholstery Trimmings	459,613	526,036	382 200	
Ladies Dress Trimmings	3,397,237	3,705,076	2,896,320	
Foulards	450,000	472,000	....	
Totals	$27,156,071	$26,592,103	$21,411,436	*$22,000,000

Importation of Silk Goods and Manufactures, at the Port of New York in each Year.

ARTICLES IMPORTED.	1875.	1876.	1877.	1878.
	$	$	$	$
Silk and Dress Goods	13,639,397	12,707,102	11,977,135	12,085,128
Satins	107,501	41,403	26,795	50,209
Crapes	47,806	504,277	397,905	383,621
Pongees	10,126	....	2,617	394
Plushes	125,722	85,668	73,777	102,718
Velvets	1,151,427	1,384,450	1,049,305	1,524,329
Ribbons	2,984,271	2,837,527	1,689,413	1,861,869
Laces	1,030,055	1,248,740	1,158,689	935,974
Embroideries	699	....	2,020	....
Shawls	71,981	5,831	5,611	5,519
Gloves	46,622	29,812	41,189	112941
Cravats	411,689	50,271	55,777	105,194
Handkerchiefs	117,368	46,294	49,932	49,184
Mantillas	....	573	....	....
Vestings	3,608	2,427	....	....
Hose	46,790	57,218	34,128	43,955
Sewings	11,367	16,557	81,764	51,994
Braid and Bindings	1,200,555	964 883	1,143,737	934,029
Silk and Worsted	421,791	165,614	136,194	136,721
Silk & Cotton and Silk & Linen	2,316,343	2,045,139	1,995,753	2,006,997
Totals	$23,168,118	$21,192,386	$19,922,741	$20,407,796

For twenty years previous to 1873, (except two years of the war), we had imported an average of about thirty million dollars worth of Silk Goods in each year. In 1872 the importations had reached $36,448,61[illegible]. Meantime the Silk Industry here had been struggling for existence for nearly thirty years, and had at last won for itself a place. It 1872 it manufactured $25,000,000 worth of goods, and in 1875 it first manufactured and marketed nearly two-fifths of the whole amount of Silk Goods consumed in this country, and it has held and increased its ascendancy ever since. It should be said in explanation of this statement, that the table of imports of Silk Goods gives the values at the place of exportation, and in *gold* (though this makes no difference now); and there is to be added to these values, the freight and duty, and the importers' profit, to reach the market value. The duty ranges from 40 to 60 per cent., so that the importations represent a market value of more than thirty millions. Then, also, in the table of goods manufactured, the first four items enter into the values of the remaining items. The desperate efforts of Silk manufacturers abroad to hold our market, has made the struggle a very difficult one, but our manufacturers are gaining slowly. Sewing Silks are not now imported to any extent. We produce about two-thirds of the ribbons consumed, most of the dress trimmings and handkerchiefs, and a constantly increasing proportion of the dress goods. Velvets, laces and mixed goods are not made here.

* Estimated by Silk Association.

EDUCATIONAL.

The Educational condition of the United States, though not yet what we may hope it will be, is far in advance of that of any other nation. Some of the German States maintain a system of compulsory education, which ensures to every child a certain amount of intellectual training, but this is surrounded by such restrictions that it is not so beneficial to the youth of the State as our more free and practical system of education. In our country, up to the close of the late war, very few of the Southern States had any thorough system of primary education, and many of their secondary and higher schools, colleges and seminaries, were very superficial; but the last ten years has witnessed a great advance in these respects in those States, and the Northern States have made equally rapid progress. The tables which follow, show that nearly 9,000,000 of our children—somewhat more than one-fifth of our entire population—are enrolled in our Public Schools; 246,654 in our secondary and special schools (these returns are so incomplete that they do not probably represent one-half of the actual number in attendance, the Catholic Secondary Schools reporting 242,000 children), the Universities and Colleges have 56,253 students, and the Scientific and Professional Schools 25,039, making a grand total of nearly 9,600,000 children and youth under instruction; more than 270,000 teachers are engaged in the work of instruction. For the purposes of this education, the investment in real estate, appliances for teaching, and libraries, is over $314,000,000; the amount of vested and permanent funds (largely increased by benefactions, sales of land, etc., every year,) is more than $127,500,000, and the annual income $108,300,000. No nation in the world can make such an exhibit as this, but we may fairly hope that another decade will show one-fourth of our population under instruction, with greatly increased facilities. The reader will find, also, in the tables which follow, an account of the private benefactions made to education since 1870, and of the large libraries which have made such a rapid growth within the past few years.

STATISTICS OF THE PUBLIC SCHOOLS OF THE UNITED STATES FOR 1876.

STATES AND TERRITORIES.	School Age.	School Population.	Number between 9 and 18 years of age.	Number enrolled in Public Schools.	*Average Daily Attendance.	Average duration of School in days.	Number of Teachers employed in Public School.	
							Male.	Female.
Alabama	5 to 21	406,270	224,389	147,340	110,253	86.5	2,702	1,297
Arkansas	6..21	184,692	138,519	73,878	42,680	.....	1,582	740
California	5..17	171,563	154,406	130,930	78,027	149.0	1,033	1,660
Colorado	5..21	23,275	16,292	12,552	7,343	116.0	172	205
Connecticut	4..16	134,976	112,480	120,189	68,993	176.0	721	2,324
Delaware	5..21	47,825	35,878	19,881	....	140.0	(4	30)
Florida	6..21	94,522	70,891	32,371	28,306	132.0	(7	96)
Georgia	6..18	394,037	354,633	156,394	96,680	....	....	....
Illinois	6..21	958,003	718,502	687,446	....	....	9,288	12,330
Indiana	6..21	667,711	500,783	502,362	300,743	120.0	7,670	5,463
Iowa	5..21	533,903	341,713	384,012	....	136 0	6,500	11,645
Kansas	5..21	199,986	129,331	142 606	85,580	102 0	2,484	2,890
Kentucky	6..20	437,100	349,680	228,000	159,000	100.0	4,236	1,732
Louisiana	6..21	274,688	206,016	74,846	....	....	797	760
Maine	4..21	221,477	143,960	157,323	100,641	117.0	1,984	4,475
Maryland	5..20	276,120	207,090	142,992	69,259	187.0	1,129	1,594
Massachusetts	5..15	294,708	294,708	302,118	216,861	177.0	1,169	8,047
Michigan	5..20	448,784	336,588	343,619	200,000	138.0	3,285	9,182
Minnesota	5..21	218,641	153,048	130,280	71,292	120.0	1,372	1,591
Missippi	5..21	318,459	222,921	168,217	106,894	140 0	2,989	1 979
Missouri	5..21	738,431	516 901	394,780	192,904	99.0	5,904	3,747
Nebraska	5..21	80,122	56,085	55,423	....	96.0	1,504	1,587
Nevada	6..18	6,315	5,683	4,811	2,884	....	35	80
New Hampshire	4..21	76,272	55,865	68,751	48,288	100 0	503	3,160
New Jersey	5..18	312,694	265 790	191,731	98,089	194.0	946	2,307
New York	5..21	1,583,064	1,108,144	1,059,238	531,835	176 0	7,428	22,585
North Carolina	6..21	348,603	261,452	146,737	97,830	50.0	(2,	690)
Ohio	6..21	1,017,726	757,138	712,129	435,349	140.0	12,306	10,186
Oregon	4..20	44,661	31,262	21,518	....	105.5	496	457
Pennsylvania	6..21	1,222,697	917,031	890,073	551,848	151.0	8,585	11,295
Rhode Island	5..15	53,316	48,321	38,554	26,163	178.0	195	861
South Carolina	6..16	239,264	239,264	110,416	....	100 0	1,773	1,082
Tennessee	6..18	426,612	383,950	199,058	136,805	100.0	3,125	1 085
Texas	6..18	313,061	281,754	184,705	125,224	78.0	(4,	030)
Vermont	5..20	89,541	67,155	78,139	50,023	111.0	667	3,739
Virginia	5..21	482,789	307,230	184 486	103,927	112.0	2,711	1,551
West Virginia	6..21	179,897	134,922	115,300	79,002	92.5	2,677	794
Wisconsin	4..20	461,829	323,280	279,854	....	149.0	(9,	451)
Totals		13,983,634	10,533,055	8,693,289			(247,	408)
Arizona	6..21	2,508	1,881	568	419	180.	6	8
Dakota	5..21	8,343	5,840	4,428	....	....	54	154
Dist. of Columbia	6..17	31,671	20,133	18,785	13,494	191.0	22	271
Idaho	5..21	4 020	2,814	3,270	....	....	....	....
Montana	4..21	3,822	2,250	2 215	1,710	92 0	43	56
New Mexico	7..18	29,312	28,984	5,151	....	132.0	132	15
Utah	4..16	35,696	29,747	19,278	13,462	140.0	220	218
Washington	4..21	8,350	5,427	6,099	....	70.0	(2	20)
Wyoming	5..20	1,095	845	1,222	....	....	7	16
Indian	6..16	....	....	3,754	....	....	....	....
Total		124,817	106,921	77,922			(1,	839)
Grand Totals		14,108,451	10,639,976	8,771,211			(249,	307)

* So many of the States do not return the average daily attendance, that the total footings are of no value, and are omitted.

STATISTICS OF THE PUBLIC SCHOOLS OF THE UNITED STATES, JAN., 1876.

STATES AND TERRITORIES.	Average Monthly Salary of Teachers.		Annual income of the Public Schools.	Annual Expenditures of Public Schools.				
	Male.	Female.		Sites, Buildings, Libraries, Furniture and apparatus.	Salaries of Superintendents.	Salaries of Teachers.	Miscellaneous.	Total Expenditures.
Alabama	$(27.	20)	$553,014	$100	34,187	$489,492	....	523,779
Arkansas	......	......	789,536	54,912	24,100	259,747	....	750,000
California	84.93	68.01	3,390,359	465,955	43,022	1,810,479	381,803	2,701,863
Colorado	60.00	48.00	254,679	76,215	7,500	102,783	31,815	218,313
Connecticut	70.05	37.35	1,592,749	220,942	20,000	1,057,242	254,399	1,552,583
Delaware	(28.	00)	192,735	....	......	....	....	....
Florida	50.00	30.00	188,952	....	15,600	....	....	107,724
Georgia	......	......	435,319	....	......	....	....	....
Illinois	48.21	33.32	8,268,540	1,090,574	......	5,326,780	971,854	8,268,540
Indiana	65.00	40.00	5,041,517	700,000	50,000	2,830,747	949,457	4,530,204
Iowa	36.68	28.33	5,035,498	1,114,68[illegible]	......	2,598,440	892,626	4,605,749
Kansas	33.98	27.25	1,042,298	182,886	34,100	689,907	113,208	1,020,101
Kentucky	(49.	40)	1,438,436	111,406	......	....	....	1,559,452
Louisiana	37.00	37.00	699,665	60,182	24,000	573,144	42,339	699,065
Maine	37.00	18.00	1,313,303	110,725	29,668	1,046,766	126,144	1,313,303
Maryland	41.73	41.73	1,376,046	272,539	25,440	1,035,755	307,313	1,641,047
Massachusetts	88.37	35.35	6,410,514	1,533,142	......	....	....	7,000,000
Michigan	51.29	28.19	4,173,551	571,109	......	1,930,928	994,745	3,516,7[illegible]2
Minnesota	41.36	28.91	1,861,158	208,030	......	702,662	247,755	1,158,447
Mississippi	55.47	55.47	1,110,248	55,000	48,650	856,950	80,000	1,040,600
Missouri	38.00	29.50	3,013,595	....	......	....	....	3,000,000
Nebraska	38.60	33.10	292,475	327,406	18,916	414,827	167,039	928,[illegible]88
Nevada	(100.	56)	146,181	22,723	......	83,548	18,030	124,301
New Hampshire	42.61	25.54	621,649	264,244	......	424,889	53,721	742,854
New Jersey	67.65	37.75	2,311,465	549,619	28,770	1,731,816	30,780	2,340,985
New York	(58.	36)	11,601,256	2,191,927	......	7,849,667	1,569,662	11,601,256
North Carolina	30.00	25.00	500,000	15,100	......	158,129	8,445	300,000
Ohio	60.00	44.00	8,711,411	1,313,515	158,773	4,787,964	1,391,704	7,651,956
Oregon	51.45	45.50	204,760	3,125	2,000	....	....	215,707
Pennsylvania	41.07	34.09	8,798,816	2,059,465	106,050	4,640,825	2,557,587	9,363,927
Rhode Island	58.18	46.17	761,796	275,835	11,681	383,284	77,059	764,643
South Carolina	31.64	29.21	489,542	22,222	......	369,685	31,554	426,461
Tennessee	30.85	30.85	740,316	44,406	19,385	582,918	42,420	703,358
Texas	(53.	00)	244,879	60,081	9,233	630,334	26,5[illegible]8	726,236
Vermont	45.62	25.65	516,252	89,789	12,643	440,536	82,089	625,057
Virginia	33.52	28.71	1,215,353	97,278	48,668	726,300	151,150	1,023,396
West Virginia	35.03	30.77	753,477	123,844	2,500	541,359	47,457	715,160
Wisconsin	50.83	33.28	2,308,187	371,496	50,000	1,350,884	241,777	2,066,375
Totals			88,390,237	14,710,475	825,486	46,448,787	11,893,524	[illegible]5,526,912
Arizona	100.00	100.00	28,759	....	......	....	....	24,151
Dakota	35.00	25.00	32,602	9,985	......	18,046	4,572	32,603
Dist. of Columbia	115.00	75.00	517,610	61,123	9,520	209,368	86,568	360,579
Idaho	55.00	55.00	22,497	....	......	....	....	17,2[illegible]0
Montana	65.00	57.00	31,821	28,726	4,500	33,921	....	67,147
New Mexico	......	......	25,473	....	......	15,432	3,458	18,890
Utah	47.00	23.00	130,799	49,568	3,450	130,800	....	183,818
Washington	......	......	....	....	......	54,720	....	54,720
Wyoming	......	......	....	....	......	16,400	....	16,400
Indian	......	......	99,929	....	......	....	....	99,000
Total			889,490	149,402	17,470	578,687	94,598	886,5[illegible]8
Grand Totals			89,288,727	14,859,877	842,956	47,027,474	11,988,122	86,407,440

STATISTICS OF THE PUBLIC SCHOOLS OF THE UNITED STATES, JAN., 1876.

STATES AND TERRITORIES.	Number of School-Houses.	Estimated value of sites, buildings and all other School Property.	Amount of Permanent School Fund.	Expenditure in the year *per capita* of the School population	Expenditure in the year *per capita* of pupils enrolled in the Public Schools.	Expenditure in the year *per capita*, of average attendance on the Public Schools.	Amount of benefaction for educational purposes reported as having been made during the year 1875.
Alabama	3,898	......	2,506,250	......	......	......	$2,825
Arkansas	2,134	355,000	1,222,500	$4.06	$10 15	$17.57	5,680
California	2,190	5,068,678	1,737,500	......	17.09	25.82	13,000
Colorado	172	474,008	......	9.38	17.39	29.73	1,300
Connecticut	1,656	......	2,807,697	11.80	12.92	22 50	34,750
Delaware	369	......	470,000	......	......	9.64	10,000
Florida	796	......	225,000	1.99	5.83	6.69	500
Georgia	3,669	......	......	1.10	2.78	4.50	66,713
Illinois	11,451	19,876,708	7,860,554	......	......	......	388,434
Indiana	9,307	10,870,338	8,799,192	6.78	9.01	15.06	51,600
Iowa	9,528	8,617,955	3,363 961	6.75	9.38	15.99	174,859
Kansas	3,715	4,140,090	1,163,000	4.28	5.93	9.99	3,200
Kentucky	4,894	1,624,000	1,327,000	......	......	......	26,495
Louisiana	1,032	896,100	400,000	2.45	9.40	......	12,809
Maine	4,180	3,019,549	400,558	5.41	7.68	12 01	307,800
Maryland	1,846	......	350,370	5.01	9.68	19.99	8,500
Massachusetts	5,551	20,856,777	2,000,000	22.00	20.00	30.00	247,399
Michigan	5,702	9,355,894	3,977,269	6.67	11.97	14.97	32 342
Minnesota	3,085	2,808,156	3,200,000	5.74	9.29	16.98	18,967
Mississippi	2,275	1,000,000	1,068,159	2.84	5.38	6.83	21,000
Missouri	7,325	6,771,163	7 248,535	......	......	......	184,455
Nebraska	1,805	1,848,239	1,212,288	7.76	11.42	......	......
Nevada	115	121,011	......	......	......	......	......
New Hampshire	2,223	2,258 000	500,000	6.57	7.31	10.41	475,760
New Jersey	2,948	6,287 267	800 000	5.85	9.55	17.97	324,901
New York	11,781	29,928,626	3,080,108	......	......	......	410,421
North Carolina	4,020	......	†2,187,564	......	......	......	33,550
Ohio	11,834	19,876,504	3,646,713	7.76	10.57	17.29	181,030
Oregon	859	350,000	1,314,000	......	......	......	3,175
Pennsylvania	17,092	24,260,789	......	......	......	......	810,672
Rhode Island	739	2,360,017	265 143	9.37	12.96	19.09	16,945
South Carolina	2,347	313,289	419,543	1.78	3.86	......	17,925
Tennessee	3,125	......	2 512,500	1.64	3.53	5.14	42 187
Texas	3,898	173,598	2,631,673	......	......	......	7,850
Vermont	2,800	1,339,864	......	7.04	8 89	12.60	25,075
Virginia	3,885	757,181	1,050,000	1.93	5.05	8,96	91,012
West Virginia	3,243	1,605,627	290,000	2 92	4.68	7.19	15,000
Wisconsin	5,260	4,979,169	2,624,240	3 64	6.05	......	40,300
Totals	162,951	192,193,598	72,681,517				
Arizona	11	20,000	......	9.62	42.41	57.66	......
Dakota	296	24,926	......	3.92	7.36	......	......
Dist. of Columbia	47	1,114,162	......	11.57	19.51	27.16	6,500
Idaho	53	......	......	......	......	......	......
Montana	76	60,000	......	8.42	14.36	18.60	......
New Mexico	138	......	......	......	......	......	500
Utah	296	438,665	......	5.15	8.53	13.00	6,671
Washington	219	......	......	......	......	......	2,400
Wyoming	13	32,500	......	......	......	......	......
Indian	163	......	......	......	......	......	2,000
Total	1,312	1,690,253					
Grand Totals	164,263	193,883,851					‡4,120,562

† Nominal, not much over 3 per cent. now available. ‡ The benefaction to education in 1874, were $6 053,304; in 1873, $11,226,977; in 1872, $9,957,494; in 1871, $8,435,990; making a total in five years of $39,800,327.

In 1876 there were 3,632 Public Libraries in the U. S., with 12,276,964 volumes. 201 contained over 10,000 volumes each; 73 over 20,000; 52 over 30,000; 29 over 40,000, and 19 over 50,000 volumes. The largest are: Library of Congress, 300,000; Boston Public Library, 199,869; Harvard University, 227,650; Astor, 152,446; Mercantile, N. Y., 160,613; Mercantile, Philadelphia, 125,168; House of Representatives, Washington, 125,000; Yale College, 114,200; Boston Athenæum, 205,000; Phila. Lib. Co., 101,000; N. Y. State, at Albany, 95,000, and several others rapidly approaching 100,000. Permanent endowment funds, about $15,000,000. Amount invested in buildings, grounds, books, manuscripts &c., $40,000,000, at least. Amount invested in Academies of Design, Art Collections, Archæology, Natural History and Science (of which there are nearly 100), aggregates from $15,000,000 to $.0,000,000.

SECONDARY INSTRUCTION.

After our Public Schools, of which we have given such full statistics in the preceding tables, some schools of secondary or superior instruction, which under a variety of names, form the connecting links between the public school and the college or university. Some of these are private schools but somewhat permanent in character; they may be schools for boys, or for girls, or both; others rank as academies, high schools or seminaries; others still, are preparatory schools for the college course; others still as schools of superior instruction for women, Female Seminaries, Colleges, Academies, or Collegiate Institutes. Still another class, are Commercial or Business Colleges. There are also Normal Schools or Colleges, sometimes private, sometimes State or City institutions, intended for training teachers—and schools of special instruction for deaf mutes, blind, feeble minded, orphans and juvenile offenders. The character of these schools is so diverse that we cannot bring them under a table, showing the number in each State, but we give below the aggregate number of each class in the entire country, with such particulars as can be collected concerning them, premising that a considerable number are not reported in any year.

CLASSES OF SCHOOLS.	No. Schools in U.S.	No. Male Teachers	No. Fem. Teachers	Total Number of Pupils.	No. Male Pupils.	No. Female Pupils.	Value of Buildings, Grounds and Apparatus.	Amount of Productive Endowment.	Income from productive Endowment of State appropriation.	Income from all Sources.	No. of Volumes in Library.
Schools & Acad. Boys.	215	830	152	15,703	15,676	117	$7,268,600	$890,850	$237,118	$1,144,637	114,816
Schools & Acad. Girls.	311	510	1,943	22,375	45	21,918	6,175,605	35,550	4,735	900,125	122,855
Schools, Boys & Girls.	617	1,239	1,407	70,067	36,978	33,029	12,193,352	2,315,513	214 230	1,255,166	206,316
Preparatory Schools.	122	(7	46)	12,954	(12,	954)	4,815,257	1,062,593	72,782	456,776	86,188
Schools, Acads. Sem. Col. & Col. Ins. for superior instruction of women..	222	585	1,592	23,975	......	23,975	10,805,100	778,650	60,699	1,259,411	217,023
Normal Schools & Col.	137	(1,0	31)	29,105	12,924	16,181	....	....	....	684,071	96,103
Com. & Business Col.	131	(5	94)	25,109	(25,	109)	....	....	....	....	19,679
Kindergarten.........	95	(2	16)	2,809	(2,	809)	....	....	....	....	....
SPECIAL INSTRUCTION—											
Schools for Deaf Mutes	41	(2	94)	5,087	2,795	2,292	6 136,815	....	1,049,524	1,144,044	29,540
Schools for the Blind.	29	(4	98)	2,054	(2,	054)	3,893,467	....	551,786	866,411	22,198
Schools, feeble minded, Idiotic, &c.....	9	(3,1	71)	1,372	816	556	....	....	....	242,514	....
Reform Schools.......	47	357	311	10,670	8,111	2,559	....	....	Earn'gs	1,145,315	85
Orphan Asylums, Soldier's Or. Homes, Infant Asylums & Indus. Schools	207	(1,3	28)	24,584	10,656	13,928	....	....	....	3,035,453	4,020
Grand Totals........	2,163	(14,0	60)	246,654	(246,	654)	51,288,406	5,083,185	2,264,202	12,132,913	1 145,071

IV. SCIENTIFIC AND PROFESSIONAL SCHOOLS.

There still remains, to complete our summary review of the Educational Institutions of this country, some account of the Scientific and Professional Schools or Institutions of the United States. The Scientific Schools are of two classes. Those organized under the law making grants of land to Agricultural Colleges, and receiving the avails of these grants, and those not receiving these avails, but endowed by State or private munificence. The Theological Seminaries and institutions can be classed under a single head, though some of them are connected with Colleges or Universities, and others are independent of these; some have a course of classical study, and others are confined to theological studies exclusively. The Law Schools come under a single head, but the Medical Schools are divided into Regular, Homœopathic and Eclectic, and the Dental and Pharmaceutical Schools are also classed with them. We give herewith such statistics as can be obtained of all these Scientific and Professional Schools.

CLASSES OF SCHOOLS OR INSTITUTIONS IN UNITED STATES.	Number of Schools.	Number of Professors or Instructors.	Whole Number of Students.	Number of Male Students.	Number of Female Students	No. in Preparatory or Partial Course.	No. in Scientific or Professional Course.	Value of Buildings, Grounds, Apparatus, &c.	Amount of Productive Endowment.	Income from Productive Endowment.	Income from all Sources.	Number of Scholarships.	Volumes in Libraries.
I. SCIENTIFIC SCHOOLS													
A—Schools endowed from Agricultural gr'nt	45	539	4,919	(4,	919	946	3,971	6,942,109	6,591,128	403,975	643,345	1,250	93,566
B—Not thus endowed	51	219	2 238	(2,	238	611	1,629	1,820,030	1,617,733	118,166	238,836	216	60,198
II. THEOLOGICAL SCH'LS	123	615	5,234	5,234	..	......	......	6,368,117	6,415,601	652,619	....	.....	599,171
III. LAW SCHOOLS.....	42	224	2,677	(2,	677	......	......	45,000	68,301	17,695	70,639	.....	63,212
IV. MEDICAL SCHOOLS													
A—Regular Practice.	65	809	7,518	(7,	518	......	......	2,477,930	160,266	12,071	388,721	.....	57,896
B—Homœopathic.....	11	136	664	(6	64)	......	......	480,400	60,000	3,108	46,174	.....	4,180
C—Eclectic	4	36	398	(3	98)	......	......	216,000	....	....	25,428	.....	1,400
Dental Schools.........	12	133	469	(4	69)	......	......	68,000	....	....	49,238	.....	1,512
Schools of Pharmacy...	14	66	922	(9	22)	......	......	111,750	39,550	3,205	26,311	.....	7,760
Totals..................	846	2,769	25,039	(25,	039	1,557	6,600	19,409,364	15,942,479	1,111,331	1,287,201		877,450

In most of the Theological Schools, the tuition is provided for by endowment and is free. The Scholarships of the Scientific Schools cover the tuition; there are also free scholarships in some of the Medical Schools—usually the result of State grants.

STATISTICS OF UNIVERSITIES AND COLLEGES IN THE UNITED STATES IN 1876.

STATES.	No. of Universities & Colleges.	Whole No. Professors and Instructors.	Whole number of Students.	Preparatory Department: Professors and Teachers.	Preparatory Department: Male Students.	Preparatory Department: Female Students.	Students not classified.	Collegiate Departments: College Professors and Instruct'rs.	Collegiate Departments: Male Students.	Collegiate Departments: Female Students.	Value of Buildings, Grounds and Apparatus.	Amount of Productive Funds.	Income from Productive Funds.	Income from all sources.	Amount of Scholarship Funds.	Number of Volumes in Libraries.
Alabama	4	49	304	1	25		131	48	148		$425,000	$320,000	$26,000	81,500		14,300
Arkansas	4	16	305		159	84		16	62		96,000	21,500	2,150	7,250		400
California	13	179	2,331	11	6[illegible]8	227	675	163	268	94	1,524,715	844,900	226,015	471,278		46,665
Connecticut	3	57	847					57	839	8	1,233,700	985,839	68,490	136,50[illegible]	60,000	141,000
Colorado	2	7	69	1	31	21		6	11	6	30,000					
Delaware	1	7	40					7	40		75,000	83,000	5,000	9,000		7,200
Georgia	6	47	714	1	174	11		46	438	90	555,600	543,000	41,50[illegible]	68,500	300	35,900
Illinois	26	342	4,766	45	2,261	842	150	297	915	310	2,817,400	1,562,000	114,193	219,523	55,500	112,519
Indiana	19	189	3,464	50	1,434	406	95	139	1,083	241	1,392,500	1,087,000	75,960	138,483	40,750	84,317
Iowa	18	203	3,864	52	1,800	1,139	200	151	457	267	560,548	73[illegible],185	62,145	133,659	38,032	42,714
Kansas	6	41	417	5	151	128		36	86	52	425,000	51,000	5,553	30,906		7,708
Kentucky	14	106	1,853	13	659	166	166	93	592	270	701,000	758,000	32,272	93,427	100,000	45,500
Louisiana	6	45	355	3	196	98		42	49	1[illegible]	355,555	138,000		14,849		21,[illegible]50
Maine	3	32	383	2	45	3		30	324	11	6[illegible]8,850	52[illegible],500	33,4[illegible]0	69,400	85,060	50,665
Maryland	8	125	917	37	347	12		88	495	63	410,000	3,000,000	100,000	27[illegible],788		4[illegible],705
Massachusetts	7	132	1,763	5	205			127	1,529	29	4,025,000	2,[illegible]76,234	761,057	[illegible]52,082	681,258	271,584
Michigan	8	115	2,151	21	737	673		94	502	239	640,250	5[illegible]6,426	47,377	169,603	15,000	41,375
Minnesota	3	44	485	3	206	57		41	161	22	190,877	319,537	16,859	40,459	3,000	15,118
Mississippi	4	31	363	6	151	35	75	25	107	70	374,[illegible]00	48,000	4,100	58,400		11,452
Missouri	20	251	2,846	4	1,555	401	271	204	643	417	1,206,850	696,000	114,447	[illegible]59,127	75,000	77,545
Nebraska	3	21	306	1	194	66		21	35	11	181,000	33,785	2,478	31,092		3,550
Nevada	1	1	31	1	15	16										
New Hampshire	1	37	357					37	357		160,000	350,000	21,00[illegible]	36,000	100,000	57,000
New Jersey	4	51	8[illegible]5	3	93			51	712		1,608,400	1,252,405	77,750	102,737	92,185	59,414
New York	26	486	5,952	75	2,299	531		411	2,588	531	6,545,332	8,877,018	503,152	1,095,452	420,392	210,832
North Carolina	7	5[illegible]	859		343	83		50	3[illegible]8	85	450,000	330,450	7,200	45,630		57,000
Ohio	33	2[illegible]9	5,824	58	2,411	1,004	106	241	1,787	622	2,80[illegible],512	1,875,145	148,185	217,917	218,612	158,465
Oregon	6	39	[illegible]27	10	429	332		29	58	68	195,851	163,349	15,494	33,72[illegible]	67,000	8,381
Pennsylvania	29	354	4,124	45	1,484	243	310	309	1,880	201	4,401,000	2,031,300	148,180	379,768	72,000	189,698
Rhode Island	1	15	255	0	0	0		15	255		1,500,000	642,155	43,04[illegible]	74,368	57,725	45,000
South Carolina	6	40	670	4	[illegible]22			35	357		784,000	484,000	26,600	75,148	48,6[illegible]0	60,250
Tennessee	21	171	2,682	31	1,176	255	185	137	1,164	190	1,327,500	948,200	55,387	116,102	24,000	40,[illegible]20
Texas	12	85	1,715	24	646	434		62	402	233	390,600	129,000	3,500	57,460	31,200	16,561
Vermont	3	22	194	0	10			22	158	20	274,400	209,250	13,581	23,181	64,500	32,521
Virginia	8	80	1,417	5	158			75	1,259		672,000	303,000	25,780	84,658	52,485	117,180
West Virginia	3	27	353	3	141	7		24	12	77	256,000	180,000	11,4[illegible]0	39,760		11,230
Wisconsin	10	133	2,101	35	1,007	352		58	580	162	943,125	762,107	53,332	194,0[illegible]2	15,000	42,113
District of Columbia	4	54	451	9	304			45	147		420,000			529		50,850
New Mexico	1	8	93	6	78			2	15		13,500			9,817		
Utah	1	8	291	4	172	119		4			1,500			6,171		2,394
Washington Territory	1	3	55					3	55							503
Totals	355	4,027	56,253	61[illegible]	22,085	7,78[illegible]	2,365	3,388	22,051	3,251	41,089,605	33,252,5[illegible]5	2,453,336	5,257,836	2,527,649	2,256,11[illegible]

RELIGIOUS STATISTICS OF THE UNITED STATES IN 1878-9.

DENOMINATIONS & SECTS.	Archbishops Bis. Supts. &c	Clergymen.	Dioc's, Syn'ds Conf. Classes Associations Presbyt's, &c	Churches, Congregat'ns and Parishes	Church Edifices.	Number of Sittings.	Communicants, or Memb'rs of Churches, Cong's, or Parishes.	Adherent Population.	Value of Church Property.	Contribut'ns for Benevolent and Church Purposes.	Additions to Church Membership within the Year.	Sunday Schools.	Sunday School Teachers & Scholars.	Denomina'al Acad's, S'h'ls & Seminar's.	Univ's, Coll'g's & Theolg. Sem's of Denom's.	Newsp'ers & Periodic'ls of Denom's.
Roman Catholic	66	5,548	67	8,170	5,634	3,178,420	3,970,000	6,078,000	$67,472,450				300,000	137	67	35
Methodist Episcopal Church	11	11,303	94	17,337	16,387	4,413,784	1,487,177	6,692,296	78,140,866	16,597,850	78,778	19,961	1,727,827	69	52	48
Do do South	7	3,721	38	7,543	7,231	1,780,427	765,337	3,444,293	19,073,425	3,2[illegible]9,706	42,346	7,947	418,405	25	53	23
United Brethren in Christ	3	1,952	43	4,078	11,909	535,230	143,881	647,627	2,823,540		7,805	2,854	163,439	12	7	6
Other Methodists, incl. Col'd	25	6,495	123	9,586	8,057	1,776,300	799,038	3,596,052	20,185,300		8,419	10,447	540,900	25	12	22
Free-Will, or Free Baptists		1,367	41	1,9[illegible]3	1,584	157,690	75,826	338,413	2,318,500		8,127			16	6	5
Regular Baptists		14,954	1,075	24,499	20,081	4,928,300	2,102,034	9,459,153	84,864,350	18,783,927	102,736	12,629	1,318,725	153	52	52
Disciples		2,371		3,893	2,313	905,400	397,246	1,787,607	5,123,200	3,006,125	6,183	2,981	349,185	16	9	26
Menn'ts, Tunkers Winebr'ns		3,688		4,031	2,710	581,500	410,600	1,847,700	2,927,320		65,000				5	6
7Day, 6Princ'l & other Bapt's		769		908	721	208,124	71,500	321,525	700,000						3	3
Presbyt'n Ch. Un. Gen. Assm		4,901	75	5,269	5,198	2,421,873	567,855	2,555,347	42,163,400		11,610		599,882			
Presbyterian Church South.		1,117	77	1,873	1,529	593,400	114,578	515,601	10,515,300	1,030,971	2,028		75,943	25	4	8
Refm'd Presbyter'ns, 4 Sects		306		322	228	72,300	28,069	126,310	578,000	391,425	873				3	2
United Presbyterians		647	65	661	638	298,058	78,048	351,216	3,985,300		1,259	709	259,243	10	7	3
Cumberland Presbyterians		1,312	112	2,347	2,109	502,725	106,253	478,012	1,741,347	601,238	3,583	587	64,829	6	8	3
Refm'd Ch. in U. S., late Ger		447	35	1,099	1,087	301,200	87,871	395,420	5,978,325	1,058,117	1,312	198	67,348	13	8	12
Refm'd Ch. in Amer. late Dut'h		543	41	503	489	238,175	79,413	357,358	12,128,500	1,496,224	1,004	648	77,541	5	4	3
Congregationalists		3,496	49	3,620	3,502	1,005,000	365,447	1,644,511	29,347,125	7,117,808	14,789		420,220	35	31	18
Protestant Episcopal Church	63	3,204	61	3,002	2,907	1,062,864	314,367	1,414,650	40,385,250	6,477,806	26,7[illegible]3	2,816	323,026	76	36	14
Reformed Episcopal Church	4	64		61	51	105,000	5,808	26,136	800,000	280,785	1,216			3		2
Lutherans		2,795	59	4,982	4,610	1,217,528	696,420	3,133,890	17,450,325	7,381,420	96,095			33	29	48
United Brethren—Morav'ns	5	98	21	75	68	25,180	9,212	40,954	135,000		913			9	1	3
Unitarians		401	39	358	360	167,000	31,780	143,100	6,504,500	450,000				7	2	5
Christian Connect'n, 3 Sects		1,271	78	1,461	1,258	131,000	98,640	447,300	1,084,250					9	7	6
Universalists		711	12	737	821	307,250	45,218	201,200	7,914,128	472,000		661	51,150	7	7	12
Friends—Orthodox			8	542	518	156,000	60,128	270,576	690,000		1,092		66,871	6	5	2
Friends—Hicksite & Progres							40,000	180,000	475,000					6	1	2
New Jerus. or Swedenborg'n		81	16	90			7,450	31,000		64,500				17	1	9
Jews		185		220	190	101,000	57,500	112,540	8,140,000					15	1	10
Mormons	155	735			95	100,000	120,000	155,000	2,500,000							8
Spiritualists					90	18,000	30,000	155,000	60,000							10
Minor Sects not included abv		3[illegible]0		425	332	63,200	50,000	150,000	280,000							6
Deist, Atheist, Rad. or Liberal								150,000								5

The above table has been prepared with great care, and in all cases from the latest authorities. The sittings, where not given by the Church authorities, are calculated from the same ratios as the table of denominations in the United States Census; and the adherent population on the ratio of 4½ adherents to each communicant, which long observation has proved to be more nearly accurate, than that of 5 to 1 usually employed. The only exceptions to this ratio, and those made for reasons which are obvious to all, are the Roman Catholic, the Jews, Mormons, and a few minor sects grouped together. In all these the members in full communion, or openly declared such, constitute a very large proportion of those who adhere to them—usually at least one half. The increase in the amount and value of Church property has been very great within the past ten years; and the recent decline in value of real estate has been in most cases more than made good by the erection of new churches and manses. It will be seen that the present estimated value is nearly $477,000,000.

CENSUS OF 1870.

POPULATION OF THE UNITED STATES.—GENERAL NATIVITY AND FOREIGN PARENTAGE.

[From the Report of the Superintendent of the Census.]

STATES AND TERRITORIES.	1870.			1860.		
	Total population.	Native born.	Foreign born.	Total population.	Native born.	Foreign born.
Total U. States	38,558,371	32,991,142	5,567,229	31,443,321	27,304,624	4,138,697
Total States	38,115,641	32,642,612	5,473,029	31,183,744	27,084,592	4,099,152
Alabama	996,992	987,030	9,962	964,201	951,849	12,352
Arkansas	484,471	479,445	5,026	435,450	431,850	3,600
California	560,247	350,416	209,831	379,994	233,466	146,528
Connecticut	537,454	423,815	113,639	460,147	379,451	80,696
Delaware	125,015	115,879	9,136	112,216	103,051	9,165
Florida	187,748	182,781	4,967	140,424	137,115	3,309
Georgia	1,184,109	1,172,982	11,127	1,057,286	1,045,615	11,671
Illinois	2,539,891	2,024,693	515,198	1,711,951	1,387,308	324,643
Indiana	1,680,637	1,539,163	141,474	1,350,428	1,232,144	118,284
Iowa	1,194,020	989,328	204,692	674,913	568,836	106,077
Kansas	364,399	316,007	48,392	107,206	94,515	12,691
Kentucky	1,321,011	1,257,613	63,398	1,155,684	1,095,885	59,799
Louisiana	726,915	665,088	61,827	708,002	627,027	80,975
Maine	626,915	578,034	48,881	628,279	590,826	37,453
Maryland	780,894	697,482	83,412	687,049	609,520	77,529
Massachusetts	1,457,351	1,104,032	353,319	1,231,066	970,960	260,106
Michigan	1,184,059	916,049	268,010	749,113	600,020	149,093
Minnesota	439,706	279,009	160,697	172,023	113,295	58,728
Mississippi	827,922	816,731	11,191	791,305	782,747	8,558
Missouri	1,721,295	1,499,028	222,267	1,182,012	1,021,471	160,541
Nebraska	122,993	92,245	30,748	28,841	22,490	6,351
Nevada	42,491	23,690	18,801	6,857	4,793	2,064
New Hampshire	318,300	288,689	29,611	326,073	305,135	20,938
New Jersey	906,096	717,153	188,943	672,035	549,245	122,790
New York	4,382,759	3,244,406	1,138,353	3,880,735	2,879,455	1,001,280
North Carolina	1,071,361	1,068,332	3,029	992,622	989,324	3,298
Ohio	2,665,260	2,292,767	372,493	2,339,511	2,011,262	328,249
Oregon	90,923	79,323	11,600	52,465	47,342	5,123
Pennsylvania	3,521,951	2,976,642	545,309	2,906,215	2,475,710	430,505
Rhode Island	217,353	161,957	55,396	174,620	137,226	37,394
South Carolina	705,606	697,532	8,074	703,708	693,722	9,986
Tennessee	1,258,520	1,239,204	19,316	1,109,801	1,088,575	21,226
Texas	818,579	756,168	62,411	604,215	560,743	43,422
Vermont	330,551	283,396	47,155	315,098	282,355	32,743
Virginia	1,225,163	1,211,409	13,754	1,219,630	1,201,117	18,513
West Virginia	442,014	424,923	17,091	376,688	360,143	16,545
Wisconsin	1,054,670	690,171	364,499	775,881	498,954	276,927
Total Territories	442,730	348,530	94,200	259,757	220,032	39,545
Arizona	9,658	3,849	5,809	....	....	....
Colorado	39,864	33,265	6,599	34,277	31,611	2,666
Dakota	14,181	9,366	4,815	4,837	3,063	1,774
Dist. of Columbia	131,700	115,446	16,254	75,080	62,596	12,484
Idaho	14,999	7,114	7,885	....	....	....
Montana	20,595	12,616	7,979	....	....	....
New-Mexico	91,874	86,254	5,620	93,516	86,793	6,723
Utah	86,786	56,084	30,702	40,273	27,519	12,754
Washington	23,955	18,931	5,024	11,594	8,450	3,144
Wyoming	9,118	5,605	3,513	....	....	....

POPULATION OF ALL THE CITIES OF THE UNITED STATES.

(This table has been carefully compiled from the census (official copy) of 1870. It embraces all the cities returned as such, with a few that appear to have been omitted as cities distinctively.

States and Cities.	Total Population.
Alabama.	
Eufaula	3,185
Huntsville	4,907
Mobile	32,034
Montgomery	10,588
Selma	6,484
Talladega	1,933
Tuscaloosa	1,629
Tuscumbia	1,214
Total	62,034
Arkansas.	
Little Rock	12,380
California.	
Los Angeles	5,728
Marysville	4,738
Oakland	10,500
Sacramento	16,283
San Diego	2,300
San Francisco	149,473
San Jose	9,089
Stockton	10,066
Total	208,177
Connecticut.	
Bridgeport	18,969
Hartford	37,180
Middletown	6,923
New Haven	50,840
Norwich	16,653
Waterbury	10,826
Total	141,391
Colorado.	
Denver	4,759
Delaware.	
Wilmington	30,841
Dist. of Columbia.	
Georgetown	11,384
Washington	109,199
Total	120,583
Florida.	
Jacksonville	6,912
Pensacola	3,347
St. Augustine	1,717
Tallahassee	2,023
Total	13,999
Georgia.	
Athens	4,251
Atlanta	21,789
Augusta	15,389
Columbus	7,401
Macon	10,810
Milledgeville	2 750
Rome	2,748
Savannah	28,235
Total	93,373
Idaho.	
Boise City	995
Idaho City	889
Silver City	599
Total	2,483
Illinois.	
Alton	8,665
Amboy	2,825
Anna	1,269
Aurora	11,162
Belleville	8,146
Bloomington	14,590
Bushnell	2,003
Cairo	6,267
Canton	3,308
Centralia	3,190
Champaign	4,625
Chicago	298,977
Danville	4,751
Illinois.—cont'd.	
Decatur	7,161
Dixon	4,055
Elgin	5,441
El Paso	1,564
Freeport	7,889
Galena	7,019
Galesburg	10,158
Jacksonville	9,203
Joliet	7,263
La Salle	5,200
Litchfield	3,852
Macomb	2,748
Mendota	3,546
Monmouth	4,662
Morris	3,138
Mound City	1,631
Mt. Carmel	1,640
Olney	2,680
Ottawa	7,736
Pekin	5,696
Peoria	22,849
Peru	3,650
Quincy	24,052
Rockford	11,049
Rock Island	7,890
Shelbyville	2,051
Springfield	17,364
Sterling	3,998
Watseca	1,551
Waukegan	4,507
Total	571,021
Indiana.	
Columbia	1,663
Connersville	2,496
Crawfordsville	3,701
Evansville	21,830
Fort Wayne	17,718
Franklin City	2,707
Goshen	3,133
Greencastle	3,227
Indianapolis	48,244
Jeffersonville	7,254
Kendallville	2,164
Lafayette	13,506
Laporte	6,581
Lawrenceburg	3,139
Logansport	8,950
Madison	10,709
Michigan City	3,985
New Albany	15,396
Peru	3,617
Richmond	9,445
Seymour	2,372
Shelbyville	2,731
South-Bend	7,206
Terre Haute	16,103
Valparaiso	2,765
Vincennes	5,440
Wabash City	2,881
Total	228,983
Iowa.	
Burlington	14,930
Cedar Falls	3,070
Cedar Rapids	5,940
Clinton	6,129
Council Bluffs	10,020
Davenport	20,038
Des Moines	12,035
Dubuque	18,434
Fairfield	2,226
Fort Dodge	3,095
Fort Madison	4,011
Glenwood	1,291
Iowa—continued.	
Independence	2,945
Iowa City	5,914
Keokuk	12,766
Lyons	4,088
Maquoketa	1,756
Marshalltown	3,218
McGregor	2,074
Muscatine	6,718
Oskaloosa	3,204
Ottumwa	5,214
Sioux City	3,401
Waterloo	4,337
Waverley	2,291
Winterset	1,485
Total	160,630
Kansas.	
Atchison	7,054
Baxter Springs	1,284
Emporia	2,168
Fort Scott	4,147
Lawrence	8,320
Leavenworth	17,873
Ottawa	2,941
Paola	1,811
Topeka	5,796
Wyandotte	2,946
Total	54,353
Kentucky.	
Covington	24,505
Frankfort	5,336
Henderson	4,171
Hopkinsville	3,136
Lexington	14,801
Louisville	100,753
Maysville	4,705
Newport	15,087
Owensboro	3,437
Paducah	6,866
Paris	2,655
Total	185,512
Louisiana.	
Baton Rouge	6,498
Donaldsonville	1,573
New Orleans	191,418
Shreveport	4,607
Total	204,096
Maine.	
Auburn	6,169
Augusta	7,808
Bangor	18,289
Bath	7,371
Belfast	5,278
Biddeford	10,282
Calais	5,944
Hallowell	3,007
Lewiston	13,600
Portland	31,413
Rockland	7,074
Total	116,235
Maryland.	
Annapolis	5,744
Baltimore	267,354
Frederick	8,526
Hagerstown	5,779
Total	287,403
Massachusetts.	
Boston	250,526
Cambridge	39,634
Charlestown	28,323
Chelsea	18,547
Fall River	26,766
Haverhill	13,092

POPULATION OF ALL THE CITIES OF THE UNITED STATES.—Continued.

States and Cities.	Total Population.
Mass.—continued.	
Lawrence	28,921
Lowell	40,928
Lynn	28,233
New Bedford	21,320
Newburyport	12,595
Salem	24,117
Springfield	26,703
Taunton	18,629
Worcester	41,105
Total	619,439
Michigan.	
Adrian	8,438
Ann Arbor	7,363
Battle Creek	5,838
Bay City	7,064
Big Rapids	1,227
Coldwater	4,381
Corunna	2,408
Detroit	79,577
East Saginaw	11,350
Flint	5,386
Grand Haven	3,147
Grand Rapids	16'507
Hillsdale	3,518
Holland	2,319
Jackson	11,447
Lansing	5,241
Lapeer	1,772
Manistee	3,343
Marshall	4,925
Monroe	5,986
Muskegon	6,002
Niles	4,630
Owasso	2,065
Pontiac	4,867
Port Huron	5,973
Saginaw	7,460
St. Clair	1,790
Wyandotte	2,731
Ypsilanti	5,471
Total	229,336
Minnesota.	
Duluth	3,131
Hastings	3,458
Mankato	3,482
Minneapolis	13,066
Owatonna	2,070
Red Wing	4,260
Rochester	3,953
St. Anthony	5,013
St. Cloud	2,161
St. Paul	20,030
Winona	7,192
Total	67,816
Mississippi.	
Columbus	4,812
Grenada	1,887
Holly Springs	2,406
Jackson	4,234
Macon	975
Natchez	9,057
Vicksburgh	12,443
Total	35,814
Missouri.	
Cape Girardean	3,585
Chillicothe	3,978
Hannibal	10,125
Independence	3,184
Jefferson City	4,420
Kansas City	32,260
Louisiana	3,639
Macon	3,678
St. Charles	5,570
St. Joseph	19,565
Missouri—cont'd.	
St. Louis	310,864
Westport	1,095
Total	401,963
Montana.	
Helena	3,842
Nebraska.	
Omaha	16,083
Nebraska City	6,050
Total	22,133
Nevada.	
Austin	1,324
Carson City	3,042
Virginia	7,048
Total	11,414
New Hampshire.	
Concord	12,241
Dover	9,294
Manchester	23,536
Nashua	10,543
Portsmouth	9,211
Total	64,825
New Jersey.	
Atlantic City	1,043
Brighton	6,830
Burlington	5,817
Camden	20,045
Elizabeth	20,832
Harrison	4,129
Hoboken	20,297
Jersey City	82,546
Millville	6,101
Newark	105,059
New Brunswick	15,058
Orange	9,348
Paterson	33,579
Plainfield	5,095
Princeton	2,798
Rahway	6,258
Trenton	22,874
Total	367,709
New Mexico.	
Santa Fe	4,765
New York.	
Albany	69,422
Auburn	17,225
Binghamton	12,692
Brooklyn	396,099
Buffalo	117,714
Cohoes	15,357
Elmira	15,863
Hudson	8,615
Lockport	12,426
Newburg	17,014
New York	942,292
Ogdensburg	10,076
Oswego	20,910
Poughkeepsie	20,080
Rochester	62,386
Rome	11,000
Schenectady	11,026
Syracuse	43,051
Troy	46,465
Utica	28,804
Watertown	9,336
Total	1,887,853
North Carolina.	
Charlotte	4,473
Fayetteville	4,660
Newberne	5,849
Raleigh	7,790
Wilmington	13,446
Total	36,218
Ohio.	
Akron	10,006
Canton	8,606
Chillicothe	8,920
Cincinnati	216,239
Circleville	5,407
Cleveland	92,829
Columbus	31,274
Dayton	30,473
Fremont	5,455
Galliopolis	3,711
Hamilton	11,081
Ironton	5,686
Lancaster	4,725
Mansfield	8,029
Marietta	5,218
Massillon	5,185
Mt. Vernon	4,876
Newark	6,698
Piqua	5,927
Pomeroy	5,824
Portsmouth	10,592
Sandusky	13,008
Springfield	12,652
Steubenville	8,107
Tiffin	5,648
Toledo	31,584
Urbana	4,276
Warren	3,457
Wooster	5,419
Xenia	6,377
Youngstown	8,075
Zanesville	10,011
Total	595,461
Oregon.	
Oregon City	1,382
Portland	8,293
Total	9,675
Pennsylvania.	
Allegheny	53,180
Allentown	13,884
Altoona	10,610
Carbondale	6,393
Chester	9,485
Columbia	6,461
Corry	6,809
Erie	19,646
Harrisburg	23,103
Lancaster	20,233
Lock Haven	6,989
Meadville	7,103
Philadelphia	674,022
Pittsburgh	86,076
Reading	33,930
Scranton	35,092
Titusville	8,639
Williamsport	16,030
York	11,003
Total	1,048,686
Rhode Island.	
Newport	12,521
Providence	68,904
Total	81,425
South Carolina.	
Charleston	48,956
Columbia	9,298
Total	58,254
Tennessee.	
Chattanooga	6,093
Knoxville	8,682
Memphis	40,226
Nashville	25,865
Total	80,866

POPULATION OF ALL THE CITIES OF THE UNITED STATES.—Continued.

States and Cities.	Total Population.	States and Cities.	Total Population.	States and Cities.	Total Population.
Texas.		*Vermont.—cont'd.*		*Wisconsin.*	
Austin	4,428	Montpelier	3,023	Appleton	4,518
Brownsville	4,905	Rutland	9,834	Beaver Dam	3,265
Galveston	13,818	St. Albans	7,014	Beloit	4,396
Houston	9,382	St. Johnsbury	4,665	Fond du Lac	12,764
San Antonio	12,256	Total	49,443	Green Bay	4,666
Total	44,789	*Virginia.*		Janesville	8,789
Utah.		Alexandria	13,570	Kenosha	4,309
Logan	1,757	Fredericksb'gh	4,046	La Crosse	7,785
Manti	1,239	Lynchburgh	6,825	Madison	9,176
Mt. Pleasant	1,346	Norfolk	19,229	Manitowoc	5,168
Ogden	3,127	Petersburgh	18,950	Milwaukee	71,440
Salt Lake City	12,854	Portsmouth	10,492	Oshkosh	12,663
Total	20,323	Richmond	51,038	Portage	3,945
Vermont.		Total	124,150	Racine	9,880
Bennington	2,501	*West Virginia.*		Sheboygan	5,310
Brattleboro	4,933	Parkersburg	5,546	Watertown	7,550
Burlington	14,387	Wheeling	19,280	Total	175,624
Middlebury	3,086	Total	24,826		

ORDER OF THE STATES IN POINT OF POPULATION, AT SEVERAL PERIODS.

	1790.	1830.	1850.	1860.	1870.
1	Virginia	New York	New York	New York	New York
2	Massachusetts	Pennsylvania	Pennsylvania	Pennsylvania	Pennsylvania
3	Pennsylvania	Virginia	Ohio	Ohio	Ohio
4	North Carolina	Ohio	Virginia	Illinois	Illinois
5	New York	North Carolina	Tennessee	Virginia	Missouri
6	Maryland	Kentucky	Massachusetts	Indiana	Indiana
7	South Carolina	Tennessee	Indiana	Massachusetts	Massachusetts
8	Connecticut	Massachusetts	Kentucky	Missouri	Kentucky
9	New Jersey	South Carolina	Georgia	Tennessee	Tennessee
10	New Hampshire	Georgia	North Carolina	Kentucky	Virginia
11	Vermont	Maryland	Illinois	Georgia	Iowa
12	Georgia	Maine	Alabama	North Carolina	Georgia
13	Kentucky	Indiana	Missouri	Alabama	Michigan
14	Rhode Island	New Jersey	South Carolina	Mississippi	North Carolina
15	Delaware	Alabama	Mississippi	Wisconsin	Wisconsin
16	Tennessee	Connecticut	Maine	Michigan	Alabama
17		Vermont	Maryland	Maryland	New Jersey
18		New Hampshire	Louisiana	South Carolina	Mississippi
19		Louisiana	New Jersey	Iowa	Texas
20		Illinois	Michigan	New Jersey	Maryland
21		Missouri	Connecticut	Louisiana	Louisiana
22		Mississippi	New Hampshire	Maine	South Carolina
23		Rhode Island	Vermont	Texas	Maine
24		Delaware	Wisconsin	Connecticut	California
25		Florida	Texas	Arkansas	Connecticut
26		Michigan	Arkansas	California	Arkansas
27		Arkansas	Iowa	New Hampshire	West Virginia
28			Rhode Island	Vermont	Kansas
29			California	Rhode Island	Minnesota
30			Delaware	Minnesota	Vermont
31			Florida	Florida	New Hampshire
32			Minnesota	Kansas	Rhode Island
33				Delaware	Florida
34				Oregon	Delaware
35					Nebraska
36					Oregon
37					Nevada

ORDER OF TERRITORIES, 1870.

District of Columbia, New Mexico, Utah, Washington, Montana, Idaho, Dacotah, Arizona, Wyoming. The census of Alaska has not been taken.

POPULATION OF STATES BY RACES.

	Whites.	*Colored.	Indians.
Alabama	521,384	475,510	98
Arizona	9,581	26	31
Arkansas	362,115	122,169	89
*California	499,424	4,272	7,241
Colorado	39,221	456	180
Connecticut	527,449	9,668	219
Dakota	12,887	94	1,200
Delaware	102,221	22,794	
District of Columbia	88,278	43,404	15
Florida	96,057	91,689	2
Georgia	638,926	545,142	4
Idaho	10,618	60	47
Illinois	2,511,096	28,762	32
Indiana	1,655,837	24,560	240
Iowa	1,188,207	5,762	48
Kansas	346,377	17,108	914
Kentucky	1,098,692	222,210	108
Louisiana	362,065	364,210	569
Maine	624,809	1,606	499
Maryland	605,497	175,391	4
*Massachusetts	1,443,156	13,947	151
Michigan	1,167,282	11,849	4,926
Minnesota	438,257	759	690
Mississippi	382 896	444,201	809
Missouri	1,603,146	118,071	75
Montana	18,306	183	157
Nebraska	122,117	789	87
Nevada	38,959	357	23
New Hampshire	317,697	580	23
*New Jersey	875,407	30,658	16
New Mexico	90,393	172	1,309
New York	4,330,210	52,081	439
North Carolina	678,470	391,650	1,241
Ohio	2,601,946	63,213	100
Oregon	86,929	346	318
Pennsylvania	3,456,609	65,294	34
Rhode Island	212,219	4,980	154
South Carolina	289,667	415,814	124
Tennessee	936,119	322,331	70
Texas	564,700	253,475	379
Utah	86,044	118	175
Vermont	329,613	924	14
Virginia	712,089	512,841	229
Washington Territory	22,195	207	1,319
West Virginia	424,033	17,980	1
Wisconsin	1,051,351	2,113	1,206
Wyoming	8,726	183	66

* Japanese:—California, 33; Massachusetts, 10; New Jersey 10.

COMPARATIVE INCREASE OF POPULATION.

Census.	*Population.*	*Increase, Per Cent.*
1790	3,929,827	....
1800	5,305,937	35.02
1810	7,239,814	36.45
1820	9,638,191	33.13
1830	12,866,020	33.49
1840	17,069,453	32.67
1850	23 191,876	35.87
1860	31,445,080	35.58
1870	38,549,987	22.59

AREA OF THE UNITED STATES.

	Acres.
Total area of the Public Lands of the States and Territories	1,792,844,160
Total area of those States where there are no Public Lands	476,546,560
Area of Indian Territory	44,154,210
Area of District of Columbia	38,400
Grand total of area of the United States, in acres	2,311,583,360

or, Three Million Six Hundred Eleven Thousand Eight Hundred and Forty-nine square Miles.

This does not include the area of the great Lakes just within and forming a portion of our Northern boundary; neither does it include the marine league on the coast.

THE STATES OF THE UNION.

STATES. (38.)	AREA.	POPULATION.							STATE GOVERNMENTS IN 1879.					
	Square Miles.	White Populat'n 1860.	Col'd Popul'n 1860.*	Total Populat'n 1860.	Total Populat'n 1870.	Incr. fr. 1860 to 1870.	Incr. Per Cent.	Electors.	CAPITALS.	GOVERNORS.	Term Expires.	Salary.	Legislature meets.	State Elections.
Alabama	50,722	526,271	*437,930	964,201	996,992	37,799	3 92	10	Montgomery	Rufus W. Cobb	Nov. 1882	$3,000	3 M. Nov.	First M. in Aug.
Arkansas	52,198	324,143	*111,307	435,450	4-4,471	37,724	8.66	6	Little Rock	William R. Miller	Jan. 1883	3,500	*T a 2 M. Ja	First M. in Sept.
California	188,981	323,177	*56,917	379,994	560,247	169,814	44.69	6	Sacramento	George C. Perkins	Jan. 1883	6,000	*1 M. Dec.	1 Wed. Sept.
Colorado	104,500	34,231	46	34,277	47,164	12,887	37.60	3	Denver	F. W. Pitkin	Jan. 1883	8,000	1 W. Jan.	1 Tuesday Oct.
Connecticut	4,750	451,504	8,627	460,147	537,454	77,270	16 79	6	Hartford	Hobart B. Bigelow	Jan. 1883	2,000	*W. a 1 M Ja	Tu. a. 1 M. Nov.
Delaware	2,120	90,589	21,727	112,216	125,015	12,799	11 41	3	Dover	John W. Hall	Jan. 1883	2,000	*1 Tu. Jan.	Tu. a. 1 M. Nov.
Florida	59,268	77,746	62,678	140,424	187,748	47,571	35.30	4	Tallahassee	W. D. Bloxham	Jan. 1885	3,500	*T. a 1 M. Jan	Tu. a. 1 M. Nov.
Georgia	58,000	591,550	465,736	1,057,286	1,184,109	117,550	11.12	11	Atlanta	Alf. H. Colquitt	Jan. 1885	4,600	*2 W. Jan.	1 Wed. Oct.
Illinois	55,410	1,704 291	7,660	1,711,951	2,539,891	817,459	47.75	21	Springfield	Shelby M. Cullom	Jan. 1885	6,000	*1 W. Jan.	Tu. a. 1 M. Nov.
Indiana	33,809	1,338,710	11,718	1,350,428	1,680,637	305,247	22 60	15	Indianapolis	Albert G. Porter	Jan. 1885	6,000	*1 W. Jan.	2 Tuesday Oct.
Iowa	55,045	673,779	1,134	674,913	1,194,020	506,446	75.04	11	Des Moines	John H. Gear	Jan. 1882	3,000	*2 M. Jan.	2 Tuesday Oct.
Kansas	81,318	106,390	816	107,206	364,299	272,291	253.99	5	Topeka	John P. St. John	Jan. 1883	3,000	*2 Tu. Jan.	Tu. a. 1 M. Nov.
Kentucky	37,680	919,484	236,200	1,155,684	1,321,011	164,723	14 99	12	Frankfort	Luke P. Blackburn	Sept. 1883	5,000	*1 M. Dec.	1 Monday Aug.
Louisiana	41,346	357,456	350,346	708,002	726,915	26,418	3.73	8	New Orleans	Louis A. Wiltz	Jan. 1884	4,000	1 M. Jan.	1 Monday Nov.
Maine	35,000	626,947	1,332	628,279	626,915	440	.07	7	Augusta	Harris H. Plaisted	Jan. 1882	2,500	1 W. Jan	2 Monday Sept.
Maryland	11,124	515,918	171,131	687,049	780,894	103,046	15 00	8	Annapolis	Wm. T. Hamilton	Jan. 1884	4,500	*1 W. Jan.	Tu. a. 1 M. Nov.
Massachusetts	7,800	1,221,432	9,634	1,231,066	1,457,351	226,285	18.38	13	Boston	John D. Long	Jan. 1882	5,000	1 W. Jan.	Tu. a. 1 M. Nov.
Michigan	56,451	736,142	*12,971	749,113	1,184,059	435,540	58.14	11	Lansing	David H. Jerome	Jan. 1883	1,000	*1 W. Jan.	Tu. a. 1 M. Nov.
Minnesota	83,531	169,395	2,628	172,023	439,706	252,520	146.79	5	St. Paul	John S. Pillsbury	Jan. 1882	3,000	T. a. 1 M. Jan.	Tu. a. 1 M. Nov.
Mississippi	47,156	353,899	437,406	791,305	827,922	50,751	6.41	8	Jackson	John M. Stone	Jan. 1882	4,000	*1 M. Jan.	Tu. a. 1 M. Nov.
Missouri	65,350	1,063,489	118,523	1,182,012	1,721,295	509,681	3 03	15	Jefferson City	Thos. T. Crittenden	Jan. 1885	5,000	1 W. Jan.	Tu. a. 1 M. Nov.
Nebraska	75,995	28,696	145	28,841	122,993	116,888	305 28	3	Lincoln	Albinus Nance	Jan. 1883	2,500	*Th a 1 M Ja	Tu. af 1 M. Nov.
Nevada	104,125	6,812	45	6 857	42,491	42,456	519.16	3	Carson City	John H. Kinkead	Jan. 1883	6,000	*1 M. Jan.	Tu. a. 1 M. Nov.
New Hampshire	9,280	325,579	494	326,073	318,300	8,633	12 56	5	Concord	Charles H. Bell	Jan. 1883	1,000	*1 M. June	Tu. a. 1 M. Nov.
New Jersey	8,320	646,699	25,336	672,035	906,096	231,009	34 37	9	Trenton	George C. Ludlow	Jan. 1884	5,000	2 Tu. Jan.	Tu. a. 1 M. Nov.
New York	47,000	3,831,590	49,145	3,880,735	4,382,759	850,111	12 63	35	Albany	Alonzo B. Cornell	Jan. 1884	10,000	1 Tu. Jan.	Tu. a. 1 M. Nov.
North Carolina	50,704	629,942	362,680	992,622	1,071,361	24,332	2 45	10	Raleigh	Thomas J. Jarvis	Jan. 1885	4,000	*W. a 1 M. Ja.	Tu. a. 1 M. Nov.
Ohio	39,964	2,302,808	36,705	2,339,511	2,665,260	312,791	13 33	22	Columbus	Charles Foster	Jan. 1882	4,000	*1 M. Jan.	Tu. a. 1 M. Nov.
Oregon	95,274	52,160	305	52,465	90,923	38,413	73 64	3	Salem	Wm. Wall. Thayer	Sept. 1883	1,500	*2 M. Sept.	1 Monday June
Pennsylvania	46,000	2,849,259	56,956	2,906,215	3,521,951	605,328	20 83	29	Harrisburg	Henry M. Hoyt	Jan. 1883	10,000	1 Tu. Jan.	Tu. a. 1 M. Nov.
Rhode Island	1,306	170,649	3,971	174,620	217,353	42,736	24.46		Newp't & Prov.	Alfred H. Littlefield	May, 1881	1,000	May & Jan.	1 Wed. April
South Carolina	34,000	291,300	412,408	703,708	705,606	2,081	.30		Columbia	Johnson Hagood	Nov. 1882	3,500	4 M. Nov.	Tu. a. 1 M. Nov.
Tennessee	45,600	826,722	283,079	1,109,801	1,258,520	116,136	10.46	12	Nashville	Alvin Hawkins	Jan. 1883	4,000	*1 Mon. Jan.	Tu. a. 1 M. Nov.
Texas	274,350	420,891	183,324	604,215	818,579	195,785	32 40	8	Austin	Oram M. Roberts	Jan. 1883	4,000	*2 Tu. Jan.	3 Tuesd. Feb.
Vermont	10,212	314,369	729	315,098	330,551	15,464	4.91	5	Montpelier	Roswell Farnham	Oct. 1882	1,000	*1 W. Oct.	1 Tuesd. Sept.
Virginia	38,352	1,047,299	549,018	1,596,318	1,225,163	56,218	3.52	11	Richmond	F. M. O. Holliday	Jan. 1882	5,000	*1 W. Dec.	Tu. a. 1 M. Nov.
West Virginia	23,000				412,014			5	Wheeling	J. B. Jackson	Mar. 1885	2,700	*2 W. Jan.	2 Tuesd. Oct.
Wisconsin	53,924	773,693	2,188	775,881	1,054,670	279,621	36 40	10	Madison	William E. Smith	Jan. 1882	5,000	2 W. Jan.	Tu. a. 1 M. Nov.

Total area (inclusive of Territories) 3,400,000 square miles. Population in 1850, 23,191,876; in 1860, 31,445,080; in 1870, 38,549,987. Whole number of Senators, 76. Congressmen, 293; total electoral vote, 369. *Including Indians and Chinese. *Biennial Sessions and Elections.

THE INDIVIDUAL STATES OF THE UNION.

HISTORICAL AND STATISTICAL TABLE OF THE UNITED STATES OF NORTH AMERICA.

[*Note.*—The whole area of the United States, including water surface of lakes and rivers, is nearly equal to four million square miles, embracing the Russian purchase.]

The Thirteen Original States.	Set-tl'd	Sq. miles	* Pop. 1870.	The Thirteen Original States.	Set-tled	Sq. miles	* Pop. 1870.
New Hampshire	1623	9,280	318,300	Delaware	1627	2,120	125,015
Massachusetts	1620	7,800	1,457,351	Maryland	1634	11,124	780,894
Rhode Island	1636	1,306	217,353	Virginia—East and West	1607	61,352	1,667,177
Connecticut	1633	4,750	537,454	North Carolina	1650	50,704	1,071,361
New York	1613	47,000	4,382,730	South Carolina	1670	34,000	705,606
New Jersey	1624	8,320	906,096	Georgia	1733	58,000	1,184,109
Pennsylvania	1681	46,000	3,521,791	....	....	......	....

* The total population of the United States in 1860 was, in round numbers, 31,500,000. In 1865 it is estimated that the population was 35,500,000, including the inhabitants of the Territories, estimated at 300,000 persons on January 1, 1865. The Census of 1870 made the whole number about 39,000,000; at the end of the present century it will be, probably, 103,000,000.

THE STATES ADMITTED INTO THE UNION.

States Admitted.	Set-tled.	Act Organizing Territory.	U.S. Statutes. Vol	Pt.	Act Admitting State.	U.S. Statutes. Vol	Page.	Area in Sq. Miles.	Population, 1870.
Kentucky	1774	....	....	....	Feb. 4, 1791	1	189	37,680	1,323,264
Vermont	1724	....	....	....	Feb. 18, 1791	1	191	a 10,212	330,558
Tennessee	1756	....	....	....	June 1, 1796	1	491	45,600	1,258,326
Ohio	1788	Ordin'c of 1787	....	....	April 30, 1802	2	173	39,964	2,675,468
Lousiana	1699	March 3, 1805	2	331	April 8, 1812	2	701	a 41,346	734,420
Indiana	1730	May 7, 1800	2	58	Dec. 11, 1816	3	399	33,809	1,668,169
Mississippi	1540	April 7, 1798	1	549	Dec. 10, 1817	3	472	47,156	842,056
Illinois	1683	Feb'ry 3, 1809	2	514	Dec. 3, 1818	3	536	a 55,410	2,567.036
Alabama	1713	March 3, 1817	3	371	Dec. 14, 1819	3	608	50,722	996,175
Maine	16[illegible]3	....	....	....	March 3, 1820	3	544	a 35,000	630,423
Missouri	1763	June 4, 1812	2	743	March 2, 1821	3	645	65,350	1,725,658
Arkansas	1685	March 2, 1819	3	493	June 15, 1836	5	50	52,198	486,103
Michigan	1670	Jan'ry 11, 1805	2	309	Jan. 26, 1837	5	144	a 56,451	1,184,653
Florida	1565	March 30, 1822	3	654	March 3, 1845	5	742	59,268	189,950
Iowa	1778	June 12, 1838	5	235	March 3, 1845	5	742	55,045	1,181,359
Texas	1694	....	....	....	Dec. 29, 1845	9	108	274,356	795,590
Wisconsin	1669	April 20, 1836	5	10	March 3, 1847	9	178	53,924	1,055,501
California	1769	....	...	....	Sept. 9, 1850	9	452	a 188,981	556,208
Minnesota	1654	March 3, 1849	9	403	Feb. 26, 1857	11	166	83,531	424,543
Oregon	1792	Aug. 14, 1848	9	323	Feb. 14, 1859	11	383	95,274	90,878
Kansas	1849	May, 30, 1854	10	277	Jan. 29, 1861	12	126	81,318	379,497
West Virginia	1607	....	....	....	Dec. 31, 1862	12	633	23,000	447,943
e Nevada	1848	March 2, 1861	12	209	Mar. 21, 1864	13	30	b 112,090	44,686
f Colorado	.....	Feb'ry 28, 1861	12	172	....	..	...	a 104,500	39,681
g Nebraska	1852	May 30, 1854	10	277	March 1, 1867	13	47	75,995	116,888

Territories.	When Settled.	Act Organizing Territory.	U.S. Statutes. Vol.	Page.	Area in Sq. Miles.	Population, 1870.
Wyoming	1866	July 25, 1868	15	178	97,883	9,118
New Mexico	1570	Sept. 9, 1850	9	446	121,201	92,604
Utah	1847	Sept. 9, 1850	9	453	c 84,746	70,000
Washington	1840	March 2, 1853	10	172	69,994	23,925
Dakota	1850	March 2, 1861	12	239	j 150,932	14,181
Arizona	1600	Feb. 24, 1863	12	664	d 113,916	9,658
Idaho	1862	March 3, 1863	12	808	k 86,294	14,882
Montana	1862	May 26, 1864	13	85	143,776	20,594
Indian	1832	....	..	...	68,991	......
h District of Columbia	1771	July 16, 1790 March 3, 1791	1 1	130 214	10 miles sq.	131,706
i North-western America, purchased by treaty of May 28, 1867	1799	July 27, 1868	15	240	557,390	67,000

NOTES TO THE FOREGOING TABLE.

a. The areas of those States marked *a* are derived from geographical authorities, the public surveys not having been completely extended over them.

b. The present area of Nevada is 112,000 square miles, enlarged by adding one degree of longitude lying between the 37th and 42d degrees of north latitude, which was detached from the west part of Utah, and also north-western part of Arizona Territory, per act of Congress, approved May 5, 1866, (U. S. Laws, 1865 and 1866, p. 43), and assented to by the Legislature of the State of Nevada, January 18, 1867.

c. The present area of Utah is 84,476 square miles, reduced from the former area of 88,056 square miles by incorporating one degree of longitude on the east side, between the 41st and 42d degrees of north latitude, with the Territory of Wyoming, per act of Congress, approved July 25, 1868.

d. The present area of Arizona is 113,916 square miles, reduced from the former area of 127,141 square miles, by an act of Congress, approved May 5, 1866, detaching from the north-western part of Arizona a tract of land equal to 12,225 square miles, and adding it to the State of Nevada. (U. S. Laws 1865 and 1866, p. 43.)

e. Nevada.—Enabling act approved March 24, 1864. (Statutes, vol. 13, p. 30.) Duly admitted into the Union. President's proclamation No. 22, dated October 31, 1864. (Statutes, vol..13, p. 749.)

f. Colorado.—Enabling act approved March 21, 1863. (Statutes, vol. 13. p. 32.) Not yet admitted.

g. Nebraska.—Enabling act approved April 19, 1864. (Statutes, vol. 13. p. 47.) Duly admitted into the Union. See President's proclamation No. 9, dated March 1, 1867. (U. S. Laws 1866 and 1867, p. 4.)

h. That portion of the District of Columbia south of the Potomac River was retroceded to Virginia, July 9, 1846. (Statutes, vol. 9. p. 35.)

i. Boundaries.—Commencing at 54° 40′ north latitude, ascending Portland Channel to the mountains, following their summits to 141° west longitude; thence north on this line to the Arctic Ocean, forming the eastern boundary. Starting from the Arctic Ocean west, the line descends Behring Straits, between the two islands of Krusenstern and Romanzoff, to the parallel of 65° 30′, and proceeds due north without limitation into the same Arctic Ocean. Beginning again at the same initial point, on the parallel of 65° 30′, thence, in a course southwest, through Behring Straits, between the Island of St. Lawrence and Cape Choukotski, to the 170° west longitude, and thence southwesterly, through Behring Sea, between the islands of Alton and Copper, to the meridian of 193° west longitude, leaving the prolonged group of the Aleutian Islands in the possessions now transferred to the United States, and making the western boundary of our country the dividing line between Asia and America.

j. The present area of Dakota is 150,932 square miles, reduced from the former area of 243,597 square miles, by incorporating seven degrees of longitude of the western part, between the 41st and 45th degrees of north latitude, with the Territory of Wyoming, per act of Congress, approved July 25, 1868.

k. The present area of Idaho is 86,294 square miles, reduced from the former area of 90,932 square miles by incorporating one degree of longitude on the east side, between the 42d and 44th degrees of north latitude with the Territory of Wyoming, per act of Congress, approved July 25, 1868.

IMMIGRATION, FROM 1783 TO 1880.

BY an Act of Congress approved March 2, 1818, Collectors of Customs were required to keep a record, and make a quarterly return to the Treasury of all passengers arriving in their respective districts from Foreign Ports, and these reports, duly condensed in the Department, are the chief bases of our knowledge of the subsequent growth and progress of Immigration. Total number of foreign-born passengers arriving at the ports of the United States in the several years from 1783 to 1880 inclusive, are as follows: Previous to

Year	Number	Year	Number	Year	Number	Year	Number
1820	250,000	1835	45,374	1851	379,466	1867	293,601
1820	8,385	1836	76,242	1852	371,603	1868	289,145
1821	9,127	1837	79,340	1853	368,645	1869	385,287
1822	6,911	1838	39,914	1854	427,833	1870	356,303
1823	6,354	1839	68,069	1855	200,877	1871	346,938
1824	7,912	1840	84,066	1856	200,436	1872	404,806
1825	10,199	1841	80,289	1857	251,306	1873	437,004
1826	10,837	1842	104,565	1858	123,126	1874	277,593
1827	18,875	1843	52,496	1859	121,282	1875	209,036
1828	27,382	1844	78,615	1860	153,640	1876	187,027
1829	22,520	1845	114,371	1861	91,920	1877	149,020
1830	23,322	1846	154,416	1862	89,005	1878	157,776
1831	22,633	1847	234,968	1863	174,523	1879	197,954
1832	60,482	1848	226,527	1864	193,191	1880	4-4,196
1833	58,640	1849	297,024	1865	248,394		
1834	65,365	1850	369,980	1866	314,840		

Of the Immigrants who landed on our shores in the *sixty years* ending with June 30, 1880 (1820 to 1880) there came from different countries as follows:

Country	Number	Country	Number	Country	Number	Country	Number
Great Britain and Ireland	4,792,207	Russia and Poland	49,658	Denmark	49,655	British North America	570,231
France	805,590	Switzerland	84,913	Portugal	7,433	Central Amer.	1,458
West Indies	76,500	China	202,054	Turkey	580	Australia, &c.	19,438
Sweden and Norway	860,292	Germany	2,994,664	Greece	860	Countries not specified	813,755
S. America	9,216	Holland	45,795	Austro-Hungary	97,881	Total 60 years	10,129,295
Africa	841	Mexico	24,077	Japan	855		
Spain	26,311	Italy	72,555	Asia, not specified	612		
		Belgium	22,909				

Of those arriving here from January 1st, 1820, to June 30, 1880, those wholly or mainly speaking English were from

Country	Number	Country	Number
Great Britain and Ireland	4,692,217	Azores and African Islands	8,076
British North America	570,231	Africa	832
English West India Islands	1,242		
Australia and adjacent Islands	19,433	Total of English speech	5,291,081

Of races mainly Teutonic or Scandinavian there were from

Country	Number	Country	Number	Country	Number
Germany	2,994,664	Switzerland	84,913	Of Sclavic races	49,658
Austro-Hungary	97,881	Denmark	49,655		
Holland	45,795	Sweden and Norway	860,292	Total	3,706,312
Belgium	22,909	Iceland	545		

Of French, Spanish, Portuguese and Italian races there were from

Country	Number	Country	Number	Country	Number
France	805,510	Central America	1,458	Miquelon	8
Spain	26,311	South American States	9,216	Corsica	13
Portugal	7,433	West Indies	76,500		
Italy	72,555	Cape Verde, Madeira and Canaries	1,298	Total	524,884
Mexico	24,077				

Of Asiatic and Polynesian races there were from

China	202,054	African Nations	841
Japan	855	Turkey	580
The rest of Asia and Asiatic Islands	612	Greece	869
Polynesia	478	Countries not specified	813,755
Total Asiatic, Etc	203,479	Total	815,536

Of the 3,734,248 passengers landed at Castle Garden from August 1, 1855, to January 1, 1879, their avowed destinations were as follows :

New York and		Florida	710	Dakota	4,729	Nova Scotia	145
undecided	1,501,531	Alabama	1,452	Colorado	2,284	New Foundl'd	2
Maine	6,164	Mississippi	1,405	Wyoming	271	New D'minion	816
New Hampsh'r	4,120	Louisiana	6,568	Utah	35,390	S. America	770
Vermont	6,210	Texas	3,329	Montana	322	Cuba	404
Massachusetts	170,024	Arkansas	626	Idaho	195	Lima	24
Rhode Island	34,273	Tennessee	6,432	Nevada	1,725	Mexico	369
Connecticut	67,800	Kentucky	16,436	Arizona	3	Bermudas and	
New Jersey	115,566	Ohio	191,434	New Mexico	2,179	other W. In.	255
Pennsylvania	381,614	Michigan	92,717	California	48,210	Central Am	116
Delaware	3,404	Indiana	46,848	Oregon and		N. W. Coast	473
Maryland	27,103	Illinois	345,894	Wash. Ter.	844	Australia	52
Dis. Columbia	11,297	Wisconsin	175,199			Sandwich Isl's	7
Virginia	10,427	Iowa	81,598	*Other Countries.*		Japan	10
W. Virginia	1,636	Missouri	67,780			China	21
N. Carolina	1,015	Minnesota	66,389	Brit. Colum	88	Vancouver's I.	
S. Carolina	3,567	Kansas	19,503	Canada	69,765	Unknown	22,036
Georgia	3,020	Nebraska	18,950	N. Brunsw'k	12,205		

The total arrivals of Immigrants into the United States in the year ending June 30, 1880, was 457,257; of whom 144,876 were from the United Kingdom of Great Britain and Ireland; 84,638 from Germany; 202,871 from other European countries; 99,706 from British America; 5,806 from China and Japan; 548 from the Azores; 1,251 from the West Indies; 23 from the East Indies; 83 from South America, and the remainder from other countries.

Passengers landed at Castle Garden from May 5, 1827, to January 1, 1879.

ARRIVED FROM	NUMBER.	ARRIVED FROM	NUMBER.
Austria	28,530	Italy	52,453
Asia Minor	98	Japan	320
Atlantic Islands	2,134	Malta	22
Australia	241	Mauritius	18
Asia, including Persia and Asiatic Russia	257	Mexico	1,260
		New Zealand	24
Africa	243	Norway, including Lapland	49,057
British America	3,224	New Brunswick	41
Belgium	10,444	Nova Scotia	1,653
Canada	1,530	Portugal	1,822
China	1,421	Russia	29,064
Central America	520	Sandwich Islands	97
Denmark	36,837	Switzerland	85,144
East India	388	Scotland	161,093
England	740,196	Sweden	124,526
France	110,529	Spain	8,876
Germany	2,163,824	South America	3,362
Greece	292	Turkey	298
Hungary	2,349	Wales	9,484
Holland	40,022	West Indies	29,635
Isle of Man	49	Born at Sea	135
Ireland	2,018,422		
Iceland	147	Total	5,720,535

THE NEW NATURALIZATION LAW.

AN ACT TO AMEND THE NATURALIZATION LAWS AND TO PUNISH CRIMES AGAINST THE SAME, AND FOR OTHER PURPOSES.

Be it enacted by the Senate and House of Representatives of the United States of America in Congress assembled, That in all cases where any oath, affirmation, or affidavit shall be made or taken under or by virtue of any act or law relating to the naturalization of aliens, or in any proceedings under such acts or laws, if any person or persons taking or making such oath, affirmation, or affidavit, shall knowingly swear or affirm falsely, the same shall be deemed and taken to be perjury, and the person or persons guilty thereof shall upon conviction thereof be sentenced to imprisonment for a term not exceeding five years and not less than one year, and to a fine not exceeding one thousand dollars.

SEC. 2.—*And be it further enacted,* That if any person applying to be admitted a citizen, or appearing as a witness for any such person, shall knowingly personate any other person than himself, or falsely appear in the name of a deceased person, or in an assumed or fictitious name, or if any person shall falsely make, forge, or counterfeit any oath, affirmation, notice, affidavit, certificate, order, record, signature, or other instrument, paper, or proceeding required or authorized by any law or act relating to or providing for the naturalization of aliens; or shall utter, sell, dispose of, or use as true or genuine, or for any unlawful purpose, any false, forged, ante-dated, or counterfeit oath, affirmation, notice, certificate, order, record, signature, instrument, paper, or proceeding as aforesaid; or sell or dispose of to any person other than the person for whom it was originally issued, any certificate of citizenship, or certificate showing any person to be admitted a citizen; or if any person shall in any manner use for the purpose of registering as a voter, or as evidence of a right to vote, or otherwise, unlawfully, any order, certificate of citizenship, or certificate, judgment, or exemplification, showing such person to be admitted to be a citizen, whether heretofore or hereafter issued or made, knowing that such order or certificate, judgment or exemplification has been unlawfully issued or made; or if any person shall unlawfully use, or attempt to use, any such order or certificate, issued to or in the name of any other person, or in a fictitious name, or the name of a deceased person; or use, or attempt to use, or aid, or assist, or participate in the use of any certificate of citizenship, knowing the same to be forged, or counterfeit, or ante-dated, or knowing the same to have been procured by fraud, or otherwise unlawfully obtained; or if any person, without any lawful excuse, shall knowingly have or be possessed of any false, forged, ante-dated, or counterfeit certificate of citizenship, purporting to have been issued under the provisions of any law of the United States relating to naturalization, knowing such certificate to be false, forged, ante-dated, or counterfeit, with intent unlawfully to use the same; or if any person shall obtain, accept, or receive any certificate of citizenship known to such person to have been procured by fraud, or by the use of any false name, or by means of any false statement made with intent to procure, or to aid in procuring, the issue of such certificate, or known to such person to be fraudulently altered or ante-dated; or if any person who has been or may be admitted to be a citizen shall, on oath or affirmation, or by affidavit, knowingly deny that he has been so admitted, with intent to evade or avoid any duty or liability imposed or required by law, every person so offending shall be deemed and adjudged guilty of felony, and, on conviction thereof, shall be sentenced to be imprisoned and kept at hard labor for a period not less than one year nor more than five years, or be fined in a sum not less than three hundred dollars nor more than one thousand dollars, or both such punishments may be imposed, in the discretion of the court. And every person who shall knowingly and intentionally aid or abet any person in the commission of any such felony, or attempt to do any act hereby made felony, or counsel, advise, or procure, or attempt to procure the commission thereof, shall be liable to indictment and punishment in the same manner and to the same extent as the principal party guilty of such felony, and such person may be tried and convicted thereof without the previous conviction of such principal.

SEC. 3.—*And be it further enacted,* That any person who shall knowingly use any certificate of naturalization heretofore granted by any court, or which shall hereafter be granted, which has been, or shall be, procured through fraud or by false evidence, or has been or shall be issued by the clerk, or any other officer of the court without any appearance and hearing of the applicant in court and without lawful authority; and any person who shall falsely represent himself to be a citizen of the United States, without having been duly admitted to citizenship, for any fraudulent purpose whatever, shall be deemed guilty of a misdemeanor, and upon conviction thereof in due course of law, shall be sentenced to pay a fine of not exceeding one thousand dollars, or be imprisoned not exceeding two years, either or both, in the discretion of the court taking cognizance of the same.

SEC. 4.—*And be it further enacted,* That the provisions of this act shall apply to all proceedings had or taken, or attempted to be had or taken, before any court in which any proceeding for naturalization shall be commenced, had, or taken, or attempted to be commenced; and the courts of the United States shall have jurisdiction of all offenses under the provisions of this act, in or before whatsoever court or tribunal the same shall have been committed.

Sec. 5.—*And be it further enacted,* That in any city having upward of twenty thousand inhabitants, it shall be the duty of the judge of the circuit court of the United States for the circuit wherein said city shall be, upon the application of two citizens, to appoint in writing for each election district or voting precinct in said city, and to change or renew said appointment as occasion may require, from time to time, two citizens resident of the district or precinct, one from each political party, who, when so designated, shall be, and are hereby, authorized to attend at all times and places fixed for the registration of voters, who, being registered, would be entitled to vote for representative in Congress, and at all times and places for holding elections of representatives in Congress, and for counting the votes cast at said elections, and to challenge any name proposed to be registered, and any vote offered, and to be present and witness throughout the counting of all votes, and to remain where the ballot boxes are kept at all times after the polls are open until the votes are finally counted; and said persons or either of them shall have the right to affix their signature or his signature to said register for purposes of identification, and to attach thereto, or to the certificate of the number of votes cast, any statement touching the truth or fairness thereof which they or he may ask to attach; and any one who shall prevent any person so designated from doing any of the acts authorized as aforesaid, or who shall hinder or molest any such person in doing any of the said acts, or shall aid or abet in preventing, hindering or molesting any such person in respect of any such acts, shall be guilty of a misdemeanor, and on conviction shall be punished by imprisonment not less than one year.

Sec. 6.—*And be it further enacted,* That in any city having upward of twenty thousand inhabitants, it shall be lawful for the marshal of the United States for the district wherein said city shall be, to appoint as many special deputies as may be necessary to preserve order at any election at which representatives in Congress are to be chosen; and said deputies are hereby authorized to preserve order at such elections, and to arrest for any offence or breach of the peace committed in their view.

Sec. 7.—*And be it further enacted,* That the naturalization laws are hereby extended to aliens of African nativity and to persons of African descent.

Approved, July 14, 1870.

ART. XII. OF AMENDMENTS TO THE CONSTITUTION OF THE UNITED STATES.--The Electors shall meet in their respective States, and vote by ballot for President and Vice President, one of whom, at least, shall not be an inhabitant of the same state with themselves; they shall name in their ballot the person voted for as President, and in distinct ballots the person voted for as Vice-President, and they shall make distinct lists of all persons voted for as President, and of all persons voted for as Vice-President, and of the number of votes for each, which lists they shall sign and certify, and transmit sealed to the seat of government of the United States, directed to the President of the Senate. The President of the Senate shall, in presence of the Senate and House of Representatives, open all the certificates, and the votes shall then be counted. The person having the greatest number of votes for President, shall be the President, if such number be a majority of the whole number of Electors appointed; and if no person have such majority, then from the persons having the highest numbers, not exceeding three, on the list of those voted for as President, the House of Representatives shall choose immediately, by ballot, the President. But in choosing the President, the votes shall be taken by States, the representation from each State having one; a quorum for this purpose shall consist of a member or members from two-thirds of the States, and a majority of all the States shall be necessary to a choice. And if the House of Representatives shall not choose a President whenever the right of choice shall devolve upon them, before the fourth day of March next following, then the Vice-President shall act as President, as in the case of the death or other constitutional disability of the President. The person having the greatest number of votes, as Vice-President, shall be the Vice-President, if such number be a majority of the whole number of Electors appointed; and if no person have a majority, then from the two highest numbers on the list, the Senate shall choose the Vice-President; a quorum for the purpose shall consist of two-thirds of the whole number of Senators, and a majority of the whole number shall be necessary to a choice. But no person, constitutionally ineligible to the office of President, shall be eligible to that of Vice-President of the United States.

(This Amendment should be read in connection with Section 1 of Article II. of the Constitution of the United States, to which it is an amendment). See Constitution of the United States, page 123

ELECTORAL VOTE OF EACH STATE FROM 1808 TO 1820.

STATES.	1808.								1812.				1816.*					1820.†				
	PRES'T			VICE-PRES'T					PR'ST		V.-P.		PRES.		V.-PRES.			PRES.		V.-PRES.		
	James Madison	Charles C. Pinckney	George Clinton	George Clinton	Rufus King	John Langdon	James Madison	James Monroe	James Madison	DeWitt Clinton	Elbridge Gerry	Jared Ingersoll	James Monroe	Rufus King	Daniel D. Tompkins	John E. Howard	Scattering	James Monroe	John Q. Adams	Daniel D. Tompkins	Richard Stockton	Scattering
Alabama																		3		3		
Connecticut		9			9					9		9		9			9	9		9		
Delaware		3			3					4		4		3			3	4				4
Georgia	6			6					8		8		8		8			8		8		
Illinois																		3		3		
Indiana													3		3			3		3		
Kentucky	7			7					12		12		12		12			12		12		
Louisiana									3		3		3		3			3		3		
Maine																		9		9		
Maryland	9	2		9	2				6	5	6	5	8		8			11		10		1
Massachusetts		19			19					22	2	20		22		22		15		7	8	
Mississippi																		3		3		
New Hampshire		7			7					8	1	7	8		8			7	1	7		1
New Jersey	8			8						8		8	8		8			8		8		
New York	13		6	13			3	3		29		29	29		29			29		29		
North Carolina	11	3		11	3				15		15		15		15			15		15		
Ohio	3					3			7		7		8		8			8		8		
Pennsylvania	20			20					25		25		25		25			25		25		
Rhode Island		4			4					4		4	4		4			4		4		
South Carolina	10			10					11		11		11		11			11		11		
Tennessee	5			5					8		8		8		8			8		8		
Vermont	6					6			8		8		8		8			8		8		
Virginia	24			24					25		25		25		25			25		25		
Total	122	47	6	113	47	9	3	3	128	89	131	86	183	34	183	22	12	231	1	218	8	6

* In 1816 Connecticut gave five votes to James Ross, of Pennsylvania, for Vice-President, and four to John Marshall of Virginia (Chief-Justice Marshall) for the same office. Delaware gave three votes for Robert G. Harper, of Maryland, for Vice-President.

† In 1820, John Quincy Adams received one Electoral Vote for President (from New Hampshire), and Richard Rush, of Pennsylvania, one for Vice-President. Richard Stockton, of New Jersey, received 8 votes from Massachusetts for the Vice-Presidency. Daniel Rodney, of Delaware, 4 from his own State, and Robert G. Harper, of Maryland, one from his own State, for the same office.

‡ There is no record of the Popular Vote by States previous to 1824 known to be existence. Many of the States chose the Electors by joint convention of the Legislatures previous to that time, as a few did later.

ELECTORAL AND POPULAR VOTE FOR PRESIDENT AND VICE-PRESIDENT FROM 1824 TO 1832.

1824.

Electors in each State in 1832	STATES.	Electoral Vote. Presid't: Andrew Jackson	John Q. Adams	Wm. H. Crawford	Henry Clay	Vice-President: John C. Calhoun	Nathan Sanford	Nathaniel Macon	Andrew Jackson	Martin Van Buren	Henry Clay	Popular Vote: John Q. Adams	Andrew Jackson	Wm. H. Crawford	Henry Clay
7	Alabama	5	..	..	..	5	..	..	..	..	..	2,416	9,443	1,680	67
8	Connecticut	..	8	..	..	....	..	..	8	..	..	7,587	....	1,978	....
3	Delaware	..	1	2	..	1	..	..	..	..	2	By	Legis	lature	
11	Georgia	..	..	9	..	....	..	..	..	9	..	By	Legis	lature	
5	Illinois	2	1	..	..	3	..	..	..	..	..	1,542	1,901	219	1,047
9	Indiana	5	..	..	..	5	..	..	..	..	..	3,095	7,343	....	5,315
15	Kentucky	..	..	..	14	7	7	..	..	..	..	....	6,453	....	16,782
5	Louisiana	3	2	..	..	5	..	..	..	..	..	By	Legis	lature	
10	Maine	..	9	..	..	9	..	..	..	..	..	6,870	2,330	....	....
10	Maryland	7	3	1	..	10	..	..	1	..	..	14,632	14,523	3,646	695
14	Massachusetts	..	15	..	..	15	..	..	..	..	..	30,687	....	6,616	....
4	Mississippi	3	..	..	..	3	..	..	..	..	..	1,694	3,234	119	....
4	Missouri	..	..	..	3	....	..	..	3	..	..	311	987	....	1,401
7	New Hampshire	..	8	..	..	7	..	..	1	..	..	4,107	643	....	....
8	New Jersey	8	..	..	..	8	..	..	..	..	..	9,110	10,985	1,196	....
42	New York	1	26	5	4	29	7	..	..	..	..	By	Legis	lature	
15	North Carolina	15	..	..	..	15	..	..	..	..	..	....	20,415	15,621	....
21	Ohio	..	..	..	16	....	16	..	..	..	..	12,280	18,457	....	19,255
30	Pennsylvania	28	..	..	..	28	..	..	..	..	..	5,440	36,100	4,206	1,609
4	Rhode Island	..	4	..	..	3	..	..	..	..	..	2,145	....	200	....
11	South Carolina	11	..	..	..	11	..	..	..	..	..	By	Legis	lature	
15	Tennessee	11	..	..	..	11	..	..	..	..	..	216	20,197	312	....
7	Vermont	..	7	..	..	7	..	..	..	..	..	By	Legis	lature	
23	Virginia	..	..	24	..	....	..	24	..	..	..	3,189	2,861	8,489	416
288	Total	99	84	41	37	182	30	24	13	9	2	105,321	155,872	41,282	46,587

1828.

Electors in each State in 1832	STATES.	Electoral Vote. Pres't: Andrew Jackson	John Q. Adams	V.-Pres't: John C. Calhoun	Richard Rush	William Smith	Popular Vote: Andrew Jackson	John Q. Adams
7	Alabama	5	..	5	..	..	17,13[illegible]	1,938
8	Connecticut	...	8	....	8	..	4,418	13,829
3	Delaware	....	3	...	3	..	4,349	4,769
11	Georgia	9	..	2	..	7	18,709	....
5	Illinois	3	..	3	..	.	6,763	1,581
9	Indiana	5	..	5	..	..	22,237	17,052
15	Kentucky	14	..	14	..	..	39,081	31,172
5	Louisiana	5	..	5	..	..	4,605	4,097
10	Maine	1	8	1	8	..	[illegible]	20,773
10	Maryland	5	6	5	6	..	24,578	25,759
14	Massachusetts	....	15	....	15	..	6,019	29,876
4	Mississippi	3	..	3	..	..	6,763	1,581
4	Missouri	3	..	3	..	..	8,[illegible]32	3,422
7	New Hampshire	...	8	....	8	..	20,6[illegible]2	24,0[illegible]6
8	New Jersey	...	8	....	8	..	21,950	23,[illegible]58
42	New York	20	16	20	16	..	140,763	135,413
15	North Carolina	15	..	15	..	..	37,857	13,918
21	Ohio	16	..	16	..	..	67,597	63,396
30	Pennsylvania	28	..	28	..	..	101,652	50,848
4	Rhode Island	....	4	....	4	..	821	2,754
11	South Carolina	4	..	11	..	..	....	....
15	Tennessee	11	..	11	..	..	44,090	2,240
7	Vermont	....	7	....	7	..	8,205	24,784
23	Virginia	24	..	24	..	..	26,752	12,107
288	Total	178	83	171	83	7	647,231	509,097

1832.

Electors in each State in 1832	STATES.	Electoral Vote. President: Andrew Jackson	Henry Clay	John Floyd	William Wirt	V.-President: Martin Van Buren	John Sargeant	William Wilkins	Henry Sée	Amos Ellmaker	Popular Vote: Andrew Jackson	Henry Clay
7	Alabama	7	..	..	..	7	..	..	..	..	unan	....
8	Connecticut	....	8	..	..	....	8	..	..	..	11,269	17,755
3	Delaware	....	3	..	..	....	3	..	..	..	4,110	4,276
11	Georgia	11	..	..	..	11	..	..	..	..	50,750	....
5	Illinois	5	..	..	..	5	..	..	..	..	14,147	5,429
9	Indiana	9	..	..	..	9	..	..	..	..	31,552	15,472
15	Kentucky	....	15	..	..	....	15	..	..	..	36,247	43,396
5	Louisiana	5	..	..	..	5	..	..	..	..	4,0[illegible]9	2,528
10	Maine	10	..	..	..	10	..	..	..	..	33,291	27,204
10	Maryland	3	5	..	..	3	5	..	..	..	19,156	19,16[illegible]
14	Massachusetts	....	14	..	..	...	14	..	..	..	14,515	33,003
4	Mississippi	4	..	..	..	4	..	..	..	..	5,919	....
4	Missouri	4	..	..	..	4	..	..	..	..	5,192	major.
7	New Hampshire	7	..	..	..	7	..	..	..	..	25,486	19,010
8	New Jersey	8	..	..	..	8	..	..	..	..	23,856	23,393
42	New York	42	..	..	..	42	..	..	..	..	163,497	154,896
15	North Carolina	15	..	..	..	15	..	..	..	..	24,862	4,563
21	Ohio	21	..	..	..	21	..	..	..	..	81,246	76,539
30	Pennsylvania	30	..	..	..	....	..	30	..	..	90,983	56,716
4	Rhode Island	....	4	..	..	....	4	..	..	..	2,126	2,810
11	South Carolina	....	..	11	..	....	..	..	11	..	....	....
15	Tennessee	15	..	..	..	15	..	..	..	..	28,740	1,436
7	Vermont	....	..	..	7	...	..	..	..	7	7,870	11,152
23	Virginia	23	..	..	..	23	..	..	..	..	33,609	11,451
288	Total	219	49	11	7	189	49	30	11	7	687,502	530,189

In the election of 1824 there were four candidates for the Presidency, each of whom received a number of Electoral Votes, but no one a majority; Andrew Jackson received a plurality of both the Electoral and Popular Vote (99 of the former and 155,872 of the latter); but as there was evidently no election, it devolved upon the House of Representatives to choose a President according to the 12th Amendment of the Constitution. The voting was by States, and 24 tellers (one member from each State) were appointed. The ballots were cast for the three highest candidates on the list, Messrs Jackson, Adams and Crawford. The friends of Mr. Clay supported Mr. Adams. When the vote was counted, thirteen States voted for Mr. Adams, seven for Gen. Jackson and four for Mr. Crawford. Mr. Adams was then declared elected. Mr. Calhoun having received a large majority of all the Electoral votes for Vice-President took the oath on the 4th of March, 1825.

The Elections of 1828 and 1832 were not specially noticeable. Gen. Jackson, whose friends had denounced the supposed coalition between Messrs. Adams and Clay, in 1824-5, as corrupt, was elected by a large majority over his competitor, both on the Popular and Electoral Vote in 1828, and re-elected by a still larger majority over Mr. Clay in 1832. John Floyd of Virginia and Wm. Wirt of Maryland received each a small number of Electoral Votes in 1832, and Mr. Clay had but 49, while Gen. Jackson received 219.

ELECTORAL AND POPULAR VOTE FOR PRESIDENT AND VICE-PRESIDENT, 1836 TO 1844.

1836.

Electoral Vote of each State in 1840.	STATES.	Electoral Vote — President: Martin Van Buren	Wm. H. Harrison	Hugh L. White	Daniel Webster	Willie P. Mangum	Electoral Vote — Vice-Pres't: Rich'd M. Johnson	Francis Granger	John Tyler	William Smith	Popular Vote: Van Buren, Democratic Nominee.	Harrison, White, Webster and Mangum, Whig Nominees.
7	Alabama	7					7				19,068	15,637
3	Arkansas	3					3				2,400	1,238
8	Connecticut	8					8				19,234	18,466
3	Delaware		3					3			4,15[illegible]	4,738
11	Georgia			11					11		22,126	24,930
5	Illinois	5					5				18,097	14,983
9	Indiana		9					9			32,480	41,281
15	Kentucky		15					15			33,435	36,955
5	Louisiana	5					5				3,653	3,383
10	Maine	10					10				22,300	15,239
10	Maryland		10						10		22,167	25,852
14	Massachusetts				14			14			43,501	41,093
3	Michigan	3					3				7,360	4,000
4	Mississippi	4					4				9,979	9,688
4	Missouri	4					4				10,995	8,337
7	New Hampshire	7					7				18,722	6,228
8	New Jersey		8					8			26,347	26,892
42	New York	42					42				166,8[illegible]5	138,543
15	North Carolina	15					15				26,910	23,626
21	Ohio		21					21			96,948	105,405
30	Pennsylvania	30					30				91,475	87,111
4	Rhode Island	4					4				2,964	2,710
11	South Carolina					11			11		By Leg	islature
15	Tennessee			15					15		26,120	35,962
7	Vermont		7					7			14,037	20,991
23	Virginia	23								23	30,261	23,368
294	Total	170	73	26	14	11	*147	77	47	23	761,549	736,656

1840.

STATES.	Electoral Vote — Pres't: Wm. H. Harrison	Martin Van Buren	Electoral Vote — Vice-Pres't: John Tyler	Rich'd M. Johnson	L. W. Tazewell	James K. Polk	Popular Vote: Wm. H. Harrison, Whig Nominee.	Martin Van Buren, Dem. Nominee	J. G. Birney, Anti-Slavery Nominee.
Alabama		7		7			28,471	33,991	
Arkansas		3		3			5,160	6,049	
Connecticut	8		8				31,601	25,296	174
Delaware	3		3				5,96[illegible]	4,884	
Georgia	11		11				40,261	31,933	
Illinois		5		5			45,537	47,47	149
Indiana	9		9				65,302	51,695	
Kentucky	15		15				58,489	32,616	
Louisiana	5		5				11,296	7,617	
Maine	10		10				46,612	46,201	194
Maryland	10		10				33,528	2[illegible],752	
Massachusetts	14		14				72,874	51,948	1,621
Michigan	3		3				22,933	21,098	321
Mississippi	4		4				19,518	16,995	
Missouri		4		4			22,972	29,760	
New Hampshire		7		7			26,158	32,670	126
New Jersey	8		8				33,351	31,034	69
New York	42		42				225,817	212,519	2,798
North Carolina	15		15				46,370	34,218	
Ohio	21		21				148,157	124,782	903
Pennsylvania	30		30				144,021	143,676	343
Rhode Island	4		4				5,278	3,301	42
South Carolina		11			11		By Leg	islature	
Tennessee	15		15				60,391	48,289	
Vermont	7		7				32,440	18,009	3·9
Virginia		23		22		1	42,501	43,893	
Total	234	60	234	48	11	1	1,275,011	1,128,702	7,05

1844.

STATES.	Electoral Vote — Pres't: James K. Polk	Henry Clay	Electoral Vote — V-Pres't: George M. Dallas	Theodore Frelinghuysen	Popular Vote: James K. Polk, Dem. Nominee	Henry Clay, Whig Nominee.	James G. Birney, Liberty Party Nominee
Alabama	9		9		37,740	26,0[illegible]4	
Arkansas	3		3		9,546	5,504	
Connecticut		6		6	29,841	32,832	1,943
Delaware		3		3	5,996	6,278	
Georgia	10		10		44,177	42,100	
Illinois	9		9		57,920	45,528	3,570
Indiana	12		12		70,181	67,867	2,106
Kentucky		12		12	51,988	61,255	
Louisiana	6		6		13,7[illegible]2	13,083	
Maine	9		9		45,719	34,378	4,836
Maryland		8		8	32,676	35,984	
Massachusetts		12		12	52,846	67,418	10,860
Michigan	5		5		27,759	24,337	3,632
Mississippi	6		6		25,126	19,206	
Missouri	7		7		41,369	31,2[illegible]1	
New Hampshire	6		6		27,160	17,866	4,161
New Jersey		7		7	37,495	38,318	131
New York	36		36		237,588	232,482	15,812
North Carolina		11		11	39,287	43,232	
Ohio		23		23	149,117	155,057	8,050
Pennsylvania	26		26		167,535	161,203	3,138
Rhode Island		4		4	4,867	7,[illegible]22	107
South Carolina	10		10		By Leg	islature	
Tennessee		13		13	59,917	60,030	
Vermont		6		6	18,041	26,770	3,954
Virginia	17		17		49,570	43,677	
Total	170	105	170	105	1,337,243	1,299,062	62,300

* In 1836, though Mr. Van Buren was chosen President, having a majority of 23 Electoral Votes and of nearly 25,000 on the Popular Vote, there was no choice of Vice-President by the Electors, Richard M. Johnson, of Kentucky, receiving 147 Electoral Votes, just one-half of the whole number cast, while 148 was necessary to a majority. Mr. Johnson was accordingly elected Vice-President by the Senate. In 1840, Gen. Harrison's majority on the Electoral Vote was 174 or almost four-fifths, but on the Popular Vote it was only 139,250 or about one-seventeenth. In 1844, Mr. Polk's majority on the Electoral Vote was 65 or nearly three-fifths, but his Popular Vote was full 24,000 short of a majority.

ELECTORAL AND POPULAR VOTE FOR PRESIDENT AND VICE-PRESIDENT FROM 1824 TO 1852.

ELECTORAL VOTES IN 1852.	STATES.	1848.							1852.							1856.								
		ELECTORAL VOTE.				POPULAR VOTE.			ELECTORAL				POPULAR VOTE.			ELECTORAL VOTE.						POPULAR VOTE		
		PRES'T		VICE-P'T					PRES'T		VICE-P					PRESIDENT			VICE-PRES'					
		Zachary Taylor	Lewis Cass	Millard Fillmore	William O. Butler	Zachary Taylor, Whig Nominee	Lewis Cass, Democratic Nominee	Martin VanBuren, Free Soil Nominee	Franklin Pierce	Winfield Scott	William R. King	Wm. A. Graham	Franklin Pierce, Dem. Nominee	Winfield Scott, Whig Nominee	John P. Hale, Free Soil Nominee	James Buchanan	John C. Fremont	Millard Fillmore	J. C. Breckenridge	William L. Dayton	And'w J. Donelson	James Buchanan, Dem. Nominee	John C. Fremont, Repub. Nominee	Millard Fillmore, American Nom.
9	Alabama		9		9	30,482	31,363		9		9		26,881	15,038		9			9			46,739		28,552
4	Arkansas		3		3	7,588	9,300		4		4		12,173	7,404		4			4			21,910		10,787
4	California								4		4		40,626	35,407	100	4			4			53,365	20,691	36,165
6	Connecticut	6		6		30,314	27,046	5,005	6		6		33,249	30,357	3,160		6			6		34,995	42,715	2,615
3	Delaware	3		3		6,421	5,898	80	3		3		6,318	6,293	62	3			3			8,004	308	6,175
3	Florida	3		3		3,116	1,847		3		3		4,318	2,875		3			3			6,358		4,833
10	Georgia	10		10		47,544	44,802		10		10		34,705	16,660		10			10			56,578		42,228
11	Illinois		9		9	53,047	56,300	15,774	11		11		80,597	64,934	9,966	11			11			105,348	96,189	37,444
13	Indiana		12		12	69,907	74,745	8,100	13		13		95,340	80,901	6,929	13			13			118,670	94,375	22,386
4	Iowa		4		4	11,084	12,093	1,126	4		4		17,763	15,856	1,604		4			4		36,670	43,954	9,180
12	Kentucky	12		12		67,141	49,720			12		12	53,806	57,068		12			12			74,642	314	67,416
6	Louisiana	6		6		18,217	15,370		6		6		18,647	17,255		6			6			22,164		20,709
8	Maine		9		9	35,125	39,880	12,096	8		8		41,609	32,543	8,030		8			8		39,080	67,379	3,325
8	Maryland	8		8		37,702	34,528	125	8		8		40,020	35,066	54			8			8	39,115	281	47,460
13	Massachusetts	12		12		61,070	35,281	38,058		13		13	44,569	52,683	28,023		13			13		39,240	108,190	19,626
6	Michigan		5		5	23,940	30,687	10,398	6		6		41,842	33,859	7,237		6			6		52,136	71,762	1,660
7	Mississippi		6		6	25,922	26,537		7		7		26,876	17,548		7			7			35,446		24,195
9	Missouri		7		7	32,671	40,077		9		9		38,353	29,984		9			9			58,164		48,524
5	New Hampshire		6		6	14,781	27,763	7,560	5		5		29,997	16,147	6,695		5			5		32,789	38,345	422
7	New Jersey	7		7		40,015	35,901	829	7		7		44,305	38,556	350	7			7			46,943	28,338	24,115
35	New York	36		36		218,603	114,318	120,510	35		35		262,083	234,882	25,329		35			35		195,878	276,007	124,607
10	North Carolina	11		11		43,550	34,869		10		10		39,744	39,058		10			10			48,246		36,886
23	Ohio		23		23	138,360	154,775	35,354	23		23		169,220	152,526	31,682		23			23		170,874	187,497	28,126
27	Pennsylvania	26		26		185,513	171,176	11,263	27		27		198,568	179,174	8,525	27			27			230,710	147,510	82,175
4	Rhode Island	4		4		6,779	3,646	730	4		4		8,735	7,626	644		4			4		6,680	11,467	1,675
9	South Carolina		9		9	By Leg	islature		8		8		By Leg	islature		8			8			By Leg	islature	
12	Tennessee	13		13		64,705	58,419			12		12	57,018	58,898		12			12			73,638		66,178
4	Texas		4		4	4,509	10,668		4		4		13,552	4,995		4			4			31,169		15,639
5	Vermont	6		6		23,122	10,948	12,837		5		5	13,044	22,173	8,621		5			5		10,569	39,561	515
15	Virginia		17		17	45,124	46,586	9	15		15		73,858	58,572		10			10			89,706	291	60,310
5	Wisconsin		4		4	13,747	15,001	10,418	5		5		33,658	22,240	8,814		5			5		52,843	66,090	579
296	Total	163	127	163	127	1,360,099	1,220,544	291,263	254	42	254	42	1,601,474	1,386,578	155,825	174	114	8	174	114	8	1,838,169	1,341,264	874,534

In the Election of 1848, Gen. Taylor, though having a majority of 36 Electoral Votes, was 151,708 short of a majority on the Popular Vote. In 1856, Mr. Buchanan, though having a majority of 52 in the Electoral College, was 377,629 short of a majority on the Popular Vote—while in the overwhelming victory of Mr. Pierce, where his majority in the Electoral College was 212, his majority on the Popular Vote was only 59,071

ELECTORAL AND POPULAR VOTES OF EACH STATE, 1860 TO 1868.

1860.

Electoral Vote in 1860	STATES.	President: Abraham Lincoln	President: J. C. Breckenridge	President: John Bell	President: Steph. A. Douglas	Vice-Pres't: Hannibal Hamlin	Vice-Pres't: Joseph Lane	Vice-Pres't: Edward Everett	Vice-Pres't: Hersch V. Johnson	Abraham Lincoln, Republican Nominee	John C. Breckenridge, HardShell Democratic Nominee	Stephen A. Douglas, Soft-Shell Democratic Nominee	John Bell, Union and Old Line Whig Nominee
9	Alabama		9				9				48,831	13,651	27,825
4	Arkansas		4				4				25,732	5,227	20,004
4	California	4				4				39,173	34,334	38,516	6,817
6	Connecticut	6				6				43,692	14,641	15,522	3,29[illegible]
3	Delaware		3				3			3,815	7,347	1,023	3,864
3	Florida		3				3				8,543	367	5,437
10	Georgia		10				10				51,889	11,590	42,886
11	Illinois	11				11				172,161	2,404	160,215	3,913
13	Indiana	13				13				139,033	12,295	115,509	5,306
4	Iowa	4				4				70,409	1,048	55,111	1,763
0	Kansas												
12	Kentucky			12				12		1,364	53,143	25,651	66,058
6	Louisiana		6				6				22,681	7,625	20,204
8	Maine	8				8				62,811	6,368	26,693	2,046
8	Maryland		8				8			2,294	42,482	5,966	41,760
13	Massachusetts	13				13				106,533	5,939	34,372	22,331
6	Michigan	6				6				88,480	805	65,057	405
4	Minnesota	4				4				22,069	748	11,920	62
7	Mississippi		7				7				40,797	3,283	25,040
9	Missouri				9				9	17,028	31,317	58,801	58,372
0	Nebraska												
0	Nevada												
5	New Hampshire	5				5				37,519	2,112	25,881	441
7	New Jersey	4			3	4			3	58,324		62,801	Fus'n
35	New York	35				35				362,646		312,510	Fus'n
10	North Carolina		10				10				48,339	2,701	44,990
23	Ohio	23				23				231,510	11,405	187,232	12,194
3	Oregon	3				3				5,270	5,006	3,951	183
27	Pennsylvania	27				27				268,030	178,871	16,765	12,776
4	Rhode Island	4				4				12,244		7,707	
8	South Carolina		8				8			By Leg	islatu	re	
12	Tennessee			12				12			64,709	11,350	69,274
4	Texas		4				4				47,548		15,438
5	Vermont	5				5				33,808	218	6,849	1,969
15	Virginia			15				15		1,929	74,323	16,290	74,681
0	West Virginia												
5	Wisconsin	5				5				86,110	888	65,021	161
303	Total	180	72	39	12	180	72	39	12	1,866,352	845,763	1,375,157	589,58[illegible]

1864.

STATES.	Electoral Vote in 1864	Pres't: Abraham Lincoln	Pres't: Geo. B. McClellan	V.-P.: Andrew Johnson	V.-P.: Geo. H. Pendleton	Abraham Lincoln, Republican Nominee	George B. McClellan, Democratic Nominee
Alabama	0						
Arkansas	0						
California	5	5		5		62,134	43,841
Connecticut	6	6		6		44,691	42,285
Delaware	3		3		3	8,155	8,767
Florida	0						
Georgia	0						
Illinois	16	16		16		189,496	158,730
Indiana	13	13		13		150,422	130,233
Iowa	8	8		8		89,075	49,596
Kansas	3	3		3		16,441	3,691
Kentucky	11		11		11	27,786	64,301
Louisiana	0						
Maine	7	7		7		61,802	44,211
Maryland	7	7		7		40,453	22,739
Massachusetts	12	12		12		126,742	48,745
Michigan	8	8		8		91,521	74,604
Minnesota	4	4		4		25,060	17,375
Mississippi	0						
Missouri	11	11		11		72,750	31,678
Nebraska	0						
Nevada	3	*2		2		9,826	6,594
New Hampshire	5	5		5		36,400	32,871
New Jersey	7		7		7	60,723	68,024
New York	33	33		33		368,735	361,986
North Carolina	0						
Ohio	21	21		21		265,154	205,568
Oregon	3	3		3		9,888	8,457
Pennsylvania	26	26		26		296,391	276,316
Rhode Island	4	4		4		13,692	8,470
South Carolina	0						
Tennessee	0						
Texas	0						
Vermont	5	5		5		42,419	13,321
Virginia	0						
West Virginia	5	5		5		23,152	10,438
Wisconsin	8	8		8		83,458	65,884
Total	234	212	21	212	21	2,216,067	1,808,725

1868.

STATES.	Electoral Vote in 1868	Pres't: Ulysses S. Grant	Pres't: Horatio Seymour	V.-P.: Schuyler Colfax	V.-P.: Francis P. Blair	Ulysses S. Grant, Republican Nominee	Horatio Seymour, Democratic Nominee
Alabama	8	8		8		76,366	72,088
Arkansas	5	5		5		22,112	19,078
California	5	5		5		54,583	54,077
Connecticut	6	6		6		50,995	47,952
Delaware	3		3		3	7,625	10,580
Florida	3	3		3			
Georgia	9		9		9	57,134	142,722
Illinois	16	16		16		250,303	199,143
Indiana	13	13		13		176,548	166,980
Iowa	8	8		8		120,399	74,040
Kansas	3	3		3		31,048	13,990
Kentucky	11		11		11	39,566	115,890
Louisiana	7		7		7	33,263	80,225
Maine	7	7		7		70,4[illegible]3	42,460
Maryland	7		7		7	30,4[illegible]	62,357
Massachusetts	12	12		12		136,477	59,408
Michigan	8	8		8		128,550	97,069
Minnesota	4	4		4		43,545	28,075
Mississippi	0						
Missouri	11	11		11		86,860	55,628
Nebraska	3	3		3		9,729	5,439
Nevada	3	3		3		6,480	5,218
New Hampshire	5	5		5		38,191	31,224
New Jersey	7		7		7	80,131	83,001
New York	33		33		33	419,883	429,883
North Carolina	9	9		9		96,769	84,601
Ohio	21	21		21		280,223	238,606
Oregon	3		3		3	10,961	11,125
Pennsylvania	26	26		26		342,280	313,382
Rhode Island	4	4		4		12,993	6,548
South Carolina	6	6		6		62,301	45,237
Tennessee	10	10		10		56,628	26,129
Texas	0						
Vermont	5	5		5		44,167	12,045
Virginia	0						
West Virginia	5	5		5		29,175	20,306
Wisconsin	8	8		8		108,857	84,707
Total	294	214	80	214	80	3,015,071	2,709,613

* In Nevada, in 1864, three Republican Electors were chosen, but one of them having died before the Electoral Vote was cast in December, the vacancy was not filled, and only two Electoral Votes were cast. In the Election of 1860, four candidates were in the field, all of whom received some Electoral Votes. Mr. Lincoln had a majority over all of 57 votes in the Electoral College, but was in a minority of 944,149 in the Popular Vote. In 1864 he had a majority of 191 in the Electoral College, and of nearly 408,000 on the Popular Vote. Gen. Grant's majority in the Electoral College, in 1868, was 134, and on the Popular Vote over 305,000.

10	Alabama	10	....	10	....	90,272	79,444	....	10	....	10	....	10	68,230	102,002	....	....	....	10	....	10	56,240	91,875	4,610	no ti	cket.	....
6	Arkansas	6	....	6	....	41,373	37 927	....	6	....	6	....	6	38,669	58,071	289	....	....	6	....	6	41,661	60,481	4,079	"	"	322
6	California	6	....	6	....	54,044	40,749	1,068	6	6	....	6	....	78,614	75,845	44	....	....	6	1	5	80,378	80,417	2,783	"	"	....
0	Colorado	....	....	....	....	....	....	....	3	3	....	3	....	By Legislature		....	....	....	3	3	....	27,450	24,647	1,435	"	"	....
6	Connecticut	6	....	6	....	50,638	45,880	204	6	....	6	....	6	59,034	61,934	774	378	....	6	6	....	67,073	64,417	869	405	"	....
3	Delaware	3	....	3	....	11,115	10,200	487	3	....	3	....	3	10 752	13,381	....	....	....	3	....	3	14,138	15,178	120	no ti	cket.	7
4	Florida	4	....	4	....	17,765	15,428	....	4	†4	....	†4	....	†23,849	†22,923	....	....	....	4	....	4	23,632	27,922	....	"	"	....
11	Georgia	....	11	....	11	62,715	76,278	4,000	11	....	11	....	11	50,446	130,088	....	....	....	11	....	11	52,652	102,522	481	"	"	....
21	Illinois	21	....	21	....	241,248	184,770	3,058	21	21	....	21	....	278,232	258,601	17,233	141	286	21	21	....	318,716	277,321	26,358	443	153	107
15	Indiana	15	....	15	....	186,144	163,637	1,417	15	....	15	....	15	208,011	213,526	9,533	....	....	15	15	....	232,164	225,522	12,986	no ti	cket.	....
11	Iowa	11	....	11	....	131,233	71,119	2,221	11	11	....	11	....	171,327	112,099	9,001	36	....	11	11	....	183,904	105 845	32,327	159	433	38
5	Kansas	5	....	5	....	66,942	32,970	596	5	5	....	5	....	78,322	37,902	7,776	110	23	5	5	....	121,549	59,801	19,851	no ti	cket.	35
12	Kentucky	....	12	....	12	88,970	100,208	2,374	12	....	12	....	12	97,156	150,690	1,944	818	....	12	....	12	106,957	148,707	11,498	257	"	....
8	Louisiana	8	....	8	....	70,553	57,029	....	8	†8	....	†8	....	†75,135	†79,636	....	....	....	8	....	8	‡38,034	65,067	442	no ti	cket.	218
7	Maine	7	....	7	....	61,402	29,087	....	7	7	....	7	....	66,300	49,823	663	....	....	7	7	....	74,039	§65,171	‖4,408	93	142	....
8	Maryland	....	8	....	8	66,750	67,685	19	8	....	8	....	8	71,981	91,780	33	10	....	8	....	8	78,515	93,706	139	no ti	cket.	....
13	Massachusetts	13	....	13	....	133,472	59,260	....	13	13	....	13	....	150 063	108,777	779	84	....	13	13	....	165,198	111,960	4,548	682	"	117
11	Michigan	11	....	11	....	138,455	78,365	2,861	11	11	....	11	....	166,534	141,095	9,060	766	71	11	11	....	185,195	131,301	34,895	942	2	¶320
5	Minnesota	5	....	5	....	54,558	34,327	....	5	5	....	5	....	72,962	48,799	2,311	72	....	5	5	....	93,903	53,316	3,267	286	"	2,113
8	Mississippi	8	....	8	....	82,406	47,287	....	8	....	8	...	8	52,605	112,173	....	....	....	8	...	8	34,854	75,750	5,797	no ti	cket.	677
15	Missouri	....	15	....	15	119,196	151,433	2,429	15	....	15	....	15	145,029	203,077	3,498	64	....	15	....	15	153,567	208,589	35,135	"	"	....
3	Nebraska	3	....	3	....	18,245	7,705	....	3	3	....	3	...	31,916	17,554	2,320	1,509	....	3	3	....	54,979	28,523	3,950	"	"	8
3	Nevada	3	...	3	....	8,403	6,236	....	3	3	....	3	....	10,383	9,308	....	....	....	3	....	3	10,145	11,215	....	"	"	....
5	New Hampshire	5	....	5	....	37,184	31,423	100	5	5	....	5	....	41,539	38,509	76	....	....	5	5	....	44,852	40,794	528	180	"	425
9	New Jersey	9	..	9	....	91,661	76,801	630	9	....	9	....	9	103,517	115,962	712	43	....	9	....	9	120,555	122,565	2,617	191	"	....
35	New York	35	...	35	....	440,749	387,279	1,454	35	....	35	....	35	489,207	521,949	1,987	2,359	....	35	35	....	555,544	534,511	12,373	1,517	75	1,806
10	North Carolina	10	....	10	....	94,304	69,474	....	10	....	10	....	10	108,417	125,427	....	....	....	10	....	10	115,616	124,204	1 136	no ti	cket.	....
22	Ohio	22	....	22	....	281,852	244,321	1,163	22	22	....	22	...	330,698	323,182	3,057	1,636	76	22	22	....	375,048	340,831	6,456	2 616	"	1,447
3	Oregon	3	...	3	...	11,820	7,746	572	3	3	....	3	....	15,206	14,149	510	....	....	3	3	....	20,618	19,950	245	no ti	cket.	....
29	Pennsylvania	29	....	29	....	349,689	211,961	....	29	29	....	29	....	384,122	366,158	7,487	1,319	83	29	29	....	444,704	407,428	20,668	1,939	44	....
4	Rhode Island	4	....	4	....	13,665	5,329	....	4	4	....	4	....	15 787	10,712	68	60	....	4	4	....	18,195	10,778	236	20	"	26
7	South Carolina	7	....	7	....	72,290	22,703	187	7	7	....	7	....	†91,870	†90,906	....	....	....	7	....	7	57,947	112,036	547	no ti	cket.	....
12	Tennessee	....	12	....	12	83,655	94,391	....	12	....	12	....	12	89,566	133,166	....	....	....	12	....	12	98 760	130,381	5,465	"	"	....
8	Texas	....	8	....	8	47,426	66,455	2,499	8	....	8	....	8	44,800	104,755	....	....	....	8	....	8	53,200	146,800	26,200	"	"	....
5	Vermont	5	....	5	...	41,487	10,926	593	5	5	....	5	....	44,092	20,254	....	....	....	5	5	....	45,091	18,182	1,212	"	105	....
11	Virginia	11	....	11	....	92,953	91,424	42	11	....	11	....	11	95,558	139,670	....	....	....	11	....	11	83,634	**128,158	501	no ti	cket.	399
5	West Virginia	5	....	5	....	32,323	29,537	600	5	....	5	....	5	42,698	56,455	1,373	....	....	5	....	5	46,243	57,391	9,079	"	"	....
10	Wisconsin	10	....	10	....	104,992	86,477	834	10	10	....	10	....	130,668	123,927	1,509	27	....	10	10	....	144,400	114,649	7,986	69	91	19
365	Total	300	*66	300	*66	3,594,109	2,833,889	29,408	369	185	184	185	184	4,033,295	4,284,265	81,737	9,522	539	369	214	155	4,438,670	4,437,902	305,339	9,799	1,072	8,084

* The 66 electors were chosen to cast their votes for Horace Greeley and B. Gratz Brown, but Mr. Greeley dying before the day on which the Electoral Colleges met, the 66 votes for President were cast as follows: 42 for Thomas A. Hendricks, 18 for B. Gratz Brown, and 6 scattering. The 66 votes for Vice-President were all cast for B. Gratz Brown. † These are the figures of the Returning Boards, the highest vote given for any elector of either party being stated. ‡ Including 9,740 votes for the Beattie electors, nominated by the Grant men; the vote for the regular Republican ticket ranged from 97,680 to 98,294, and the vote for the Beattie ticket between 9,727 and 10,340; the votes given here (98.294 for Charles Dillingham and 9,740 for Edward Heath) best represent the entire Republican vote. § Fusion vote (Greenback and Democratic). ‖ Vote received by the three candidates on the Straight Greenback ticket, who were not on the Fusion ticket; the Fusion ticket contained the names of 4 Greenback men and 3 Democrats, and the Straight Greenback ticket contained the names of the 4 Greenback men on the Fusion ticket, and the names of three new men; the Fusion vote ranged between 65,171 for Samuel Watts (who was not on the Straight ticket) and 64,453 for Charles R. Whidden, who was a candidate on the Fusion and Straight tickets; had the Fusion ticket been elected, 3 of the electors would have voted for Hancock and 4 for Weaver. ¶ For "American-Labor" ticket. ** 96,599 regular (or Funder) votes and 82,559 Readjuster votes, all for Hancock. Summing up results in 1880, we find that 9,200,460 votes were cast for President this year. The Republicans cast 404,025 more votes this year than in 1876, the Democrats 151,560, the Greenback men 223,534, the Prohibitionists 78, and the Anti-Masonic party 604—making a total increase of 780,678 in the vote of the five parties. The net increase in the total of all the votes cast, however, is 772,678, there having been a falling off of 7,900 in the scattering votes.

HISTORY OF THE PRESIDENTIAL ELECTION AND INAUGURATION,

SUBSEQUENT TO THE MEETING OF THE ELECTORAL COLLEGES.

The doubt in regard to the result of the Presidential Election was not removed by the returns from the Electoral Colleges which met December 6, 1876, for in South Carolina, Florida and Louisiana two or more lists of Electors were returned, though some of them lacked the required authentication, and in Oregon, one name was returned who had confessedly not been elected, and there were in consequence three Electoral Certificates from that State, one containing the elected list, one substituting one name not elected for an elector declared to have been ineligible, and one made up of the names of this substituted elector and two others whom he had appointed. The confusion seemed constantly growing more hopeless, and the danger of revolution or violence constantly greater. Investigating Committees had been sent to South Carolina, Florida and Louisiana by both houses of Congress, and informal commissions sent by the President and by the Chairman of the National Democratic Committee. A joint committee was at last appointed from the Senate and House of Representatives, with instructions to consider and report a bill for regulating the counting of the votes for President and Vice-President. The questions which were to be solved were these: whether as one party claimed, the Vice-President or Acting Vice-President of the United States was vested with the exclusive power of opening and counting, or causing to be counted, the electoral vote; whether his functions in this matter were purely ministerial; whether in case of two returns he alone had the right to decide which were valid; and if not, whether the Senate or the House, or either or both, separately or together, as a joint convention, or the House voting by States, had a right to decide the question for him; whether the House had a right, after objecting to the electoral vote of any State, to declare that there was no election, and to proceed to vote for a President by States, the Senate thereupon electing the Vice-President. There were other but minor questions also involved, and it was felt that there was need of great caution and wisdom in digesting a plan which would prove satisfactory to both parties and avert the threatened conflict. The committee was selected with great care, and consisted of some of the ablest men in each house. The President of the Senate named four Republicans and three Democrats, and the Speaker of the House four Democrats and three Republicans, so that each party might be represented by an equal number. The Senators on the committee were Messrs. Edmunds, Frelinghuysen, Morton, Conkling, Thurman, Bayard and Ransom, and the members of the House, Messrs. Payne, Hunton, Hewitt, Springer, McCrary, Hoar and Willard. The committee thus constituted, after long and careful deliberation, reported the following act on the 18th of January, 1877.

THE ACT PROVIDING FOR THE ELECTORAL COMMISSION.

AN ACT to provide for and regulate the counting of votes for President and Vice-President, and the decision of questions arising thereon, for the term commencing March Fourth, Anno Domini eighteen hundred and seventy-seven.

Be it enacted by the Senate and House of Representatives of the United States of America in Congress assembled, That the Senate and House of Representatives shall meet in the hall of the House or Representatives, at the hour of one o'clock post meridian, on the first Thursday in February, Anno Domini eighteen hundred and seventy-seven, and the President of the Senate shall be their presiding officer. Two tellers shall be previously appointed on the part of the Senate, and two on the part of the House of Representatives, to whom shall be handed, as they are opened by the President of the Senate, all the certificates, and papers purporting to be certificates, of the electoral votes, which certificates and papers shall be opened, presented, and acted upon in alphabetical order of the States, beginning with the letter A; and said tellers having then read the same in the presence and hearing of the two Houses, shall make a list of the votes as they shall appear from the said certificates; and the votes having been ascertained and counted as in this act provided, the result of the same shall be delivered to the President of the Senate, who shall thereupon announce the state of the vote, and the names of the persons, if any, elected, which announcement shall be deemed a sufficient declaration of the persons elected President and Vice-President of the United States, and, together with a list of the votes, be entered on the journals of the two Houses. Upon such reading of any such certificate or paper when there shall be only one return from a State, the President of the Senate shall call for objections, if any. Every objection shall be made in writing, and shall state clearly and concisely, and without argument, the ground thereof, and shall be signed by at least one Senator and one member of the House of Representatives before the same shall be received. When all objections so made to any vote or paper from a State shall have been received and read, the Senate shall thereupon withdraw, and such objections shall be submitted to the Senate for its decision; and the speaker of the House of Representatives shall, in like manner, submit such objections to the House of Representatives for its decision; and no electoral vote or votes from any State from which but one return has been received shall be rejected, except by the affirmative vote of the two Houses. When the two Houses have voted, they shall immediately again meet, and the presiding officer shall then announce the decision of the question submitted.

SEC. 2. That, if more than one return, or paper purporting to be a return from a State, shall have been received by the President of the Senate, purporting to be the certificates of electoral votes given at the last preceding election for President and Vice-President in such State (unless they shall be duplicates of the same return), all such returns and papers shall be opened by him in the presence of the two Houses when met as aforesaid, and read by the tellers, and all such returns and papers shall thereupon be submitted to the judgment and decision as to which is the true and lawful electoral vote of such State, of a commission constituted as follows, namely: During the session of each House, on the Tuesday next preceding the first Thursday in February, eighteen hundred and seventy-seven, each House shall, by viva voce vote, appoint five of its members, who with the five associate justices of the Supreme Court of the United States, to be ascertained as hereinafter provided, shall constitute a commission for the decision of all questions upon or in respect of such double returns named in this section. On the Tuesday next preceding the first Thursday in February, Anno Domini eighteen hundred and seventy-seven, or as soon thereafter as may be, the associate justices of the Supreme Court of the United States now assigned to the first, third, eighth, and ninth circuits shall select, in such manner as a majority of them shall deem fit, another of the associate justices of said court, which five persons shall be members of said commission; and the person longest in commission of said five justices shall be the president of said commission. The members of said commission shall respectively take and subscribe the following oaths: "I, ——— ———, do solemnly swear (or affirm, as the case may be) that I will impartially examine and consider all questions submitted to the commission of which I am a member, and a true judgment give thereon, agreeably to the Constitution and the laws: so help me God;" which oath shall be filed with the Secretary of the Senate. When the commission shall have been thus organized, it shall not be in the power of either House to dissolve the same, or to withdraw any of its members; but if any such Senator or member shall die or become physically unable to perform the duties required by this act, the fact of such death or physical inability shall be by said commission, before it shall proceed further, communicated to the Senate or House of Representatives, as the case may be, which body shall immediately and without debate proceed by viva voce vote to fill the place so vacated, and the person so appointed shall take and subscribe the oath hereinbefore prescribed, and become a member of said commission; and, in like manner, if any of said justices of the Supreme Court shall die or become physically incapable of performing the duties required by this act, the other of said justices, members of the said commission, shall immediately appoint another justice of said court a member of said commission, and, in such appointments, regard shall be had to the impartiality and freedom from bias sought by the original appointments to said commission, who shall thereupon immediately take and subscribe the oath hereinbefore prescribed, and become a member of said commission to fill the vacancy so occasioned. All the certificates and papers purporting to be certificates of the electoral votes of each State shall be opened, in the alphabetical order of the States, as provided in section one of this act; and when there shall be more than one such certificate or paper, as the certificates and papers from such State shall so be opened (excepting duplicates of the same return), they shall be read by the tellers, and thereupon the President of the Senate shall call for objections, if any. Every objection shall be made in writing, and shall state clearly and concisely, and without argument, the ground thereof, and shall be signed by at least one Senator and one member of the House of Representatives before the same shall be received. When all such objections so made to any certificate, vote, or paper from a State shall have been received and read, all such certificates, votes and papers so objected to, and all papers accompanying the same, together with such objections, shall be forthwith submitted to said commission, which shall proceed to consider the same, with the same powers, if any, now possessed for that purpose by the two Houses acting separately or together, and by a majority of votes, decide whether any and what votes from such State are the votes provided for by the Constitution of the United States, and how many and what persons were duly appointed electors in such State, and may therein take into view such petitions, depositions, and other papers, if any, as shall, by the Constitution and now existing law, be competent and pertinent in such consideration; which decision shall be made in writing, stating briefly the ground thereof, and signed by the members of said commission agreeing therein; whereupon the two Houses shall again meet, and such decision shall be read and entered in the journal of each house, and the counting of the votes shall proceed in conformity therewith, unless, upon objection made thereto in writing by at least five Senators and five members of the House of Representatives, the two Houses shall separately concur in ordering otherwise, in which case such concurrent order shall govern. No votes or papers from any other State shall be acted upon until the objections previously made to the votes or papers from any State shall have been finally disposed of.

Sec. 3. That, while the two Houses shall be in meeting, as provided in this act, no debate shall be allowed and no question shall be put by the presiding officer, except to either House on a motion to withdraw; and he shall have power to preserve order.

Sec. 4. That when the two Houses separate to decide upon an objection that may have been made to the counting of any electoral vote or votes from any State, or upon objection to a report of said commission, or other question arising under this act, each Senator and Representative may speak to such objection or question ten minutes, and not oftener than once; but after such debate shall have lasted two hours, it shall be the duty of each House to put the main question without further debate.

Sec. 5. That at such joint meeting of the two Houses, seats shall be provided as follows: For the President of the Senate, the Speaker's chair; for the Speaker, immediately upon his left; the Senators in the body of the hall upon the right of the presiding officer; for the Representatives, in the body of the hall not provided for the Senators; for the tellers, Secretary of the Senate, and Clerk of the House of Representatives, at the Clerk's desk; for the other officers of the two Houses, in front of the Clerk's desk and upon each side of the Speaker's platform. Such joint meeting shall not be dissolved until the count of electoral votes shall be completed and the result declared; and no recess shall be taken unless a question shall have arisen in regard to counting any such votes, or otherwise under this act, in which case it shall be competent for either House, acting separately, in the manner hereinbefore provided, to direct a recess of such House not beyond the next day, Sunday excepted, at the hour of ten o'clock in the forenoon. And while any question is being considered by said commission, either House may proceed with its legislative or other business.

Sec. 6. That nothing in this act shall be held to impair or affect any right now existing under the Constitution and laws to question, by proceeding in the judicial courts of the United States, the right or title of the person who shall be declared elected, or who shall claim to be President or Vice-President of the United States, if any such right exists.

Sec. 7. That said commission shall make its own rules, keep a record of its proceedings, and shall have power to employ such persons as may be necessary for the transaction of its business and the execution of its power.

Approved, January 29, 1877.

This act passed the Senate January 25, 1877. forty-seven Senators voting for it, seventeen against it, and ten not voting. It passed the House, Jan. 26, one hundred and ninety-one voting for it, eighty-six against it, and fourteen not voting. It was approved by the President, Jan. 29, 1877.

On the 30th of January the Senate and House each elected their members of the Commission, and the four Judges of the Supreme Court virtually named in the act, proceeded to elect a fifth, choosing Justice Joseph P. Bradley, of N. J. The Commission was thus constituted as follows:

Justices of the Supreme Court.	*Senators.*	*Representatives.*
NATHAN CLIFFORD, President, Me.	GEORGE F. EDMUNDS, Vt.	JAMES A. GARFIELD, Ohio.
SAMUEL F. MILLER, Iowa.	FRED. T. FRELINGHUYSEN, N. J.	GEORGE F. HOAR, Mass.
WILLIAM STRONG, Penn.	OLIVER P. MORTON, Ind.	HENRY B. PAYNE, Ohio.
STEPHEN J. FIELD, Cal.	ALLEN G. THURMAN, Ohio.	EPPA HUNTON, Va.
JOSEPH P. BRADLEY, N. J.	THOMAS F. BAYARD, Del.	JOSIAH G. ABBOTT, Mass.

On the 31st of January the Commission met and adopted the following rules:

RULES OF THE COMMISSION.

RULE I. The Committee shall appoint a Secretary, two Assistant Secretaries, a Marshal, and two Deputy Marshals, a Stenographer, and such messengers as shall be needful; to hold during the pleasure of the Commission.

RULE II. On a y subject submitted to the Commission, a hearing shall be had; and counsel shall be allowed to conduct the case on each side.

RULE III. Counsel, not exceeding two in number on each side, will be heard by the Commission, on the merits of any case presented to it, not longer than two hours being allowed to each side, unless a longer time and additional counsel shall be specially authorized by the Commission. In the hearing of interlocuting questions, but one counsel shall be heard on each side, and he not longer than fifteen minutes, unless the Commission allow further time and additional counsel; and printed arguments will be received.

RULE IV. The objectors to any certificate or vote, may select two of their number to support their objections in oral argument, and to advocate the validity of any certificate or vote, the validity of which they maintain; and in like manner the objectors to any other certificate may select two of their number for a like purpose; but, under this rule, not more than four persons shall speak, and neither side shall occupy more than two hours.

RULE V. Applications for process to compel the attendance of witnesses, or the production of written documentary testimony may be made by counsel on either side, and all process shall be served and executed by the Marshal of the Commission or his deputies. Depositions hereafter taken for use before the Commission shall be sufficiently authenticated if taken before any Commissioner of the Circuit Courts of the United States, or any clerk or deputy clerk of the United States.

RULE VI. Admission to the public sittings of the Commission shall be regulated in such manner as the President of the Commission shall direct.

RULE VII. The Commission will sit, unless otherwise ordered, in the room of the Supreme Court of the United States, and with open doors (excepting when in consultation), unless otherwise directed.

WASHINGTON, D. C., January 31, 1877.

The first case requiring the action of the Commission was that of the electoral vote of Florida. There were three certificates presented to the President of the Senate, two of them certifying—though on different grounds—to the election of the Hayes Electors; one of them having been issued by order of the Supreme Court of Florida some weeks after the meeting of the Electoral College, on account of an alleged defect in the count, and the third certifying to the election of the Tilden Electors, but not signed by the requisite authority. There was also a further question regarding the eligibility of F. C. Humphreys, one of the Hayes Electors, who, it was alleged, was a U. S. Shipping Commissioner when chosen an Elector. After a long and able argument on each side, the Commission voted Feb. 9—eight in the affirmative and seven in the negative—"That the four Hayes Electors were duly appointed, and that the votes cast by them are the votes provided for by the Constitution of the United States; that neither the second or the third certificates presented were the certificates of votes prescribed by the Constitution, and that the evidence did not show that F. C. Humphreys held the office of a Shipping Commissioner of the U. S. at the time of his election."

This decision having been reported to Congress, it was sustained by the Senate: yeas, 44; nays, 24; not voting, 7; and rejected by the House: yeas, 168; nays, 103; not voting, 19; and, according to the Act, was counted, Feb. 10.

The Louisiana case was reached and laid before the Commission Feb. 13, where it was debated till Feb. 16, when the Commission decided, by a vote of eight to seven, that the eight Hayes Electors were the lawful electors of the State of Louisiana, and their votes the votes provided by the Constitution of the

United States, and should be counted for President and Vice-President. This decision, like that in the Florida case, rested on the basis that the Electoral Commission did not possess any more or greater power than the Congress which had created it, and, therefore, had no power to go behind the legally-authorized report of the Returning Board, Board of Canvassers, or other authority prescribed by the State for this purpose.

This decision was reported to Congress on the 16th of February, but was not acted upon until the 19th, when the Senate sustained the decision of the Commission by 41 yeas; nays, 28; not voting, 6. The House rejected it by—yeas, 173; nays, 99; not voting, 18; and the vote was counted Feb. 20. Objection was made to one of the Electors in the Michigan, and one in the Nevada, certificate; but as there was but one certificate in each case, and the objections were evidently invalid, they were not referred to the Commission.

The Oregon case was reached Feb. 21, and referred to the Commission, which reassembled Feb. 22. The arguments on both sides were heard, and on Feb. 23 the Commission decided "That W. H. Odell, John C. Cartwright and John W. Watts, the persons named as Electors in certificate No. 1, were the lawful Electors of the State of Oregon, and that their votes are the votes provided for by the Constitution of the United States, and should be counted for President and Vice-President of the United States." This decision passed by the usual vote of eight yeas and seven nays.

The fact of the election of three Hayes Electors in Oregon was not in dispute, but it was claimed that one of these, J. W. Watts, was a postmaster at the time of his election, and so ineligible; and Gov. Grover had assumed to throw out his name and give the certificate to Messrs. Odell, Cartwright, and E. A. Cronin, who had been Mr. Watts' competitor, but had fallen 1,000 votes short of an election. Thus, while the Secretary of State (the canvassing authority of the State) had certified to the election of Messrs. Odell, Cartwright and Watts, Gov. Grover had certified to the election of Messrs. Odell, Cartwright and Cronin. Mr. Cronin, failing to persuade Messrs. Odell and Cartwright to act with him, had resolved himself into an Electoral College, and had chosen two men who had not been voted for at all, as Electors, and sent—or rather brought in—a third certificate, declaring E. A. Cronin, J. N. T. Miller and John Parker the duly appointed Electors. This certificate was rejected, as was Cronin's appointment, by the entire Commission. On the 24th of February the Senate sustained the decision of the Commission by—yeas, 40; nays, 24; and 11 did not vote. The House rejected it by—yeas, 151; nays, 106; not voting, 33. On the 26th of Feb. objection was made to Electors in the Pennsylvania and Rhode Island Colleges; but as there were only single certificates in each case, they were not referred to the Commission.

The case of South Carolina was reached Feb. 26, and Hon. A. G. Thurman having withdrawn on account of illness from the Commission, Hon. Francis Kernan, of N. Y., was chosen in his place The case of South Carolina differed from those which had preceded it in some important particulars. Although there were two certificates, it was not seriously contended that the Hayes Electors had not received a majority of votes, but it was urged that, owing to the failure of the Legislature to provide a system of registration, and to the disorders, irregularities and frauds attending the Presidential election, that election should be declared void, and that the State, being at that time under duress from the United States troops stationed there, was incapable of holding a valid election. The Commission, after hearing the arguments, decided unanimously that the Tilden Electoral ticket should be rejected, and, by a vote of eight to seven, that the Hayes Electors were lawful Electors for the State of South Carolina, and that the State was entitled to have her vote counted. The Senate the same day sustained the action of the Commission by—yeas, 39; nays, 22; not voting, 14; and the House rejected it by—yeas, 190; nays, 72; not voting, 28. To the vote was counted.

Objection was made to Electors on the certificates of Vermont and Wisconsin, but these did not come within the provisions of the Commission.

On the morning of March 2, the completion of the count of Electors was reached, and at 4:10 A. M., of that day, Mr. Allison, one of the Tellers on the part of the Senate, announced the result of the footings as 185 votes for the Republican candidates, and 184 votes for the Democratic candidates, whereupon his Honor Thomas W. Ferry, President of the Senate, declared RUTHERFORD B. HAYES, of Ohio, the duly elected President, and WILLIAM A. WHEELER, of New York, the duly elected Vice-President of the United States for the term of four years, commencing on the 4th of March, 1877.

DECLARATION OF INDEPENDENCE.

WHEN, in the course of human events, it becomes necessary for one people to dissolve the political bands which have connected them with another, and to assume among the POWERS OF THE EARTH the separate and equal station to which the LAWS OF NATURE and of NATURE'S GOD entitle them, a decent respect to the opinions of MANKIND requires that they should declare the causes which impel them to the separation. We hold these truths to be self-evident: That all men are created EQUAL; that they are endowed by their CREATOR with certain Unalienable Rights; that among these are Life, Liberty, and the Pursuit of Happiness: That to secure these rights, governments are instituted among men, deriving their just powers from the consent of the governed: That whenever any form of government becomes destructive of these ends, it is the RIGHT of the PEOPLE to alter or abolish it, and to institute NEW GOVERNMENT, laying its foundation on SUCH PRINCIPLES, and organizing its powers in SUCH FORM as to them shall seem most likely to effect their SAFETY AND HAPPINESS. Prudence, indeed, will dictate, that governments long established should not be changed for light and transient causes; and accordingly all experience hath shown, that mankind are more disposed to suffer, while evils are sufferable, than to right themselves by abolishing the forms to which they are accustomed. But when a long train of ABUSES and USURPATIONS, pursuing invariably the same object, evinces a design to reduce them under absolute DESPOTISM, it is their RIGHT, it is their DUTY, to throw off SUCH GOVERNMENT, and to provide new guards for their future SECURITY. Such has been the patient sufferance of these Colonies; and such is now the necessity which constrains them to alter their former systems of Government. The history of the present king of GREAT BRITAIN is a history of repeated Injuries and Usurpations, all having in direct object the establishment of an absolute Tyranny over these States. To prove this, let FACTS be submitted to a candid world. He has refused his assent to Laws, the most wholesome and necessary for the public good. He has forbidden his Governors to pass laws of immediate and pressing importance, unless suspended in their operation till his assent should be obtained; and when so suspended, he has utterly neglected to attend to them. He has refused to pass other Laws for the accomodation of large districts of people, unless those people would relinquish the right of Representation in the Legislature; a right inestimable to them, and formidable to tyrants only. He has called together legislative bodies at places unusual, uncomfortable, and distant from the depository of their Public Records, for the sole purpose of fatiguing them into compliance with his measures. He has dissolved Representative Houses repeatedly, for opposing with manly firmness his invasions on the Rights of the People. He has refused for a long time, after such dissolutions, to cause others to be elected; whereby the Legislative powers, incapable of annihilation, have returned to the people at large for their exercise; the State remaining, in the meantime, exposed to all the dangers of invasion from without, and convulsions within. He has endeavored to prevent the population of these States; for that purpose obstructing the Laws of Naturalization of Foreigners; refusing to pass others to encourage their migrations hither, and raising the conditions of new appropriations of lands. He has obstructed the administration of Justice, by refusing his assent to Laws for establishing Judiciary powers. He has made Judges dependent on his will alone for the tenure of their offices, and the amount and payment of their salaries. He has erected a multitude of new offices, and sent hither swarms of officers to harass our people, and eat out their substance. He has kept among us, in times of peace, Standing Armies, without the consent of our Legislatures. He has affected to render the military independent of, and superior to, the Civil power. He has combined with others to subject us to a jurisdiction foreign to our Constitution, and unacknowledged by our laws, giving his assent to their acts of Pretended Legislation:—For quartering large bodies of Armed Troops among us:—For protecting them by a Mock Trial, from punishment for any Murders which they should commit on the inhabitants of these States:—For cutting off our Trade with all parts of the world:—For imposing Taxes on us without our consent:—For depriving us, in many cases, of the benefits of TRIAL BY JURY:—For transporting us beyond seas to be tried for pretended Offences:—For abolishing the free system of English Laws in a neighboring Province, establishing therein an Arbitrary Government, and enlarging its boundaries, so as to render it at once an example and fit instrument for introducing the same absolute rule into these Colonies:—For taking away our CHARTERS, abolishing our most valuable Laws, and altering fundamentally the forms of our Governments:—For suspending our own Legislatures, and declaring themselves invested with power to legislate for us in all cases whatsoever. He has abdicated Government here, by declaring us out of his protection, and waging war against us. He has plundered our Seas, ravaged our coasts, burnt our Towns, and destroyed the lives of our People. He is at this time transporting large armies of foreign mercenaries to complete the works of death, desolation, and tyranny, already begun with circumstances of Cruelty and Perfidy, scarcely paralleled in the most BARBAROUS AGES, and totally unworthy the head of a CIVILIZED NATION. He has constrained our fellow-citizens taken captive on the high seas, to bear arms against their country, to become the executioners of their friends and Brethren, or to fall themselves by their hands. He has excited Domestic Insurrection among us, and has endeavored to bring on the inhabitants of our frontiers the merciless Indian Savages, whose known rule of warfare is, an undistinguished destruction of all ages, sexes and conditions. In every stage of these OPPRESSIONS, we have Petitioned for REDRESS in the most humble terms: Our repeated Petitions have been answered only by repeated injury. A Prince, whose character is thus marked by every act which may define a TYRANT, is unfit to be the ruler of a FREE PEOPLE. Nor have we been wanting in attentions to our British brethren. We have warned them, from time to time, of attempts by their legislature to extend an unwarrantable jurisdiction over us. We have reminded them of the circumstances of our emigration and settlement here. We have appealed to their native justice and magnanimity, and we have conjured them by the ties of our common kindred to disavow their usurpations, which would inevitably interrupt our connections and correspondence. They, too, have been deaf to the voice of justice and consanguinity. We must, therefore, acquiesce in the necessity which denounces our SEPARATION, and hold them as we hold the rest of mankind, enemies in War—in Peace, Friends. We, therefore, the Representatives of the United States of America, in General Congress assembled, appealing to the Supreme Judge of the world for the rectitude of our intentions, do, in the name, and by authority of the good people of these Colonies, solemnly publish and declare: That these United Colonies are, and of right ought to be, FREE AND INDEPENDENT STATES; that they are absolved from all allegiance to the British Crown, and that all political connection between them and the State of Great Britain is, and ought to be, *totally dissolved;* and that as FREE AND INDEPENDENT STATES they have full power to levy War, conclude Peace, contract Alliances, establish Commerce, and to do all other Acts and Things which Independent States may of right do. And for the support of this DECLARATION, with a firm reliance on the protection of DIVINE PROVIDENCE, we mutually pledge to each other our LIVES, our FORTUNES, and our sacred HONOR.

CONSTITUTION OF THE UNITED STATES.

WE, the people of the United States, in order to form a more perfect Union, establish justice, insure domestic tranquility, provide for the common defense, promote the general welfare, and secure the blessings of liberty to ourselves and our posterity, do ordain and establish this Constitution of the United States of America:

ARTICLE I.—Congress.

SECTION I.—*Legislative Powers.*

1. All legislative powers herein granted shall be vested in a Congress of the United States, which shall consist of a Senate and House of Representatives.

SECTION II.—*House of Representatives.*

1. The House of Representatives shall be composed of members chosen every second year by the people of the several States, and the electors in each State shall have the qualifications requisite for electors of the most numerous branch of the State Legislature.

Qualifications of Members.—Apportionment.

2. No person shall be a Representative who shall not have attained to the age of twenty-five years, and been seven years a citizen of the United States, and who shall not, when elected, be an inhabitant of that State in which he shall be chosen.

3. Representatives and direct taxes shall be apportioned among the several States which may be included within this Union, according to their respective numbers, which shall be determined by adding to the whole number of free persons, including those bound to service for a term of years, and excluding Indians not taxed, three-fifths of all other persons. The actual enumeration shall be made within three years after the first meeting of the Congress of the United States, and within every subsequent term of ten years, in such manner as they shall by law direct. The number of Representatives shall not exceed one for every thirty thousand, but each State shall have at least one Representative; and until such enumeration shall be made, the State of New Hampshire shall be entitled to choose three, Massachusetts eight, Rhode Island and Providence Plantations one, Connecticut five, New York six, New Jersey four, Pennsylvania eight, Delaware one, Maryland six, Virginia ten, North Carolina five, South Carolina five, and Georgia three.

4. When vacancies happen in the representation from any State, the executive authority thereof shall issue writs of election to fill such vacancies.

5. The House of Representatives shall choose their Speaker and other officers, and shall have the sole power of impeachment.

SECTION III.—*Senate.*

1. The Senate of the United States shall be composed of two Senators from each State, chosen by the Legislature thereof for six years; and each Senator shall have one vote.

2. Immediately after they shall be assembled in consequence of the first election, they shall be divided as equally as may be into three classes. The seats of the Senators of the first class shall be vacated at the expiration of the second year, of the second class at the expiration of the fourth year, and of the third class at the expiration of the sixth year; so that one third may be chosen every second year; and if vacancies happen by resignation, or otherwise, during the recess of the Legislature of any State, the Executive thereof may make temporary appointments, until the next meeting of the Legislature, which shall then fill such vacancies.

3. No person shall be a Senator who shall not have attained to the age of thirty years, and been nine years a citizen of the United States, and who shall not, when elected, be an inhabitant of that State for which he shall be chosen.

4. The Vice-President of the United States shall be President of the Senate, but shall have no vote unless they be equally divided.

5. The Senate shall choose their other officers, and also a President *pro tempore*, in the absence of the Vice-President, or when he shall exercise the office of President of the United States.

6. The Senate shall have the sole power to try all impeachments; when sitting for that purpose, they shall be on oath, or affirmation. When the President of the United States is tried, the Chief Justice shall preside, and no person shall be convicted without the concurrence of two-thirds of the members present.

7. Judgment in cases of impeachment shall not extend farther than to removal from office, and disqualification to hold and enjoy any office of honor, trust, or profit under the United States; but the party convicted shall nevertheless be liable and subject to indictment, trial, judgment and punishment, according to law.

SECTION IV.—*Election of Members.*

1. The times, places, and manner of holding elections for Senators and Representatives, shall be prescribed in each State by the Legislature thereof, but the Congress may at any time by law make or alter such regulations, except as to the places of choosing Senators.

2. The Congress shall assemble at least once in every year, and such meeting shall be on the first Monday in December, unless they shall by law appoint a different day.

SECTION V.—*Powers of each House.*

1. Each House shall be the judge of the elections, returns, and qualifications of its own members, and a majority of each shall constitute a quorum to do business; but a smaller number may adjourn from day to day, and may be authorized to compel the attendance of absent members, in such manner, and under such penalties, as each House may provide.

2. Each House may determine the rules of its proceedings, punish its members for disorderly behavior, and, with the concurrence of two-thirds, expel a member.

3. Each House shall keep a journal of its proceedings, and from time to time publish the same, excepting such parts as may in their judgment require secrecy; and the yeas and nays of the members of either House on any question shall, at the desire of one-fifth of those present, be entered on the journal.

4. Neither House, during the session of Congress, shall, without the consent of the other, adjourn for more than three days, nor to any other place than that in which the two Houses shall be sitting.

SECTION VI.—*Compensation, Privileges, Etc.*

1. The Senators and Representatives shall receive a compensation for their services, to be ascertained by law, and paid out of the Treasury of the United States. They shall, in all cases, except treason, felony and breach of peace, be privileged from arrest during their attendance at the session of their respective Houses, and in going to and returning from the same; and for any speech or debate in either House, they shall not be questioned in any other place.

2. No Senator or Representative shall, during the time for which he was elected, be appointed to any civil office under the authority of the United States, which shall have been created, or the emoluments whereof shall have been increased during such time; and no person holding any office under the United States, shall be a member of either House during his continuance in office.

SECTION VII.—*Bills and Resolutions, Etc.*

1. All bills for raising revenue shall originate in the House of Representatives; but the Senate may propose, or concur with amendments, as on other bills.

2. Every bill which shall have passed the House of Representatives and the Senate, shall, before it becomes a law, be presented to the President of the United States; if he approve he shall sign it, but if not he shall return it, with his objections, to that House in which it shall have originated, who shall enter the objections at large on their journal, and proceed to reconsider it. If, after such reconsideration, two-thirds of that House shall agree to pass the bill, it shall be sent,

together with the objections, to the other House, by which it shall, likewise, be reconsidered; and if approved by two-thirds of that House, it shall become a law. But in all such cases the votes of both Houses shall be determined by yeas and nays, and the names of the persons voting for and against the bill shall be entered on the journal of each House respectively. If any bill shall not be returned by the President within ten days (Sundays excepted) after it shall have been presented to him, the same shall be a law in like manner as if he had signed it, unless the Congress by their adjournment prevent its return, in which case it shall not be a law.

3. Every order, resolution, or vote, to which the concurrence of the Senate and House of Representatives may be necessary (except on a question of adjournment,) shall be presented to the President of the United States; and before the same shall take effect shall be approved by him, or being disapproved by him, shall be repassed by two-thirds of the Senate and House of Representatives, according to the rules and limitations prescribed in the case of a bill.

SECTION VIII.—*Powers of Congress.*

1. The Congress shall have power to lay and collect taxes, duties, imposts and excises to pay the debts and provide for the common defense and general welfare of the United States; but all duties, imposts and excises, shall be uniform throughout the United States.

2. To borrow money on the credit of the United States.

3. To regulate commerce with foreign nations, and among the several States, and with the Indian tribes.

4. To establish a uniform rule of naturalization, and uniform laws on the subject of bankruptcies throughout the United States.

5. To coin money, regulate the value thereof, and of foreign coin, and fix the standard of weights and measures.

6. To provide for the punishment of counterfeiting the securities and current coin of the United States.

7. To establish post-offices and post roads.

8. To promote the progress of science and useful arts, by securing for limited times to authors and inventors the exclusive right to their respective writings and discoveries.

9. To constitute tribunals inferior to the Supreme Court.

10. To define and punish piracies and felonies committed on the high seas, and offences against the law of nations.

11. To declare war, grant letters of marque and reprisal, and make rules concerning captures on land and water.

12. To raise and support armies, but no appropriation of money to that use shall be for a longer term than two years.

13. To provide and maintain a navy.

14. To make rules for the government and regulation of the land and naval forces.

15. To provide for calling forth the militia to execute the laws of the Union, suppress insurrections and repel invasions.

16. To provide for organizing, arming and disciplining the militia, and for governing such part of them as may be employed in the service of the United States, reserving to the States, respectively, the appointment of the officers and the authority of training the militia according to the discipline prescribed by Congress.

17. To exercise exclusive legislation, in all cases whatsoever, over such district (not exceeding ten miles square) as may, by cession of particular States, and the acceptance of Congress, become the seat of the Government of the United States, and to exercise like authority over all places purchased by the consent of the Legislature of the State in which the same shall be, for the erection of forts, magazines, arsenals, dock-yards, and other needful buildings; and,

18. To make all laws which shall be necessary and proper for carrying into execution the foregoing powers, and all other powers vested by this Constitution in the Government of the United States, or in any department thereof.

SECTION IX.—*Prohibitions and Privileges.*

1. The migration or importation of such persons as any of the States now existing shall think proper to admit, shall not be prohibited by the Congress prior to the year 1808, but a tax or duty may be imposed on such importation, not exceeding ten dollars on each person.

2. The privilege of the writ of *Habeas Corpus* shall not be suspended, unless when in cases of rebellion or invasion the public safety may require it.

3. No bill of attainder or *ex-post facto* law shall be passed.

4. No capitation or other direct tax shall be laid, unless in proportion to the census or enumeration herein before directed to be taken.

5. No tax or duty shall be laid on articles exported from any State.

6. No preference shall be given by any regulation of commerce or revenue to the ports of one State over those of another; nor shall vessels bound to, or from, one State, be obliged to enter, clear, or pay duties in another.

7. No money shall be drawn from the Treasury but in consequence of appropriation made by law; and a regular statement and account of the receipts and expenditures of all public money shall be published from time to time.

8. No title of nobility shall be granted by the United States; and no person holding any office of profit or trust under them, shall, with-

out the consent of the Congress, accept of any present, emolument, office, or title of any kind whatever, from any king, prince, or foregin state.

Section X.—*State Restrictions.*

1. No State shall enter into any treaty, alliance, or confederation; grant letters of marque and reprisal, coin money, emit bills of credit, make anything but gold and silver coin a tender in payment of debts, pass any bill of attainder, *ex-post facto* law, or law impairing the obligation of contracts, or grant any title of nobility.

2. No State shall, without the consent of the Congress, lay any imposts or duties on imports or exports, except what may be absolutely necessary for executing its inspection laws, and the net produce of all duties and imposts, laid by any State on imports or exports, shall be for the use of the Treasury of the United States; and all such laws shall be subject to the revision and control of the Congress.

3. No State shall, without the consent of Congress, lay any duty on tonage, keep troops, or ships of war in time of peace, enter into any agreement or compact with another State, or with a foreign power, or engage in war, unless actually invaded, or in such imminent danger as will not admit of delay.

ARTICLE II.—President.

1. The executive power shall be vested in a President of the United States of America. He shall hold his office during the term of four years, and together with the Vice-President, chosen for the same term, be elected as follows:

2. Each State shall appoint, in such manner as the Legislature thereof may direct, a number of Electors, equal to the whole number of Senators and Representatives to which the State may be entitled in the Congress; but no Senator or Representative, or person holding an office of trust or profit under the United States, shall be appointed an Elector.

3. The electors shall meet in their respective States, and vote by ballot for two persons, of whom one, at least, shall not be an inhabitant of the same State with themselves. And they shall make a list of all the persons voted for, and of the number of votes for each; which list they shall sign and certify, and transmit sealed to the seat of the Government of the United States, directed to the President of the Senate. The President of the Senate shall, in the presence of the Senate and House of Representatives, open all the certificates, and the votes shall then be counted. The person having the greatest number of votes shall be the President, if such number be a majority of the whole number of electors appointed; and if there be more than one who have such majority, and have an equal number of

votes, then the House of Representatives shall immediately choose by ballot one of them for President; and if no person have a majority, then from the five highest on the list the said House shall in like manner choose the President. But in choosing the President, the votes shall be taken by States, the representation from each State having one vote; a quorum for this purpose shall consist of a member or members from two-thirds of the States, and a majority of all the States shall be necessary to a choice. In every case, after the choice of the President, the person having the greatest number of votes of the electors shall be the Vice-President. But if there should remain two or more who have equal votes, the Senate shall choose from them by ballot the Vice-President.]

[*This clause altogether altered and supplied by the XII Amendment.*]

4. The Congress may determine the time of choosing the Electors, and the day on which they shall give their votes, which day shall be the same throughout the United States.

5. No person, except a natural born citizen, or a citizen of the United States at the time of the adoption of this Constitution, shall be eligible to the office of President; neither shall any person be eligible to that office who shall not have attained to the age of thirty-five years, and been fourteen years a resident within the United States.

6. In case of the removal of the President from office, or of his death, resignation, or inability to discharge the powers and duties of the said office, the same shall devolve on the Vice-President, and the Congres may by law provide for the case of removal, death, resignation, or inability both of the President and Vice-President, declaring what officer shall then act as President, and such officer shall act accordingly, until the disability be removed, or a President shall be elected.

7. The President shall, at stated times, receive for his services a compensation, which shall neither be increased nor diminished during the period for which he shall have been elected, and he shall not receive within that period any other emolument from the United States or any of them.

8. Before he enter on the execution of his office, he shall take the following oath or affirmation:

"I do solemnly swear (or affirm) that I will faithfully execute the office of President of the United States, and will, to the best of my ability, preserve, protect, and defend the Constitution of the United States."

SECTION II.—*Powers of the President.*

1. The President shall be commander-in-chief of the army and navy of the United States, and of the militia of the several States,

when called into the actual service of the United States; he may require the opinion, in writing, of the principal officer in each of the executive departments upon any subject relating to the duties of their respective offices, and he shall have power to grant reprieves and pardons for offenses against the United States, except in cases of impeachment.

2. He shall have power, by and with the advice and consent of the Senate, to make treaties, provided two-thirds of the Senators present concur; and he shall nominate, and by and with the advice and consent of the Senate, shall appoint ambassadors, other public ministers and consuls, judges of the Supreme Court, and all other officers of the United States whose appointments are not herein otherwise provided for, and which shall be established by law; but the Congress may by law vest the appointment of such inferior officers as they think proper in the President alone, in the courts of law, or in the heads of departments.

3. The President shall have power to fill up all vacancies that may happen during the recess of the Senate, by granting commissions which shall expire at the end of their next session.

SECTION III.—*Duties of the President.*

1. He shall from time to time give to the Congress information of the state of the Union, and recommend to their consideration such measures as he shall judge necessary and expedient; he may, on extraordinary occasions, convene both Houses, or either of them, and, in case of disagreement between them, with respect to the time of adjournment, he may adjourn them to such time as he shall think proper; he shall receive ambassadors and other public ministers; he shall take care that the laws be faithfully executed, and shall commission all the officers of the United States.

SECTION IV.—*Impeachment of Officers.*

1. The President, Vice-President, and all civil officers of the United States, shall be removed from office on impeachment for, and conviction of, treason, bribery, or other high crimes and misdemeanors.

ARTICLE III.—Judiciary.

SECTION I.—*Courts—Judges.*

1. The Judicial power of the United States shall be vested in one Supreme Court, and in such inferior Courts as the Congress may from time to time ordain and establish. The Judges, both of the Supreme and inferior Courts, shall hold their offices during good behavior, and shall, at stated times, receive for their services a compensation which shall not be diminished during their continuance in office.

Section II.—*Judicial Powers—Civil—Criminal.*

1. The judicial power shall extend to all cases in law and equity, arising under this Constitution, the laws of the United States, and treaties made, or which shall be made under their authority; to all cases affecting ambassadors, other public ministers, and consuls; to all cases of admiralty and maritime jurisdiction; to controversies to which the United States shall be a party; to controversies between two or more States—between a State and the citizens of another State—between citizens of different States—between citizens of the same State claiming lands under grants of different States—and between a State, or the citizens thereof, and foreign States, citizens or subjects.

2. In all cases affecting ambassadors, other public ministers and consuls, and those in which a State shall be a party, the Supreme Court shall have original jurisdiction. In all the other cases before mentioned, the Supreme Court shall have appellate jurisdiction, both as to the law and fact, with such exceptions, and under such regulations as the Congress shall make.

3. The trial of all crimes, except in cases of impeachment, shall be by jury; and such trial shall be held in the State where the said crimes shall have been committed; but when not committed within any State, the trial shall be at such place or places as the Congress may by law have directed.

Section III.—*Treason.*

1. Treason against the United States shall consist only in levying war against them, or in adhering to their enemies, giving them aid and comfort. No person shall be convicted of treason unless on the testimony of two witnesses to the same overt act, or on confession in open court.

2. The Congress shall have power to declare the punishment of treason, but no attainder of treason shall work corruption of blood, or forfeiture, except during the life of the person attained.

ARTICLE IV.—State Rights.

Section I.—*Restitution and Privileges.*

1. Full faith and credit shall be given in each State to the public acts, records, and judicial proceedings of every other State. And the Congress may by general laws prescribe the manner in which such acts, records and proceedings shall be proved, and the effect thereof.

Section II.—*Privilege of Citizens.*

1. The citizens of each State shall be entitled to all privileges and immunities of citizens in the several States.

2. A person charged in any State with treason, felony, or other crime, who shall flee from justice, and be found in another State, shall

on demand of the Executive authority of the State from which he fled, be delivered up, to be removed to the State having jurisdiction of the crime.

3. No person held to service or labor in one State under the laws thereof, escaping into another, shall, in consequence of any law or regulation therein, be discharged from such service or labor, but shall be delivered up on claim of the party to whom such service or labor may be due.

SECTION III.—*New States.*

1. New States may be admitted by the Congress into this Union; but no new State shall be formed or erected within the jurisdiction of any other State; nor any State be formed by the junction of two or more States, or parts of States, without the consent of the Legislatures of the States concerned, as well as of the Congress.

2. The Congress shall have power to dispose of and make all needful rules and regulations respecting the territory or other property belonging to the United States, and nothing in this Constitution shall be so construed as to prejudice any claims of the United States, or of any particular State.

SECTION IV.—*State Governments—Republican.*

1. The United States shall guarantee to every State in this Union a republican form of Government, and shall protect each of them against invasion; and on application of the Legislature, or of the Executive (when the Legislature cannot be convened), against domestic violence.

ARTICLE V.—Amendments.

1. The Congress, whenever two-thirds of both Houses shall deem it necessary, shall propose amendments to this Constitution, or, on the application of the Legislatures of two-thirds of the several States, shall call a convention for proposing amendments, which, in either case, shall be valid to all intents and purposes, as part of this Constitution when ratified by the Legislatures of three-fourths of the several States, or by conventions in three-fourths thereof, as the one or the other mode of ratification may be proposed by the Congress; provided that no amendment which may be made prior to the year 1808 shall in any manner affect the first and fourth clauses in the ninth section of the first article; and that no State, without its consent, shall be deprived of its equal suffrage in the Senate.

ARTICLE VI.—Debts.

1. All debts contracted, and engagements entered into, before the adoption of this Constitution, shall be as valid against the United States under this Constitution, as under the confederation.

2. This Constitution, and the laws of the United States which shall be made in pursuance thereof; and all treaties made, or which shall

be made, under the authority of the United States, shall be the supreme law of the land; and the judges in every State shall be bound thereby, anything in the Constitution or laws of any State to the contrary notwithstanding.

3. The Senators and Representatives before mentioned, and the members of the several State Legislatures, and all executive and judicial officers, both of the United States and of the several States, shall be bound, by oath or affirmation, to support this Constitution; but no religious test shall ever be required as a qualification to any office or public trust under the United States.

ARTICLE VII.—Ratification.

1. The ratification of the conventions of nine States shall be sufficient for the establishment of this Constitution between the States so ratifying the same.

Done in Convention, by the unanimous consent of the States present, the seventeenth day of September, in the year of our Lord, one thousand seven hundred and eighty-seven, and of the Independence of the United States of America, the Twelfth.

In witness whereof, we have hereunto subscribed our names.

GEORGE WASHINGTON,
President, and Deputy from Virginia.

ATTEST:
WM. JACKSON, *Secretary.*

AMENDMENTS.

Articles in addition to, and amendment of the Constitution of the United States of America, proposed by Congress, and ratified by the Legislatures of the several States, pursuant to the Fifth article of the original Constitution.

ARTICLE I.

Congress shall make no law respecting an establishment of religion, or prohibiting the free exercise thereof; or abridging the freedom of speech, or of the press; or the right of the people peaceably to assemble, and to petition the Government for a redress of grievances.

ARTICLE II.

A well regulated militia being necessary to the security of a free State, the right of the people to keep and bear arms shall not be infringed.

ARTICLE III.

No soldier shall, in time of peace, be quartered in any house without the consent of the owner, nor in time of war but in a manner to be prescribed by law.

ARTICLE IV.

The right of the people to be secure in their persons, houses, papers and effects, against unreasonable searches and seizures, shall not be violated; and no warrants shall issue, but upon probable cause, supported by oath or affirmation, and particularly describing the place to be searched, and the persons or things to be seized.

ARTICLE V.

No person shall be held to answer for a capital or otherwise infamous crime, unless on a presentment or indictment of a grand jury, except in cases arising in the land or naval forces, or in the militia when in actual service, in time of war or public danger; nor shall any person be subject, for the same offense, to be twice put in jeopardy of life or limb; nor shall be compelled in any criminal case to be a witness against himself; nor be deprived of life, liberty or property, without due process of law; nor shall private property be taken for public use without just compensation.

ARTICLE VI.

In all criminal prosecutions, the accused shall enjoy the right to a speedy and public trial by an impartial jury of the State and district wherein the crime shall have been committed, which district shall have been previously ascertained by law; and to be informed of the nature and cause of the accusation; to be confronted with the witnesses against him; to have compulsory process for obtaining witnesses in his favor; and to have the assistance of counsel for his defense.

ARTICLE VII.

In suits at common law, where the value in controversy shall exceed twenty dollars, the right of trial by jury shall be preserved; and no fact tried by a jury shall be otherwise re-examined in any court of the United States, than according to the rules of the common law.

ARTICLE VIII.

Excessive bail shall not be required, nor excessive fines imposed, nor cruel and unusual punishments inflicted.

ARTICLE IX.

The enumeration in the Constitution of certain rights shall not be construed to deny or disparage others retained by the people.

ARTICLE X.

The powers not delegated to the United States by the Constitution, nor prohibited by it to the States, are reserved to the States respectively, or to the people.

ARTICLE XI.

The judicial power of the United States shall not be construed to extend to any suit in law or equity commenced or prosecuted against one of the United States, by citizens of another State, or by citizens or subjects of any foreign State.

Article XII.

The Electors shall meet in their respective States, and vote by ballot for President and Vice-President, one of whom, at least, shall not be an inhabitant of the same State with themselves; they shall name in their ballots the person voted for as President, and in distinct ballots the person voted for as Vice-President, and they shall make distinct lists of all persons voted for as President, and of all persons voted for as Vice-President, and of the number of votes for each, which lists they shall sign and certify, and transmit, sealed, to the seat of the Government of the United States, directed to the President of the Senate; the President of the Senate shall, in presence of the Senate and House of Representatives. open all the certificates, and the votes shall then be counted. The person having the greatest number of votes for President shall be the President, if such number be a majority of the whole number of Electors appointed; and if no person have such majority, then from the persons having the highest numbers, not exceeding three, on the list of those voted for as President, the House of Representatives shall choose immediately, by ballot, the President. But in choosing the President, the votes shall be taken by States, the representation from each State having one vote; a quorum for this purpose shall consist of a member or members from two-thirds of the States, and a majority of all the States shall be necessary to a choice. And if the House of Representatives shall not choose a President whenever the right of choice shall devolve upon them, before the fourth day of March next following, then the Vice-President shall act as President, as in case of the death or other constitutional disability of the President.

The person having the greatest number of votes as Vice-President shall be the Vice-President, if such number be a majority of the whole number of Electors appointed, and if no person have a majority, then from the two highest numbers on the list the Senate shall choose the Vice-President; a quorum for the purpose shall consist of two-thirds of the whole number of Senators, and a majority of the whole number shall be necessary to a choice.

But no person constitutionally ineligible to the office of President, shall be eligible to that of Vice-President of the United States.

[An article intended as a thirteenth amendment to the Constitution was proposed at the Second Session of the Eleventh Congress, but was not ratified by a sufficient number of States to become valid as a part of the Constitution. It is erroneously given in an edition of the Laws of the United States, published by Bioren and Duane in 1815.]

[Note.—The eleventh article of the amendments to the Constitution was proposed at the Second Session of the Third Congress; the twelfth article, at the First Session of the Eighth Congress; and the thirteenth article at the Second Session of the Eleventh Congress.]

Article XIII.

Neither slavery nor involuntary servitude, except as a punishment for crime, whereof the party shall have been duly convicted, shall exist within the United States, or any place subject to their jurisdiction.

Article XIV.

Section 1. All persons born or naturalized in the United States, and subject to the jurisdiction thereof, are citizens of the United States, and of the State wherein they reside. No State shall make or enforce any law which shall abridge the privileges or immunities of citizens of the United States; nor shall any State deprive any person of life, liberty, or property, without due process of law, nor deny to any person within its jurisdiction the equal protection of the laws.

Sec. 2. Representatives shall be apportioned among the several States according to their respective numbers, counting the whole number of persons in each State, excluding Indians not taxed. But when the right to vote at any election for the choice of electors for President and Vice-President of the United States, representatives in Congress, the executive and judicial officers of a State, or the members of the Legislature thereof, is denied to any of the male inhabitants of such State, being twenty-one years of age, and citizens of the United States, or in any way abridged, except for participation in rebellion or other crime, the basis of representation therein shall be reduced in the proportion which the number of such male citizens shall bear to the whole number of male citizens twenty-one years of age in such State.

Sec. 3. No person shall be a Senator or Representative in Congress, or elector of President and Vice-President, or hold any office, civil or military, under the United States, or under any State, who, having previously taken an oath, as a member of Congress, or as an officer of the United States, or as a member of any State Legislature, or as an executive or judicial officer of any State, to support the Constitution of the United States, shall have engaged in insurrection or rebellion against the same, or given aid or comfort to the enemies thereof. But Congress may, by a vote of two-thirds of each House, remove such disability.

Sec. 4. The validity of the public debt of the United States, authorized by law, including debts incurred for payment of pensions and bounties for services in suppressing insurrection or rebellion, shall not be questioned. But neither the United States nor any State shall assume or pay any debt or obligation incurred in aid of insurrection or rebellion against the United States, or any claim for the loss or emancipation of any slave; but all such debts, obligations and claims shall be held illegal and void.

SEC. 5. The Congress shall have power to enforce, by appropriate legislation, the provisions of this article.

ARTICLE XV.

SECTION 1. The right of citizens of the United States to vote shall not be denied or abridged by the United States, or by any State, on account of race or color, or previous condition of servitude.

SEC. 2. The Congress shall have power to enforce this article by appropriate legislation.

AGRICULTURAL STATISTICS, 1870-1878.

—

I.—CROPS.

1. INDIAN CORN—In this crop Illinois ranks first; Iowa, second; Missouri, third; Kansas, fourth.

Years.	Bushels.	Acres.	Value.	Yield	Price.	Value per Acre.
1870	1,094,255,000	38,646,977	$601,839,030	28 3	$0 54 9	$15 57
1871	991,898,000	34,091,137	478,275,900	29 1	48 2	14 02
1872	1,092,719,000	35,526,836	435,149,290	30 7	39 8	12 24
1873	932,274,000	39,197,148	447,183,020	23 8	48 0	11 41
1874	850,148,500	41,036,918	550,043,080	20 7	64 7	13 40
1875	1,321,069,000	44,841,371	555,445,930	29 4	42 0	12 38
1876	1,283,827,500	39,033,364	475,491,210	26 1	37 0	9 69
1877	1,342,558,000	50,369,113	480,643,400	26 6	35 8	9 54
1878	1,371 000,000	51,400,000	436 800,000	26.7	31.9	9 04
Total	10,279,740,000	384,151 864	$4,460,870,860	26 7	44 7	$11 92
Average	1,142,194,333	42,683,540	$495,652,318	26.7	44.7	$11 92

2. WHEAT—Iowa and Minnesota lead on the wheat crop; Illinois and California not far behind.

Years.	Bushels.	Acres.	Value.	Yield	Price.	Value per Acre.
1870	235,884,700	18 992,591	$245,865,045	12 4	$1 04 2	$12 94
1871	230,722,400	19,943,893	290,411,820	11 5	1 25 8	14 50
1872	249,997,100	20,858,359	310,180,375	11 9	1 24 0	14 87
1873	281,254,700	22,171,076	323 594,805	12 7	1 15 0	14 50
1874	308,102,700	24,967,027	291,107,895	12 3	94 4	11 66
1875	292,136,000	26,381,518	294,580,990	11 0	1 00 0	11 13
1876	289,356,500	27,627,021	300,259,300	10 4	1 03 7	10 89
1877	365,094,800	26,193,407	395,155,375	13 9	1 08 2	15 08
1878	422,000,000	23,492,000	320,000,005	14 2	78 2	10 97
Total	2,674,550,900	215,758,486	$2,780 155,605	12 2	$0 97.3	$12 95
Average	297,172,322	23,973,165	$308,906,178	12.2	$0 97.3	$12 95

3. OATS—Illinois takes the lead on this crop; New York follows, and then Iowa and Pennsylvania.

Years.	Bushels.	Acres.	Value.	Yield	Price.	Value per Acre.
1870	247,277,400	8,792,395	$107,136,710	28 1	$0 43.3	$12 18
1871	255,743,000	8,365,809	102,570,030	30 5	40 1	12 36
1872	271,747,000	9,000,769	91,315,710	30 1	33 6	10 14
1873	270,340,000	9,751,700	101,175,750	27 7	37.4	10 37
1874	240,369,000	10,897,412	125,047,530	22 0	52 0	11 47
1875	354,317,600	11,915,075	129,499,930	29 7	36 5	10 86
1876	320,884,000	13,358,908	112,865,90	24 0	35 1	8 41
1877	406,394,000	12,826,148	118,661,550	31 6	29 2	9 25
1878	411,835,500	13,176,000	140,544,000	30 9	96.0	11 07
Total	2,779,326,900	98,084,216	$1,028,817.110	28 4	$0 38 1	$10 67
Average	308,815,211	10,878,246	$114,313,012	28.4	$0 38.1	$10 67

4. Barley—California, New York and Iowa are the States which raise the largest part of the Barley crop.

Years.	Bushels.	Acres.	Value.	Yield	Price.	Value per Acre.
1870	26,295,400	1,108,924	$22,244,584	23 7	$0 84 5	$20 05
1871	26,718,500	1,177,666	21,541,777	22 6	80 6	18 29
1872	26,846,400	1,397,082	19,837,773	19 2	73 8	14 19
1873	32,044,491	1,387,106	29,333,529	23 1	91 5	21 15
1874	32,552,500	1,580,626	29,984,768	20 6	92 1	18 96
1875	36,908,600	1,789,902	29,952,082	20 6	81 1	16 73
1876	38,710,500	1,766,511	25,735,110	21 9	66 4	14 56
1877	34,441,400	1,614,654	22,028,641	21 3	63 9	13 61
1878	42,000,000	1,790,050	26,166,000	23 4	62 8	14 63
Total	296,517,791	13,612,471	$246,823,268	....	....	....
Average	31,814,724	1,477,809	$25,082,158	22 3	$0 77 3	$16 91

5. Rye—Pennsylvania, New York, Illinois, Wisconsin and Kansas are in their order the principal States engaged in raising this crop.

Years.	Bushels.	Acres.	Value.	Yield	Price.	Value per Acre.
1870	15,473,600	1,176,137	$12,612,605	13 1	$0 81 5	$10 72
1871	15,365,500	1,069,531	12,145,646	14 3	79 0	11 35
1872	14,888,600	1,048,654	11,363,693	14 1	76 3	10 83
1873	15,142,000	1,150,355	11,548,126	13 1	70 2	10 04
1874	14,990,900	1,116,716	12,870,411	13 4	85 8	11 53
1875	17,722,100	1,359,788	13,631,900	13 0	76 9	10 03
1876	20,374,800	1,468,374	13,635,826	13 8	66 9	9 28
1877	21,170,100	1,412,902	12,542,895	14 9	59 2	8 87
1878	25,800,000	1,621,000	16,847,400	15 9	55 3	10 39
Total	160,927,600	11,423,453	$117,198,502	.....	....	....
Average	17,880,844	1,269,272	$13,022,056	13.9	$0 74 1	$10 33

6. Buckwheat—This is not a large crop, nor is it rapidly extending; about four-fifths of the whole is grown in New England, New York, and Pennsylvania, and most of the remainder in three or four of the north-western States.

Years.	Bushels.	Acres.	Value.	Yield	Price.	Value per Acre.
1870	9,841,500	536,992	$7,725,044	18 3	$0 78 4	$14 38
1871	8,328,700	413,915	6,900,268	20 1	82 8	16 67
1872	8,133,500	448,497	6,747,618	18 1	82 9	15 04
1873	7,837,700	454,152	6,382,043	17 2	81 4	14 05
1874	8,016,600	452,590	6,477,885	17 7	80 8	14 31
1875	10,082,100	575,530	7,166,267	17 5	71 0	12 43
1876	9,668,800	666,441	7,021,498	14 5	72 6	10 53
1877	10,177,000	649,923	6,998,810	15 6	68 7	10 76
1878	12,247,000	673,000	7,225,230	18 2	59 0	10 74
Total	84,332,900	4,871,040	$62,816,663	.....	....	....
Average	9,370,322	541,226	$6,979,629	17.4	$0 75 3	$13 21

7. Potatoes—New York takes the lead in the Potato crop, and Pennsylvania, Wisconsin and Ohio follow, but the crop is a large one in most of the northern States.

Years.	Bushels.	Acres.	Value.	Yield	Price.	Value per Acre.
1870	114,775,000	1,325,119	$82,668,59[illegible]	86 6	$0 72 0	$62 38
1871	120,461,700	1,220,912	71,836,671	98 6	59 6	58 83
1872	113,516,000	1,331,331	68,091,12[illegible]	85 2	59 9	51 14
1873	106 089,000	1,295,139	74,774,89[illegible]	81 9	70 5	57 73
1874	105,981,000	1,310,041	71,823,33[illegible]	80 9	67 7	54 82
1875	166,877,000	1,510,041	65,019,42[illegible]	110.5	39 9	43 05
1876	124,827,000	1,741,983	83,861,39[illegible]	71.6	65 5	48 14
1877	170,092 000	1,792,287	76,249,500	94.9	44 8	42 54
1878	124,027,000	1,627,000	73,000,000	70.3	58 8	41 23
Total	1,146,645,700	14,053,853	$667,324,771	......	....	....
Average	127,405,077	1,561,539	$74,147,212	85 7	$0 59 7	$51 10

8. HAY—New York leads in this great crop, and Illinois and Pennsylvania follow. We give only the statistics of 1876 and 1877, those of 1878 and the early years of this decade being unreliable.

Years.	Tons.	Acres.	Value.	Yield	Price.	Value per Acre.
				Tons.		
1876	30 876,300	24,769,60[illegible]	$300,901,000	1 24	$0 9 7[illegible]	$12 15
1877	31,629,300	25,367,70[illegible]	271,934,950	1 32	8 60	10 72
Total	62,505,600	50,137,31[illegible]	$572,835,950	......	....	....
Average	31,252,800	25,068,65[illegible]	$286,417,975	1 28	$0 9.1[illegible]	$11 44

9. COTTON—This product being only reported at the ports whence it is shipped, it is difficult to ascertain the exact product of each State. We give, therefore, only the gross amount of the crops and their values, premising that Cotton is grown as a marketable crop only in North Carolina, South Carolina, Georgia, Florida, Alabama, Mississippi, Louisiana, Texas, Arkansas, Tennessee and Southern Missouri. A few bales may be grown one or two degrees further north, but not enough to produce any effect upon the market.

Years.	Bales Produced	Value.	Average Price per Pound	Amount Exported.	Value of Exports.	Am't retained for Home Consumption.	Value.
				Bales.			
Sept. 1, 1876-7	4,811,265	$212,000,000	12 25	3,346,640	$171,1[illegible]8,508	1,463,625	$71,000,000
Sept. 1, 1877-8	5,200,000	194,000,000	8 25	3,785,000	145,500,000	1,415,000	48,500,000
Total	10,011,265	$436,000,000	......	7,131,640	$316,618,508	2,878,625	$119,005,200
Average	5,005,632	....	......	....	....	....	....

10. TOBACCO—All the chewing, and a large proportion of the smoking tobacco and snuff used in this country are produced on our own soil, while about two thirds of the cigars and cigarettes are made here from native tobacco, the other third being imported either in the manufactured or unmanufactured state.

Years	Tobacco Crop of the Year.	Value of Crop.	Amount returned for Rev. Tax.	Amount of Tax.	Pr'ct lb. Unmanf	Am'nt of Tobacco Imported	Value of Imports	Amount Tobacco Exported	Value of Exports.
		$						Lbs.	$
1875	408,000,000	63,220,000	Lbs. Manuf. Tob. & Snuff 12 .615.1?0 No. of Cig'rs & Cigaret's. 1,967.959,6?2	On Man.Tob and Deal's in $23.675,276 On Cigars &c and Manuf's ?.494.147	c 16 0	6,063,843	6,812,496	§ 120174377 Re-Expts 759,798	28,547,862 Re-Exp'ts 547,278
1876	290,000,000	45,217,000	Lbs Manuf. Tobacco. 119,796,727 No Cigars & Cigaret's 1,908,141,?70	On Man.Tob & Dealers in 28,526 823 On Cgrs, Cg's and Manufs. 11,268,517	12 5	Lbs. Tobacco, &c. 6,598,410 No. of Cigars, &c. 599,086	6,081,647	* 106200734 Re-Exprt 706,393	25,682,670 Re-Exp'ts 398,278
1877	420,000,000	28,437,000	Lbs. Manuf. Tobacco. 127.481.149 No. Cigars & Cigarett's. 1,958,391,482	On Man.Tob & Dealers in 29,281.507 On Cigars &c & Manufct's 11,224.6?0	8.3	Lbs. 7,188,718	5,720,966	† 149347670 Re-Exprt 266,?01	32,079,047 Re-Exp'ts 292,315
1878	392,000,000	22,000,000	Lbs. Manuf. Tobacco. 119,406,588 No. Cigars & Cigarett's. 2,082,356,362	On Man.Tob and Deal's in 28.204,045 Cigars &c. & Manf'ctor's 11,887,7?0	5.6	8,003,041	6,420,868	‡ 283280557 Re-Exprt 404,421	28,434,493 Re-Exp'ts 313,691

* Besides Cigars and other manufactures of Tobacco, to the value of $2,804,975. † Besides 330,000 Cigars. ‡ Besides 2,002,000 Cigars and other manufactures of Tobacco, to the value of $3,073,492. § Besides a large number of Cigars and other forms of manufactured Tobacco, valued at $3,228,740.

11. RICE.—This crop has passed through great fluctuations within the past thirty years, both in the quantity produced and the districts in which it is grown. Formerly the crop was very large, and was almost wholly produced on the Atlantic coast, in the States of South Carolina and Georgia, and in a small district of lower North Carolina, and ranged from 200 to 215 millions of pounds. Now, the total product in the best years, does not exceed 85,000,000 pounds, of which about one-half is grown in Louisiana.

Years	Amount of Crops.	Value of Crop.	Price pr lb.	Imports.	Value.	Re-Exports.	Value	Dom'stc Exports	Value Dom. Expts	Total Exports.	Total Value Expts.
	Pounds.	$	Cts.	Pounds.	$	Pounds.	$	Pounds.	$	Pounds.	$
1869	73,635 000	5,154,450	7.00	53,065,191	1,325 234	8.836,164	284632	2,232.833	145934	11.101.497	430466
1870	50,244,000	3,517,080	7.00	43,121,939	1.007.612	15 212,833	454316	2,133.014	127655	17,345,847	581971
1871	39,350.000	3,361,750	8 50	64,655,827	1,876,786	10,21 .920	280463	445,842	22502	10,658.762	302965
1872	42,646,3 0	3,517,493	8.25	74.642.631	3,317.172	12.651.959	378996	403,835	2 768	13,055,794	407764
1873	4?,548,000	3,765,694	7.60	83,755,225	2,304.696	20 204.714	591417	276,637	19740	20,479,401	611157
1874	55,123,290	3,858,630	7 00	71.257 716	2.083.248	25.840.877	763497	558,922	27075	26.399,799	790572
1875	84,635 001	5,770.815	6 90	59,414.749	1 547,697	12,352.330	342894	277.337	19831	12.629,667	362725
1876	86,000,000	5,160,000	6.00	71,561,852	1,093,547	16 610.614	406553	439,991	30918	17,050 605	437471
1877	60,?05,950	3,932,886	6.50	60.978,659	1.439.767	14 483 645	369235	1,306,982	78112	15.790,627	447347

12. SUGAR AND MOLASSES.—The cultivation of Cane Sugar in the United States is conducted under such disadvantages that the amount produced has not, since 1862, much if at all exceeded one-eighth of the amount imported. The production of Maple and Sorghum Sugar has been increasing, but has not yet reached an amount of more than one-sixth of the whole domestic production. It has lately been charged by the Government, that owing to frauds in grading imported sugars, the annual income from sugars is from seven to ten millions dollars less than it should be. The following tables give all the facts relative to the production, importation, exportation, and duties on sugars and molasses, from 1870 to 1879.

1.—SUGARS, including Cane, Maple and Sorghum, Sugar Candy and Melado.

Year.	Domestic.		Foreign.			Value of Foreign Sugar Consumed.			Total Consumption.		
	Production.	Exports.	Imports.	Re-Exports.	Difference.	Foreign Value	Paid for Customs.	Total Value.	Foreign.	Domestic.	Total.
	Lbs.	Lbs.	Lbs.	Lbs.	Lbs.				Lbs.	Lbs.	Lbs.
1870.	132,979,178	4,501,221	1,196,289,389	18,333,902	1,178,495,487	$30,270,688	$36,829,037	$67,099,725	1,216,459,872	128,477,957	1,344,937,829
1871.	208,196,046	3,945,923	1,277,525,009	10,364,161	1,267,160,848	60,849,370	30,758,657	91,608,027	1,231,883,061	204,250,123	1,436,133,184
1872.	186,106,426	4,590,932	1,509,249,507	12,122,280	1,497,127,227	76,029,865	28,876,131	104,905,996	1,412,219,438	181,515,494	1,594,434,932
1873.	163,955,047	10,222,728	1,568,393,877	23,930,453	1,544,463,424	79,513,278	29,842,942	109,356,220	1,485,657,191	153,742,319	1,639,389,510
1874	141,629,424	15,585,587	1,701,354,312	19,310,777	1,682,043,535	81,491,851	32,499,835	113,991,686	1,644,765,505	126,043,837	1,770,809,342
1875.	184,536,695	35,694,888	1,797,586,806	11,200,857	1,786,385,949	71,800,598	34,662,057	106,462,655	1,649,100,179	148,841,807	1,797,941,986
1876.	214,974,473	52,024,916	1,494,065,427	15,870,600	1,478,194,827	67,030,351	39,450,917	106,481,268	1,658,719,324	162,949,557	1,821,668,881
1877.	241,286,958	54,073,314	1,623,973,537	3,122,956	1,620,850,581	73,780,829	35,274,468	109,055,297	1,505,086,114	187,213,644	1,692,299,758
1878.	278,000,000	44,089,039	1,505,120,551	6,016,855	1,499,103,696	70,464,869	37,075,427	107,540,296	1,589,506,338	233,910,931	1,823,516,299

2.—MOLASSES, of Cane, Sorghum, Maple, &c.

Year.	Domestic.		Foreign.			Value of Foreign Molasses Consumed.			Total Consumption.		
	Production.	Exports.	Imports.	Re-Exports.	Difference.	Foreign Value	Paid for Customs.	Total Value.	Foreign.	Domestic.	Total.
	Gallons.	Gallons.	Gallons.	Gallons.	Gallons.				Gallons.	Gallons.	Gallons.
1870.	26,632,763	299,672	56,373,537	1,606,272	54,767,265	$11,345,631	$3,821,461	$15,167,092	47,768,267	26,333,091	74,101,358
1871.	30,242,501	2,946,113	44,401,359	1,002,084	43,399,175	10,953,639	3,826,462	13,779,491	47,260,021	27,296,398	74,556,419
1872.	27,830,428	2,726,848	45,214,403	310,588	44,903,815	10,108,889	2,102,896	12,211,785	42,057,924	25,103,570	67,161,494
1873.	25,406,254	3,055,836	43,533,909	558,289	42,975,620	10,424,652	2,205,621	12,630,273	44,112,413	22,350,418	66,462,831
1874.	24,905,796	2,447,905	47,189,837	958,280	46,231,557	11,122,174	2,360,282	13,482,456	47,205,641	22,457,893	69,663,534
1875.	26,438,084	4,769,292	49,112,255	648,488	48,463,767	10,409,255	2,495,189	12,904,444	43,220,697	21,668,792	64,889,489
1876.	27,585,545	4,408,412	39,026,200	1,058,815	37,967,385	8,712,156	2,447,658	11,159,774	39,213,805	23,177,133	62,390,938
1877.	28,347,079	3,470,827	30,188,963	302,891	29,886,072	7,335,194	1,812,525	9,147,719	29,000,397	24,876,252	53,876,649
1878.	30,350,000	1,477,047	27,490,007	844,206	26,645,801	6,860,317	1,678,485	8,538,802	26,855,764	28,872,953	55,728,717

II.—LIVE STOCK.

This department of agricultural production increases in a much more rapid ratio than the population, much of the land west of the Mississippi, as well as the prairie lands, east of the river, being admirably adapted to grazing, and the breeding of neat cattle and swine for slaughter, and sheep, both for their fleece and for slaughter, being conducted on a large scale. Horses and mules are also reared in great numbers for domestic use and for exportation. For many years past we have exported large quantities of salted and smoked meats to Europe, mess beef, mess pork, hams, shoulders, jerked beef, bacon, &c., as well as lard, and in moderate quantities, tallow, butter, cheese and condensed milk; but for the last three or four years, a large export trade has sprung up in live stock for slaughter, neat cattle and sheep, and in fresh beef and fresh mutton, as well as much greater quantities of butter, cheese, and liquid condensed milk. This has speedily developed into an enormous traffic. Oysters and fresh fruits are also exported in considerable quantities. In the following tables we have given the numbers, average price and estimated value of the live stock of the country in 1876, 1877 and 1878, and also the exports of animals and animal products for the last three years. We deem these statistics of great importance to the farmer, agricultural settler, and to the shipper, as indicating the directions in which agricultural labor may be most profitably employed.

1.—FARM ANIMALS at the End of each Year.

Animals.	December, 1876.			December, 1877.			December, 1878.		
	Number.	Av. Pr	Value.	Number.	Av. Pr	Value.	Number.	Av. Pr	Value.
			$		$	$		$	$
Horses.....	10,401,527	58 60	610,372,845	10,329,700	58 10	600,813,681	10,012,800	61 25	610,401,500
Mules......	1,609,429	64 57	103,916,231	1,637,500	63 70	104,323,930	1,667,000	64 01	106,604,670
Milch Cows	10,758,120	28 29	304,347,205	11,300,100	26 41	299,499,866	12,206,600	22 91	279,653,206
Oxen & other Cattle..	17,647,381	19 64	336,006,128	19,223,300	17 14	329,541,703	21,077,000	18 10	331,493,700
Sheep & G'ts	33,981,725	2 31	81,000,000	35,740,500	2 25	80,603,062	38,432,600	2.40	92,338,240
Swine......	34,633,280	5 03	171,343,321	32,262,500	4 98	160,838,532	34,331,400	5 00	171,657,000

2.—ANIMALS and ANIMAL PRODUCTS Exported in each Year.

These are for the Fiscal year ending June 30, except where marked with a *.

Animals and Animal Products.	1876. Number or Quantity.	1876. Value.	1877. Numb'r or Quantity.	1877. Value.	1878. Numb'r or Quantity.	1878. Value.	Totals for 3 Years. Numb'r or Quantity.	Totals for 3 Years. Value.
LiveSt'k Expt		$		$		$		$
Hogs........	68,044	670,042	65,107	699,180	29,284	217,259	162,435	1,636,481
Horned Cattle	51,593	1,110,703	50,001	1,593,080	80,040	3,896,818	181,631	6,600,601
Horses	2,030	234,964	2,040	301,134	4,104	798,723	8,174	1,334,821
Mules........	1,784	224,800	3,441	474,434	3,860	501,513	9,085	1,201,807
Sheep	110,312	171,101	179,017	234,480	183,995	333,499	473,324	739,080
Others & fowls	....	24,617	....	18,895	....	46,811	....	90,353
Fresh Beef, lbs	....	....	49,210,990	4,552,523	54,046,771	5,009,856	103,257,761	9,562,379
* Fr'h Beef, lbs	19,838,895	1,743,211	55,362,736	5,241,668	53,340,696	4,808,612	128,542,354	11,796,491
Bac'n, Hmslbs	327,730,172	39,664,456	460,057,146	49,512,412	592,797,481	51,750,205	1380584799	140,927,073
B'f, Salt, Cornd	36,596,150	3,186,304	39,155,153	2,950,952	38,831,379	2,973,234	114,582,682	9,110,490
Meats Pres'rvd	....	998,052	....	3,939,977	....	5,099,918	....	10,037,947
Mut'n, frsh, lbs	....	....	349,368	26,480	130,582	9,272	479,950	45,752
Butter, lbs ..	4,644,894	1,109,496	21,527,242	4,424,616	21,837,117	3,931,822	48,009,253	9,464,934
Cheese, lbs ..	97,676,264	12,270,083	107,364,666	12,700,627	123,783,736	14,103,529	328,824,666	39,074,239
Condns'd Milk	....	118,549	....	123,401	....	128,818	....	371,168
Eggs, dozen..	29,633	8,300	32,591	8,429	94,265	14,880	156,489	31,609
Pork, lbs	54,195,118	5,744,022	69,671,894	6,297,414	71,889,155	4,913,646	195,755,167	16,954,082
Anm'l Oils, gal	168,954	173,654	631,247	430,381	2,216,676	1,241,718	3,016,968	1,845,753
Lard	168,405,839	22,429,485	234,741,233	25,562,665	343,097,464	30,014,023	746,245,036	78,006,173
Total Values	....	89,881,809	....	114,576,625	....	124,814,330	....	329,271,854

* These amounts are for the calendar year.

WEIGHT OF A BUSHEL.

REVISED TABLE SHOWING THE STATES AND TERRITORIES OF THE UNITED STATES WHICH HAVE ESTABLISHED BY LAW THE WEIGHT AND POUNDS AVOIRDUPOIS OF A BUSHEL OF DIFFERENT GRAINS AND OTHER COMMODITIES.

STATES AND TERRITORIES.	Wheat.	Rye.	Oats.	Barley.	Buckwheat.	Indian Corn.	Corn on the Cob.	Corn Meal and Rye Meal.	Bran.	Malt.	Potatoes, Irish.	Potatoes, Sweet.	Carrots.	Onions.	Turnips, English.	Beets.	Beans.	Peas.	Apples, Peaches, Pears and Quinces.	Dried Apples.	Dried Peaches.	Castor Beans.	Flax-Seed.	Hemp Seed.	Millet Seed.	Timothy Seed.	Blue-Grass Seed.	Hungarian Grass S'd.	Clover Seed.	Salt.	Coal, Bituminous.	Coal, Anthracite.	Lime.	Hair.	LEGISLATIVE ENACTMENTS.
Maine	60	..	30	48	48	56	..	50	..	..	60	..	50	52	50	60	64	60	44	..	..	..	..	..	..	..	..	..	..	......	......	..	..	11	Acts of January 23, 1871, and February 17, 1874.
New Hampshire	60	56	30	..	..	56	..	50	..	..	60	..	..	..	..	..	60	60	..	..	..	..	..	..	..	..	..	..	..	......	......	..	..	..	Revised Statutes, 1867.
Vermont	60	56	32	48	46	56	..	......	..	..	60	..	50	52	60	60	60	60	46	..	..	..	..	..	..	45	..	..	60	......	......	..	..	..	Revised Statutes, 1870; Act November 28, 1878.
Massachusetts	60	56	32	48	48	56	..	50	..	..	60	..	..	52	..	..	..	..	..	..	..	..	..	..	..	..	..	..	..	70	......	..	..	..	General Statutes, 1860.
Rhode Island	..	56	32	48	..	56	..	50	..	..	60	..	..	50	..	..	..	..	..	..	..	..	..	..	..	..	..	..	..	......	......	..	..	..	General Statutes, 1872.
Connecticut	60	56	32	48	48	56	..	50	..	..	60	..	55	50	50	60	60	60	..	..	..	..	..	..	..	..	..	..	..	......	......	..	..	..	General Statutes, 1875.
New York	60	56	32	48	48	58	..	......	..	..	60	..	..	..	..	..	62	60	..	..	..	..	55	..	..	44	[illegible]	..	60	......	......	..	..	..	Revised Statutes, 1875.
New Jersey	60	56	30	48	50	56	..	......	..	..	60	54	..	57	..	..	60	60	50	25	33	..	55	..	..	..	..	..	64	a b c	......	..	..	..	Acts of March 17, 1870, and March 25, 1873.
Pennsylvania	60	56	30	47	48	56	..	......	..	..	..	..	..	..	..	..	..	..	..	..	..	..	..	..	..	..	..	..	62	85 70 62	......	..	..	..	Digest of 1872.
Delaware	60	..	..	..	..	56	..	d44–48e	..	..	..	..	..	..	..	..	..	..	..	..	..	..	..	..	..	..	..	..	..	......	......	..	..	..	Revised Statutes, 1874.
Maryland	60	56	26	47	48	56	..	......	..	..	..	56	..	..	..	..	..	..	..	..	..	..	..	..	..	..	..	..	..	......	......	..	..	..	Acts of March 6, 1860, and April 1, 1872.
Virginia	60	56	32	48	52	56	70	50	..	38	60	56	..	57	55	..	60	60	..	28	32	..	56	[illegible]	50	45	14	48	60	50	......	80	80	8	Act of March 20, 1877.
West Virginia	60	56	32	48	52	56	..	......	..	..	60	..	..	..	..	..	60	..	..	25	33	..	56	..	..	45	..	..	60	......	80	..	..	..	Revised Code, 1868.
Georgia	60	56	32	47	52	56	70	48	20	..	60	55	..	57	55	..	60	60	..	24	33	..	56	44	..	45	14	..	60	......	......	80	80	8	Act of February 20, 1875.
Louisiana	60	32	32	32	..	56	..	......	..	..	..	..	..	..	..	..	..	..	..	..	..	..	..	..	..	..	..	..	..	......	......	..	..	..	Revised Statutes, 1876.
Ohio	60	56	32	48	50	56	[illegible]	......	..	34	58	50	..	50	..	..	60	60	..	22	33	..	56	44	50	45	..	50	60	......	f80 g80	..	70	..	Acts Mr. 21, 1863, Mr. 15, 1869, Apr. 29, 1872, Mr. 10, 1876.
Indiana	60	56	..	48	50	56	68	50	..	..	60	..	..	48	..	..	60	..	..	25	33	46	..	44	..	45	14	..	60	50	h70 i70	..	..	..	Revised Statutes, 1876.
Kentucky	60	56	32	47	56	46	70	50	20	..	60	55	..	57	60	..	60	60	..	21	39	45	56	44	50	45	14	50	60	55	......	76	35	[illegible]	General Statutes, 1873.
Illinois	60	56	32	48	52	56	70	48	20	38	60	55	..	57	55	..	60	..	..	24	33	46	56	44	..	45	14	..	60	50 c55	......	80	80	8	Revised Statutes, 1874.
Michigan	60	56	32	48	48	56	70	50	..	..	60	56	..	54	58	..	60	60	48	22	28	46	56	44	50	45	14	50	60	56	80	..	70	..	Compiled Laws, 1872; Act of April 20, 1877.
Wisconsin	60	56	32	48	50	56	70	......	..	..	60	..	50	50	42	50	60	..	57	28	28	..	56	..	..	45	..	..	60	......	......	..	..	..	R. S. 1871; Acts Feb. 20, 1872; Mr. 10, 1873; Mr. 8, 1877.
Minnesota	60	56	32	48	42	56	..	......	..	..	60	..	..	..	..	..	..	..	..	28	28	..	..	..	..	..	..	..	60	......	......	..	..	..	Statutes at Large, 1873.
Iowa	60	56	32	48	52	56	70	......	20	..	60	46	..	57	..	..	60	..	48	24	33	46	56	44	45	45	14	45	60	50	......	80	80	..	Revised Code, 1873; Acts Mar. 8, 1876, & Mar. 14, 1876.
Nebraska	60	56	34	48	52	56	70	50	20	30	60	50	..	57	55	..	60	60	..	24	33	46	56	44	[illegible]	45	14	60	60	50	......	80	80	8	General Statutes, 1873
Missouri	60	56	32	48	52	56	..	......	20	..	60	..	..	57	..	..	60	..	48	24	33	46	56	44	..	45	14	..	60	50	80	..	..	..	General Statutes, 1872; Act of April 13, 1877.
Kansas	60	56	32	48	50	56	70	50	20	32	60	50	..	57	55	..	60	..	..	24	33	44	54	44	50	45	14	50	60	50	......	80	[illegible]	8	General Stat's, 1876; Acts Mar. 2, 1876, & Mar. 10, 1877.
Colorado	60	56	32	48	52	56	70	50	..	..	60	..	..	57	..	..	60	..	..	..	..	..	..	44	..	45	14	..	60	80	80	..	80	..	General Laws, 1877.
California	60	54	32	50	40	52	..	......	..	..	..	..	..	..	..	..	..	..	..	..	..	..	..	..	..	..	..	..	..	......	......	..	..	..	General Statute, 1876.
Oregon	60	56	36	46	42	56	..	......	..	..	60	..	..	..	..	..	..	..	45	28	28	..	..	..	..	..	..	..	60	......	......	..	..	..	General Laws, 1872.
Arizona	60	56	32	45	..	54	..	......	..	..	..	..	..	..	..	..	60	..	..	..	..	..	..	..	..	..	..	..	..	......	......	..	..	..	Compiled Laws, 1871.
Dakota	60	56	32	48	42	56	70	......	20	..	60	46	..	52	60	60	60	60	..	..	..	..	56	..	..	42	..	..	60	80	......	80	80	..	Revised Code, 1877.
Montana	60	56	35	48	52	56	..	50	..	..	60	..	50	57	50	50	60	..	..	..	..	..	..	44	..	45	14	..	60	50	......	..	..	..	Codified Statutes, 1872.
Washington	60	56	36	45	42	56	..	......	..	..	50	..	..	50	50	50	60	60	45	28	28	..	..	..	..	40	..	..	60	......	......	..	..	..	Acts of Jan. 28, 1876; Jan. 29, 1863; November 6, 1877.
District of Columbia	60	56	32	..	..	56	..	48	..	..	60	..	..	..	..	..	..	..	..	..	..	..	..	..	..	..	..	..	..	......	......	..	..	..	Wells's Digest, 1878.

a Coarse. b Ground. c Fine. d Sifted. e Unsifted. f & h Bituminous, and mined in the State. g & i Cannel, or mined out of the State.

ADDITIONAL TO THE FOREGOING TABLE.

In addition to the articles named in the foregoing table, the following weights per bushel, of the following articles, are established by law in the States indicated, viz:

Coke: Pennsylvania, 40 pounds to the bushel; Ohio, 40 pounds to the bushel; Iowa, 38 pounds to the bushel.

Hominy: Massachusetts, 50 pounds to the bushel; Ohio, 60 pounds to the bushel.

Peas, ground: Georgia, 25 pounds to the bushel; Kentucky, 24 pounds to the bushel.

Parsnips: Connecticut, 45 pounds to the bushel; Wisconsin, 44 pounds to the bushel; Montana, 50 pounds to the bushel.

Ruta-bagas: Maine, 60 pounds to the bushel; Connecticut, 60 pounds to the bushel; Wisconsin, 56 pounds to the bushel.

Mangel-wurzel: Maine, 60 pounds to the bushel; Connecticut, 60 pounds to the bushel; Washington Territory, 50 pounds to the bushel.

Vegetables not specified: Rhode Island, 50 pounds to the bushel; Washington Territory, 50 pounds to the bushel.

Onion top sets: Virginia, 28 pounds to the bushel; Nebraska, 25 pounds to the bushel.

Dried fruit—Plums: Michigan, 28 pounds to the bushel.

Peaches, peeled: Virginia, 40 pounds to the bushel; Georgia, 38 pounds to the bushel.

Currants, gooseberries, and grapes: Iowa, 40 pounds to the bushel.

Other berries: Rhode Island, 32 pounds to the bushel; Michigan, 40 pounds to the bushel; Iowa, 32 pounds to the bushel.

Chestnuts: Virginia, 57 pounds to the bushel.

Peanuts: Virginia, 22 pounds to the bushel.

Seeds—Broom-corn: Iowa, 30 pounds to the bushel; Dakota, 30 pounds to the bushel.

Cotton: Georgia, 30 pounds to the bushel; Missouri, 33 pounds to the bushel.

Osage Orange: Virginia, 34 pounds to the bushel; Michigan, 33 pounds to the bushel; Iowa, 32 pounds to the bushel; Nebraska, 32 pounds to the bushel.

Rape: Wisconsin, 50 pounds to the bushel.

Sorghum: Iowa, 30 pounds to the bushel; Nebraska, 30 pounds to the bushel.

Orchard grass: Virginia, 14 pounds to the bushel; Michigan, 14 pounds to the bushel.

Redtop: Virginia, 12 pounds to the bushel; Michigan, 14 pounds to the bushel.

Sand: Iowa, 130 pounds to the bushel.

THE LABOR QUESTION.

In a work like this, devoted to the highest interests of the workingmen of all classes, whether their labor is mechanical, agricultural, commercial, manufacturing or intellectual, it is due to the large and intelligent clientage which we desire to represent, that questions pertaining to the employment of labor, the hours of working, the average remuneration of different classes of workingmen, and the advantages and disadvantages of labor unions, should be fairly though briefly considered.

There is a prevalent disposition among workingmen to regard the employer and employed as classes hostile to each other, and as having interests which are diametrically opposed to each other.

This we believe to be not only a very narrow, but an entirely false view. Were it true, there would be no work done in civilized countries, except what every man could do for himself. A man wants a house built; he must build it for himself, on this theory, though there might be a hundred workmen who desire to labor on it; for, the moment he seeks to employ others to do this work, he becomes an employer, a capitalist, and his position is hostile to that of the men he employs, and he can have no object in life, but to use his money to oppress and distress them; while they, in return, look upon him with envy and hatred, because he has more money than they, and is their natural antagonist and oppressor. The theory oncestated in this plain way, even the most ignorant can see its fallacy. What we have to say in regard to the labor question here, concerns only labor in the United States. We have nothing to do with the labor question in Russia, Germany, France, Italy or Great Britain. The government of those countries, and the conditions under which alone labor is possible there, are entirely different from ours, and whatever excuse there may be for making the labor question a political one there, no such excuse avails here. So long as he violates no law, and does no injustice to his fellow man, the workingman possesses the same rights and privileges as the capitalist. For him to resort to violence, and oppose the government which he himself has had a hand in making, is as absurd as it was for the petted child who when his wearied mother said "Well, let him have what he wants," to exclaim, "I won't have what I want."

If the workingman has not all his just rights under our government, it is his fault. He is one of the law makers; let him ask for these just laws and he will get them.

A word, then, about that much abused title, "Capitalist." What is a Capitalist in this country? He is, in most cases, a man who, beginning as a workingman, and often in early life steeped to the lips in poverty, has, by industry, economy and good management, saved his earnings to such an extent, as to be able to employ others; and his income being thus increased, extends his business till he employs hundreds and perhaps thousands of his late fellow workmen. Is it supposable that such a man will forget that he himself has been a workingman, or that he will become hostile to the interests of those with whom he has wrought day after day? I suppose that the late Cornelius Vanderbilt was the largest Capitalist employing labor, in our time. Yet who that has read his history does not know that in early life he was not only a workingman, but one of the most laborious of workingmen? The venerable Peter Cooper is another example of the advancement of an industrious and prudent workingman to the ranks of the employers; Asa Packer, the largest proprietor of Coal Mines in America, and the man who single handed, has been able, for many months, to prevent the great Coal Companies from forming a combination which would prove disadvantageous to the public, was, at the age of 28, a day-laborer, earning but fifty or sixty cents a day. Thomas Scott, the controlling spirit of the Pennsylvania Central Railway and all its affiliated roads, came up from the ranks of the workingmen. So did William Orton, late President of the Western Union Telegraph Co., and hundreds more whom we might name.

These men have, or had, large amounts of capital at their disposal, and they chose to dispose of it in such a way as to employ great numbers of men. This was certainly no wrong, but a benefit, they were obliged to fix upon some terms on which they would employ such help as they needed. No one was compelled to work for them, if their rate of compensation was less than could be obtained for the same work elsewere; and it is not, we believe, pretended that they paid, on the average, less wages than the others. So far, then, there is nothing to awaken hostility between employers and employed. It was not assumed that these men were perfect, or honest, upright, and benevolent in their business, beyond the average of men. They were men of like passions and dispositions with the rest of us.

But now, after a season of excessive commercial prosperity, and high prices, the result in part of an inflated currency, there comes a time of financial depression.

If our capitalist is a manufacturer, he finds his goods will not sell, or if they are sold at all, it must be at a price below their actual cost, and consequently, in the long run, he must reduce the cost of manufacture, or become a bankrupt. The cost of the raw material has depreciated, and he tries to make up his losses by buying it lower, but if the depression is of long continuance he is still a heavy loser. His employes have been receiving high wages in the past; is it wrong, that he should say to them, I cannot afford to pay the highest prices. I must reduce your wages by such a percentage. If others will pay more, of course they have the right to go where they can receive the largest wage, but if a part of their number, or others, who are out of work, choose to accept his terms, which it is fair to presume are the best he can afford, those who leave his employ have no right to molest or obstruct those who choose to remain in it.

If the capitalist has reduced his wages too low, below those paid by others in the same business or below what is, under the circumstances, a living rate, and all his employes leave him, and others as competent will not take their places, he soon finds out his mistake, and is ready to compromise.

Much is said of the soullessness of corporations, and it is often asserted that the cases of oppression of workingmen are more frequent where they are employed by corporations than elsewhere. We doubt this—a company or corporation which is honestly and ably managed, is governed by the same motives and principles as an individual capitalist. It must manage its affairs carefully and economically or its stockholders will suffer loss; as a general rule, corporations pay higher wages, especially in prosperous times, than individual capitalists, and the difference comes out of the pockets of the stockholders. Happy is that corporation whose stock is mainly or largely owned by its employes. Individual capitalists and corporations, engaged in the same or similar lines of business, sometimes associate themselves together, and through this association, act in concert in regard to the amount of production, wages and other matters appertaining to their united interests. Workingmen often take exception to these associations, and denounce them as oppressive and as hostile to the working classes.

We cannot see the reasonableness of this. It is a fundamental principal in our republican form of government, that men have a right to associate together for the protection of their just and lawful interests, though not for purposes of wrong and violence. As a general rule, these associations have proved beneficial to both employers and employed. A comparison of views has tended to shorten rather than protract the hours of labor, and to advance as fast as it could justly be done the amount of wages. It has also led to what workingmen should be thankful for, a classification and discrimination in regard to the skill and capacity of employes, by which higher wages have been paid to the industrious and skilled workman, while the indolent and incapable have either been dismissed, or remanded to low wages till their work was improved.

This much we have felt it right and just to say for the employers. Now let us see what, the rights and privileges that the workingman and workingwoman may claim.

Let us begin negatively. No human being has an absolute right to compel another to employ him, be that other an individual capitalist, a corporation, or the state. Man *has* a right to live, if he can, by honest toil, of hand, of foot, or brain; but he has no right to compel an individual, a corporation or the state, to support him. He has no right to obtain his living by theft or violence. In a normal condition of society, there is enough work to employ every honest, intelligent, temperate and industrious man who has the health to work. But for the purpose of bringing the employers and employes together it is sometimes necessary that there should be changes of location, or, in other words, emigration on the part of some of those desiring employment.

In a normal state of society, when business is depressed, the intemperate, the improvident, the ignorant, and the worthless are sure to be thrown out of employment. This result is inevitable, no Trades Union or organization can prevent it. Hence the necessity, that workingmen and their children should be educated for their business, that they should be strictly temperate, honest and industrious. They should be more than this. The employe who seeks to make the interest of his employer his own interest, and is watchful against any loss or injury to it, may think his faithful services unappreciated, but in the time of trial, in ninety-nine cases out of a hundred, he will find that his faithfulness has been noticed, if it has not been commended, and that though others may be dismissed, he will be retained, if his retention is possible.

It is the undoubted right of every workingman to refuse to work for an employer, if his wages are reduced, below what he regards as a just and living compensation; it is the right of any number of workingmen who are thus aggrieved, or who feel satisfied that they should receive a higher price for their work than they are now receiving, to refuse to work any longer at those wages. This is usually called "a strike," and whether it produces its intended effect or not, that of compelling the employers to raise the price of work, it is none the less the right and privilege of the workingman to refuse the work.

But when the strike is made, *he has no right* to take any steps to prevent others from obtaining the work he has refused.

When an employer, from whatever motive, reduces the wages of his employes, or refuses to advance them, and they strike, it is his right and privilege to obtain other equally competent help at the reduced price, if he can. He may be actuated by good or bad motives in doing this; it may be, and often is, the case that the condition of the market for his goods, renders it impossible for him to go on giving his present wages without becoming bankrupt, and thus this act, hard as it seems, may be really one of kindness to his employes, by furnishing them employment at moderate wages, instead of throwing them out of employment entirely by failure. But whether his motives are good or bad, as soon as he has applicants for work at the reduced price, who are competent for the work, and employs them, the law throws around them and him its protection. Those who had previously been in his employ, must not obstruct the new-comers, or use violence toward them in any way. If they do, they become law-breakers and will receive punishment, and justly too; for these new workingmen are only doing what they in their circumstances would do.

The workingmen on a strike may remonstrate, may urge the restoration of the higher wages, may protest or petition, for redress. *That* is their right.

We have alluded to the association of workingmen together in strikes. This, too, is one of their rights, and we would not confine this association of workingmen to the time of a strike.

Trades Unions are not objectionable in themselves, on the contrary they may be, and often times are, the means of doing great good to the workingmen who are members, and to their families. It is only when they are perverted from their true purpose that they become mischievous. In the early history of the Trades Unions in Great Britain they were hot-beds of crime. The workingmen goaded to revenge by the oppression which they suffered, resisted by arson, assassination and murder, all the attempts of the employers to employ non-union men, or to employ any greater or less number of men, or men of greater efficiency, or at any other wages than they prescribed. Charles Reade in his "Put yourself in his Place," has drawn with perfect fidelity the picture of the horrors of that time, and we have had an example of them of nearly as great enormity, in the Molly Maguires organization among the miners of Pennsylvania.

But these times and deeds have passed away, never again to return. Workingmen now understand better than they did formerly the natural laws which govern labor; they know very generally that in a period of financial depression, such as we have been passing through, that no force can compel the capitalist to pay for any length of time, higher prices than he can afford; and if it could, the end would be still more disastrous, because capital would be annihilated, or rendered so timid, that it would not venture to employ labor at all.

Trades Unions, as at present constituted, are mainly Mutual Benefit Associations, which by small weekly payments, usually of from 20 to 30 cents per week, provide a fund for the care of sick members, the burial of the dead, the providing for the widows and orphans, the aid of the infirm, disabled or unemployed, if temperate and of reputable character. They also negotiate with the employers, with whom they endeavor to maintain friendly relations, keep a general supervision over wages, recognizing the difference (which the old Trades Unions did not) between skilled and unskilled workmen, prevent strikes, when possible, by mediation, and where they prove inevitable, grant such assistance to the strikers in money or supplies as may be required. The best and strongest of these Unions avoid carefully any political action, and will not sell themselves to any party.

In Great Britain within the past twenty-five years these Unions have attained to great influence, and embody great numbers of members, the total number of members in England in 1878, being, it is said, about 1.500,000. Among their other work there they encourage emigration, and aid emigrant members to find a new home in Canada, Australia, Tasmania, New Zealand, and to some extent in the United States.

One of the largest and most efficient of these Unions is the Amalgamated Society of Engineers, Machinists Millwrights, Smiths and Pattern Makers, founded in Jan.

1851, but reorganized after severe misfortunes toward the close of 1852. Its membership has risen from 9,737 in Jan. 1853, to 45,472 in 1878; its funds from $25,000 in the first named years to $1,376.350 in 1877. It has about 400 branches in all parts of the world, of which 36 are in the United States. Its discipline of its members is very strict. "All persons," says its constitution, "admitted into this Society, shall be possessed of good ability as workmen, of steady habits and good moral character," and their records show that their rules are enforced with great rigor. The dues are from 25 to 60 cents per week. The benefits are considerable. The unemployed members, where the lack of employment is the result of an authorized strike, or of the general depression of business, receives $3 per week for 14 weeks, and $2.10 per week for the next thirty, if he is unemployed so long. Sick benefits are $3 per week for 26 weeks, and $1.25 for a longer period. Funeral benefits, (to members $60, to the wives $30,) are a considerable item. Accidents resulting in permanent injury, causing further inability to work, are compensated by a payment of $500. The disabled member by keeping up his contribution of 12 cents per week is still entitled to receive sick and funeral benefits provided that the sickness is not the same complaint for which he received the $500. The superannuated members receive an allowance varying in different cases, and cases of exceptional distress receive extra allowance. Their expenses are light. The following statement of the President of the Society, John Bennett, will explain very fully its principles and purposes:

"But the great and primary object of this organization is to maintain the condition of the trade, is to see that the benefit to members out of work is so much, and given under such circumstances as will leave them no excuse for underselling their labor, or of agreeing to regulations which are injurious to their fellow-workmen—all these benefits are instituted for the purpose of providing for the wants of members when in adverse circumstances, of cementing a feeling of brotherhood throughout the society, and enlisting every member in the good work of supporting the best interest of the trade. To provide only for merely benevolent benefits is to satisfy the sympathetic feelings of our nature; but we must never lose sight of the great and all-absorbing fact that we are a Trade Society, established to protect the interests of trade; and the consideration, far above all others, should be how that protection can be secured with the means at our disposal."

In general, Trades Unions of the better class have not been as successful in the United States as in Great Britain. There is some reason to hope that they may become more so in the future. They have in many cases been only organizations of a single trade, as the Typographical Unions for the Printers, the St. Crispins for the Shoemakers, the Locomotive Engineers for that class, &c., and have, in many instances, come into violent and protracted collisions with the employers which have engendered a bitter hostility. Of late the inclination to consolidate several trades or callings in one society, has been gaining ground, and every such organization is to be encouraged, as it liberalizes and enlarges the field of the workingmen, and renders them more tolerant of the rights of employers, and less disposed to violence. The Workingmen's Central Union of Boston is one of the latest and most successful of these. The movements for Trade Protection by means of Secret Societies, (the Patrons of Husbandry and the Sovereigns of Industry) combined too many objects, Co-operation, Trade Protection, Mutual Benefits, Intellectual and Social Culture, and the forms of Secret Societies, to be able to give each its full necessary attention. Still these organizations have accomplished some good for the working classes, and given a new impulse to Co-operative Stores, Manufactories, and business operations.

The tables heretofore inserted in this work of the wages paid for labor in Great Britain in 1872 and 1873, and of the prices of Provisions, Groceries and other leading articles in the Provincial Towns and Cities, are now valueless; since the terrible depression in every department of trade since 1878, has effected such changes in the rate of wages and the prices of provisions that they afford no clue to the present condition of things. Emigration has largely increased, and the great reduction in the amount of goods exported to the United States, and the equally vast increase of food products imported from thence, have revolutionized the price of provisions, &c. The future for British workingmen has a gloomy outlook, while in our own country we seem to be passing into an era of great prosperity.

The following table gives the wages actually paid in Massachusetts, on the gold standard, in 1860, 1872 and 1878, the last being a year of great depression. The probabilities are that there, as well as elsewhere, wages will appreciate to a moderate degree with returning prosperity. We also give the average retail prices of Groceries, Provisions, Fuel, Dry Goods, Rents, &c., for the same years.

AVERAGE WEEKLY WAGE—1860, 1872 AND 1878.

OCCUPATIONS.	Average Weekly Wage, Gold Stand'rd 1860.	1872.	1878.	Inc & Dec 1860 & 1878 comp'd
Agriculture.				
Lab'rs per mo. & board	$13 63	$23 00	$15 72	$2 00
Lab'rs pr day, no bo'rd	90		1 25	35
Arms & Ammunition.				
Machinist	11 00		15 00	4 00
Machinists, foremen	37 50		37 50	=
Inspectors	12 00		15 00	3 00
Inspectors, foremen	30 00		30 00	=
Fitters	13 00		16 50	3 50
Tool-Maker	9 75		17 12	7 37
Armorers	9 45		14 25	4 80
Watchmen	10 00		12 50	2 50
Firemen	11 00		13 50	2 50
Engineers	12 00		15 00	3 00
Laborers	6 00		8 00	2 10
Boys	5 10		6 00	90
Artisans' Tools.				
Pattern-Makers			13 00	
File-Cutters	8 00		8 10	=
Machinists			12 75	
Hardeners	6 50		8 00	1 50
Forgers	11 30		15 00	3 67
Moulders			11 40	
Wood-Workers	11 00		11 50	50
Finishers	10 50		13 50	3 00
Helpers	6 80		8 80	2 00
Laborers	5 00		6 75	1 75
Blacksmiths	9 20	13 44	13 75	4 45
Bleach'g, Dy'ng, Prn'tg				
Overseers	27 50	20 77	20 77	*6 73
Engine Tenders		12 00	11 00	
Printers	25 00	21 3.	23 40	1 40
Back Tenders	5 00	7 0.	6 65	1 65
Dyers	5 50	8 0.	6 00	50
Designers	25 00	26 0.	25 00	=
Engravers	23 50	21 3	23 80	30
Driers	5 00		5 50	50
Starchers	5 50		5 75	25
Finishers and Packers	6 00	6 8.	7 07	1 0.
Soapers			6 00	
Dyers and Steamers		8 00	6 00	
Singers		6 0.	6 75	
Engineers			9 00	
Carpenters		13 37	9 00	
Teamsters		10 67	8 40	
Mechanics, repairs	11 10	14 67	13 50	2 40
Color-Mixers	5 00	8 00	6 12	1 12
Watchmen	7 00	12 00	8 90	1 90
Firemen	6 00		7 50	1 50
Men	5 50		6 33	83
Women	4 25		4 95	70
Boys	3 37	3 21	3 90	53
Girls			4 80	
Boys and Girls	2 75		3 00	25
Laborers	5 25		6 37	1 12
Bookbinders.				
Gilders	17 00		20 00	3 00
Finishers	14 85	13 32	17 77	2 92
Forwarders	13 89	18 36	16 20	2 31
F'ldrs & Sewers, w'mn	5 21	6 66	6 05	84
Collators, women	5 66	6 74	6 32	66
Boots and Shoes.				
Cutters	12 00	14 81	11 05	* 95
Bottomers	10 50	16 00	10 71	21
Machine-Closers	13 50		14 25	75
Boot-Treers	10 50		12 00	1 50
Crimpers	10 50		10 00	* 50
Fitters		14 22	12 00	
Finishers	14 50	16 00	11 75	*2 75
Buffers			19 50	
Heelers		17 78	13 75	

OCCUPATIONS.	Average Weekly Wage, Gold Stn'd 1860.	1872.	1878.	Inc & Dec 1860 & 1878 comp'd
Boots & Shoes—Con'd	$	$	$	$
Edge-Setters	12 00	17 78	13 00	1 00
Shoemakers	10 33	14 66	8 00	2 33*
Machine Hands, w'mn	8 25	8 89	7 31	92*
McKay Operators		22 22	17 75	
Beaters	11 50		8 00	3 50*
Beaters out		16 89	15 00	
Trimmers	15 00	17 78	12 25	2 75*
Women	5 50		8 00	2 50
Boxes.				
Men	11 20	13 33	11 57	37
Women and Girls	5 71	5 48	5 09	62*
Boys	3 50	4 77	5 00	1 50
Bread, Crackers, Etc				
Bread-Bakers	8 06	13 10	11 57	3 51
Cracker-Bakers	7 83	12 41	12 00	4 17
Drivers	12 00		16 01	4 01
Shippers	9 55		12 00	2 47
Packers, Women	6 93		7 87	94
Breweries.				
Teamsters	9 95	13 00	12 00	2 05
Engineers	13 50	14 78	14 75	1 25
Watchmen	8 60	12 15	9 66	1 06
Carpenters	10 00	16 00	12 00	2 00
Painters	10 50	16 00	12 00	1 50
Wash-House	9 60	11 11	10 90	1 30
Mash-Floor	12 19	11 55	12 81	62
Coopers	12 00	16 66	15 00	3 00
Bricks.	with b'rd.	No b'rd	with b'rd	
Moulders	3 10	11 26	3 37	27
Sorters	2 97	7 00	3 12	15
Loaders	3 15	7 00	3 96	81
Barrow-men	3 44	8 82	3 87	43
Overseers	7 50	13 33	8 50	1 00
Engineers	6 00	15 92	7 50	1 50
Carpenters	6 00	14 1.	6 00	=
Pressers	6 00	10 08	5 3.	61*
Face-Brick men	6 00	10 07	7 0.	1 07
Burners' Assistants	9 83	14 1.	13 57	3 74
Laborers	2 96	8 40	3 00	04
Teamsters	3 23	7 7.	3 74	51
Hostlers	3 00	7 7.	3 00	=
Blacksmiths	4 00	12 82	4 00	=
Brushes.				
Finishers	11 00	16 8.	13 4.	0 52*
Finishers, low gr'd w'k	7 0.		6 0.	1 00*
Nailers	14 10	15 5.	7 1.	2 30
Paint-Brush Makers	13 06	17 75	18 0.	4 31
Do Fine Work	21 00		25 0.	4 00
Painters		17 77	15 1.	
Borers	12 04	14 41	15 1.	3 47
Combers	12 47	14 5.	14 24	1 77
Combers, low gr'd w'k			8 00	
Washers	7 50		8 00	50
Pan-hands, women	5 27	6 23	5 01	26*
Drawers, women	5 15	4 18	4 70	35*
Boys	4 00	4 45	5 00	1 00
Building Trades.				
Carpenters	9 9.	1 06	11 33	1 41
Painters & Glaziers	11 0.	. 11	13 85	2 83
Steam & Gas Fitters	10 2.	. 55	12 16	1 83
Slaters	14 5.	16 00	13 50	1 80*
Paper-Hangers	12 9.	14 82	16 45	3 48
Plumbers	14 05	14 22	18 00	3 95
Plasterers	10 18	21 33	12 25	2 07
Masons	11 45	21 33	13 37	1 92
Carpenters' Laborers	7 16		8 29	1 13
Mas. & Plast. laborers	7 14	12 22	8 13	99

OCCUPATIONS.	Average Weekly Wage, Gold Stand'rd 1860.	1872.	1878.	Inc. & Dec. 1860 & 1878 comp'rd
Cabinet Making.				
Chair-Makers	$10 11	$11 50	$11 00	$0 89
Decorators	20 50	22 2[illegible]	24 00	3 50
Gilders	15 00	17 35	17 00	2 00
Turners	11 80	15 11	11 40	40*
Carvers	12 80	16 00	12 33	47*
Cabinet-Makers	10 56	14 00	11 03	47
Mill-Men	10 05	12 44	10 67	62
Polishers & Finishers	10 00	11 54	10 25	25
Upholsterers	10 90	14 00	11 42	52
Upholst. sewers, w'mn	6 00	6 0[illegible]	7 00	1 60
Carpetings.				
Wool-Sorters	6 50		9 25	2 75
Wool-Washers	5 50		7 25	1 75
Wool-Preparers	5 50		6 50	1 00
Combers	6 00		6 30	30
Finishers	5 25	6 1[illegible]	5 57	32
Dyers and Dryers	6 00	9 [illegible]	7 50	1 50
Drawing in	4 80		7 13	2 33
Filling Boys	2 50		3 50	1 00
Drawers	6 00		6 50	50
Dressers	7 50		10 50	3 00
Weavers	6 50	7 40	8 50	2 00
Burlers	3 50		4 70	1 20
Section Hands	7 50		10 33	2 83
Drawers and Spinners			4 37	
Doffers	3 00		3 00	=
Frame-Spinners	4 50	4 05	5 00	50
Twisters	7 50		9 00	1 50
Carders			13 75	
Firemen	6 00		7 00	1 00
Packers			7 50	
Overseers	24 00	22 07	27 00	3 00
Machin'sts & Carpnt'rs	9 00	9 87	11 00	2 00
Watchmen	7 00		10 00	3 00
Laborers	5 00		7 05	2 05
Laborers' Boys			3 75	
Carriages.				
Body-Makers	11 82	19 55	15 70	3 89
Painters	11 90	17 3	14 56	2 66
Carriage-Part Makers	9 50	17 48	14 14	4 64
Wheelwrights	10 64	17 77	13 70	3 06
Trimmers	12 62	17 7[illegible]	15 80	3 18
Blacksmiths	11 20	16 00	15 21	4 14
Blacksmiths' Helpers	7 50	12 43	9 00	1 50
Corsets.				
Forewoman		10 67	7 00	
Overlookers		7 11	5 71	
Embroiderers		7 11	6 47	
Needle-Hands		7 11	5 37	
Finishers & Packers			4 50	
Machine-Hands		8 00	6 02	
Boners		7 11	4 00	
Eyeleters		7 11	6 37	
Binders			6 78	
Cutters			7 00	
Cutters, men		16 00	12 00	
Pressers		8 89	7 50	
Pressers, men			11 00	
Custom Work			5 00	
Clothing-Ready-Made				
Overseers	19 45	24 45	24 82	5 37
Cutters	13 92	19 85	16 00	2 08
Trimmers	11 06	11 26	14 31	3 25
Pressers	9 17	16 0[illegible]	10 28	1 11
Basters, women	6 32	7 7[illegible]	6 46	14
Mach'n-oper's, women	5 53	10 61	5 92	39
Finsh'rs at home, w'mn	4 00		3 46	54*
Finishers, shop, wm'n	4 56	4 74	4 58	02
Finishers, contr. w'mn			3 50	
Finishers, cust'm, w'mn	6 00		8 00	2 00
Pants, Vest, Cust. Wrk	5 58		6 90	1 32

OCCUPATIONS.	Average Weekly Wage, Gold St'nd 1860	1872.	1878	Inc. & Dec. 1860 & 1878 compr'd
Cotton Goods.				
Openers and Pickers	$4 76	$7 35	$6 23	$1 47
Do Boys	2 57	4 55	3 45	88
Strippers	4 48	7 00	5 06	58
Strippers & Grinders	4 50	7 7[illegible]	7 95	3 45
Grinders	6 51	7 50	7 34	83
Frame Tenders	3 48	5 0[illegible]	4 47	99
Drawers	2 33		3 70	1 37
Railway & Alley Boys	2 70		3 45	75
Slubbers	3 50	3 30	4 80	1 30
Overseers of Carding	16 70	26 0[illegible]	18 72	2 02
Section Hands	12 00		11 40	60*
Second Hands	8 00	16 00	10 00	2 00
Overseers of Spinning	17 70	26 0[illegible]	19 45	1 75
Second Hands	7 00	14 0[illegible]	8 00	1 00
Section Hands	9 00		11 40	2 40
General Hands	6 00		6 44	44
Young Persons	3 46	4 59	3 72	26
Spare Hands	3 45	4 53	4 00	55
Mule-Spinners	6 25	10 70	7 4[illegible]	1 63
Mule Spinners, wm'n		6 50	4 00	
Mule Spinners, boys	1 [illegible]		1 [illegible]	30*
Back-Boys	2 07	3 68	2 32	25
Doffers	3 00		4 65	1 65
Frame Spinners	3 28		3 96	68
Frame Sp'nrs, b's & g's	2 6[illegible]	4 55	3 34	66
Frame Spinners, girls	2 37		3 5[illegible]	1 15
Frame Spinners, boys			2 70	
Frame Spinners, w'mn		4 90	2 8[illegible]	
Ring Spinners, overs'rs	11 5[illegible]		18 00	6 43
Ring Spinners, 2d h'nds	7 50		9 00	1 50
Ring Spinners, 3d h'nds	4 00		5 50	1 50
Ring Spinners, girls	3 60		4 30	70
Do spare h'nds, g'ls	3 30		3 90	60
Doffers, boys & girls	1 50		2 42	93
Doffers, Boys	2 56	4 00	2 80	24
Fly & J'k Fr'm T'ndrs	3 50		5 80	2 30
Reel'g & Warp'g, ov'rs	9 00	14 67	15 00	6 00
Do second hands	4 50	9 3[illegible]	9 00	4 50
Do spare h'ds, girls	2 40	1 48	4 20	1 80
Do spoolers	1 62	4 85	3 9[illegible]	1 34
Do do overseers	13 50		16 50	3 00
Do young persons	2 53	4 5[illegible]	3 00	47
Reelers	3 54	6 40	5 35	1 81
Reamers	7 35		9 25	1 90
Warpers	4 22	5 90	5 30	1 08
Dressers	8 19	13 4[illegible]	11 27	3 08
Dressers' overseers	21 91	31 33	20 40	1 51*
Slasher tenders		10 00	9 79	
Thread-dressers	6 75		7 95	1 20
Drawers	4 56	5 64	5 55	99
Drawers, second h'nds	8 25	11 57	12 08	3 83
Drawers, sect'n hands	6 25	10 67	8 34	2 09
Drawers, third hands	6 00	8 80	6 90	90
Drawers, room hands	5 00		6 00	1 00
Quillers	2 77	3 08	3 67	90
Twisters	6 00	8 00	9 00	3 00
Twisters, women	4 50	5 33	5 00	50
Winders	8 33		11 33	3 00
Winders, women	4 45		5 94	1 49
Winders, overseers	15 00		18 00	3 00
Weavers	4 44		5 88	1 44
Weavers, overseers	17 41		20 00	2 59
Weavers, second h'nds	7 00		9 00	2 00
Weavers, sect'n h'nds	7 74	10 67	9 71	1 97
Weavers, spare hands	4 50	6 [illegible]	5 25	75
Weavers, 4 looms		5 78	3 96	
Weavers, 5 looms		7 81	4 50	
Weavers, 6 looms		9 50	5 01	
Weavers, 8 looms		11 3[illegible]	6 30	
Bobbin-boys	4 00		4 50	50
Cloth-room, overseers	18 10	14 67	17 25	85*
Cloth-room, sec'd h'ds	7 17	8 64	9 30	2 13
Cloth-room, men	5 44	8 16	6 45	1 01
Cloth-room, wm. & b'ys	4 06	4 80	4 27	21
Packing-room, g's & b's	4 03		4 70	67
Dyers	5 87	8 93	8 13	2 26

OCCUPATIONS.	Average Weekly Wage, Gold Stnd'rd 1860.	1872.	1878.	Inc & Dec 1860 & 1878 comp'rd
Cotton Goods—Cont'd.				
Bundlers	$6 00	$8 07	$8 88	$2 88
Overseers of Repairs	17 10	17 33	20 00	2 90
Mechanics	8 35	12 16	10 72	2 37
Mechanics' Laborers	5 47	6 72	6 94	1 47
Engineers	9 00		11 37	2 37
Firemen	7 09		8 33	1 24
Overseers of Yard	11 56		15 96	4 40
Yard Hands	5 22	8 75	6 32	1 10
Watchmen	6 83		8 12	1 29
Teamsters	5 40	10 07	8 00	2 60
Cutlery.				
Forgers	9 40		12 00	2 60
Forgers' helpers	6 00		6 00	=
Grinders	12 60		11 65	95*
Sawyers	8 25		9 00	75
Hafters and Finishers	9 00		10 62	1 62
Hafters & Fin'rs boys	3 00		3 30	30
Machinists	11 00		14 25	3 25
Packers	5 75		6 00	25
Inspectors	10 00		10 50	50
Inspectors, women	6 50		7 50	1 00
Stampers, boys & girls	8 37		9 00	63
Men	13 00		13 00	=
Women	5 17		5 17	=
Boys	4 53		4 53	=
Laborers	5 50		6 00	50
Dressmaking.				
Managers	9 94	13 33	12 19	2 25
Dressmakers	6 52	7 11	7 43	91
Envelopes.				
Cutters	10 50	13 44	13 50	3 00*
Trimmers	12 05		10 86	1 19*
Folders, women	7 75	7 23	6 75	1 00*
Machine hands, wom'n	7 75	6 89	6 75	1 00*
Overseer of Ruling	18 00		15 00	3 00*
Rulers, women	6 00		4 50	1 50*
Printers	11 00		9 60	1 40*
Printers, women	4 00		3 00	1 00*
Box-makers, women	9 00		8 00	1 00*
Sewers, women	10 00		9 00	1 00*
Packers	10 50		9 75	75*
General Help	5 00		4 50	50*
Laborers	6 00		6 00	=
Foremen	21 00		21 00	=
Glass.				
Blowers		8 00	12 00	
Kiln-men		12 41	10 50	
Cutters		13 33	9 00	
Polishers		17 78	12 00	
Gaffers		15 00	20 00	
Servitors		13 33	13 00	
Foot-makers		13 33	11 00	
Pressers		12 00	13 00	
Gatherers		10 67	12 00	
Stickers-up		7 11	8 00	
Ware-wheelers		9 11	6 00	
Engravers		13 22	12 00	
Mixers		10 67	12 00	
Men, not in deprtm'ts			10 50	
Boys		3 50	4 50	
Women and girls		4 44	4 00	
Hosiery.				
Overseer of Carding			13 50	
Young persons, card'g			6 00	
Overs'r, bl'chg & dye'g			16 02	
Men, ble'ch'g & dye'g.			7 87	
Overseer of Spinning.			13 50	
Men & boys, spinning			6 75	
Shapers			7 50	
Finishers, women			5 10	
Cutters and boarders			8 40	

OCCUPATIONS.	Average Weekly Wage, Gold Stn'd 1860.	1872.	1878.	Inc & Dec 1860 & 1878 comp'rd
Hosiery—Cont'd.	$	$	$	$
Winders			6 00	
Knitters			6 85	
Twisters			6 00	
Sewing-girls			6 00	
Menders			5 70	
Rotary knitters, men.			15 00	
Engineers			12 00	
Yard hands & watch'n			7 80	
Leather.				
Liners and Beamers	7 50		11 00	3 50
Tanners	6 83	10 41	8 60	1 77
Shavers	9 00		15 00	6 00
Finishers	8 50		11 00	2 50
Splitters	14 25	15 00	16 00	1 75
Knife men	12 00	13 77	13 50	1 50
Table-men	7 00	13 25	8 00	1 00
Foremen	15 00		20 00	5 00
Linen Goods.				
Hacklers	5 75		6 75	1 00
Preparers	5 00		6 15	1 15
Preparers, boys	2 62		3 30	68
Preparers, women	4 55		5 45	90
Preparers, girls	2 60		3 00	40
Bleachers	5 00		6 80	1 80
Finishers	6 00		7 50	1 50
Spinners			5 18	
Spinners, boys			3 00	
Spinners, girls	2 3		3 00	63
Spinners, women	4 00		4 80	80
Spinners, men	8 00		11 40	3 40
Ruffers	5 00		5 70	70
Spoolers	1 75		1 80	05
Warpers	4 50		5 40	90
Dressers	5 75		7 50	1 75
Winders	3 25		3 55	30
Machine boys	3 12		3 90	78
Mechanics	8 00		10 09	2 09
Jute Goods.				
Carders		6 57	6 00	
Weavers		7 84	6 78	
Rovers		5 78	3 90	
Drawers		4 00	4 20	
Feeders		5 78	5 40	
Bundlers		7 56	4 50	
Callenderers		8 80	7 02	
Batchers		6 22	5 70	
Shifters		3 3.	2 40	
Piecers		3 50	3 00	
Bobbin carriers		6 17	5 10	
Winders		3 5.	3 00	
Reelers		7 11	4 80	
Oilers		6 82	6 30	
Yard hands	5 62		8 10	2 48
Machines & Machinery				
Pattern Makers	11 50	17 00	15 24	3 74
Iron Moulders	9 50	14 67	12 30	2 80
Brass Moulders	10 00	14 67	13 25	3 25
Core Makers	5 00		6 00	1 00
Blacksmiths	9 15	16 00	12 15	3 00
Blacksmith's helpers	6 50	10 20	7 70	1 20
Machinists	9 64	14 40	13 05	3 41
Cleaners and Clipper	6 00		7 50	1 50
Chuckers	6 75		9 75	3 00
Fitters	8 83	14 40	10 16	1 33
Polishers	8 00		9 75	1 75
Setters up	10 00	12 80	12 00	2 00
Rivet-heaters, boys	4 00		5 00	1 00
Riveters	9 90	14 67	12 00	2 10
Wood-workers	9 16		10 39	1 23
Painters	6 00		8 60	2 60
Laborers	6 00	8 50	7 27	1 27
Watchmen	7 00		9 00	2 00
Teamsters	7 50		10 00	2 50

OCCUPATIONS.	Average Weekly Wage, Old Stand'rd 1860.	1872.	1878.	Inc. & Dec. 1860 & 1878 comp'r'd
Matches.				
Men		$16 00	$10 50	
Women		4 00	4 00	
Girls		4 00	3 00	
Boys			3 50	
Metals & Metallic Goods				
Hammersmen			12 00	
Heaters		21 25	23 40	
Rollers		10 67	11 80	
Puddlers		14 00	18 00	
Shinglers		24 00	19 50	
Helpers			12 75	
Wire-drawers			12 75	
Annealers & Cleaners			9 50	
Butlers			21 00	
Finishers			27 00	
Filleters			9 00	
Stockers			9 00	
Reelers			10 80	
Strikers-in			8 10	
Brick-masons			13 00	
Brick-masons' helpers			7 87	
Sinkers			22 50	
Sinkers' helpers			12 00	
Machinists	$10 65		11 42	$0 77
Laborers	6 35	9 23	7 38	1 03
Met'ls & Met'lic G'ds, Fine				
Wood-workers	9 00		10 50	1 50
Women	4 50		6 00	1 50
Men	7 50		10 50	3 00
Boys and Girls	3 75		4 05	30
Moulders	8 50		11 75	3 25
Gold-workers	15 00		18 00	3 00
Steel-workers	10 50		12 00	1 50
Metal-workers	7 00		9 00	2 00
Watchmen	7 50		10 57	3 07
Engineers	10 50		12 00	1 50
Millinery.				
Managers	7 84	13 33	9 62	1 78
Milliners	5 72	7 11	7 16	1 44
Musical Instruments.				
Case Makers	13 50		13 12	38*
Varnishers	7 85		10 12	2 27
Finishers	10 85		14 46	3 61
Mill-men	12 78		14 19	1 41
Action-Makers	13 67		14 09	42
Action-makers, wom'n	6 72		7 11	39
Tuners	16 40		15 00	1 40*
Laborers	7 17		7 70	53
Paints.				
Foremen	15 00		18 50	3 50
Mixers and Grinders	7 93		10 46	2 53
Boys	3 91		5 41	1 50
Paper.				
Foremen	16 63	16 00	26 49	9 86
Millwrights	9 86	16 00	15 21	5 35
Rag-engine tenders	7 90	14 67	10 41	2 51
Paper-machine tend'rs	10 00	16 00	15 25	5 25
Thresher-women	5 70	8 09	7 40	1 70
Rag-cutters	7 50		8 40	90
Finishers	7 70	11 33	10 20	2 50
Finishers, girls	3 92	6 93	5 27	1 35
Finishers, boys	5 50		7 00	1 50
Finishers' helpers	5 80		7 27	1 47
Cutters	6 30	8 88	7 95	1 65
Cutters, girls	3 40	5 35	5 00	1 60
Bleachers	6 70	8 19	7 56	86
Rag-sorters	3 27	4 00	4 53	1 26
Men on Stock	5 88	9 33	6 57	69
Mechanics	9 75		13 20	3 45
Engineers & Firemen	6 64	10 52	8 77	2 13
Laborers	5 50	8 33	6 55	1 05

OCCUPATIONS.	Average Weekly Wage, Gold Stn'd 1860	1872.	1878.	Inc. & Dec. 1860 & 1878 comp'r'd
Preserved Meats, Fruits and Pickles.	$	$	$	$
Men	11 67	12 67	12 30	63
Women and Girls	5 00	4 44	4 05	95*
Printing.				
Job Compositors	10 19		14 12	3 93
Job Compositors	12 71		15 47	2 76
Proof-readers	17 45	23 89	20 09	2 64
Proof-readers, women	8 67		11 07	2 40
Job Pressmen	9 95	14 44	12 60	2 65
Job Pressmen	10 60	16 89	16 53	5 93
News-work	8 77		15 11	6 34
Press Feeders	5 17		6 40	1 23
Press Feeders	5 65		6 38	1 73
Press Feeders, wom'n	4 77		5 80	1 03
Compositors, daily	14 83	25 77	18 28	3 45
Proof Readers	19 54		25 26	5 72
Pressmen, daily	13 19	17 55	18 11	4 92
Book Compositors	10 28	15 22	12 87	2 59
Book Comps., women	5 42	7 11	7 22	1 80
Rubber Goods, Elastic Fabrics.				
Rubber-workers			12 00	
Rubber-workers, wmn			5 55	
Overseer of Weavers			15 00	
Weavers, women			5 40	
Dyers			7 87	
Dyers, Foremen			18 00	
Sewing girls			6 50	
Overseer of Spoolers			15 00	
Spoolers, men			8 75	
Spoolers, women			4 75	
Overseer, Leather w'k			16 50	
Men on Leather work			8 40	
Boys on Leather work			4 37	
Quillers, boys & girls			2 75	
Wood-workers			14 25	
Safes.				
Safe Makers	10 00	15 33	12 67	2 67
Painters	10 33		11 11	78
Helpers	6 28	8 18	7 56	1 28
Ship-Building.				
Carpenters, old work	21 00	21 50	9 00	12 00*
Carpenters, new work	21 00	16 00	7 50	13 50*
Calkers, old work	27 00	21 00	12 00	15 00*
Calkers, new work	24 00	16 00	10 50	13 50*
Joiners, old work	23 50	21 00	13 00	10 50*
Joiners, new work	21 00	16 00	9 00	12 00*
Painters	18 00	13 32	12 00	6 00*
Riggers	15 00	18 00	15 00	==
Blacksmiths	15 00		9 75	5 25*
Silk.				
Winders	4 20		5 40	1 20
Doublers	4 80		5 40	60
Spinners	5 35		6 75	1 40
Spoolers and Skeiners	4 80		5 70	90
Dyers	6 75		10 50	3 75
Silk Cleaners	3 00		3 60	60
Watchmen	7 50		12 00	4 50
Machinists	7 50		15 00	7 50
Engineers & Firemen	7 50		10 50	3 00
Soap and Candles.				
Men	8 50	12 19	9 47	97
Candle Makers	9 50	10 67	11 00	1 50
Stone.				
Quarrymen	5 70		6 80	1 10
Paving-cutters	6 00		6 75	75
Stone-cutters	13 50		12 00	1 50*
Polishers	7 50		9 00	1 50
Blacksmiths	10 22		10 50	28
Teamsters	8 17		9 75	1 58
Laborers	5 00		6 00	1 00

OCCUPATIONS.	Average Weekly Wage, Gold Stand'rd 1860.	1872.	1878.	Inc & Dec 1860 & 1878 comp'rd
Straw Goods.				
Bleachers			9 00	
Blockers			12 00	
Pressers			12 00	
Packer			12 00	
Machine Sewers			10 50	
Plaster-Block makers			11 25	
Whittlers			18 00	
Menders			7 50	
Tippers			9 00	
Trimmers			9 00	
Wirers			10 50	
Braid-winders			9 00	
Machinists			18 00	
Tobacco.				
Strippers	$4 50	$6 66	7 80	$3 30
Cigar-makers	12 00	16 00	12 75	75
Cigar-makers, women	7 50		9 00	1 50
Packers	16 00	17 77	18 00	2 00
Type.				
Casters	11 70	16 00	13 56	1 86
Dressers	17 14	22 00	19 00	1 86
Not designated	18 00		20 00	2 00
Rubbers		7 1[illegible]	7 57	
Setters			5 89	
Breakers			4 44	
Woollen Goods.				
Wool-sorters	6 58	9 50	8 10	1 52
Washers & Scourers	5 48	8 60	6 66	1 18
Dyers	5 72	7 85	6 66	94
Dryers	5 68	7 13	6 12	44
Young Persons	5 00		6 00	1 00
Dyers and Scourers	4 27		6 50	2 23
Washers	6 33		8 15	1 82
Dyers and Dryers	4 10		6 10	2 00
W'sh'rs S'our's, Dry's	5 50		7 12	1 62
Dryers and Pickers	4 50		6 00	1 50
Scourers	4 50		5 75	1 25
Carders	5 32	7 50	6 19	87
Carders, women	3 74	4 12	4 54	80
Carders, wm'n, b'ys, g'ls	4 00		4 91	91
Carders, young pers'ns	4 00		4 50	50
Carders, boys & girls	2 62	4 40	4 00	1 38
Carders, overseers	12 00		18 00	6 00
Strippers	4 97		6 19	1 22
Strippers, boys	3 50		4 45	95
Strippers, boys & girls	2 50		3 00	50
Spinners	6 79	9 20	7 64	85
Spinners, boys	3 00		3 00	=
Spinners, women	4 75	6 85	6 15	1 40
Spinners, y'ng persons	4 00	4 80	4 50	50
Jack-spinners	6 41		8 01	1 60
Jack-spinners, boys	2 71		3 91	1 20
Jack sp'n'rs, y'ng p'r's	3 50		5 00	1 50
Spoolers, women	4 08		5 61	1 53
Spoolers, girls	3 37		4 22	85
Spoolers, wom'n & girls	2 40		4 60	2 20
Dressers and Warpers	6 48		7 68	1 20
Dress'rs & W'rp'rs, wom'n	4 61		6 73	2 12
Dressers	7 60		9 18	1 58
Dressers, men	9 00	9 40	12 75	3 75
Weavers	5 50		7 00	1 50
Weavers, men	7 50		9 50	2 00
Weavers, women	5 25		6 95	1 70
Weavers, men & wm'n	5 55	7 47	7 15	1 60
Fullers	5 23	7 41	6 89	1 66
Shearers	5 40		6 60	1 20
Woollen Goods—Cont'd.	$	$	$	$
Shearers, men & boys	5 00	$6 33	5 81	81
Shearers, men & wm'n	5 26		6 60	1 34
Shearers, boys	4 00		5 40	1 40
Fullers, giggers, and Shearers	5 28		6 75	1 47
Giggers	5 04	7 26	5 90	86
Burlers	5 08	7 61	6 34	1 26
Burlers, women	3 81	6 25	4 59	78
Burlers, girls	3 00	4 98	3 25	25
Finishers	6 04	7 68	7 08	1 04
Finishers, women	3 08	4 91	4 95	1 87
Pickers	5 00	8 00	7 21	2 21
Packers, women	3 78	6 17	5 23	1 45
Mechanics	8 90	12 47	12 33	3 43
Boys and girls	3 05		3 50	45
Pressmen	6 50		7 50	1 00
Section hands	7 33		9 33	2 00
Firemen	6 56	9 97	8 78	2 22
Engineers & firemen	9 00		10 50	1 50
Laborers	5 44	7 8[illegible]	6 69	1 25
Watchmen	7 08		9 41	2 33
Teamsters	7 50		9 00	1 50
Engineers	12 00		18 00	6 00
Wool Hats.				
Carders		10 94	10 66	
Carders, boys		5 33	3 70	
Carders, foremen			21 00	
Carders, second hands			9 00	
Dyers, first grade			12 00	
Dyers, men			9 00	
Hardeners, foremen			10 50	
Hardeners, men		10 67	9 00	
Hardeners, boys			6 00	
Machine girls			12 00	
Trimmers, women		8 89	7 50	
Carpenters			15 00	
Blockers		14 40	9 81	
Blockers, overseers			21 00	
Finishers		17 33	15 00	
Plankers		10 22	9 50	
Plankers, foremen			21 00	
Plankers, second h'nd's			7 50	
Plankers, boys			6 00	
Worsted Goods.				
Wool-sorters	7 00		9 00	2 00
Wool Washers	6 40		7 50	1 10
Wool-Preparers	6 00		7 50	1 50
Wool-Combers	5 75		7 50	1 75
Wool-Finishers	4 70		5 04	34
Drawers	5 60		6 13	53
Roping tenders	4 00		5 82	1 82
Spinners	4 80		5 70	90
Doffers	3 00		3 30	30
Bobbin-setters	3 00		2 70	* 30
Dyers	6 00		7 14	1 14
Dressers	12 00		4 93	2 93
Twisters	13 00		4 94	1 94
Drawers-in	6 75		9 18	2 43
Sleyers	3 00		3 80	80
Weavers	6 50		7 02	52
Section hands	9 00		2 12	3 12
Filling-tenders	4 00		5 58	1 58
Burlers	4 20		5 40	1 20
Finishers	6 50		7 02	53
Crabbers	6 50		7 50	1 00
Driers	6 80		7 98	1 18

* Indicates decrease in wages. = No change in wages. Blanks, wages not obtained.

LIVING EXPENSES.

The above result concerning wages being arrived at, the subject of the cost of living becomes an interesting question. We present a table showing the prices of groceries, provisions, fuel, dry goods, boots, rent, and board, for 1860, 1872, and 1878, together with a column showing the per centage of increase or decrease on each item of expense for 1878, as compared with 1860:

Quantities.	ARTICLES.	Average Retail Prices. Standard, Gold.			Per Centage of Increase or Decrease for 1878, as compared with 1860.
		1860.	1872.	1878.	
	Groceries.				
Barrel.....	Flour, Wheat, superfine......	$7 61	$10 75	$8 63	13
Barrel.....	Flour, Wheat, family.........	7 14	12 75	7 95	19
Pound.....	Flour, Rye....................	3	3	3	16
Pound.....	Corn Meal.....................	2	1	2	* 4
Pound	Codfish, dry..................	5	8	5	13
Pound.....	Rice..........................	7	11	9	23
Quart	Beans.........................	8	9	8	5
Pound.....	Tea, Oolong..................	54	60	60	10
Pound.....	Coffee, Rio, green............	21	34	23	10
Pound.....	Coffee, roasted..............	23	42	26	13
Pound.....	Sugar, good brown............	8	10	8	5
Pound.....	Sugar, coffee................	9	10	9	3
Pound.....	Sugar, granulated............	10½	12	10	* 3
Gallon.....	Molasses, New Orleans........	50	70	57	13
Gallon.....	Molasses, Porto Rico.........	57	76	68	18
Gallon	Syrup.........................	63	75	85	35
Pound.....	Soap, common..................	8	8	7½	* 7
Pound.....	Starch........................	11	12	9	*15
	Provisions.				
Pound.....	Beef, roasting................	11	15	14	28
Pound.....	Beef, soup....................	4	7	5	10
Pound.....	Beef, rump steak..............	14	20	20	41
Pound.....	Beef, corned..................	6	10	8	26
Pound.....	Veal, fore-quarter............	7	10	10	39
Pound.....	Veal, hind-quarter............	11	17	15	40
Pound.....	Veal, cutlets.................	14	28	20	40
Pound.....	Mutton, fore-quarter..........	7	10	10	39
Pound.....	Mutton, leg...................	13	19	17	30
Pound.....	Mutton Chops..................	13	15	18	38
Pound.....	Pork, fresh...................	11	12	10	* 7
Pound.....	Pork, salted..................	11	11	9	*11
Pound.....	Hams, smoked..................	13	13	12	* 4
Pound.....	Shoulders, corned.............	8	10	9	7
Pound.....	Sausages......................	11	13	11	* 1
Pound.....	Lard..........................	13	12	10	*19
Pound.....	Mackerel, pickled.............	9	13	12	33
Pound.....	Butter........................	21	30	25	15
Pound.....	Cheese........................	13	17	12	* 7
Bushel....	Potatoes......................	50	1 03	47	65
Quart.....	Milk..........................	4	8	5	13
Dozen.....	Eggs..........................	20	30	25	23
	Fuel.				
Ton.......	Coal..........................	6 40	9 25	6 45	1
Cord......	Wood, hard....................	6 49	10 13	6 71	4
Cord......	Wood, pine....................	4 42	7 00	5 01	14
	Dry Goods.				
Yard......	Shirting, 4-4 brown...........	9	13	7	*18
Yard......	Shirting, 4-4 bleached........	10	16	9	*13
Yard......	Sheeting, 9-8 brown...........	10	14	9	*16
Yard......	Sheeting, 9-8 bleached........	13	19	11	*11
Yard......	Cotton Flannel................	13	27	11	* 7
Yard......	Ticking.......................	17	24	17	⅛
Yard......	Prints........................	11	11	7	*36
Yard......	Saltnet.......................	56	50	54	* 3
	Boots.				
Pair......	Men's heavy...................	2 73	3 24	3 24	18
	Rents.				
Month	Four-rooms tenement...........	4 43	11 75	5 53	25
Month	Six rooms tenement............	7 54	18 00	9 43	25
	Board.				
Week.....	Men...........................	2 79	5 62	4 19	50
Week.....	Women.........................	1 79	3 73	2 63	47

* Decrease. All the rest Increase in cost.

ADVICE TO THOSE SEEKING NEW HOMES.

"GO WEST, YOUNG MAN."—*Horace Greeley.*

For some years after the late civil war, emigration from Europe increased, and the average number of arrivals of immigrants, for the port of New York alone, for the nine years 1865-1873, both inclusive, was 240,000. But in 1874 there was a sudden reduction in the number of arrivals; falling off from 266,818 in 1873 to 104,041 in 1874; 84,560 in 1875; 68,264 in 1876, and 54,536 in 1877. In 1878 the trade began to rise again—75,347 coming to the port of New York, and 138,469 at all points. It should be said, also, that a larger number than formerly came into the country by way of the Dominion of Canada, and other Atlantic and Pacific ports. In all about 4,6[illegible]2,000 immigrants have arrived in this country since 1861. The past falling off in immigration was due to several causes; the depression in business and finances, which had lasted from 1873 to 1878, had caused many business failures, and the reduction in values, a necessary prelude to resumption, had almost paralyzed manufacturing. Our immense agricultural crops were sold at very low prices, because there was not, until 1877 and 1878, a large demand for them from Europe, the cereals of Southern Russia being marketed at a lower price—and the production was too great for the consumption of the home market. Meanwhile the demand for labor at remunerative prices was, until 1877, taking all things into account, better in Europe than here—and the number of emigrants who returned to their homes in Europe was greater than at any previous period. As our condition began to improve, and business grew more brisk, and manufacturing revived here, the state of affairs in Europe became rapidly worse; in Great Britain the indebtedness in India was crushing the wealthy firms engaged in that trade; the demand for their manufactures from this country and other countries was rapidly diminishing, and, to a large extent, our goods were taking their place. There was little demand, except from India, which could not pay, for British iron and steel: Belgium, France and Germany were underbidding English iron masters on their own soil. The goods of Manchester and Sheffield remained on their shelves, and American goods of better quality were offered in those cities at lower prices. The failure of the Bank of the City of Glasgow in October, 1878, of the West of England Bank in December, and of one or two smaller institutions subsequently, caused great numbers of failures; and the extensive strikes which followed the attempt of the manufacturers, ship builders and mine owners to reduce wages, added to the general gloom. While this reduction was a matter of necessity on the part of the capitalists, it bore with great severity on the working classes. When, in addition to this, the government was carrying on war in Afghanistan and in Zululand, and had accepted heavy responsibilities in Asia Minor, Cyprus and Egypt, involving increased taxation, and India was hopelessly in debt, there was great room for apprehension, and the tendency to emigration is a natural consequence of that apprehension.

On the Continent the condition of things was not much better. Germany, Italy, Spain and France were in a condition of upheaval. Socialism on the one side and Ultra-montanism on the other, are threatening the peace of all four, and attempts at repression only aggravate the difficulty. Russia is permeated by Nihilism, the worst form of socialism, because it is only destructive, with no desire or intention of reconstruction. Turkey is in a deplorable state, but her people do not migrate westward. From the other countries named, as well as from the Scandinavian States, the probabilities are strong of a greater immigration to this country than we have ever seen. Neither Canada nor Australasia offer any such inducements to the industrious and peace-loving immigrants as we can offer—and we shall, unquestionably, receive the larger portion of them.

Let us, then, give some friendly and disinterested advice to those who are intending to come and make their homes in our country. We are not interested in any land scheme—any railroad or transportation company; we are not citizens of any of the so-called land States or Territories, and do not own an acre of land in any one of them: we are simply intelligent citizens of the United States, patriotic enough to desire the growth and prosperity of our country, and its settlement by honest, upright, law-abiding, industrious citizens, who will build up for themselves and their children homes here in which they may enjoy long life and prosperity.

We have taken the utmost pains to obtain the most thorough information possible in regard to the different States and Territories which are inviting immigration, and what we have to say here, will be found to be entirely true, and without any coloring of personal interest.

But it is not alone for European emigrants that we have collected this information. Since 1873 more than two million American citizens have migrated from the Eastern States to the States and Territories west of the Mississippi; and perhaps as many more, most of them mechanics and young farmers, though including also other professions and trades, are fully determined to go within the next year or two. We would not seek to detain them at the East, for there is a grand field for development in the West, and the greater the number of intelligent, industrious and patriotic American citizens who shall settle its vast prairies and carry thither the religious, literary and political institutions which have caused the East to prosper in the past, the stronger will be the guaranty of the perpetuity of our Union with its noble heritage of free institutions.

To both classes, then—the emigrants from foreign lands and our own sons, brothers and friends—who are setting their faces westward, we would address our counsels.

1. We would say, first, to all intending emigrants, whether from our own or foreign countries, do not go West without some ready money beyond your travelling expenses, and the amount necessary to secure your lands. If you are intending to be farmers, you will need money to stock your farm, to buy seed and food for your stock, and to support your family until you can realize on your first crop. The emigrant who is thus unprovided will fare hard in a new country, though the settlers there are as generous and helpful as they can be. The larger the amount of ready money an emigrant can command, the more easily and pleasantly will he be situated. The building of a rude house, and furnishing it in the plainest way, will consume considerable money—and the first breaking up of his land, the necessary agricultural implements and machines, and the hire of help in putting in his crops, aside from the cost of stock and fodder, will add to his early expenses. The man who can go to any of the western States or Territories and take up a farm and have on hand, after paying the necessary fees and land expenses, $1,000 (£200), will have a very comfortable time, and will, under ordinary circumstances, be well situated for the future. The man who has a much smaller sum will find that he has many hardships to undergo, and will do better to seek employment as a hired laborer for the first year, purchasing his land meanwhile, and if possible, getting in a crop.

The mechanic or operative who goes West for a home also needs capital, though perhaps not as much, if his calling is one of those which are indispensable in a new country. A good carpenter, mason, blacksmith, miller, sawyer, stone-cutter, brick-maker, painter and glazier will be reasonably sure of remunerative work very soon; but two or three hundred dollars at least, and as much more as they can command, will be needed. For professional men there may be a longer waiting required. The clergyman may have a congregation to preach to, but the salary he will receive from them at first will be very small, and unless he can derive at least a part of his salary from other sources, he will be very sure to suffer. The physician will find his services in demand but his fees will, many of them, be collected with difficulty. The lawyer may have to wait long for business, but will generally manage to get his pay for his services. The editor, the artist, the bookseller, and the dealers in luxuries generally must wait till society reaches its second stage of development.

2. Be deliberate in the choice of a location, and do not decide until you have carefully weighed all the advantages and disadvantages of each. It is our purpose to set these before you so fully and fairly as to aid you in this matter.

It is not necessary to go to the West in order to find land at a reasonable price, in good and healthy locations, and within moderate distance of a good market. There are large tracts in Maine of very fair land, with ready access by river or railroad to good, though not large, markets. The soil is not as rich as that at the West, and the winters are long and cold; the climate is healthy, except a strong tendency to pulmonary consumption, which is the scourge of most cold climates on the seaboard; but these lands compare very well with the new Canadian lands, and are more accessible to markets. Wheat, rye and barley can be grown to advantage, but the summers are not generally long enough for Indian corn, though a very large business is done at Saco, Biddeford, &c., in canning the green corn for consumption. The long winters make the rearing of cattle and sheep less profitable than in southern regions. The other New England States have but little land which, at the prices at which it would be sold, would be attractive to emigrants.

The State of New York has much desirable land for settlers. The eastern two-thirds of Long Island has a light, friable soil, easily cultivated, inclined to be sandy, but yielding very large crops when properly manured, with abundant manures, and railroad lines giving it speedy access to the New York and Brooklyn markets, the best on the Continent. The whole island might and should be covered with market gardens, and flower gardens. Much of this land is purchasable at from three to ten dollars an acre, and for market gardening from 10 to 20 acres is sufficient. The climate is mild and healthful, and the prompt returns for labor sure It is necessary that the settler should know something of the business of market gardening; but this is as easily acquired as any other agricultural business. The Island is, in it's greatest length. 104 miles long, and from 7 to 15 miles broad. The difficulties in regard to this region in the past have been due to the want of good railroad communication; but these have now disappeared, and the railroads will multiply from year to year. Within ten years these lands will increase in value, certainly five fold and possibly ten fold. There are extensive tracts of land in eastern New Jersey which might also be easily transformed into rich market gardens, as some of them have already been. But to return to New York. In the northern part of the State there is a vast tract known as the John Brown Tract, covering the greater part of several large counties, of excellent farming lands, much of it forest, with numerous lakes and streams—valuable land for grain crops, especially wheat, barley, rye, oats and buckwheat, and much of it excellent grazing land. It has been proposed to set it apart as a public park, with a view to the utilization of its lakes and streams for the supply of the canals and the upper waters of the Hudson. There are railroads and navigable streams on all sides of this vast tract, but as yet no railroad through it, though this difficulty would be readily overcome if it were fairly opened for settlement. All the cereals except Indian corn could be produced abundantly. There is much wild game in the tract, deer especially, and feathered game of all sorts, and delicious fish in great abundance. There are some bears, catamounts, lynxes, badgers, and many foxes, woodchucks, rabbits, squirrels, &c., &c. The markets are Ogdensburgh, Oswego, Watertown, Rome, Utica, Little Falls, Schenectady and Albany. Land can be purchased at from 50 cents to $5 per acre.

Pennsylvania has, near the centre of the State, a similar tract of desirable though mountainous land.

But perhaps, in some respects, the most desirable region for some classes of immigrants and settlers is to be found in West Virginia. The region is hilly and parts of it too mountainous for cultivation, but wherever it can be cultivated the soil is rich and productive. The whole region abounds in valuable timber—black walnut, oak, ash, beech, hickory, chestnut, and other hard woods, with a fair proportion of hemlock and pine. These command high prices at markets readily accessible. Its mineral wealth of coal, of the best quality, petroleum, salt, lime, baryta, &c., is inexhaustible—and the markets of Cincinnati, Pittsburgh, Richmond, Norfolk and Baltimore are easily accessible from nearly all points of the State. Three railroads cross the State, one at its northern border, one at its southern, and one nearly through the centre. The Ohio River also skirts the border of the State on the north-west and is navigable for large steamers. The climate is excellent. Land can be purchased in this State at from $3 to $10 per acre, and tracts not so desirable at lower prices. The Governor of the State will furnish all the information needed.

In the Southern Atlantic States there is a fine climate and much good land offered at reasonable prices, but, with the exception of Florida, the social, political, educational and financial conditions of these States are not such as to make emigration to them desirable. The only way in which emigration to Virginia, North Carolina, South Carolina Georgia, Alabama, Mississippi, Louisiana, or Arkansas, is practicable, is by colonies; and in most of those States, there would still be difficulties and disabilities which would make a residence there unpleasant. These States are ruled too much by the pistol, the rifle, and the shot-gun, to make life agreeable there. Florida is obtaining a large population of northern settlers, and though some portions of the State are subject to malarious fevers, and its principal towns suffer occasionally from yellow fever, the climate in the interior is delightful, and the culture of the orange, lemon and fig, and other semi-tropical fruits, is becoming large and profitable. Lands in desirable portions of the State are much in demand and are bringing higher prices than those we have named from other States.

Texas has, since 1870, been a favorite resort for those emigrants who desire a warm climate. The interior of the State is very healthy, and for rearing cattle, sheep and horses, its advantages are superior to those of any other State. The lands, especially in eastern and middle Texas, are very fertile and yield immense crops of Indian corn, sorghum, sugar-cane, cotton, rice and tobacco. The best mode of settlement here is by colonies, and the region to be settled should be carefully explored by a committee of the colonists in advance. Western Texas is very dry, and along the Mexican and northern borders, Mexican raiders, and Apache and Comanche Indians very often make plundering expeditions, carrying off horses and cattle, and destroying property and occasionally murdering the settlers. The finances of the State are not so well administered as they should be, and the taxes are largely in arrears. It is easier to obtain a clear title to lands here than in most of the States where the title does not come either from the U. S. Government or from the railways to which the government has made grants. Land can be obtained, unimproved, at from $1 to $5 per acre.

Tennessee (East Tennessee in particular) has much desirable land. The valleys along the Appalachian chain, in eastern Kentucky and Tennessee, extending into northern Georgia and Alabama, have a delightful climate, great mineral wealth, and much valuable timber, and in many places a fertile soil. For capitalists, miners, workers in iron, copper or zinc, colliers, and the mechanical trades generally, this region gives better promise of obtaining a competence than most others. A number of large colonies from Great Britain have already located themselves here, and, even under the financial pressure of the past five years, most of them have done well. Middle Tennessee has also much desirable land for settlers, and it is offered at low prices. The financial condition of the State is not good, and the party in power have shown a proclivity for repudiation of their past debts, which has given them a bad reputation abroad. East Tennessee is traversed by several railways and has for its markets, Chattanooga, Cincinnati, Charleston and Savannah. Middle and Western Tennessee raise large quantities of cotton, Indian corn and peanuts, as well as sorghum, wheat, barley, oats, &c. East Tennessee produces very little cotton, but more of the food products. Land can be obtained at low prices, especially if purchased for colonies in large tracts.

Arkansas has in its western portion large tracts of very fair land, hilly but productive, and with great mineral wealth. The mountains are well covered with heavy timber. The climate is salubrious and especially adapted for those having any tendency to pulmonary diseases. Rheumatic and gouty diseases are much benefited by the Hot Springs. Yet the social, political and financial condition of the State is such that we hesitate to recommend it as a home for emigrants.

While Missouri has many tracts of land suited for emigrants, we must, until she repeals her repudiation laws, regard her as an undesirable State for our own citizens or those seeking a home from foreign countries to make their residence. Mechanics and machinists will often find in St. Louis good and remunerative employment, and miners may find work in her iron, lead and coal mines.

In Indiana, Illinois and Iowa there are no very desirable lands belonging to the United States Government, and certainly none which could be taken under the Homestead, Pre-emption or Timber Culture laws—and very little in Wisconsin. The Illinois Central R. R., Chicago & North Western, Chicago, Rock Island & Pacific, Burlington & Missouri River, and several others have land grants and will sell alternate sections to settlers at from $5 to $10 per acre. These lands being on trunk railroad lines are, in many cases, desirable as investments.

But in the States of Minnesota, Nebraska, Kansas, and Colorado, east of the Sierra Nevada, and the Territories of Dakota, Wyoming, Montana, Idaho, Utah, New Mexico and Arizona, there are still very considerable quantities of government lands; though in each of the States and in the Territories of Wyoming, Utah and New Mexico, there have been large grants to railroads.

Of these States and Territories some are more desirable than others, though all have their advantages and disadvantages. Minnesota has a fertile soil, great enterprise, and a magnificent future. The climate in winter is cold, but dry and uniform; in summer it is delightful. The western portion of the State, which forms a part of the valley of the Red River of the North, is the best land for Spring wheat in the United States, and the larger portion of the Minnesota wheat, which has a world-wide reputation, is raised there. This region is attracting great numbers of immigrants, and is traversed by several railroads—the Northern Pacific, and the railroad now building through the Red River Valley from Pembina southward, are the most important. Lands every way desirable can now be procured in this region, by the use of cash or bounty land scrip, under the Homestead Act or under the Timber Culture Act. We shall explain these processes of obtaining lands further on. Lands can also be obtained by individual settlers from the railroads which gridiron the State, at somewhat higher prices, but with the advantages of a ready access to good markets. Considerable portions of the State are well adapted to grazing, but the cattle and sheep must be carefully housed during the lo g winter, and hence the cost of raising stock for food purposes is greater than in most Southern S ates and Te ritories. Butter, cheese and wool are largely produced, and with much profit. The principal cities and towns have had a very rapid but healthy growth, and are goo l plac s for industrious and enterprising mec anics to find abundant and remunerative employment.

Dakota Territory, which joins Minnesota and Iowa on the west, is one of our newest territories. An effort likely to be successful is now making to divide it and to organize from it, with perhaps the addition of a small portion of Wyoming and Montana Territories, a new territory to be called Lincoln, which shall include the whole of the Black Hills region, where recent gold discoveries have built up a thriving district. This measure would work no ill to Dakota and would greatly fac litate the development of the new territory. The greater part of the settl ments of the Territory of Dakota, as it will be after this new territory is organized, are in the eastern a d south-eastern port ons; the Northern Pacific Railroa l crosses the State just below the 47th parallel, and Bismarck, its station on the Missouri River, is a town of some imp rtance, and other towns a e growing up on the line of that road. The eastern or rather north-eastern counties adjoining Minneso'a are in the fertile valley of the Red River of the North, and are admirably adapted to wheat culture. South-eastern Dakota has also a very rich soil, and is equally well suited for grazing, and the culture of cereals or root crops. A correspondent of the Milwaukee (Wis.) *Sentinel*, who had spent s me time in S. E. Dakota in the autumn of 1878, says that in Hanson County, 60 miles north of Yank on (the capital of the territory), on the 1st of December, 1878, "the ground was free from snow, and cattle and horses were f eding on the wild prairie grass. No coun ry in the world produces a more nutritious grass; oxen need no other food. For stock and she p raising this region has perhaps no rival in a northern latitude, and offers special attractions to the dairyman." Another correspondent, writing about the same time, says of this region: "Dakota is *par excellence* a stock country, as the natural grasses are rich, and yield heavy crops of hay. All that is to be done is to pay for herding in summer, a d to cut hay and cure it for winter use. The cost of herding is about ten shillings per head for a season of five months. Sheep pay well, the climate being dry and the lands rolling. The soil will grow anything to perfection adapted to the latitude, as it contains an almost inexhaustible supp'y of pla t food. I saw a carrot two and a half feet long, and it was not cosnidered much of a carrot eith r." Mr. W. H. Swartz, for some years a highly respected citizen of that part of Dakota, writes to the *Examiner and Chronicle*, New York, in March, 1879, that "the chief business of the region is agriculture. Stock raising will return 100 per cent. on investmen t every three or four years, and can be carried on regardless of grasshoppers (the Rocky Mountain locust, which has in some ye rs destroyed the grain crops) and the influences that sometimes affect the small grains. Water is to be found at a depth of from 15 to 25 fee', mostly of a very goo l quality."...... "The soil is equal to any in the world. The climate is milder than in the same latitude east by some degrees. The Spring opens fully as early, ordinarily, as at Pittsburgh, Penn. The fall season is exceptionally fine, affording the farmer amp e time to secure his crops. There is a railroad to Yankton, the cap tal, in the south-east corner of the Ter itory, and several others projected but not finished; there is also the Northern Pacific Railroad, already mentioned, just below the 47th parallel and crossing the territory from east to west. The Missouri River is navigable through nearly the whole of its extent in the territory, for steamers. The eastern counties in the Red River Valley can send their grain to market by Minneso'a railroads. Still it must be acknowledged that the want of railroads increases the expense of transportation of crops and goods. This is a present objection to Dakota, but it will soon cease to be so for railroads in the west keep pace with the increase of the population. Meantime, as this territory is the most accessible of any of those which contain a large amount of government land, with a healthful climate, abundant streams, and other advantages for emigrants, we may as well describe here the processes by which an emigrant farmer can obtain 480 acres of government land of the best quality at a very moderate cost. The same process will procure these lands in the other States and Territories where desirable government lands are yet for sale—but it is not to be forgotten that desirable government lands are fast becoming scarce.

The method of obtaining them is thus described by Mr. W. H. Swartz, a practical business man, thoroughly familiar with Dakota, but now residing at Eyota, Minnesota:

There being but few railroad land grants in Dakota, the only way to obtain these lands is to enter them under the Homestead laws of the U. S. A. Every citizen of the United States, or those who declare their intention to become such, over twenty-one years of age, whether male or female, except the married wife, possesses three rights entitling them to 480 acres of government land: the right of pre-emption, homestead, and an entry under the Timber Culture Act. A pre-emption is a fourth of a section, or 160 acres of land, obtained by occupancy and improvement, and the payment of $1 25 per acre, or $200 for 160 acres. Payment can be made at any time after 6 months or within 33 months from date of entry, and a deed obtained allowing to dispose of or hold the purchase at will. A homestead is a similar tract obtained by the payment of $14 government fees, and the continued occupancy and improvement of the land for five successive years. Persons are not required to remain on it uninterruptedly, but an abandonment for six months works a forfeiture. Those who prefer, and are able, can secure a title after six months by paying the pre-emption price. A claim under the Timber Culture Act is secured by paying $14 government fee, and the planting of tree seeds or cuttings to the amount of ten acres. Three years' time are allowed in which to do this, making the cost merely nominal. Persons entering a claim for timber culture are not required to occupy it, or even go upon it, if they do not desire to. The improvements can be made by employed help. Two years are allowed before any trees need be planted, and the entire expense, if done by employed labor, will not exceed $120 for the entry. Every individual may enter either pre-emption or homestead and a claim under the Timber Culture Act at the same time, making 320 acres, and after fulfilling the requirements of the law regulating either of the former two, can exercise his remaining unoccupied right, giving him 480 acres. Persons wishing to enter these lands must appear in person at a Territorial United States Land-Office, or before a Clerk of the Court for the county in which the land is located. All persons, however, who have served in the army or navy of the U.S.A., or their widows or orphans, can enter a homestead through power of attorney for the sum of $2, and hold the land one year without occupying it. They have also the privilege of changing their entry to any other selection within six months, and if they fail to ratify their application at the end of the six months and enter upon their claim, no forfeiture is made excepting the privilege of filing again by power of attorney.

Nebraska is one of the newer States of the Union, admitted in 1867. Its area is nearly 76,000 square miles, a little less than that of England and Scotland together. Its population, which was 122,993 in 1870, was not less than 450,000 in 1879. The increase by immigration alone, in the year ending June 30, 1878, was not less than 100,000. There were sold to immigrants in that year 614,774 acres of pre-empted, homestead and timber culture lands by the government, and 303,991 acres of railroad lands, making nearly 920,000 acres beside all sales of private farms and all the uncompleted sales of government lands. The unsold government lands amounted at that time to about twenty-eight million acres, but only a portion of these were desirable.

The climate is excellent, though the heat of summer is sometimes intense for a few days, and the winds in winter sweep over the prairies with great force. Western Nebraska, beyond the 100th Meridian W. from Greenwich, is subject to drought, the rainfall being comparatively small; but the influence of settlement and cultivation, and especially of tree-planting, has been remarkable in increasing the amount of rain fall. The crop of cereals in 1877 in the State was about 50,000,000 bushels; in 1878 over 80,000,000 bushels. Much of the country is admirably adapted to grazing purposes—and with, at the utmost, a few weeks shelter, cattle can obtain their own living from the prairie grass. Many of the settlements are by colonies, and these have generally done well. Of the more recent immigrants, the greater portion are from the Eastern and Atlantic States. The Missouri River forms the entire eastern boundary of the State, and is navigable and navigated by large steamers for the whole distance; the Platte River and the Niobrara, which traverse the breadth of the State from east to west, are not navigable throughout the year or for any considerable distance. The Platte is a broad but shallow stream, and receives many affluents from its north bank, but very few from the south bank. The numerous branches of the Kansas River, which water the southern and south-eastern part of the State, largely supply this deficiency. The Union Pacific R.R., which follows the Valley of the Platte, Lodge Pole Creek, and the South Fork of the Platte, crosses the State near the middle from east to west; and the Burlington and Missouri River, the Atchison and Nebraska, St. Joseph and Denver City, Midland Pacific, and other railroads, afford ready access to southern and south-eastern Nebraska. Portions of the State have suffered from the grasshopper or locust plague, but it is believed that the measures proposed for their repression will be found effective. The Colorado beetle or potato bug, which threatened at one time the destruction of that valuable tuber, is now regarded with indifference. Its prevalence in such vast numbers, and perhaps that of the Rocky Mountain locust also, was due to the wanton destruction of the prairie hens and other descriptions of grouse, which had been carried on for several years. North-western Nebraska offers less inducements for settlers than the rest of the State. It is dry and sandy, and the soil is covered in summer with alkaline deposits. Water is scanty, and many of the small lakes or ponds are saline or alkaline.

Kansas, the state next south of Nebraska, is an older state than Nebraska, but admitted into the Union so lately as 1859. It lies between the parallels of 37° and 40° N. Lat., and the meridians of 95° and 102° W. longitude from Greenwich, and is the Central State of the United States, and in some sense, the heart of the North American Continent. Its area is 81,318 square miles, about the same as that of England and Scotland. Its population in 1860, was 109,000, in 1870, 364,399, and is now probably not less than 730,000. In the year ending June 30, 1878, 1,711,572 acres of government lands were sold, and probably over a million acres of railroad lands. The climate of Kansas is healthful and pleasant, occasionally the heat is intense in summer, and the average rainfall, especially in Western Kansas, though increasing, is yet somewhat less than is desirable. Much of the soil is very fertile, and that portion of the state lying west of the 100th meridian, though alkaline, is tolerably well watered, and the profuse planting of trees there has so much increased the rainfall, that these lands bid fair to yield excellent wheat and barley crops.

The State is rapidly settling, and in productiveness ranks with the older states. Its crops of Indian Corn rank third or fourth in the Union, and the Wheat crops seventh or eighth. Its soil is well adapted to the growth of cereals and root crops, while it has excellent facilities for stock-raising. Though for so new a state it is traversed by an unusual number of railroads, and all portions except the north-west are readily accessible by means of the great lines and their branches and feeders, yet southern and south-western Kansas seem to be at present the regions most sought by settlers. Like its neighbors in the north and west, Kansas has had its visitations of drought, of grasshoppers or Rocky Mountain locusts, and of Colorado beetles, but has survived them all, and by the abundance of its crops for three or four years past, has recovered from its losses. It is hardly probable that it will be desolated by either of these scourges again very soon. The educational advantages of both Nebraska and Kansas are excellent, and the two states are in a good financial condition. The principal towns in Kansas are thriving and growing rapidly, and offer good opportunities of employment to industrious and intelligent mechanics.

Colorado is the latest accession to the sisterhood of states, having been received in the Centennial year, 1876. It lies between the parallels of 37° and 41° N. Lat., and the meridians of 102° and 109° west longitude from Greenwich. Its area is 104,500 square miles, a little less than that of the United Kingdom of Great Britain and Ireland, and its population, which in 1870 was 38,864, now probably exceeds 200,000. Unlike the states and territories previously described, it is a mountain state; the Rocky Mountains in two nearly parallel ranges, pass through it from north to south nearly centrally, and have within the bounds of the state some of their loftiest peaks. The table-lands and foot-hills by which the Rocky Mountains are approached from the east, are themselves elevated, and most of the arable and pastoral lands of the state are from 4,000 to 7,000 feet above the level of the sea. The mountain peaks rise to an altitude of from 12,000 to 15,000 feet. On the western portion of the state beyond the Rocky Mountains, the surface is exceedingly rough, though with some beautiful valleys. The Grand, Green and San Juan Rivers and their affluents, which are the sources of the Colorado of the West, plough through these broken lands in canons varying in depth from 2,000 to 4,000 feet. This is one of the new mining regions, and gold and silver are found in paying quantities by those who are willing to undergo the hardships of the way and the still greater hardships which attach to the miner's life in such a region.

Another peculiar feature of Colorado is its vast natural parks. There are several of these, the largest being the North, the Middle, the South and the San Luis Parks. They are extensive fertile valleys, surrounded by the lofty mountain walls of the Rocky Mountains, and are undoubtedly the beds of ancient lakes of vast extent, which, in some of the upheavals of the geologic periods, have been drained, and formed these beautiful valleys. These parks are six or seven thousand feet above the sea. Their whole surface is covered with a rich and abundant herbage, and in the season, with the gayest flowers.

Colorado has much good soil, but for the most part is better adapted to grazing than to the culture of the cereals and root crops. Its grasses are eagerly sought by cattle and sheep, and both thrive and fatten on them. At the close of the last year this new state had over half a million of cattle and 750,000 sheep in its pastures. Notwithstanding the elevation, both cattle and sheep seldom require to be sheltered and fed during the winter. Most of the arable lands require irrigation, for which, in many sections, provision has been made, and if properly irrigated, the lands yield almost incredible crops. In the table lands of Weld County, in the N. N. E. part of the state, irrigated fields are reported by the very highest authority, to have yielded in successive years, over 300 bushels of Indian corn to the acre, a yield never equalled elsewhere. To the enterprising farmer with a small capital, perhaps no portion of the west offers a better opportunity of profitable investment and labor. The grains, vegetables and root crops, which by irrigation yield so abundantly, are in immediate demand at profitable prices, by the mining and other population. Those farmers who are engaged in stock raising, are large purchasers of vegetables and grain, and as from the salubrity, dryness and elevation of the country, Colorado has become a favorite resort for invalids, the towns form excellent markets for produce. Eastern Colorado is well provided with railroads. The Denver Pacific, the Atchison, Topeka and Santa Fe, the Colorado Central, and several minor roads, some of them of narrow gauge, traverse these table lands, while the Union Pacific skirts its northern border. As yet the principal range of the Rocky Mountains in the State has not been crossed, and Western Colorado has no railroads in operation, but at the present rate of progress this will not long be the case. The recent discoveries of gold and silver in enormous quantities at Leadville, Silver Cliff, Rosita, and further West, near Ouray, are producing a stampede in that direction, and will compel the quick completion of railroads now in progress.

Wyoming Territory lies between 41° and 45° of north latitude, and between the meridians of 104° and 111° of west longitude from Greenwich. The Rocky Mountains cross it diagonally from north-west to south-east, covering a breadth of more than 200 miles, though between the ranges there are some fine, arable valleys, especially those of Big Horn River and its affluents, and the north fork of the Platte River. Between the 42d and 43d parallels the Sweet Water Mountain range crosses the Territory from west to east, terminating at the east in Laramie Park. The two parallel diagonal ranges, are the Wind River Mountains on the west, and the Big Horn on the east. A small portion of the Black Hills region, now noted for its gold mines, is in the north-east of this Territory, and the Yellowstone National Park, covering 3575 square miles, containing the most wonderful natural curiosities in the world, is in the north-west corner. Wyoming has an area of 97,-883 square miles, or 62,645,120 square acres, considerably more than England, Wales and Scotland, but only one-eighth of the whole had been surveyed, to July, 1878. The mineral wealth of Wyoming is perhaps less abundant than that of some of the other States and Territories, though gold in paying quantities is produced at several points. The whole amount of deposits of gold and silver at the mint or its branches, from Wyoming Territory since its first settlement, is only $684,000. Copper is found at several points, but awaits development. There are, also, iron, lead and gypsum in large quantities. But the most profitable mineral product of the country is coal. It is supposed to be lignite, being found in tertiary deposits, but it is of very good quality, and is used not only on the Union and Central Pacific Roads, which travers the southern part of the Territory, but in the towns and villages along those lines.

Wyoming is better adapted to the raising of cattle than to the culture of grain and root crops. In many quarters there is a good hay crop, but for cereals or roots, irrigation is required, and in valleys, with this aid, large crops are raised.

The presence of a large population of consumers of food will insure a prompt and ready market at high prices for vegetables and cereals, and will justify considerable outlay for irrigation.

The rush of travel toward Yellowstone National Park, will make the stations on the route thither excellent markets for all kinds of produce. The Indians in the Territory are generally peaceful and friendly.

Montana Territory lies north and north-west of Wyoming, extending to the boundary of the Dominion of Canada on the north, joining Dakota on the 55th meridian, and extending to the Bitter Root and Wind River Mountains, the westernmost range of the Rocky Mountains on the west. It lies between the 45th and 49th parallels of north latitude, the west portion dipping down to the 44th parallel, and between the 104th and the 116th meridians west from Greenwich. Its area is 143,776 square miles, or 92,016,640 acres, or one seventh larger than the United Kingdom of Great Britain and Ireland. It is a mountainous country, though it has many beautiful and some fertile valleys, and some extensive plains. The various ranges of the Rocky Mountains traverse the whole western portion, covering a width of from 150 to 180 miles. The Bitter Root range divides it from Idaho Territory. There are also lower ranges dividing the Yellowstone from the Missouri, as well as north of the Missouri, and south of the Yellowstone; they run from west to east.

The Territory is well watered. The sources of the largest rivers of the continent, the Missouri with its great tributaries, the Yellowstone and the Madison, Jefferson and Gallatin, and the head waters of the Snake and Clark's Fork, the two great tributaries of the Columbia River, are in this Territory. The climate is mild and temperate except on the high elevations. The rainfall is from 12 to 16 inches annually, and is increasing, but the facilities for irrigation are generally good.

The Territory is rich in mineral wealth, 120 millions of dollars of gold and silver, mostly gold, having been produced in its mines since 1861. The yield in 1878 exceeded $5,000,000. There are also valuable copper ores, coal beds, (lignite) and petroleum springs in this Territory.

About one-ninth of the whole land in Montana has been surveyed; while there is much of the Territory which is unsurveyable, and worthless for agricultural and pastoral purposes, there is also a much larger amount of valuable land than has hitherto been supposed. The sage-brush lands, covered with alkali, and formerly supposed to be worthless, prove, under the increased rainfall, and especially with moderate irrigation, the most fertile lands for cereals in the world. The wheat and oats produced on these lands, surpass all others in the market in weight and quality. But this Territory is especially adapted for stock raising, and has already very large herds and flocks. The returns in 1878 show 300,000 cattle and 100,000 sheep, about 40,000 horses and mules. There are no railroads as yet, in the Territory, but it is very accessible by the Missouri and Yellowstone, and has good wagon roads. The Indians are not likely to be very troublesome.

Idaho Territory lies between the parallels of 42° and 49° north latitude and meridians of 111° and 117° west longitude from Greenwich. It is of irregular form, narrow at the north and broad at the south, its eastern boundary being the Bitter Root and Wind River range of the Rocky Mountains, the westernmost range of these mountains.

It is for the most part in the Valley of the Snake or Lewis River, the main tributary of the Columbia River, and part of the great basin lying between the Rocky and the Sierra Nevada or Cascade Mountains, but is crossed by several considerable ranges, those on the south-east and south forming the borders of the Great Salt Lake Basin, the Coeur d' Alene Mountains in the north being outlying spurs of the Bitter Root Mountains, and the vast irregular mass of the Salmon River Mountains near the centre, dividing the upper Snake River Valley from the Salmon River, or lower Snake River Valley. The area is 86,294 square miles, about as large as New York and Ohio. The Territory is mainly drained by the Snake River and its affluents, the Owyhee, Salmon and Spokane Rivers, through the Clark's Fork of the Columbia, and some of its affluents cross it in the north, and the Bear River, a tributary of the Great Salt Lake, enters the Territory on the south. The climate of Idaho is temperate and mild except at the highest elevations. Much of the land requires irrigation, but under a moderate amount of irrigation it yields very large crops of cereals and vegetables. The mountain slopes are covered with heavy timber. There are considerable tracts of good pastoral lands. Only about one-twelfth of the area of the Territory has as yet been surveyed. Much of what are known as sage-brush lands might be profitably settled, by companies or colonies who would provide for irrigation on a large scale, by which the most bounteous crops could be secured.

The mineral wealth of the Territory is very great, over 23 millions of bullion, mostly gold, having been deposited in the mint and branches, previous to July 1, 1878. The yield in 1878 was at least $1,500,000, and might be almost indefinitely increased. There is one railroad in the southern part of the Territory, the Utah, extending from the Union Pacific at Ogden, to Old Fort Hall on the Snake River. The settlement by colonies is the best method in this Territory.

Utah, "the land of the Mormons," lies between the parallels of 37° and 42° north latitude, and between 109° and 114° west longitude from Greenwich. It is for the most part in a deep basin surrounded by high mountains, the Wahsatch range forming the eastern rim of the basin. East of this range the country belongs to the Rocky Mountain system. It is drained by the Colorado and its tributaries, the Grand, Green and San Juan Rivers, all of which flow through deep canons, from 2,000 to 5,000 feet below the surface of the elevated plain.

West of the Wahsatch Mountains there are a succession of valleys, forming together a part of the Great Salt Lake Basin, and the lakes and rivers have no outlet. The Great Salt Lake is 100 miles long and 50 broad, and has an area of 1,900 square miles.

In the north-west and west the plains are alkaline, treeless and covered with sagebush, but by irrigation, even these produce 40 to 50 bushels of wheat, 70 to 80 bushels of oats and barley, and from 200 to 400 bushels of potatoes, to the acre. The Mountains are generally covered with timber, which belongs to the California forest growth, though not attaining its great height. There is about 4,000 square miles of timber of the 84,000 square miles in the Territory. The lower portion of the valley around Utah Lake, and the Jordan and Sevier, is fertile and requires less irrigation. The Mormon system of irrigation is very effective.

The climate, though dry and cool from the general elevation of the surface, is very healthy. The rainfall is somewhat more than 15 inches annually, except in the north-west. Eastern Utah has a climate and soil much like Colorado; the soil yields large crops when irrigated. About three-fourths of the inhabitants are Mormons, a peculiar people acknowledging Joseph Smith, Brigham Young, and their successors, as their supreme religous leaders and prophets, holding many strange and crude views, practicing polygamy, and defying the authority of the United States in regard to it. The remainder of the people are not Mormons, and are engaged in mining, agriculture and other business pursuits.

Utah is very rich in minerals. Mining for the precious metals has been discouraged by the Mormons, but the yield of silver is now more than $5,000,000 a year, and considerable quantities of gold are also produced. It is richer in the best iron ores than any other portion of the United States. It has also copper, lead and sulphur in abundance, and has immense beds of both lignite and bituminous coals of excellent quality. The Union Pacific Railroad passes across the northern portion, and the Utah Railroad, 54 miles in length, extends from Ogden southward. There are 350 irrigating canals.

NEW MEXICO, a Territory largely inhabited by Spanish Americans and the Mexican or Pueblo (village) Indians, lies between the parallels of 31° 20′ and 37° north latitude, and between the meridians of 103° 2′ and 109° 2′ west longitude from Greenwich. Its area is 121,201 square miles, almost precisely that of the United Kingdom of Great Britain and Ireland. It forms a part of the elevated table land which forms the foundation of the Rocky Mountains, as well as of the Sierra Nevada. At Santa Fe it is 6,682 feet above the sea, in the Upper Rio Grande Valley, 5,000 to 6,000 feet, at Albuquerque, 4,800 feet, on the Llano Estacado, or Staked Plain, and at El Paso, 3,000 to 3,500 feet. From this elevated plain rise hundreds of peaks from 3,000 to 10,000 feet above the plain. The Staked Plain, in the south-east, is a broad, almost level, treeless and waterless plain, sterile, but where it can be irrigated, capable of yielding immense crops, and producing abundantly the mesquite, a small but very valuable and deep rooted shrub of the Acacia family. West of the Rio Grande, wherever irrigation is possible, the soil yields abundantly, grain and vegetables, while the gramma grass on the hill slopes furnishes a delicious and fattening food for cattle. The raising of cattle is likely to become the favorite agricultural pursuit in the Territory, and many portions are admirably adapted for fruit raising. The climate is unrivalled for health. The rainfall in Santa Fe is about 13 inches annually; at Mesilla, in the south part of the Territory, on the west bank of the Rio Grand, it is not quite six inches. There are two railroads entering the Territory. The Atchison, Topeka and Santa Fe comes from the east, and is now completed to Santa Fe. The Denver and Rio Grande comes from the north, and has also reached Santa Fe. The population is about 130,000; 100,000 whites and nearly 90,000 of them Mexicans, the remainder mostly from the Eastern States—there are 25 to 30,000 Indians of various races, including about 8,000 Pueblo or Village Indians, of the ancient Mexican races. Education is in a very low condition; more than three-fifths of the population cannot read or write. The public Schools and most of the private Schools are under control of the Jesuits, or other Catholic orders, and the instruction is more religious than literary. Colonies will do well in this Territory.

ARIZONA TERRITORY is sandwiched between California and Nevada on the west, and New Mexico on the east, having Utah on the north, and Mexico on the south.

It is between 31° 37' and 37° north latitude, and between the meridians of 109° and 114° 25' west longitude from Greenwich. Its area is 113,916 square miles, or a little more than the united area of Michigan and Illinois. The north and west of the Territory are drained by the Colorado River and its principal tributaries, the San Juan and little Colorado, with their affluents. These rivers plough through the *mesas* or table-lands, in canons from 3,000 to 5,000 feet deep, and the lands through which they pass are dry, parched and sterile, except where they can be irrigated. A few artesian wells furnish a scanty supply of water, and among the ruins of the Aztec towns are large reservoirs for holding the rain water, which rarely falls. The southern part of the Territory is watered by the Gila and its numerous tributaries, and is more easily cultivated, as there is a large rainfall, and the banks of the Gila and lower Colorado are overflown in summer. The heat in summer in south and south-west Arizona is terrible, 120° and 126° in the shade, and 160° or more in the sun, is not an uncommon temperature in summer, but the winters are mild and delightful. On the table lands the temperature is pleasant during the year. Irrigation is necessary to agricultural production everywhere in the Territory, but it contains excellent grazing lands, and a sufficient amount of arable land to insure a sufficient supply of vegetables and cereals for the population. There is considerable timber on the Mountain slopes, and the various species of cactus attain great size there.

The mineral wealth of Arizona is enormous, gold, silver, quick-silver, platina, tin, nickel, very pure copper ores, lead, the best ores of iron, bituminous coals of excellent quality, salt, sulphur, gypsum and many of the precious stones, abound there. $500,000 of gold and $3,000,000 of silver were sent from this Territory in 1878, and that amount is constantly increasing with the increasing population. The Indians are no longer troublesome. For miners, engineers, or herdsmen, the Territory is very attractive, and intelligent farmers can do well there.

NEVADA was admitted as a State when its population was notoriously too small, and though the number of inhabitants is increasing, it is still below the quota for a member of Congress, though it is represented by one member in the lower house of Congress. It lies between the 35th and 42d parallels of north latitude, and between the 114th and 120th meridians of west longitude from Greenwich. Its area is 112,090 square miles, about the same as Arizona. Its mineral wealth surpasses that of any of the western States or Territories. In 1877 the yield of silver from the mines was $41,594,616; in 1878 $47,676,863. The silver mines are scattered over the whole State.

Its production of gold, mostly parted from the silver, is nearly 20 millions of dollars, and both gold and silver are increasing. It has also quick-silver, lead, copper, iron, antimony, sulphur, arsenic, graphite, borax, carbonate of soda, in immense quantities, rock salt, lignite or brown coal of good quality, &c., &c.

The climate varies with the latitude and elevation. The cold of winter is intense in the mountains and lofty valleys, the mercury falling to—10°—16°, and much lower in the mountains, and the heat in the summer, is equally intense, rising to 105° in June, but the nights in summer are cool; July and August are not so hot. In south-east Nevada, there is much less cold, and cotton and the sugar cane are both cultivated there.

The climate is generally healthy. The rainfall is larger than in the States and Territories lying east of it, but much of the land needs irrigating to be successfully cultivated. Much of the mountain slopes is well adapted to grazing, and the State has already a large amount of live stock, for its population. The sage-brush lands where irrigated, yield very large crops of the alfalfa clover, the cereals and vegetables. Provision was made in 1878 for irrigating more than 100,000 acres of these sage-brush lands.

The State has many lakes, mostly without outlet, the water in some is pure, in others brackish or alkaline, in a few salt. Pyramid Lake with its natural pyramid in the centre, the three Mud Lakes, Holloway, Humboldt, Carson, Walter's, Preuss, Franklin, Pahranagat, and on the border line of California, the beautiful Lake Tahoe, 1,500 feet deep, and 6,000 feet above the sea. Southern Nevada is a barren and desolate region, but has valuable mines. The Central Pacific Railroad crosses the State in a west-south-west direction, between the parallels of 41° 20' and 39° 30', and there are several local railroads. Nevada is a good State for miners, smelters, engineers, intelligent farmers, grazers, and enterprising mechanics.

CALIFORNIA has been so often described, that we can only speak of it now in reference to its adaptation to receive emigrants. It has a vast territory, extending from 32° 28′ to 42° north latitude, and lying between the meridians of 114° 30′ and 124° 45′ west longitude from Greenwich. Recent surveys have reduced somewhat its supposed area, which was formerly stated at 188,980 square miles, but is now said, by the United States land office, to be 157,801 square miles, a territory about as large as that of the Kingdom of Sweden.

The climate varies through all the gradations of the temperate and semi-tropical regions The average mean temperature of the year ranges from 51° 5′ at Humboldt Bay, and 56° 6′ at San Francisco, to 73° 5′ at Fort Yuma. The summer mean temperature has a range of 33 degrees between Humboldt Bay and Fort Yuma, while the winter mean varies but 14°. The annual rainfall is equally varied, at Humboldt Bay, from 57 to 64 inches; in Klamath Co., from 81 to 110 inches, in Nevada Co., at latitude 39° 20′, 64 inches to 81 inches; in San Francisco, 20.79 inches; in Sacramento, 18.23; in San Diego, 10.43; in Fort Yuma, 3.24 inches. It is a land of lakes, rivers and mountains, with some of the most beautiful and fertile lands in the world, and some of the most desolate and forbidding. Its golden grain is famous the world over, and its vineyards and olive gardens, luscious fruits and abundant crops of every thing which will grow anywhere, are well known. About 50 millions of acres of its lands are arable, but they are mostly taken up in large ranches or plantations, though these are now being divided, in many instances, into small farms. For the most part, arable lands are too dear for the farmer of small means. Many of these large ranches are on unsurveyed lands, and must eventually come into market, when there will be a good opportunity for purchasing farms.

There are nearly 40,000,000 acres of grazing lands, and though stock-raising is generally carried out upon a large scale, it is possible for an intelligent stock grower to do well in the business. South-east California is a wild volcanic region, with its dry lakes covered with salt or bitumen, its vast sinks, many of them below the surface of the ocean, and its Death Valley, most appropriately named. It is now proposed, by a short ship canal, to turn the waters of the Pacific into this valley and render it habitable, where it is not submerged.

The mineral wealth of California is very great. Its production of gold and silver since 1849 has been nearly 700 million dollars, and it is still producing over 20 millions a year, mostly in gold, quick-silver to the amount of about 2,000,000 annually; copper, tin, coal, &c., &c., are also produced. Most parts of the State are easily reached by railroads and steamers.

California is a good State for artisans, gardeners, vine growers and dressers, and farmers who are content to be employed at first by others; miners, metal workers, machinists, and operators in woollen mills, &c., &c., but less so for those who wish to purchase farms.

OREGON, one of the two States lying on the Pacific. It is between the parallels of 42° and 46° 18′ north latitude, and the meridians of 116° 33′ and 124° 25′ west longitude from Greenwich. Its area is 95,274 miles. About five-sevenths of its northern boundary is formed by the Columbia, or what is sometimes called the Oregon River, the largest river flowing into the Pacific Ocean, and at least three-fifths of its eastern boundary is washed by the Snake or Lewis River, the largest tributary of the Columbia.

Most of the State is well watered, mainly from the affluents of the Columbia and Snake, though the Klamath, a California river, rises in the State, and the Umpqua, Rogue and other small streams fall into the Pacific. It is divided by the Cascade and Blue ranges of Mountains into three sections, known as Western, Middle, and Eastern Oregon. Western Oregon, that part lying west of the Cascades, a strip about 110 miles wide, though broken and hilly from the presence of the coast range, which is from 3,000 to 4,000 feet in height, is generally fertile, and the Mountains are clothed with heavy timber to their summits. The Willamette Valley, lying between the Coast and Cascade ranges, and containing about 5,000,000 acres, is exceedingly fertile and beautiful. The rainfall in Western Oregon ranges from 44 to 60 inches, the highest amount being reached at the mouth of the Columbia in the north, and near the Klamath Lakes in the south. The temperature is mild and delightful. The mean for the year being 52° 13′, and the range very moderate. Middle Oregon is dryer, not so well watered nor so fertile. The rainfall is about 20 inches. The climate is agreeable, except in the south, where the high mountains make it sometimes excessively cold. Eastern Oregon is dry, but has many well watered and fertile valleys. The winters are cold, with deep snow. Western Oregon is traversed for almost its entire length from south to north by the California branch of the Northern Pacific. The rivers abound with valuable fish. The salmon fisheries send out about $10,000,000 worth annually, mostly in cans, and canned beef is also largely exported. The agricultural crops are good, and command a fair price; wheat, oats and potatoes yield largely. The timber trade is very large, the finest trees of Oregon being very large, and the wood durable. Fruit is also largely cultivated. It is an excellent country for raising live stock, especialy cattle and sheep. The wool product of the State is considerable, and mostly consumed in Oregon woollen factories.

The mineral wealth of the State is very great, but not so fully developed as it should be. Nearly $2,000,000 of gold and silver, principally the former, are mined annually; other metals abound. Most of the mines are in eastern and middle Oregon. Miners, lumbermen, fishermen, herdsmen, and industrious, intelligent farmers, will find Oregon the best place for them. There is much Government land yet in market.

WASHINGTON TERRITORY is, except Alaska, the extreme north-western Territory of the United States, and Alaska is not as yet, in a condition to invite immigration.

The Territory may be said in general terms, to lie between the parallels of 45° 30' and 49° north latitude, and between 117° and 125° west longitude from Greenwich. The Columbia River, which drains about two-thirds of the Territory forms its southern boundary, for three-fourths of its width from east to west, and its western shores are washed by the Pacific, and the waters of the Strait of Juan de Fuca and the Gulf of Georgia. The area of the Territory is 69,994 square miles. Western Washington like western Oregon, has much broken land, but the valleys, especially around both sides of Puget Sound, are very fertile, and the slopes of the mountains are heavily timbered, and valuable. There are 200 miles of railroad in operation in the Territory, and the Columbia River, Snake River and Clark's Fork are navigable, except at four points, throughout their entire course in this Territory.

The climate of Western Washington is much like that of England, mild and moist, the extreme heat of summer seldom exceeding 80 degrees F., and the nights cool and agreeable. The winters are so mild that it is seldom necessary to house the live stock. Mean annual temperature 52°, annual range only about 40 degrees. Rainfall 100 to 130 inches on the coast, 36 inches at Cascade Mountains; in Eastern Washington, from 12 to 24 inches. The summers in Central and Eastern Washington are dry and hot, winters much like those of Pennsylvania, cold, but not severe. Only about one-third of the public lands are yet surveyed. There is some gold in the Territory, but more coal, iron, and other minerals.

The coal in the Puyallup Valley is anthracite, of excellent quality, and a railroad now runs to the mines. There are other beds of both anthracite and bituminous coal, along the Cascade Mountains. The soil is, much of it, very fertile, and the finest trees are but little inferior to the giant sequoias of California.

The Territory is well adapted to the culture of the cereals, which can be brought to a good market, by the Columbia and Snake Rivers, which have now 500 miles of uninterrupted navigation. It is also a good region for wool growing and stock raising. The salmon and other fisheries in Puget Sound, and in the Columbia, are very profitable. A grand future awaits the citizens of Oregon and Washington.

HOMESTEAD FOR SOLDIERS.

DEPARTMENT OF THE INTERIOR,
GENERAL LAND OFFICE, Aug. 8, 1870.

GENTLEMEN:—The following is the twenty-fifth section of the act of Congress, approved July 15, 1870, entitled "An act making appropriations for the support of the army for the year ending June 30, 1871, and for other purposes," viz.:

SEC. 25.—*And be it further enacted*, That every private soldier and officer who has served in the army of the United States during the rebellion, for ninety days, and remained loyal to the Government, and every seaman, marine, and officer or other person who has served in the navy of the United States, or in the marine corps or revenue marine during the rebellion, for ninety days, and remained loyal to the Government, shall, on payment of the fee or commission to any Register or Receiver of any Land Office required by law, be entitled to enter one quarter section of land, not mineral, of the alternate reserved sections of public lands along the lines of any railroads or other public works in the United States, wherever public lands have been or may be granted by acts of Congress, and to receive a patent therefor under and by virtue of the provisions of the act to secure homesteads to actual settlers on the public domain, and the acts amendatory thereof, and on the terms and conditions therein prescribed; and all the provisions of said acts, excetp as herein modified, shall extend and be applicable to entries under this act, and the Commissioner of the General Land Office is hereby authorized to prescribe the necessary rules and regulations to carry this section into effect, and determine all facts necessary thereto.

By these provisions the Homestead Law of 20th May, 1862, and the acts amendatory thereof, are so modified as to allow entries to be made by the parties mentioned therein, of the maximum quantity of one quarter-section, or 160 acres of land, held at the double minimum price of $2.50 per acre, instead of one-half quarter-section, or eighty acres as heretofore.

In case of a party desiring to avail himself thereof, you will require him to file the usual homestead application for the tract desired, if legally liable to entry, to make affidavit according to the form hereto annexed, instead of the usual homestead affidavit, and on doing so allow him to make payment of the $10 fee stipulated in the act of 20th May, 1862, and the usual commissions on the price of the land at $2.50 per acre, the entry to be regularly numbered and reported to this office in your monthly homestead returns.

Regarding settlement and cultivation, the requirements of the law in this class of entries are the same as in other homestead entries.

Very respectfully your obedient servant,

JOSEPH S. WILSON,
Commissioner, Register, and Receiver.

INTERNAL REVENUE.

[See "LITTLE TARIFF LAW," p. 66].

THESE rates are those of the new Internal Revenue Law, passed June, 1872, and taking effect October 1, 1872.

TAXES.

Ale, per bbl. of 31 gallons........ $1 00
Banks, on average amount of deposits, each month........ 1-24 of 1 per ct.
Bank deposits, savings, etc., having no capital stock, per six months ¼ of 1 per ct.
Banks, on capital, beyond the average amount invested in United States bonds, each month........ 1-24 of 1 per ct.
Banks, on average amount of circulation, each month........ 1-12 of 1 per ct.
Banks, on average amount of circulation, beyond 90 per cent. of the capital, an additional tax each month........ 1-6 of 1 per ct.
Banks, on amount of notes of any person, state bank, or state banking association, used and paid out as circulation........ 10 per ct.
Beer, per bbl. of 31 gallons........ $1 00
Brandy, made from grapes, per gallon........ 70
Brewers, special tax on........ 100 00
Chewing tobacco, fine cut, plug, or twist, per lb........ 20
Cigars, manufacturers of, special tax........ 10 00
Cigars, of all descriptions, made of tobacco or any substitute therefor, per 1,000........ 5 00
Cigars, imported, in addition to import duty to pay same as above.
Cigarettes, not weighing more than 3 lbs. per 1,000, per 1,000........ 1 50
Cigarettes, weight exceeding 3 lbs. per 1,000, per 1,000........ 5 00
Dealers in leaf tobacco, wholesale........ 25 00
Dealers in leaf tobacco, retail........ 5 00
Dealers in leaf tobacco, for sales in excess of $1,000, per dollar of excess........ 5
Distilled spirits, every proof gallon........ 70
Distillers, producing 100 bbls. or less, (40 gallons of proof spirits to bbl.) per annum........ 400 00
Distillers, for each bbl. in excess of 100 bbls........ 4 00
Distillers, on each bbl. of 40 gallons in warehouse when act took effect, and when withdrawn........ 4 00
Distillers of brandy from grapes, peaches, and apples exclusively, producing less than 150 bbls. annually, special tax $50, and $4 per bbl. of 40 gallons.
Distillery, having aggregate capacity for mashing, etc., 20 bushels of grain per day, or less per day........ 2 00
Distillery, in excess of 20 bushels of grain per day, for every 20 bushels, per day........ 2 00
Fermented liquors, in general, per bbl........ 1 00

Gas, coal, illuminating, when the product shall not be above 200,000 cubic feet per month, per 1,000 cubic feet	10
Gas, coal, when product exceeds 200,000, and does not exceed 500,000 cubic feet per month, per 1,000 cubic feet	15
Gas, coal, when product exceeds 500,000, and does not exceed 5,000,000 cubic feet per month, per 1,000 cubic feet	20
Gas, coal, when product exceeds 5,000,000 feet per month, per 1,000 cubic feet	25
Imitation wines and champagne, not made from grapes, currants, rhubarb, or berries, grown in the United States, rectified or mixed, to be sold as wine or any other name, per dozen bottles of more than a pint and not more than a quart	2 40
Imitation wines, containing not more than one pint, per dozen bottles..	1 20
Lager beer, per bbl. of 31 gallons	1 00
Liquors, dealers in, whose sales, including sales of all other merchandise, shall exceed $25,000, an additional tax for every $100 on sales of liquors in excess of such $25,000	1 00
Manufacturers of stills	50 00
Manufacturers of stills, for each still or worm made	20 00
Porter, per bbl. of 31 gallons	1 00
Rectifiers, special tax	200 00
Retail liquor dealers, special tax	25 00
Retail malt liquor dealers	20 00
Snuff, manufactured of tobacco, or any substitute, when prepared for use, per lb	32
Snuff-flour, sold or removed, for use, per lb	32
Stamps, distillers', other than tax-paid stamps charged to collector, each	10
Tobacco, dealers in	10 00
Tobacco, manufacturers of	10 00
Tobacco, twisted by hand, or reduced from leaf, to be consumed, without the use of machine or instrument, and not pressed or sweetened, per lb.	20
Tobacco, all other kinds not provided for, per lb	20
Tobacco peddlers, traveling with more than two horses, mules, or other animals (first class)	50 00
Tobacco peddlers, traveling with two horses, mules, or other animals (second class)	25 00
Tobacco peddlers, traveling with one horse, mule, or other animal (third class)	15 00
Tobacco peddlers, traveling on foot, or by public conveyance (fourth class)	10 00
Tobacco, snuff and cigars, for immediate export, stamps for, each	10
Wholesale liquor dealers	100 00
Wholesale malt liquor dealers	50 00
Wholesale dealers in liquors whose sales, including sales of all other merchandise, shall exceed $25,000, each to pay an additional tax on every $100 of sales of liquors in excess of $25,000	1 00

STAMP DUTIES.

THE latest Internal Revenue Act of the United States (that of June, 1872), provides for the following stamp duties after October 1, 1872. All other stamp duties in Schedule B are repealed.

SCHEDULE B.

Bank check, draft, or order for the payment of any sum of money whatsoever, drawn upon any bank, banker, or trust company, or for any sum exceeding $10, drawn upon any other person or persons, companies, or corporations, at sight or on demand........................ 2

Medicines or Preparations.

SCHEDULE C.

For and upon every packet, box, bottle, pot, vial, or other inclosure, containing any pills, powders, tinctures, troches, or lozenges, syrups, cordials, bitters, anodynes, tonics, plasters, liniments, salves, ointments, pastes, drops, waters, essences, spirits, oils, or other preparations or compositions whatsoever, made and sold, or removed for consumption and sale, by any person or persons whatever, wherein the person making or preparing the same has, or claims to have, any private formula or occult secret or art for the making or preparing the same, or has, or claims to have, any exclusive right or title to the making or preparing the same, or which are prepared, uttered, vended, or exposed for sale under any letters patent, or held out or recommended to the public by the makers, venders, or proprietors thereof as proprietary medicines, or as remedies or specifics for any disease, diseases, or affections whatever affecting the human or animal body, as follows: where such packet, box, bottle, vial, or other inclosure, with its contents, shall not exceed, at the retail price or value, the sum of twenty-five cents, one cent 1

Where such packet, box, bottle, pot, vial, or other inclosure, with its contents, shall exceed the retail price or value of 25 cents, and not exceed the retail price or value of 50 cents, two cents........................ 2

Where such packet, box, bottle, pot, vial, or other inclosure, with its contents shall exceed the retail price or value of 50 cents, and shall not exceed the retail price or value of 75 cents, three cents................ 3

Where such packet, box, bottle, pot, vial, or other inclosure, with its contents, shall exceed the retail price or value of 75 cents, and shall not exceed the retail price or value of $1, four cents...................... 4

Where such packet, box, bottle, pot, vial, or other inclosure, with its contents, shall exceed the retail price or value of $1, for each and every 50 cents or fractional part thereof over and above the $1, as before-mentioned, an additional two cents 2

Perfumery and Cosmetics.

For and upon every packet, box, bottle, pot, vial, or other inclosure, containing any essence, extract, toilet water, cosmetic, hair oil, pomade, hair dressing, hair restorative, hair dye, tooth wash, dentifrice, tooth paste, aromatic cachous, or any similar articles, by whatsoever name the same have been, now are, or may hereafter be called, known, or distinguished, used or applied, or to be used or applied as perfumes or applications to the hair, mouth, or skin, made, prepared, and sold or removed for consumption and sale in the United States, where such packet, box, bottle, pot, vial, or other inclosure, with its contents, shall not exceed, at the retail price or value, the sum of 25 cents, one cent 1

Where such packet, bottle, box, pot, vial, or other inclosure, with its contents, shall exceed the retail price or value of 25 cents, and shall not exceed the retail price or value of 50 cents, two cents 2

Where such packet, box, bottle, pot, vial, or other inclosure, with its contents, shall exceed the retail price or value of 50 cents, and shall not exceed the retail price or value of 75 cents, three cents 3

Where such packet, box, bottle, pot, vial, or other inclosure, with its contents, shall exceed the retail price or value of 75 cents, and shall not exceed the retail price or value of $1, four cents 4

Where such packet, box, bottle, pot, vial, or other inclosure, with its contents, shall exceed the retail price or value of $1, for each and every 50 cents or fractional part thereof over and above the $1, as before mentioned, an additional two cents 2

Friction matches, or lucifer matches, or other articles made in part of wood, and used for like purposes, in parcels or packages containing 100 matches or less, for each parcel or package, one cent 1

When in parcels or packages containing more than 100 and not more than 200 matches, for each parcel or package, two cents 2

And for every additional 100 matches, or fractional parts thereof, one cent 1

For wax tapers, double the rates herein imposed upon friction or lucifer matches; on cigar lights, made in part of wood, wax, glass, paper, or other materials, in parcels or packages containing 25 lights or less in each parcel or package, one cent 1

When in parcels or packages containing more than 25 and not more than 50 lights, two cents 2

For every additional 25 lights or fractional part of that number, one cent additional 1

THE FINANCE BILL.

Passed June 20, 1874.

SECTION 1.—The Act entitled "An Act to provide National Currency, secured by a Pledge of United States Bonds, and to provide for the Circulation and Redemption thereof," approved June 3, 1864, shall be hereafter known as the National Bank Act.

SEC. 2. That Section 31 of the National Bank Act be so amended that the several Associations therein provided for shall not be required to keep on hand any amount of money whatever, by reason of the amount of their respective circulations; but the moneys required by said section to be kept at all times on hand shall be determined by the amount of deposits, as provided for in the said section.

SEC. 3. That every association organized or to be organized under the provisions of the said act, and of the several acts amendatory thereof, shall at all times keep and have on deposit in the Treasury of the United States, in lawful money of the United States, a sum equal to five per centum of its circulation, to be held and used for the redemption of such circulation, which sum shall be counted as a part of its lawful reserve, as provided in Section 2 of this act, and when the circulating notes of any such associations, assorted or unassorted shall be presented for redemption in sums of $1,000 or any multiple thereof to the Treasurer of the United States, the same shall be redeemed in United States notes. All notes so redeemed shall be charged by the Treasurer of the United States to the respective associations issuing the same, and he shall notify them severally on the first day of each month or oftener, at his discretion, of the amount of such redemptions, and whenever such redemptions for any association shall amount to the sum of $500 such association so notified shall forthwith deposit with the Treasurer of the United States a sum in United States notes equal to the amount of its circulating notes so redeemed; and all notes of National Banks worn, defaced, mutilated, or otherwise unfit for circulation shall, when received by any Assistant Treasurer, or at any designated depository of the United States, be forwarded to the Treasurer of the United States for redemption, as provided herein; and when such redemptions have been so reimbursed the circulating notes so redeemed shall be forwarded to the respective associations by which they were issued; but if any such notes are worn, mutilated, defaced, or rendered otherwise unfit for use, they shall be forwarded to the Controller of the Currency and destroyed and replaced as now provided by law. Provided, that each of such associations shall reimburse to the Treasury the charges for transportation and the costs for assorting such notes, and the associations hereafter organized shall also generally reimburse to the Treasury the cost of engraving such plates as shall be ordered by each association respectively, and the amount assessed upon each association shall be in proportion to the circulation redeemed, and be charged to the fund on deposit with the Treasurer; and provided further, that so much of Section 32 of said National Bank Act recognizing, or permitting the redemption of its circulating notes elsewhere than at its own counter, except as provided in this section, is hereby repealed.

SEC. 4. That any association organized under this act, or any of the acts to which this is an amendment, desiring to withdraw its circulating notes, in whole or in part, may upon the deposit of lawful money with the Treasurer of the United States, in sums not less than $9,000, take up the bonds which said association has on deposit with the Treasurer for the security of such circulating notes, which bonds shall be assigned to the banks in the manner specified in the 19th section of the National Bank Act, and the outstanding notes of said association to an amount equal to the legal-tender notes deposited, shall be redeemed at the Treasury of the United States and destroyed, as now provided by law; provided the amount of the bonds on deposit for circulation shall not be reduced below $50,000.

SEC. 5. That the Controller of the Currency shall, under such rules and regulations as the Secretary of the Treasury may prescribe, cause the charter numbers of the association to be printed on all National Bank notes which may be hereafter issued by him.

SEC. 6. That the amount of United States notes outstanding, and to be issued as a part of the circulating medium, shall not exceed the sum of $382,000,000, which said sum shall appear in each monthly statement of the public debt, and no part thereof shall be held or used as a reserve.

SEC. 7. That so much of the act, entitled An Act to provide for the redemption of the three per centum temporary loan certificates, and for an increase of National Bank notes, as provided, that no circulation shall be withdrawn under the provisions of Section 6 of said Act, until after the $54,000,000 granted in Section 1 of said Act shall have been taken up, is hereby repealed, and it shall be the duty of the Controller of the Currency, under the direction of the Secretary of the Treasury, to proceed forthwith, and he is hereby authorized and required, from time to time, as application shall be duly made therefor, and until the full amount of the $54,000,000 shall be withdrawn, to make a requisition on each of the National Banks described in said section, and in the manner therein provided, organized in States having an excess of circulation, to withdraw and return so much of this circulation as by said Act may be apportioned to be withdrawn from them, or in lieu thereof to deposit in the Treasury of the United States lawful money sufficient to redeem such circulation, and upon the return of the circulation required, or the deposit of lawful money as herein provided, a proportionate amount of the bonds held to secure the circulation of such association as shall make such return or deposit, shall be surrendered to it.

SEC. 8. That upon the failure of the National Banks upon which requisitions for circulation shall be made, or of any of them, to return the amount required, or to deposit in the Treasury lawful money to redeem the circulation required within thirty days, the Controller of the Currency shall at once sell, as provided in Section 49, of the National Currency Act, approved June 3, 1864, bonds held to secure the redemption of the circulation of the association or associations which shall so fail to an amount sufficient to redeem the circulation required of such association or associations, and with the proceeds which shall be deposited in the Treasury of the United States so much of the circulation of said association or associations shall be redeemed as will equal the amount required and not returned; and if there be any excess of proceeds over the amount required for such redemption, it shall be returned to the association or associations whose bonds shall have been sold; and it shall be the duty of the Treasurer, Assistant Treasurers, designated depositaries and National Bank depositaries of the United States, who shall be kept informed by the Controller of the Currency of such associations as shall fail to return circulation as required, to assort and return to the Treasurer for redemption the notes of such associations as shall come into their hands until the amount required shall be redeemed, and in like manner to assort and return to the Treasury for redemption the notes of such National Banks as have failed or gone into voluntary liquidation for the purpose of winding up their affairs or such as shall hereafter so fail or go into liquidation.

SEC. 9. That from and after the passage of this act it shall be lawful for the Controller of the Currency, and he is hereby ordered, to issue circulating notes without delay as applications are therefor made, not to exceed $55,000,000, to associations organized or to be organized, in those States and Territories having less than their proportion of circulation under an apportionment made on the basis of population and of wealth as shown by the returns of the census of 1870, and every association hereafter organized shall be subject to and be governed by the rules, restrictions, and limitations, and possess the rights, privileges, and franchises now or hereafter to be prescribed by law as National Banking Associations, with the same power to amend, alter and repeal, provided by the National Bank Act, provided that the whole amount of circulation withdrawn, and removed from the banks transacting business shall not exceed $55,000,000, and that such circulation shall be withdrawn, and redeemed as shall be necessary to supply the circulation previously issued to the banks in those States having less than their apportionment; and provided further, that not more than $30,000,000 shall be withdrawn and redeemed as herein contemplated, during fiscal year ending June 30, 1875.

The title of the bill is amended to read as follows:—"An act to fix the amount of United States notes, provide for the redistribution of the National Bank Currency, and for other purposes."

CUSTOM HOUSE FEES,

REQUIRED BY LAW TO BE PAID AT THE SEVERAL CUSTOM HOUSES ELSEWHERE THAN ON THE NORTH, NORTH-EAST AND NORTH-WEST FRONTIERS.

For admeasurement of tonnage, and certifying the same, for every transverse section under the tonnage deck	$1.50
For each between decks above tonnage deck	3.00
For each poop, or closed-in space above the upper or spar deck, required by law to be admeasured	1.50
Certificate of registry or record	2.00
Indorsement on Certificate of registry or record	1.00
For every bond under the Registry Act	.25
Certificate of Enrollment	.50
Indorsement on Certificate of Enrollment of Change of Master, &c	.20
License and granting the same, including bond, if not over 20 tons	.25
Above 20 and not over 100 tons	.50
Over 100 tons	1.00
Indorsement on a License, of Change of Master, &c	.20
Certifying manifest, and granting permit for *licensed* vessel to go from district to district—Under 50 tons	.25
Over 50 tons	.50
Certifying manifest, and granting permission to *registered* vessels to go from district to district	1.50
Receiving certified manifest and granting permit on arrival of such registered vessel	1.50
Granting permit to a vessel not belonging to a Citizen of the United States, to go from district to district, and receiving manifest	2.00
Receiving manifest, and granting permit to unload, for last-mentioned vessel, on arrival at one district from another	2.00
Granting permit for vessel carrying on fishery to trade at a foreign port	.25
Report and entry of foreign goods imported in such vessel	.25
Entry of vessel of 100 tons and more	2.50
Clearance of vessel of 100 tons and more	2.50
Entry of vessel under 100 tons	1.50
Clearance of vessel under 100 tons	1.50
Post Entry	2.00
Permit to land or deliver goods	.20
Bond taken officially	.40
Permit to lade goods for exportation entitled to drawback	.30
Debenture, or other official certificate	.20
Bill of Health	.20
Official documents, required by any merchant, owner or master of any vessel, not before enumerated	.20
Services, other than admeasurement, to be performed by the Surveyor, in vessels of 100 tons and more, having on board merchandise subject to duty	3.00
For like services in vessels under 100 tons, having similar merchandise	1.50
For like services in all vessels not having merchandise subject to duty	.66⅔
Protection	.25
Crew List	.25
General permit to land passenger's baggage	.20
Weighing of weighable articles exported per 100 lbs	.03
Weighing of salt, to cure fish, (See Art. 122 Warehouse Regulations)	
Weighing of other weighable articles in the districts of Boston, New York, Philadelphia, and Baltimore, per 112 lbs	.01⅞
Weighing of other weighable articles in the district of Norfolk	.02¼
Weighing of other weighable articles in all other districts	.03
Gauging of gaugable articles exported, per cask	.10
Gauging other articles.—Casks each	.12
Cases and Baskets, each	.04½
Ale, Porter, &c., per dozen bottles	.01½
Measuring, per 100 bushels—Coal, chalk, brimstone	.90
Salt	.75
Potatoes, seeds, grain and all similar measurable articles	.45
Marble, lumber, and other similar articles, the actual expense incurred	
For recording bill of sale, mortgage, hypothecation, or conveyance of vessel, under Act of July 29, 1850	.50
For recording certificate for discharging and canceling any such conveyance	.50
For furnishing a certificate, setting forth the names of the owners of any registered or enrolled vessel, the parts or properties owned by each, and also the material facts of any existing bill of sale, mortgage, hypothecation, or other incumbrance, the date, amount of such incumbrance, and from and to whom made	1.00
For furnishing copies of such records, for each bill of sale, mortgage or other conveyance	.50

For licenses to Steamers, as a compensation for the inspection and examination made for the year, and furnishing the required copies of the inspection certificate, under the Steamboat Law, approved August 30 1852, in addition to the fees above mentioned, for issuing enrollments and licenses to vessels:

For each steam vessel of 100 tons or under	25.00
and for each ton in excess of 100 tons	.03
For licensing of pilots and engineers	10.00

THE WEST:

WHO SHOULD MIGRATE THITHER.

THERE have been in our country, as in other countries of Christendom, periodical crazes—times when nations, states, and communities were completely under the influence of a single dominating idea, which, with the great masses of the people, drove out all other ideas and thoughts from their minds. Eating or drinking, waking or sleeping, they could think and talk of nothing else. These crazes sometimes seem very absurd to us, as we look back upon them; but at the time, they are intensely real. They may do some good: perhaps they always do; but they do much evil also. They may be industrial, scientific after the fashion of popular science, political, agricultural, educational, or religious; but whatever may be the subject of the craze, its effect is much the same.

THE MORUS MULTICAULIS CRAZE.

The *Morus Multicaulis* fever of 1835–38 was an example of the agricultural and industrial sort. Men of sound judgment and of good business abilities, were deluded into the belief, that by planting or starting a half-dozen or a dozen cuttings of a foreign shrub or tree they would speedily amass an immense fortune; that from these little sticks, not so large as a pipe stem, there would presently grow stately mulberry-trees, on which millions of silkworms to be somehow procured, would feast and form cocoons, which any girl could reel, and which would, by some hocus-pocus process, be transmuted into elegant dress-silk, dress-goods, velvets, satins, ribbons, and lace, all of which would be furnished without cost, to the fortunate possessor of the mulberry-slips.

The whole thing looks supremely ridiculous to us now; but then, every man and woman invested all that they could earn, or beg, or steal in these precious twigs; and when the bubble burst, as it did in 1837, it involved millions of people in heavy, and some of them in ruinous losses.

THE SECOND ADVENT CRAZE OF 1843.

There followed this a religious delusion, the Second Adent craze of 1843, when people made up ascension robes, and some, in their zeal stole the muslin which they used in their manufacture.

THE WESTERN CRAZE OF 1847–48.

A few years later there was an emigration craze. *The West*, which then meant Indiana, Illinois, Michigan, Wisconsin, Iowa, and Missouri, and the cities of Chicago, Milwaukee, and St. Louis, was on every man's lips; tens of thousands of miles of railroads were projected, thousands of cities laid out on paper, stocks and bonds issued without stint, every kind of wild-cat paper issued as money, and the most fabulous stories told, of the fortunes amassed in a single day, by the advance in lands, city lots, and stocks. This craze, too, died out from sheer absurdity, but with frightful losses.

OTHER CRAZES.

Time would fail me to tell of the crazes since that time ; of the petroleum mania, the shoddy speculation, the mining fever of a dozen years ago, the new railroad excitement, all ending in general disaster, and in long years of gloom; now to be replaced, perhaps, by an emigration fever, and a reckless speculation in mining properties, almost as absurd as the earlier manias, and even more disastrous. It seems to be the fate of the Yankee to be at one moment on the top of Pisgah, and the next in the Valley of Humiliation.

THE PRESENT MINING CRAZE.

There are at the present time (May, 1880) over 1500 mining companies or organizations in the region west of the Mississippi, nine tenths of them formed within two years past, and having a nominal capital of about $2,000,000,000. From ignorance of the business, bad management, and often from misrepresentation in regard to their value, more than nine tenths will prove unproductive, and the stockholders will meet with heavy losses. One hundred and forty mining companies, incorporated in San Francisco within a few years past, have assessed their stockholders $47,000,000, besides their original capital, and have paid in all only $6,000,000 dividends.

THE DESIRE TO GO WEST.

"But," it may be asked, "what has all this to do with going West?" Much more than you may think, my friend. You are a working-man, a machinist, an operative in a manufactory, a builder, or an artisan in some one of the trades or callings which are followed in our Eastern communities, or you have been farming in a moderate way, or engaged in trade. You have laid up a little, have perhaps a home of your own, though there may be a small mortgage on it; but you do not get rich so fast as you would like, and, as you look upon your wife and little ones, you think to yourself, "I have not much to leave to them if I were taken away, and they might be left to suffer. I must try in some way to accumulate property faster, so as to be able to leave them in better circumstances." As you look about you, there seems to be no chance in your present circumstances and position, for doing this. If you are a working-man, your wages are only likely to be advanced, when there are such advances in food and clothing and living expenses, as will leave you no more net gain than you have had in the past. If you are following a trade or calling, any advance in price is necessarily accompanied by an advance in material, or wages of employés, and in living expenses, which leaves you no better off than you were before. In trade, there is perhaps a little advantage in prosperous times, because there are not so many bad debts, but very few can lay up money in retail trade. You are apparently cut off from any considerable improvement of your circumstances.

THE EMIGRATION FEVER.

Meantime the spirit of emigration is abroad in the air. Every other man whom you meet is talking of the West—the West, with its rich and constantly developing mines of gold and silver; the West, with its productive farms and its agricultural wealth; the West, with its immense herds of cattle, and its hundreds of thousands of sheep and goats. You ask yourself, "Why not go to this great West and accumulate wealth, as others have done, in a few years, instead of wasting my time here for a mere pittance?"

WHAT IS INVOLVED IN EMIGRATION TO THE WEST.

The mania is abroad, and you are in a fair way to become one of its victims. Still your question is a reasonable one. Allow us to answer it, after the Yankee fashion, by asking some others. Have you a very clear, distinct idea of what is included in emigration to a new State or Territory?

THE DISCOMFORTS.

You have a good, comfortable home, with all its appliances and conveniences. It may be small, but it is a good home. If you emigrate to the frontier, even if you have a good sum of money to pay your living expenses, your home for the first year or two must be of sods, of logs, or of canvas. You must content yourself with the fewest possible conveniences for comfortable housekeeping, and the roughest and poorest food; all those thousand little comforts, which go to make up our Eastern civilization, will be wanting, for a year or two at least. If you make your new home on the prairie, the summer's sun will scorch and burn you, and the winter's snow may bury your little cabin out of sight. Neighbors at first will be few and far apart. Schools and churches will come in time, but you will have to lift heavily to make them come, and for a year or two you will be obliged to go without them. If your home is in the timbered land, other disabilities, equally severe, will try you. Wolves, panthers, lynxes, and now and then a bear, will pay you visits, not so much because they care for your society, as because they hope to find some food, on or about your premises. You will have a vigorous appetite, though it may sometimes be difficult to satisfy it; and the exposure to the pure open air may improve your health, though there are some chances of malarial fever or catarrhal affections. You may have been particular about your clothing at the East, but you will very soon present an appearance which would well befit a tramp.

DANGERS TO HEALTH.

We do not speak of the risks to health, because, with only a few exceptions, the region west of the Mississippi is healthy. The region bordering immediately on the Mississippi, from the Iowa line southward, and the lower Missouri, as well as Southeast Kansas, much of the Indian Territory and the lower lands of Texas, are to some extent subject to billious, remittent, and intermittent fevers, and care should be taken, if a location is sought there, to select elevated lands, with good drainage and no standing water, and to avoid the night air and heavy dews.

RISKS OF LOSS.

There are also some risks in investing the money you have been able to save in the past. If you have saved $1000 or $2000, and buy or secure a farm in some one of these new States or territories, by whatever mode you have obtained or are to obtain a title to it, it will probably be about twenty months before you can realize anything on your first crop. Meantime you must make your first payments on your land, which will be more or less, according to the mode of purchase; pay for having it broken up, which will cost you from four to eight dollars per acre, according to the thoroughness with which it is done; must pay for seed, and buy the horses, mules, oxen, or cows needed, and the wagons, carts, ploughs, harrows, cultivators, and, if you can, a harvester for your first grain crop. You must also buy or build your cabin and furnish it, or, which will be about the same thing, pay the freight on your furniture from the East. And whatever you or your family need in the way of food or clothing, before you receive anything from the first crop, must also come out of this reserve.

THE CHANCES OF SUCCESS AND FAILURE.

It is true that, if you are successful, your money will have been put out at good interest—ten, twelve, or even twenty per cent. perhaps—but there are chances of failure, and the risk should be fairly considered. Even if you are able to pre-empt your land, and so delay paying the Government price for it for thirty-three months, or take it up under the Homestead or Timber Culture acts, or buy it of the railway companies, on long time, you will still find ample use for your $1000 or $2000 in paying your necessary expenses, and maintaining your family, until the crop money comes in.

WHAT A SUCCESSFUL FIRST CROP WILL ACCOMPLISH.

If this first crop has been twenty acres in root crops and twenty in wheat (you will hardly be able to crop more than forty acres at first), and there have been no drawbacks, but a full crop of both, you should be able to raise about $2000 from the forty acres, and cultivating besides a large garden plot, to provide your family with all the vegetables they need. A pig and a calf will add to your meat rations, and your cow should furnish the butter and milk needed. Under these circumstances, if you are a good manager, you may be able to make your next payment, if necessary, on your farm; to improve your dwelling, and break up an additional twenty or forty acres; support your family in better style than the previous year, and still lay up a small sum toward replacing your reserve.

THE POSSIBILITIES OF FAILURE.

But suppose that your wheat is consumed while growing, by the grasshopper or Rocky Mountain locust, and your root crops by the Colorado beetle or potato bug, and the gophers, or the moles; or that your farm is desolated by drought; that your horses or mules, your oxen or cows, or the pig or pigs, whose luscious flesh you have been looking forward to, as a part of your winter's supply, are destroyed by wolves, lynxes, or bears, or are seized with the diseases not infrequently prevalent; your supplies for the coming year will be cut off, and if your reserve has all been expended, you will be very hard pressed to find the means for supporting your family, and obtaining the seed necessary to be planted or sown for the next year. You may say that it is not probable that all these disasters will come at once; so would have said many thousands of farmers, who put in their first or second crops in the autumn of 1873 or the spring of 1874, and yet it was exactly these disasters which did come in that year, and thousands of families were only kept from starvation, by the public and private bounties bestowed upon them, largely by Eastern people.

ROSE-COLORED PICTURES OF THE EMIGRATION AGENTS.

This is not the sort of talk you will be likely to hear from the agents of emigration societies, or land-grant railroad companies; they will represent to you that the climate, soil, and productions render the country a perfect paradise; that there are no disturbing or discouraging influences, but that everything is perfectly lovely. The crops are grown without labor, the houses are builded without effort, the live stock takes care of itself, the rain irrigates thoroughly the long-parched soil, so soon as the immigrant plants his foot upon it. Such unthinking advocates of emigration will accuse us of hostility to it, but most unjustly; for while we have presented frankly and without exaggeration the troubles and privations which the emigrant must encounter in the early months of his settlement, there is a bright future before him, if he has only the nerve, patience, enterprise, and good fortune to triumph over them all.

WHY THE DARK SIDE AS WELL AS THE BRIGHT SHOULD BE PRESENTED.

No man of true courage is ever discouraged by the presentation of difficulties to be surmounted in attaining a desired end; he is only stimulated to greater effort to overcome them. If, on the other hand, only the bright side is presented to him, and all knowledge of difficulties and discouragements is carefully withheld from him when he is called unexpectedly to encounter serious trials and privations, of which he had no previous warning, the probability of disappointment and despair is greatly increased. He is the best friend of the emigrant who shows him what clouds and storms will darken his way, as well as the glowing sunshine which will gladden it.

GARIBALDI'S PROCLAMATION.

When Garibaldi was about to enter upon his campaign for the capture of Rome and its annexation to the kingdom of Italy, he sent out this proclamation: "Italians, I am about to move forward for the conquest of Rome, and I call upon the brave patriots of Italy to volunteer for my help. Whoso joins my army will have but scanty and poor rations; his couch will be the cool ground, his shelter-tent the starry skies; if he is wounded or sick, no hospital will open its gates to him; if he falls, no priest will give him extreme unction, or say masses for his soul's repose—but at the end of the fight, *there is a free, a redeemed Italy!* Comrades, brothers, forward and enlist!" And they did come forward and enlist by thousands, and though many fell, the great end was at last gained.

WHAT THE EMIGRANT HAS TO ENCOUNTER.

Your warfare is not with human foes, or despotisms hastening to decay, but only with the inertia of the natural world, with the difficulties and privations incident to a new settlement, and possibly with insect foes, diseases, and summer droughts. These once overcome, and you will have established yourselves in homes whose value is constantly increasing, and will have ere long an income sufficiently ample for your family and yourselves. You who are enterprising, courageous, and persevering, come forward and enlist!

THE CHANCES FOR THE MEN WHO HAVE TRADES.

Those working-men who have good trades, and are skilful in them, may find profitable employment in their respective lines of business much sooner than the farmer, and have an opportunity of obtaining better social positions, than they can usually do here; but they will do well to secure some land—enough for their own needs. To keep two or three cows and a few sheep; to raise what grain and root crops are needed for home consumption; to have a comfortable home, with pleasant surroundings of flowers, shrubs, fruit and forest-trees, and a good vegetable garden, will not be very expensive, if there are young hands to help; and if in, or near one of the growing towns of the West, it will be not only a source of pleasure, but of constantly-increasing profit. And in many instances there will be opportunities for the cultivation of special crops on a small scale, the raising of poultry, the rearing of silk-worms, the care of bees, etc., etc., which will add materially to the revenues of the household.

We can hardly advise our friends to go into the business of stock-raising or wool-growing in the West, unless they have a considerable capital at command.

HEAVY CAPITAL NEEDED IN STOCK-RAISING.

A cattle-ranche, even on the smallest scale which will pay a profit, requires at least $20,000 to start with, and would be more speedily profitable with $50,000. As many of the large cattle-farms or ranches are owned by joint stock companies, some stock might be taken in them with a smaller sum, say $5,000 or $10,000; but their capital is usually from $500,000 to $1,000,000, and the dividend on a small sum would be nothing for two or three years, and not a large amount for several more. Eventually it might pay.

BECOMING A HERDER.

Another way of working into this business would be to become a herder or "cow-boy" at first, and, buying a few cows and calves, herd them with the rest of the stock. At "rounding up" time, brand them with the herder's own brand (which must be recorded), and in the course of five or eight years there will be a herd of respectable size from this small beginning, so that it will answer to set up a separate ranche. This can be done to much better advantage in Texas than elsewhere; but the Texas cattle bring lower prices in the market than those of the States farther north.

SHEEP-FARMING.

As to the sheep, $14,000 or $15,000 will answer to start a sheep farm if a man understands the business, though a larger sum is better. The profit from raising sheep is sooner realized than from raising cattle, and is nearly as great. A single man with a little money, who will be content to serve as a shepherd for five years, and pasture his own sheep with his employer's flock, can lead out a very respectable flock at the end of that time, but it would be difficult, if not impossible, to support a family in that way before the five years were up. The wages of a herder or a shepherd vary from $18 to $25 a month and keeping; but their lives are very lonely, and the danger to life and limb is considerable.

THE MINING CRAZE.

There is at the present time a great craze in regard to the fortunes to be made in *mining operations*, especially for gold and silver in the West. You will hear every day that Mr. A. or Mr. B., Senator C., or Judge D., or Col. E. has become a millionaire, through the valuable mines in which he has invested. Sometimes you will be told that some of these fortunate men have accumulated five, six, ten, or twenty millions in a very short time. This may be true, or it may not.

HOW GREAT FORTUNES ARE MADE IN MINING OPERATIONS.

If it is true, you may be sure of these three things: First, that these millionaires were men of comfortably large fortunes before they took hold of those great enterprises; that they investigated very thoroughly, and, having their money at command, took advantage of the circumstances, and bought for a small sum what has brought them a large profit. Second, that a great part of their profit has been realized by selling shares in a company which they have formed, putting in a property which cost them perhaps $30,000, as the equivalent for a capital stock of $3,000,000 to $5,000,000. The mine may have been worth five or ten times what they actually paid for it, but most of these concerns are watered prodigiously. Third, that however many millions this fortunate mine-owner may suppose himself to be worth, or make others believe he is worth, it is by no means certain, that within one, two, or three years he may find that he is not worth as much money as he was, when he made his first investment in mining property.

A STRIKING EXAMPLE.

Take an example. Not six months ago Col. C.'s name was in all the papers; he had come to one of the great mining centres with a fair property, most of it in ready money, a year or so before, and had investigated the condition of a newly-opened mine there, had taken an interest in it before it was much developed, had bought other claims on the same lode, till with a trusty partner he owned three fourths of this mine and the adjacent claims. He then organized a company, with a capital of ten millions, and large amounts of the stock were sold; what capital was necessary was used for the full development of the mine, and a smelter purchased and kept running on the ores. For several months the dividends were large; the amount of rich ore smelted was sufficient to justify them, and the stock—of which the par value was $25—rose to $32 or $33. Suddenly it began to fall, and when it reached $13 our capitalist gave orders to sell all his stock; but too late! it continued to sink till it reached $4.50 per share, where it stood a few days ago. The "ore on the dump," that is, the ore which was mined and brought to the surface, was exhausted, and the miners had come to a wall of porphyry, or, as they call it, a "horse," which contained no silver. Expensive explorations were made, and there was some ground for hope, that beyond this wall of stone, there might be another lode or vein which would prove as profitable as the former ones. The capitalist was honest and well-meaning, but when he looks around and sees the wreck of his own property and the property of others who bought the stock from their faith in him, he doubtless wishes he was back where he was two years ago.

MORALS TO THIS STORY.

There are several morals to this story—indirect ones, it is true, but none the less serviceable, if you will only heed them. One is, that it is not all gold that glitters, and that even the shrewdest man who is not practically acquainted with mining, may make a great mistake in purchasing mining property. Another is that you should never be beguiled into buying mining stocks, no matter at what price they may be offered. The par value of these stocks represents from ten to one hundred times the actual cost of the mining property; and even at that, most of them are liable to assessments beyond the original purchase, "to develop the mine."

WHAT SHOULD BE KNOWN BEFORE BUYING MINING PROPERTY.

No! if you *will* put your money into mining property, wait until you can see the property for yourself; until you can learn how much ore has been taken out, what its probable value per ton is, what is the condition of the mine behind "the ore on the dump"—*i.e.*, whether the veins or lodes not yet worked or excavated, promise as rich ore as that already raised—whether there are any obstructions to future success in mining, such as accumulation of water, intense heat of the mine, "horses" in the veins, or barren tracts in the lodes. It is necessary also to know what is the character of the product of the mine: if it is gold, whether it is free milling gold, which needs only to be crushed by the stamps and run over the amalgamated plates to yield up the quarter part of the gold; or whether it is combined with sulphur and copper, or sulphur and zinc, or with lead. Where sulphur is present in the form of sulphides or sulphurets, roasting, and sometimes chlorination or lixiviation, is required to expel the sulphur; and these are costly processes, and will only pay when the ores are rich. If the ores are silver, you should know whether it is combined with lead, zinc, or copper; whether it is a carbonate, a sulphate, a chloride, a telluriate, or a sulphuret of silver, or of silver-bearing lead. Most of the silver ores require smelting, some of them roasting, some chloridinizing, and some lixiviation.

TRANSPORTATION.

At some mines, distant from railroads, and requiring difficult and expensive methods for the complete reduction of their ores, there is a process of concentration carried on which preserves in a kind of base bullion all the valuable portions of the ore, rejecting that which is worthless, and reduces the weight from four fifths to nine tenths, so that they can be transported at much less cost to the works where the silver can be completely reduced and the full value of the lead retained. The questions of transportation and of the proximity of a railroad are, next to the reduction works, of great importance in estimating the value of a mine. If your ore or base bullion has to be packed on the backs of mules over a mountain trail for twenty, thirty, or fifty miles, or if it must be carried one hundred or one hundred and fifty miles in wagons, at $12, $15, or $20 a ton, it must needs be very good ore to pay for the transportation, and yield any profit to the miner; but if it is near a railroad, where the ore can be carried without too much handling, and if it is ore that can be easily or readily reduced or concentrated, ore which will yield from $6 to $10 a ton will pay a handsome profit.

If, then, you will buy an interest in a mine, look it over thoroughly before buying; be sure to "come in on the hard pan," as the miners say, *i.e.*, pay only the first cost of the mine, before they have begun to water the stock, and pay for the mine, only the value of the ore in sight. You cannot be badly defrauded if you do this.

FOLLY OF BUYING AN INTEREST IN A PLACER MINE.

Do not be beguiled into buying an interest in a placer mine, even if it is worked on the hydraulic system. It may pay magnificent dividends for a time, but it is sure to be completely exhausted before long, and will leave no hope of any further profit, unless the tailings can be re-worked by Edison's process, and generally, John Chinaman has already extracted every available grain of gold from them.

PROSPECTING FOR A MINE NOT ADVISABLE.

If you visit the mining districts, you may be tempted to try your hand at prospecting for a new mine. Unless you are an educated mining engineer, please take our advice—which is, in one word, "Don't!" No "tenderfoot" (the mining phrase for *greenhorn*), or, at least, not one in a thousand, has ever tried that with success, certainly not in these later days. You run a much better chance of being struck with lightning, than of discovering a mine worth working, or one which, when found, you could develop without a considerable amount of capital. It is much better to join forces with an honest expert, if you can find such a one, and putting your capital, in part or in whole, against his knowledge, work away together at the mine, till you have developed it sufficiently to be able to command the necessary capital to make it a success.

PURCHASING A PARTLY-DEVELOPED MINE.

There is no lack of good mines, as yet not much developed, in all the Rocky Mountain region, and there is not likely to be, for many years to come. But if you have, by thus joining forces with an expert, found a really good and valuable mine, do not give it away to the capitalists, in return for their establishing smelting works or stamp mills near you. If you have a good thing, hold on to it, and they will come to you for your custom. In some sections, as in the Black Hills, for instance, the large mine owners who have an abundance of capital, make it a rule to buy up every new mine which promises fairly, that they may be able to hold a monopoly of the mining business of that region. Although the ores there are all of low grade, very few of them yielding more than from $6 to $13 a ton, and some not more than $5, yet from the convenience and economy of their reduction works, they are able to make their poor ores pay a better profit, than higher grade ores pay elsewhere.

THE LIFE OF THE PRACTICAL MINER.

Having thus briefly placed before you the difficulties and dangers incident to investments in mining property, let us say a few words concerning the life of the practical miner and his work. By the practical miner we mean here, not, necessarily, the dull, uneducated mining laborer, who pursues his daily task and receives his daily wage, with no thought beyond these, but in many instances the owners of new and undeveloped mines, who, with but moderate means, and with great intelligence and commendable industry, are working diligently, to open a mine and ascertain its real value. In many instances, in Colorada, Montana and Utah, graduates of our great universities, professional men, merchants, mining engineers, master mechanics, and machinists have bent their backs, begrimed their faces, and blistered their hands, at their unaccustomed toil with the pick or shovel, the winch, the pan or the sieve, in washing, amalgamating, digging shafts, opening winzes and tunnels, drawing up and lowering the miner's bucket, and stoping, or opening the veins or lodes, above or below the levels, which they had cut in the rocky ridge in which their principal lode was found.

This is hard work; and it is only the hope of gain sufficient to remunerate these volunteer working-men for their toil, which gives strength to their arms and vigor to their blows. For a long and steady pull, they would have to give place to the sturdy and stolid laborer; but their energy and will power may hold out, till they have sufficient encouragement in their prospects, to warrant their employment of men of greater brawn and muscle, though of less intellectual ability.

HARDSHIPS OF THE IMMIGRANT TO A MINING REGION.

The lot of the immigrant to the mining districts, even if he has a moderate capital at command, is harder, and his condition more uncomfortable, than that of the immigrant who has a farmer's vocation in view. The farmer can have a rude yet comparatively comfortable shelter from sun, wind, and storm reared very soon. His farm is on the prairie or the edge of the forest, and at all events not on broken or rocky ground. He can command generally food sufficient for himself and his family, either from the nearest town, or, if on the extreme frontier, by the use of his rifle or his fishing-rod. Before he realizes anything from his own farm, there is always opportunity for earning good wages by working for his neighbors.

But the immigrant to the mining regions finds them invariably in a rough and broken country; and if he seeks a place anywhere in the Rocky Mountain ranges, especially on their western slopes, which are richest in gold and silver, he will soon discover that he has come upon a region, which has hardly a parallel on the earth's surface in the boldness of its cliffs, the ruggedness of its precipices, the depth and gloominess of its cañons, and the wonderful character of its eroded and water-worn rocks and caverns. Sharp, treeless ridges, upheaved by earthquakes or displaced by volcanic action, are the most frequent localities of the larger fissure veins and lodes.

A MINING VENTURE.

If, then, you determine to try your fortune in mining operations, having located a promising claim by the assistance of such an honest and capable expert as we have spoken of, who becomes your partner on "the grub stake plan," as it is called in the mining region, you furnishing the necessary money and provisions (mostly canned meats, fish, and vegetables) against his experienced mining knowledge and skill, in both directing and working personally, you may as well go to work yourself with him, and with what other mining laborers you can find means to employ, for the sooner your lode is partially developed, the sooner you will be likely to receive a return for your money invested. You have found a lode not already claimed, and you and your partner have made such examination and assay as to satisfy you that it probably contains paying ore.

STAKING OFF YOUR CLAIM.

Your first business is to stake off your claim. By the United States mining laws, unless restricted by local laws, as they sometimes are, you can claim 1500 feet in length upon the line of the lode, and a width of 300 feet on each side of it, making a tract of 1500 by 600 feet, unless this extends into other claims previously made. This is about 20¼ acres. To make sure of the course and dip of your fissure vein, you should run a tunnel or drift into it or sink a shaft of small size before recording it.* Next you stake this off and have it recorded within twenty days at the district Register's office, describing it by its metes and bounds, in connection with some prominent natural object, stating also the precise extent of your claim, and whether it is taken on one or both sides of the point of discovery of the existence of the lode, and obtain your certificate of location. At the same time, or if possible before recording it, you should post on your claim a notice of its extent, the names of the locators, the number of feet claimed,

* This is important, as the Government now refuses to admit a claim which has not been thus explored.

and the direction from the point of discovery shaft. The bounds of the claim must be defined by good sized posts of wood or stone, set at suitable distance from each other.

HOW TO ENTER SEVERAL CLAIMS.

If several others are associated with you, you can, if you choose, claim a similar tract of 1500 feet by 600 feet for each person, not exceeding eight in all, having, however, made exploration by a discovery shaft tunnel or drift on each plat, and having staked it off and posted a notice of it at the discovery shaft, giving all the particulars already specified for each plat. But these several plats must not run into any other claim, and each must have in its central line a well defined lode or vein—and all these particulars must be given for each plat in the application for a recorder's certificate. The fees for this filing are five dollars each to the Register and Receiver for each plat.

HOLDING POSSESSION.

In order to hold possession of these mining plats it is required that until the patent is issued—which may not be under one, two, or three years—the locator or locators must perform work, or make improvements on each plat, to the value of not less than one hundred dollars each year. It may happen that the lode or vein dips at such an angle as to come outside of the claim on one side or the other, at a depth which is not too great to be worked; where this is the case the locator or his grantors and legal successors can claim this vein, between the vertical lines of 1500 feet (the extent of the claim), although these lines may be extended beyond the three hundred feet limit on either side.

BLIND LODES AND TUNNELLING CLAIMS.

If in tunnelling their lode the owners of a claim come upon blind lodes, *i.e.*, those not appearing at the surface, extending at a greater or less angle from the original lode, and not previously known to exist, they have a right to tunnel these blind lodes to an extent not exceeding 3000 feet, though they must be worked with reasonable diligence, and a failure to work them for six months is considered an abandonment of them. If they are worked continuously, no surface claimant of the land beyond the limits of the 300 feet and within 3000 feet of their commencement can make a valid claim to the surface under which they run. These are called tunnel rights.

CONTESTING CLAIMS.

Where a contesting claim is brought against an original one, the law requires that both parties should file a survey, which must be endorsed by the Surveyor General, and the Register publishes a full notice of both claims, at the expense of the claimants, for sixty days in some newspaper published nearest the claim.

MAKING PAYMENT FOR THE CLAIM.

Or if there is no adverse claimant, the publication may be made for the protection of the title of the original claimant, who at the end of the sixty days files his affidavit showing the posting of the claim during the sixty days, and that he has complied with the other requirements of the law, and asks for his patent, paying to the Receiver, in addition to the other fees, five dollars for each acre and five dollars for each fraction of an acre in his claim. Thus in the case of a single claim the payment will be for the twenty and four-seventh acres, one hundred and five dollars. The Receiver issues the usual duplicate receipt for this money and forwards all the papers to the General Land Office at Washington, where a patent for the land is issued if it is found regular.

PROSECUTING AN ADVERSE CLAIM.

If there is an adverse claimant who persists in his claim, after the sixty days' publication the Receiver gives notice in writing to both parties, requiring the adverse claimant to proceed within thirty days to prosecute his claim before a court of competent jurisdiction, and if he fails to do so within that time, it will be considered waived, and the application of the original claimant for a patent will be allowed to proceed on its merits.

These are all the provisions of the law in regard to lode or vein mining, and they apply as well to the newly discovered form of deposits known as contact lodes, except so far as "tunnel rights" are concerned.

PLACER MINING UNCERTAIN.

Placer mining comes under different provisions, but as we cannot advise you to invest in placer mining on account of its uncertainty, it is hardly worth while to specify the lengthy provisions of the law in regard to it.

WORKING THE CLAIM.

Now, then, your claim to your mine being reasonably secured, you have time to find out what value there is to it, present or prospective. Here come in your uncertainties and perplexities. It may prove a fortune for you, and then again it may not. The chance is perhaps about one in five that if your prospector was skillful, you have a good thing.

THE DISCOUNT NECESSARY ON THE ASSAY.

If it is a true fissure vein, and the dip is at such an angle that it can be worked without too much expense, it may prove profitable; but you must not suppose that because the lode at or near the surface yields on assay (if it is gold) eighty or a hundred dollars to the ton of ore or gangue, that you will be able to realize that amount per ton from it in practically working the vein. Even if it proved as rich at a greater depth as at the surface, which is not probable, as the productiveness usually diminishes to some extent as you penetrate deeper, the assay must be reduced at least twenty-five per cent. to estimate the actual working product.

"POCKETS" AND "CHIMNEYS" *vs.* "HORSES."

There may be "pockets" and "chimneys," spurs from the main vein, of exceptional richness yielding three, four or five hundred dollars or more per ton; but these are rare; while the occurrence of "horses" or boulders of porphyry or quartz, entirely barren of gold, blocking the vein for some feet, are far more frequent, and tracts of barren rock in the vein, extending for a hundred feet or more, are not uncommon.

LOW GRADE ORES SOMETIMES PROFITABLE.

There are very few gold veins in the whole mining region whose average yield is as much as forty dollars to the ton; hundreds of veins are worked and yield a good profit under favorable circumstances where the yield does not exceed from six to thirteen dollars per ton. If your gold mine has a stamp mill near at hand, and you can transport your ore or quartz there without too heavy expense, and the gold is what is known as free milling gold, that is, pure or nearly pure gold in the quartz, and not a sulphuret, or other combination which requires, for its reduction, roasting or chloridinizing or lixiviation (all expensive processes), you have no reason to be discouraged if it does not yield over $15 or $20 to the ton.

CONTACT LODES.

But it is possible that, instead of a fissure vein, you have a contact lode. You do not know what that is? Very probably; but we will tell you. It is a newly-discovered form of mineral deposit, so far as we yet know confined to silver-bearing lead ores, in which, however, there may be some gold in combination with the silver and lead. These contact lodes were first discovered in the vicinity of Leadville, where their character was not for a long time understood; but they have since been found in other localities on the western slope of the Rocky Mountains, in Colorado, and elsewhere, and it is possible that some of the mines in the Black Hills, may prove to be of the same character. In the fissure veins or lodes the gold or silver (oftenest the gold) was found mixed with quartz and other broken down rock between walls of porphyry or other hard rock. These veins, and the fissure which they fill, may incline at any direction, but they are generally very narrow, varying from two or three inches, or even less, to perhaps, at the widest, four or five feet. When, therefore, the carbonate of silver deposits in the vicinity of Leadville began to uncover to a width of forty, fifty, and finally one hundred and even one hundred and fifty feet, people wondered at the tremendous dimensions of this vast fissure vein, and were ready to think they had hit upon the mother-vein of the Rocky Mountains. After a time, however, they began to find that, though so very broad, these deposits were not very thick; that, while the true fissure veins penetrated for an unknown distance into the earth, the miner in these, going down vertically, soon came to entirely barren rock. Penetrating through this, he might come to another layer of silver ore, or he might not.

WHAT CONTACT LODES ARE.

It was a considerable time after these discoveries were made before their real significance was understood. They are layers or strata of the argentiferous carbonate of lead, interposed between the strata of rock, sandstone, limestone, slate, hornblende, gneiss, or granite, as the case may be, and they may extend to the right or left indefinitely, thinning out in some places and thicker in others; but their vertical thickness is not very great. In some instances, on penetrating through the underlying stratum of rock, one, and we believe, in one instance two, similar deposits were found between lower strata. The name given to these deposits—contact lodes—expresses their character very well, for they are in contact with the strata above and below them.

THESE CONTACT LODES NO RICHER THAN THE FISSURE VEINS.

You are not to suppose that these deposits are entirely of pure ore, or indeed that they contain any larger proportion of pure silver or lead than the deposits contained in fissure veins. The average yield of silver and lead from the mines in the vicinity of Leadville is from $50 to $75 to the ton. A few have exceeded this for a time, but the yield of larger amounts, as of $200 to $350 per ton, has very soon fallen off.

COSTLY REDUCTION WORKS NECESSARY.

Like all silver mining, this cannot be carried on successfully without costly reduction works, smelters, or works for roasting, chloridinization, lixiviation, etc. These, if owned by other parties than the owners of the mines, generally absorb the largest share of the profits, and in the end often become the proprietors of the mine, if it is a good one.

LARGE CAPITAL NECESSARY FOR SILVER MINING.

The point where the small mining proprietor begins to lose ground, and make losses instead of profits, is the one where he finds that more capital is indispensable for the development of his mine, and, in order to secure that capital, parts with a controlling interest in it, and soon is crowded out by his wealthier associates, who take advantage of his toil and sacrifices, without making him any adequate return for them.

There are not to-day a dozen mines in all the West which are in the hands of their original discoverers or owners.

MINING IN THE SMALL WAY IN ARIZONA.

In Arizona, to those who are disposed to brave the climate, and the often protracted drought, and the isolation from the great centres of life and civilization, there are good opportunities for mining, even on a small scale. The lodes, both of gold and silver, are exceptionally rich, and even the simplest and rudest processes yield large returns. In no other region among civilized nations can a farmer do as General Frémont says many of the Arizona farmers are in the habit of doing—viz.: having found a gold mine upon their farms, which they have not the means of working on a large scale, they pursue their ordinary farm-work, and, when a leisure day comes, dig a quantity of gold ore from the vein, pound it up in a wooden or stone mortar with a log pestle, wash it in an old tin pan, or pick out the gold if it is in large grains, or amalgamate it if it is in small scales or powder, after the rude Mexican way, and then expel the mercury by heat. At the next market-day, with their other produce, they bring their bag of gold dust and sell it, repeating the process when spending money runs low. This method of mining is rather wasteful, as much of the gold is lost; but there is more money made by it there than in many of the mines by more expensive processes.

The vein and lodes in Arizona are so rich in gold and silver that there is a much better opportunity for men of small means to unite together and reduce the ores in a small way and with inexpensive apparatus, and obtain large profits, than anywhere else.*

THE MINING OF OTHER MINERALS.

But gold and silver are not the only minerals to be mined in this Western country, nor the only minerals which will yield a large profit. The production of gold and silver in the United States amounts to from eighty to ninety million dollars a year, and in the coming years will undoubtedly exceed one hundred millions; but it constitutes only about one twelfth of the entire mineral production of the country. The coal mines yield a much larger annual amount than the mines of gold and silver—at least three, and perhaps four, times as much. Copper, lead, and zinc are produced annually to the amount of more than one hundred millions, while iron and steel, the latter now made directly from the ore, exceed two hundred millions. The other mineral products, such as petroleum, salt, plaster of Paris, cement, sulphur, borax, nitrates and carbonates of soda and potassa, etc., etc., make up another large sum. The production and marketing of some of these minerals will yield a more certain, and in the end, a larger profit than most of the gold and silver mining.

PETROLEUM AND COAL.

Petroleum and coal production, in particular (the former found in great abundance in Wyoming Territory and in California, and probably in some of the other States and Territories, and the latter in many parts of the West),†

* There is, however, a strong probability that the marked tendency, which is now manifested, to invent or discover processes by which the severe labor and large expense now incurred in the reduction of gold and silver ores may be materially lessened, will not prove unavailing in other regions than Arizona. The recent invention of Mr. Edison by which the tailings from the stamp mills and amalgamated plates may be made to yield up a large percentage of gold hitherto lost, and another process, even more successful, now about to be brought to public notice, gives us great reason to hope that we are about to see cheap *gold* mining at least.

† The coal-beds west of the Mississippi are of all known qualities, and are valuable for fuels, for gas-making, for smelting, and the production of iron and steel. Many of them are geologically lignite, or coals of the tertiary formation; but in New Mexico, and perhaps at other points, we have a phenomenon which is not know to exist elsewhere on the globe—viz: these soft, lignite, bituminous coals transformed into anthracite by volcanic action.

are industrious, which cannot fail to prove profitable and to be largely developed within the next five or ten years. The production of copper and lead is already very large, and it is not necessary now to send the ores of the former to Europe to be smelted.

SALT, BORAX, AND SULPHUR.

Salt, a prime necessity of human life, and used extensively in mining processes and in meat packing, is found in all forms: by evaporation at the salt lakes and on the ocean shores, by boiling and solar evaporation from brine springs, and by mining in the numerous deposits of rock-salt. Borax (bi-borate of soda) is found as a natural product in California and Nevada, in such quantities, that its gathering and exportation is a large and growing business. The alkaline plains yield at certain points carbonates and nitrates of soda and potassa (cooking-soda, saleratus, saltpetre, etc.) in large quantities, and nearly chemically pure sulphur is very abundant in California, Nevada, and Utah, and can be exported with great profit. An industry in which there is not too much competition is much more certain to yield success than one of greater promise into which thousands are rushing.

THE ARTISAN IN THE WEST.

But it may be tha you have no fancy for mining or the exploiting of mineral products. You have not been brought up on a farm, nor been accustomed to the rearing of live stock. You have a good trade, and are skilful in it, and you have been accustomed from boyhood to the care of a garden, and to the cultivation of vegetables, fruit trees, and flowers; but your present quarters are too contracted for any considerable indulgence of your tastes. You have, moreover, a great desire to go West. What shall you do? Go, by all means, friend. You will find abundant employment, and a good opportunity to acquire a competence. You may have to rough it at first, but in a short time you will find yourself in a position of comfort.

WHAT CALLINGS ARE MOST SUCCESSFUL.

If your calling is one of the indispensable ones—builder, mason, plasterer, painter, glazier, paper-hanger, blacksmith, butcher, baker, hatter and furrier, or perhaps tanner, shoemaker, harness-maker, brick-maker, watchmaker and jeweller, bookbinder, stationer and news-dealer, miller, saw-mill tender, tinman, roofer, etc., etc.—you will find plenty of work in any of the new mining towns or farming villages, and at good prices; but take our advice: secure, before it is too high, a forty-acre lot of good land in the immediate vicinity, have it broken up, build a house on it, small at first, but so it can be enlarged easily. Sow your land to wheat or root crops, and you can sell this crop at home, with but little trouble, and add a comfortable amount to your income. Then plant young trees—shade trees, fruit trees of well-known and choice varieties—and devote your spare moments and hours to them; plant eight or ten acres, as soon as you can, with all the vegetables and truck which go to make up a market garden, and you will soon find that however profitable your trade may be, your market garden brings in twice as much; and your nursery of young trees will soon be thronged with purchasers. If you have children who are growing up, add flowers, build a greenhouse, and as fast as you can learn the art of floral cultivation, work into the florist's business.

NURSERIES, MARKET GARDENS, AND GREENHOUSES.

If work at your trade is dull, push your flowers, your market garden, your nursery, the more; if work is brisk, train your children to attend to this, giving them your oversight as often as you can.

Following up this course, you need not break your heart if your neighbor A, who is a mine owner, finds a pocket in his mine which yields him many thousand dollars; or if your neighbor B sells out his shares for fifty or a hundred thousand dollars more than they cost him. You are adding to the earth's production; you are making two blades of grass grow where only one grew before, or a hundred trees where none grew previously; your neighbor who speculates in shares produces nothing; he only gambles on what others have produced. You may acquire property more slowly than he, but your course is sure and safe, and the chances are that ten years hence, you will be much the richer man of the two, though he may have won and lost a dozen fortunes in that time.

THE TEACHER AT THE WEST.

If you are a teacher, and would better your condition by emigrating to the West, our advice would be much the same. Good teachers are always in demand, even in the newest towns. The Yankee must have a school-house, and, generally, a church too, in his new village, quite as soon as a house for himself; the school-house, at all events, is sure to come very soon, whatever the nationality of the settlers of the town. But while you are teaching the young idea how to shoot, teach the shrubs, the young trees, and the flowers and vegetables to put forth their shoots too. Secure your forty acres as near to the town as possible, and make and keep it productive. Then, when teaching becomes a drudgery, and you desire to be relieved from its cares, you will have a valuable property, and a profitable business to make your declining years comfortable. Keep bees, if you can, or pigeons or poultry, rabbits or hares, or pet birds, anything except cats and curdogs. Teach your children botany and natural history, and lead their minds up from the beautiful flowers to Him who painted them with His sunbeams, and from the wise and curious animals, so well adapted to their modes of living, to Him whose omniscience guides all the actions of His creatures, and whose providence provides for their needs.

PROFESSIONAL MEN, CLERGYMEN.

The members of the several learned professions hardly need our advice in regard to emigration. Clergymen, in the exercise of their clerical duties, will find their positions at first trying, because of the present poverty of most of the settlers. When a man has expended all his means in paying for his land and its first cultivation, and the food which his family must consume before he realizes on his first crop, he cannot aid in supporting a minister, however strong may be his desire to do so. Moreover, these new immigrants must aid in building a church edifice of some kind, as well as in supporting a pastor, and this, while still straitened in regard to their own means living. After a few years this will be easy, but meantime they cannot with safety dispense with the church or clergyman. If the clergyman has any spare money he will do well to buy some land, or at least to secure the title of it to himself; it may be very convenient by and by. In most instances the Home Missionary Societies, of the different denominations, in the East will grant aid to deserving churches and ministers, till the churches are able to stand alone.

LAWYERS AND PHYSICIANS.

Lawyers and physicians are plenty enough, but they fare rather better than clergymen. The lawyers find a great deal of business in the abundant litigation in the mining districts and in conveyancing, and most of them have an additional resource in politics, which sooner or later bring them into official positions. The physicians, beside their professional duties, are mostly either chemists, metallurgists, or botanists, and find employment which is profitable, either in connection with some of the mining, assaying or smelting companies, or in a professor's chair.

ENGINEERS AND ARTISTS.

Engineers are sure of constant employment, whether mining or civil engineers, if they understand their business.

Artists generally come as visitors, not immigrants, but are often employed by the wealthy mine owners very profitably.

OPERATVES AND EMPLOYES IN FACTORIES, ETC.

Employés and operatives in manufactories may find employment in some kinds of manufacture in the States nearest the Mississippi, for there is a large amount of manufacturing in Minnesota, Iowa, Missouri, Nebraska, and Kansas, and manufactures are increasing in Arkansas, Louisiana, and Texas. There is some opportunity for millers, saw-mill hands, sash, door and blind makers, coopers, agricultural machinery hands, iron and steel rail makers, iron furnace and foundry hands, stove and hollow ware founders and finishers, smelters, and in California and Oregon, salmon packers and a few woollen factory hands. In Kansas, Arkansas and Texas there are some cotton factories, and many oil mills for expressing cotton-seed oil, castor oil, linseed oil, etc.

COTTON AND WOOLLEN FACTORIES.

The factories for manufacturing cotton and wool are likely to increase largely within a few years. A machine has been invented, and is now in use to some extent, for spinning cotton with the seed in it, unginned, and the yarn is much better and more beautiful and durable than can be produced from ginned cotton. The yarn produced by these machines is destined to be manufactured largely in the vicinity of the cotton fields, and will thus create a home demand for cotton. Wool is now produced so largely throughout this whole region, that much saving of freight will result from its manufacture near the centres of wool production. When this is accomplished, the operatives from Eastern cotton and woollen factories will find it for their interest to emigrate westward.

IS IT NECESSARY TO GO WEST?

But, after all, is it not barely possible that there are lands east of the Mississippi, where, all things being taken into the account, a man or family can live as well and make as much money as in the West, and at the same time avoid the hardships and discomforts of a life on the frontier?

There is the same choice of occupations here as at the West. Land is not quite so low, generally, but on the other hand you avoid the long and expensive journey to the West. The agricultural production, under favorable circumstances, does not differ materially; but there prices are low and the cost of transportation to a better and higher market is very heavy, while here you have a market almost at your doors, and that, one which pays the highest price for produce. If there is a difference, as there certainly is in some sections, the Eastern climate is healthier, neither the heat nor the cold so oppressive, the rainfall sufficient to prevent any apprehension of a drought, the insect pests much less formidable, and the danger from malarial fevers less serious. The intensity of the cold of winter is greater in the northern tier of States and Territories of the West than in the middle Atlantic States, and the heat of the south-western States and Territories in summer, has no parallel in the East.

WHERE THE NEW LANDS ARE—MAINE AND NEW ENGLAND GENERALLY.

"But where," you will ask, "are these lands, to which you refer in the Atlantic States, and how can we reach them?" We answer, Not perhaps in Maine, though there is much good land in the State which is to be had at from three to five dollars per acre; but it is, for the most part, somewhat remote from good markets, and the winter's cold is severe and protracted. Yet if you wish to engage in silver or copper mining there is a very fair opportunity for doing so in Maine, and with perhaps as good results as most men will attain at the West, and with lighter expenses.

Northern New Hampshire and Vermont have some good lands to be purchased at low prices, but the winters are hard and the soil rocky. Massachusetts, Connecticut, and Rhode Island are too densely populated to have much cheap land. Still there are old farms to be bought very low in the two former states, which need only the energy of a thorough farmer, to bring them into a thrifty condition and to make them yield very profitable crops. There are more or less mines and quarries in all three, which would pay well if well managed.

NEW YORK—NORTHERN NEW YORK.

New York has two large tracts of land and several smaller ones which, all things considered, are as favorably situated for profitable settlement as most of the Western lands. These are, first, the region known as "the Adirondacks," "John Brown's Tract," etc., in Northern New York. The country is well watered, the soil is mostly a virgin soil, with considerable timber of excellent quality on it, and will yield large crops of spring wheat, rye, and barley, the early sorghum, and in some sections Indian corn. The land can be purchased for from two to five dollars per acre, except where there is heavy timber on it, when it would probably be worth from eight to ten dollars. It is not at present traversed by any railroads, but these would soon be constructed if settlements were made there. The winter is very cold, but so it is in the valley of the Red River of the North. Wheat, rye, oats, and barley, as well as potatoes and other root crops for which it is well adapted, can be brought to market at a moderate expense, and the prices they will command are much higher than those paid in the West.

LONG ISLAND.

The second region which is eligible for settlement in New York, is on Long Island, and mainly in Suffolk County. It seems almost incredible that half a million of acres of land lying between thirty-five and ninety miles from New York City, the best and most inexhaustible market in the world, with a good soil, a very healthful climate, well watered, and having a sufficient but not excessive annual rainfall, should lie unimproved, and be at the present time for sale at from five to twelve dollars per acre. And the wonder is all the greater, when we find that a railroad passes through the whole length of this tract, with several branches, and that no part of it is more than twelve miles from the railroad, and much of it within from one to five miles of it, and that this railroad is now offering every facility to farmers, to transport their produce to market, and to bring from the city the needed fertilizers. The shores of the island abound in the best qualities of edible fish, oysters, clams, mussels, scollops, lobsters, crabs, etc., and the game birds and four-footed game of the whole region are abundant. On the island are forty factories for the production of oil from the menhaden, and the fish-scrap, or guano, one of the best fertilizers known, is now sent away from the island, because there is little or no demand for it there.

WHY IT HAS NOT BEEN SETTLED HITHERTO.

The only causes which can be assigned for the non-settlement of these lands, are the apathy of the inhabitants, and their lack of enterprise, and the evil report which has been made, falsely, of the barrenness of the lands, by those who preferred to supply themselves with wood from these lands, rather than to have them cultivated and populous, and be obliged to purchase coal for fuel. This state of affairs is now passing away.

ITS ADVANTAGES.

The land can be cleared at from five to ten dollars per acre, some of the timber being large enough for building purposes or for railroad ties. It will yield from twenty-five to thirty-five bushels of wheat or from twenty to twenty-eight bushels of rye to the acre, from two hundred and fifty to three hundred and fifty bushels of potatoes of the best quality, and with good cultivation and fair manuring, the whole region can be transformed into market gardens, fruit orchards, and strawberry, blackberry, and raspberry lands of the greatest productiveness, and for all these products there is an unfailing demand at the highest prices, in New York and Brooklyn and the cities adjacent.

MARKET-GARDEN FARMING MORE PROFITABLE HERE THAN AT THE WEST.

With the same capital, a young farmer, who is intelligent and enterprising, can do better on these lands, than he can in Kansas, Minnesota, Dakota, or Montana, and can be so conveniently situated to the great city that he or his family can visit it as often as they please. The great summer resorts of Cony Island, Rockaway Beach, Long Beach, Fire Island, and Montauk, which are visited by nearly two millions of people every season, afford additional markets for produce. The island affords also great opportunities for successful manufacturing. The great city of Brooklyn at its western extremity, has more than 250 millions of dollars invested in manufacturing, and there is now rapid progress in the establishment of manufactories in the counties of Queens and Suffolk.

NOT ADAPTED TO MINING.

There are not, at present, any known mineral deposits of great value on the island, whatever there may be in the future. The man whose heart is set on obtaining wealth from mining, will do better to go elsewhere; but even he need not go to the Rocky Mountains or the Pacific coast to find employment suited to his tastes, as we shall presently show.

NEW JERSEY.

If "Long Island's rock-bound shore" does not satisfy your longings for a new home, what have you to say to New Jersey?

Just listen to a few facts in relation to the lands which can be furnished to immigrants in that State. These facts are officially published, during the present year, by the Secretary of the Bureau of Statistics of Labor and Industry of New Jersey.

A MILLION ACRES.

There are more than a million of acres of uncleared lands in the eight southern counties of New Jersey, which can be purchased at from $5 to $20 per acre. They have been held by large proprietors, and most of them have their titles direct from the "Lords Proprietors," Penn, Fenwick, Byllinge, and others, who received their grants from Charles II. These great proprietors held their estates of from 17,000 to 80,000 acres of woodlands, and increased their fortunes by selling wood, timber and charcoal to the forges, iron furnaces, and glass-works of the vicinity. These great estates are now broken up, and the use of anthracite and other coals for the furnaces and glass-works, and for fuel, has rendered their former business less productive.

THE SOIL AND CLIMATE—FERTILIZERS.

The soil of these lands is good, a light loam, but easily cultivated; it can be readily fertilized by the use of marl, which is abundant in the immediate vicinity, and is worth from $1 to $1.75 per ton; lime, which is worth from twelve to fifteen cents a bushel; or fish guano, which is a very powerful manure, worth from $15 to $18 per ton. It will produce almost any crop which you may desire to cultivate, and yields fine crops of the cereals and Indian corn (thirty to sixty bushels of the latter), root crops, melons, market-garden vegetables of excellent quality, fruit of great excellence, and all the small fruits. Railroads traverse all these counties, and both New York and Philadelphia furnish excellent markets.

The climate is very mild, the mean annual range of the thermometer being only 43½° and the extremes being about 90° and 15° F.

RAINFALL, GRAPE CULTURE, MANUFACTURES, ETC.

The rainfall is about 48 inches. Ploughing can be done every month in the year. The culture of the grape is a favorite industry, and the grape attains great perfection from the long season without frost. The region is remarkably healthy and free from all malarious influences. It is especially commended for sufferers from pulmonary complaints.

Here are glass-works, silk factories, iron mines, artificial-stone works, iron furnaces, and a great variety of other manufacturing and mining industries.

WEST VIRGINIA.

If, however, you still prefer a country abounding in mineral wealth, turn your face westward or rather south-westward, and you will find in West Virginia, western North Carolina, or east Tennessee all that your heart can desire in the way of mineral wealth. In West Virginia the most abundant minerals are petroleum, salt, coal, and iron, and all are found in the greatest abundance. The salt springs along the banks of the Great Kanawha yield a salt of the very best quality. The petroleum wells yield mostly the heavy lubricating oils, though some of them produce the lighter illuminating oils. The quantity seems to be inexhaustible. The coal is of several varieties, but all of excellent quality. There are cannel coals, gas coals, smelting coals, analogous to the Indiana block coal, and some semi-anthracite coals for fuel. At some points in the cañon of New River and elsewhere, the best iron ores and furnace coals are in such close proximity, that the pig iron can be produced at the lowest possible cost, lime and other fluxes being also at hand, and the cars of the Chesapeake and Ohio Railway passing close at hand to carry it away. The climate is salubrious and pleasant, except on the mountain summits, where the snow lies long. The mountain slopes are covered with valuable timber, furnishing the principal supply of black walnut and other hard woods to the manufacturers of furniture. The soil in the valleys is excellent, the rainfall sufficient, and the crops satisfactory. Land is cheap here, but the settler, though nearer the great markets than at the West, is very much isolated.

NORTH CAROLINA,

In her mountainous region, in the west of the State, has veins of gold and silver, which, though not very rich, yield a fair competence to the industrious miner. She has also mountains of mica, from which the best large sheets are procured; and some iron and lead. The soil is not very rich, and the method of tilling it is primitive. There is much timber in the mountains. The climate is agreeable, and there are valuable mineral springs at several points. Land is held at low prices, but its quality is not such as to make it very desirable.

EAST TENNESSEE.

East Tennessee has valuable iron mines, copper mines, and coal-beds, and at several points is largely engaged in the production of iron which is of excellent quality. There is also gold, salt, and some petroleum in her hills. Much of her land is covered with heavy timber. Land is cheap, but the soil is poor, and requires fertilizers to enable the settler to procure good crops. But the mineral wealth of the region will eventually enrich it. Northern Georgia and Alabama have considerable quantities of gold and silver, but the ores are poor, or the precious metals have not been thoroughly extracted. These regions are not very attractive to the emigrant.

FLORIDA.

Florida offers many advantages to the settler in her fine climate, her generally fertile soil, and her early seasons. The cultivation of the orange has been greatly developed there, and is profitable to those who can wait for the maturity of the orange groves. This takes about ten years, and then the income is permanent and constantly increasing. Some parts of the peninsula are subject to malarial diseases.

THE MORAL.

The moral of our long dissertation is, that with health, industry, enterprise, and economy a man can achieve a competence almost anywhere; without them, he will not succeed, even under the most favorable circumstances.

"ONE HUNDRED YEARS AGO."

HISTORICAL CHRONOLOGY OF THE UNITED STATES.

1761.

Excitement in the colonies against the British Government, caused by enforcement of Navigation Act against illegal traders.

1765.

Protests against Stamp Act (passed March 22) by the colonists, who object to taxation without representation ....Oct. 7—First Colonial Congress met in New York.

1766.

Stamp Act repealed.

1767.

New duties levied on glass, paper, printers' colors and tea, and against which the colonial assemblies protest.

1768.

Gen. Gates sent to Boston to overawe the colonists.

1770.

March 5—Boston Massacre, when the first blood was spilt in the dispute with England....Daniel Boone explores Kentucky.

1771.

Armed protest against taxation in the Carolinas, and Governor Tyron suppresses the rebellion.

1773.

British Parliament repeals the duties, except threepence a pound on tea....Dec. 16—Dutiable tea emptied into Boston Harbor by men in disguise.

1774.

Boston closed by British Parliament as a port of entry. ....Sept. 5—The first Continental Congress assembled in Carpenter's Hall, Philadelphia....Declaration of Colonial Rights issued....April—Tea thrown overboard in New York Harbor....Dec. 25—British tea ship forbidden to land at Philadelphia.

1775.

April 19—Battle of Lexington, Mass., and beginning of the War of Independence....May 10—Fort Ticonderoga captured by Col. Ethan Allen....Crown Point and Whitehall taken....June 17—Battle of Bunker Hill, and death of General Warren....20—George Washington commissioned Commander-in-chief of the Army of the United Colonies....Bills of credit, known as Continental money, issued by Congress....Americans invade Canada....Surrender of Montreal....Death of General Montgomery before Quebec....Kentucky first settled by whites, near Lexington.

1776.

March 17—The British evacuate Boston....Americans driven out of Canada....July 4—Declaration of Independence. Aug. 2—Signed by the representatives of the thirteen States....July 8—Read to the people by John Nixon from the Observatory, State-house yard, Philadelphia....Aug. 27—Americans defeated on Long Island ....Sept. 9—Title of "United States" adopted by Congress ....Sept. 15—New York City taken by the British ...Oct. 11, 12—Battle on Lake Champlain....Retreat of Washington over the Hudson and across the Jerseys to Pennsylvania....Oct. 18—Kosciusko commissioned an officer in U. S. army....Oct. 29—Battle of White Plains, N. Y.... Dec.—Congress adjourns to Baltimore....25—Washington crosses the Delaware; 26—Captures 1.000 Hessians at Trenton, and recrosses the Delaware....Dec.—Benjamin Franklin and Arthur Lee, U. S. Embassy to solicit aid from France, arrive in Paris.

1777.

Jan. 3—Battle of Princeton....Washington in Winter quarters at Morristown, receives 24,000 muskets from France....Congress returns to Philadelphia....April—British burn Danbury, Ct....May—Americans destroy British stores at Sag Harbor, L. I....June 30—British army crosses from Jersey to Staten Island....July 10—Seizure of British Gen. Prescott in Rhode Island by Col. Wm. Barton....July 5—Burgoyne takes Crown Point and Ticonderoga....31—Lafayette commissioned a major-general, and introduced to Washington in Philadelphia, Aug. 3....Aug. 16—Battle of Bennington....Sept. 11—Battle of Brandywine and retreat of Americans to Chester, and to Philadelphia 12....Sept. 18—Congress retires to Lancaster, and then to York....26—British Gen. Howe marches to Philadelphia, and encamps at Germantown....Oct. 4—Washington attacks the enemy at Germantown....Burgoyne advances to Saratoga....17—Surrender of Burgoyne and his whole army to Gen. Gates, at Saratoga, N. Y....22—Battle of Red Bank, on Delaware River, and death of Count Donop....Howe's army goes into Winter quarters in Philadelphia, and Washington's at Valley Forge.

1778.

Feb. 6—Treaty of alliance with France....May 5—Baron Steuben created a major-general in American army.... June 18—Howe's army evacuates Philadelphia, and retreats towards New York... 28—Attacked by Americans on the plains of Monmouth, and retreats again 29....July 8—A French fleet arrives in the Delaware....30—Congress meets in Philadelphia....Shoes worth $700 a pair in the Carolinas....Aug. 12—French and English fleets disabled in a storm off Rhode Island....29—Battle of Rhode Island....Wyoming Valley pillaged by Tories and Indians....Nov. 3—French fleet sails for West Indies.... 11, 12—Cherry Valley attacked by Indians and Tories.... Dec. 29—The British capture Savannah, Ga.

1779

March—Major-general Israel Putnam's famous ride down Horseneck Hill....May 11—British advance to Charleston, S. C., but retreat at the approach of Gen. Lincoln....June 6—Patrick Henry dies....June—Norfolk, Va., burnt by the British....June 20—Americans repulsed at Stone Ferry....July—New Haven, Ct., plundered, and East Haven, Fairfield and Norwalk burned... Stony Point, on the Hudson, captured by the Americans.... Sept. 22—Paul Jones, in the Bon Homme Richard, captures the British ship Serapis....Oct. 9—Repulse of French and Americans, and death of Count Pulaski.... 25—Withdrawal of British troops from Rhode Island.... Gen. Sullivan chastises the Six Nations....Dec. 25—Sir Henry Clinton, with his forces, sails for the South.... Washington in Winter quarters at Morristown, N. J.

1780.

Washington sends Baron DeKalb to aid the Patriots in the Carolinas....Feb. 11—Clinton's troops land below Charleston....May 12—Surrender of Charleston....Subjugation of South Carolina....Gen. Gates marches South and is defeated by the British at Camden, S. C., Aug. 16; Baron DeKalb killed....British again land in Jersey, and attempt to capture Washington's stores at Morristown, but are repulsed at Springfield, June 23....July 10—Arrival of a French fleet and 6,000 troops, under the Count de Rochambeau, at Newport, R. I....Sept. 22—Arnold meets Andre at Haverstraw to arrange for the surrender of West Point....23—Capture of Major Andre and discovery of Benedict Arnold's treason.....Oct.—Andre hanged as a spy....American Academy of Arts and Sciences at Boston founded.

1781.

Continental money almost worthless....Jan. 17—Defeat of the British at Cowpens by Gen. Morgan, and retreat of the Americans into Virginia....March 15—Battle of Guilford....Retreat of the British to Wilmington....May 26—Act of Congress authorizing Bank of North America to be established at Philadelphia....Battle of Eutaw Springs, South Carolina....New London, Ct., burnt by the British....Arnold, in the British service, commits depredations in Virginia....Aug.—Cornwallis fortifies himself at Yorktown....Arnold devastates the New England coast....Sept. 28—Washington and Rochambeau arrive before Yorktown....Oct. 19—Surrender of Cornwallis at Yorktown, which secures the ultimate triumph of the United States....Rochambeau remains in Virginia, and Washington marches North, and goes into Winter quarters on the Hudson.

1782.

British flee from Wilmington, S. C., at the approach of Gen. St. Clair....Clinton and his army blockaded in New York by Washington....March 4—British House of Commons resolves to end the war ...May 5—Arrival of Sir Guy Carleton to treat for peace.....July 11—British evacuate Savannah....First war ship constructed in the United States at Portsmouth, N. H....John Adams, John Jay, Dr. Benjamin Franklin, Thomas Jefferson and Henry Laurens appointed by the United States, Commissioners to conclude a treaty of peace with Great Britain. ....Four of them meet English commissioners in Paris, and sign preliminary treaty Nov. 30....Dec. 14—British evacuate Charleston, and Gen. Francis Marion ("The Swamp Fox") disbands his brigade.

1783.

Jan—Bank of North America opened in Philadelphia ....Jan. 20—French and English commissioners sign treaty of peace....A cessation of hostilities proclaimed in the army.....Feb. 5—American Independence acknowledged by Sweden; Feb. 25, acknowledged by Denmark; March 24, by Spain; July, by Russia....Sept. 3—Definite treaty of peace signed at Paris, and America's

Independence acknowledged by Great Britain....June 19—Society of the Cincinnati formed by officers of the army at Newburg....Nov. 3—United States army formally disbanded ...25—New York City evacuated by the British, and General Washington at head of American army, entered the city....26—Congress assembles at Annapolis, Md ..Dec. 4—Washington takes leave of his comrades-in-arms, New York City....Dec. 23—Washington resigns his commission to Congress.....Slavery abolished in Massachusetts....The parties known as Federalists and Anti-Federalists originated.

1784.

First voyage of an American ship to China from New York....New York Chamber of Commerce founded.... Jan. 4—Treaty of Paris ratified by Congress.

1785.

John Adams, first American ambassador to England, has an audience with the King....First Federal Congress organized in New York.

1786.

Shay's insurrection in Massachusetts.

1787.

May 25—A convention to amend articles of Confederation composed of delegates from all the States except Rhode Island, met in Philadelphia. Federal constitution formed and submitted to Congress Sept. 28....July—Northwestern Territory, embracing the present States of Ohio, Indiana, Illinois, Michigan and Wisconsin established.

1788.

Quakers of Philadelphia emancipate their slaves.

1789.

March 4—Federal Constitution ratified by the requisite number of States, and becomes the organic law of the Republic... March 11—Philadelphia incorporated as a city ...April 6—Washington chosen the first President of the United States, and John Adams Vice-President....30—Washington inaugurated at the City Hall, Wall Street, New York....Departments of Treasury, War and Foreign Affairs created, and a national judiciary established ....Nov. 21—North Carolina adopts the Constitution.

1790.

District of Columbia ceded to the United States by Maryland and Virginia....April 17—Death of Benjamin Franklin....May 29—Rhode Island adopts the Constitution, being the last of the original thirteen States to do so Aug 12—Congress adjourns in New York, and, Dec. 6, meets in Philadelphia....First census of the United States: population 3,929,326....Territory South-west of the Ohio established. A United States ship circumnavigates the globe....Troubles with the Indians, which continue until '94. ..The Anti-Federalists become known as the Republican party.

1791.

Feb. 18—Vermont admitted as a State....City of Washington founded....First bale of cotton exported to England since the war.

1792.

April 2—Act past establishing United States Mint at Philadelphia....June 1—Kentucky admitted as a State ...Washington and Adams re-elected....June 21.... Philadelphia and Lancashire Turnpike Company Chartered. Road opened in 1795—the first turnpike in the United States.

1793.

Cotton-gin invented by Eli Whitney.

1794.

Congress appropriates $700,000 to establish a navy. Insurrection among the Dutch in Western Pennsylvania on account of duties on distilled liquor....John Jay appointed Envoy Extraordinary to England to settle disputes between the two Governments.

1795.

Treaty with Western Indians...Yellow-fever pestilence in New York....Oct.—Treaty with Spain.

1796.

June—Tennessee admitted as a State....Credit of the Government re-established, and all disputes with foreign powers, except France, adjusted....Sept.—Washington issues a farewell address.

1797.

John Adams inaugurated President; Thomas Jefferson Vice-President....Envoys appointed to adjust difficulties with France are refused an audience with the French Directory.

1798.

Preparations for hostilities with France....July—Washington again appointed Commander-in-chief of the Army....Navy Department created, with Benjamin Stoddart of Maryland, as Secretary....French Directory make overtures for peace.

1799.

Jan.—Lafayette returns to France....Feb. 26—Three Envoys proceed to France to negotiate for peace.... Dec. 14—Washington dies at Mount Vernon, aged 68 years.

1800.

Removal of the Capital from Philadelphia to Washington....May—Formation of Mississippi Territory....Sept. 30—American Envoys to France conclude a treaty with Napoleon Bonaparte.

1801.

March 4—Thomas Jefferson inaugurated President.... Tripoli declares war against the United States....U. S. Navy Yard at Philadelphia established.

1802.

April—Ohio admitted as a State...Yellow Fever ravages Philadelphia.

1803.

April—Louisiana purchased from the French, and divided into Territory of New Orleans and District of Louisiana...Alien and sedition laws passed....Amendments to the Constitution adopted....Com. Preble sails for Tripoli....U. S. frigate Philadelphia captured by the Tripolitans.

1804.

Lewis and Clarke start on an exploring expedition up the Missouri and down the Columbia River to the Pacific Ocean....Feb. 15—Lieut. Decatur burns the Philadelphia in the harbor of Tripoli....Middlesex canal, first in the United States, completed.....July 12—Alex. Hamilton killed in a duel by Aaron Burr....Aug.—Com. Preble bombards Tripoli.

1805.

Michigan created into a Territory....June 3—The Pasha of Tripoli makes terms of peace....Yellow-fever pestilence in New York.

1807.

May 22—Beginning of trial of Aaron Burr on a charge of treason, Richmond. Va.; Sept. 15, acquitted; recommitted, but never tried....Robert Fulton navigates the Hudson in a steamboat....June 22—The Chesapeake fired upon by the British ship Leopard ..Retaliatory measures between England and France cripple the American shipping trade abroad....Congress decrees an embargo, which detains all vessels, both American and foreign, in port.

1809.

March 1—Congress repeals the embargo on shipping, and at the same time passes a law forbidding all commercial intercourse with England or France until their obnoxious restrictions on commerce shall be removed. ....March 4—James Madison inaugurated President.

1811.

Congress refuses to recharter the Bank of the United States....Nov. 5—Battle of Tippecanoe—General Harrison defeats the Indians.

1812.

June 19—The President formally declares war against Great Britain.....General Dearborn appointed Commander-in-chief....New England States threaten to secede....July 12—Gen. Hull crosses the Detroit River to attack Fort Malden, Canada.... 17—Fort Mackinaw captured by British and Indians ...Aug. 7—Hull retires from Canada ..13—The Essex, Captain Porter, captures the Alert—first vessel taken from the British in that war ....16—Surrender of Detroit to British....Several skirmishes on the frontier... 19—U S. frigate Constitution, Commodore Isaac Hull, captures and burns the Guerriere. ....Oct. 18—U S. sloop Wasp, Capt. Jones, captures the Frolic, and both are taken by the British ship Poictiers 25—U S. frigate United States, Com. Decatur, captures the Macedonian.....Dec. 28—The Constitution, Com. Bainbridge, makes a prize of the British frigate Java ....April 8—Louisiana admitted as a State.

1813

Jan. 22—British Gen. Proctor defeats the Americans at Frenchtown, prisoners and wounded massacred by the Indians....Admiral Cockburn destroys shipping in the Delaware and ravages the Southern coast....New England coast blockaded by Com. Hardy Feb. 21—Battle of Ogdensburg, N Y ...March 4—Second inauguration of President Madison.....Successful defense of Forts Meigs and Sandusky....April—Americans capture York (now Toronto). ..May—Fort George taken... June 1—U. S. frigate Chesapeake surrenders to the Shannon (British). Capt. James Lawrence—("Don't give up the ship!")—mortally wounded and dies June 5....General Dearborn succeeded by Gen. Wilkinson....Aug. 30—Massacre by Creek Indians at Fort Minims, Alabama River ... Generals Andrew Jackson and Coffee prosecute the war against the Indians ...Sept. 10—Battle of Lake Erie—Com. Perry defeats and captures the British Fleet.... 28 or 29—Americans take possession of Detroit....Oct. 5—Battle of the Thames. Americans, under Gen. Harrison almost annihilate the British, under Proctor. Tecumseh killed ...Termination of the war on the Northwest boundary....12—Americans compelled to abandon Fort George. British and Indians surprise and capture Fort Niagara and burn Buffalo and several other villages and towns....Power loom introduced in the United States.

1814.

March—The Essex taken by British ships Phœbe and Cherub....Gen. Wilkinson repulsed on Canadian frontier and superseded by Gen. Izard May 5—British attack Oswego and withdraw 7 .. July 3—Fort Erie captured ....4—Battle of Chippewa; British defeated . 25—Battle of Niagara; British again defeated . .Aug. 9-12—Com. Hardy makes an unsuccessful attack on Stonington. Aug. 15—Repulse of assault on Fort Erie....24—Ross defeats the Americans at Bladensburg, and on the same day captures the City of Washington, burning the Capitol, White House and other buildings....25—British retreat to their ships....Sept. 12-14—Unsuccessful attack on Baltimore; Gen. Ross killed....Sept. 13—Key composes "The Star-Spangled Banner."....Sept. 15—British attack on Mobile repulsed....Sept.—Com. McDonough's victory on Lake Champlain. The British land forces, under Provost, are defeated at Plattsburgh, N. Y..... Americans destroy Fort Erie, and Nov. 5 go into Winter quarters at Buffalo....Nov. 7—Gen. Jackson storms and captures Pensacola, Fla., and leaves for Mobile 9....15—Hartford Convention—Federalists oppose the war, and threaten a secession of the New England States....Dec. 2—Gen Jackson arrives at New Orleans....24—Treaty of peace with Great Britain signed at Ghent.

1815.

Jan. 8—Battle of New Orleans....15—U. S. ship President captured by the Endymion....Feb. 17—Treaty of Ghent ratified and peace proclaimed....March 23—The Hornet captures the Penguin....War with Algiers ... Com. Decatur humbles the Mediterranean pirates.... April 6—Massacre of American prisoners at Dartmoor, England.

1816.

Congress charters a new United States Bank....Indiana admitted as a State....The Republican party in N. Y. City adopt, for the first time, the title of Democrats.

1817.

James Monroe inaugurated President....The United States suppresses piratical establishments in Florida and Texas....Trouble with the Seminole and Creek Indians....Dec.—Mississippi admitted as a State....July 4.—Erie Canal begun.

1818.

Gen. Jackson pursues the Indians into Florida, takes Pensacola and banishes the Spanish authorities and troops....Aug. 24—Centre foundation of present Capitol laid at Washington, D. C.....Dec.—Illinois admitted as a State.

1819.

Florida ceded by Spain to the United States....Steamer, named the Savannah, first crossed the Atlantic.... First lodge of Oddfellows opened in the States....Territory of Arkansas formed....Dec.—Alabama admitted as a State.

1820.

March—Maine admitted as a State....James Morroe re-elected President.

1821.

Aug. 21—Missouri admitted as a State, with the famous "Compromise," under which it was resolved that in future no slave State should be erected north of northern boundary of Arkansas....Streets of Baltimore lighted with gas.

1822.

Piracy in the West Indies suppressed by the United States....Boston, Mass., incorporated as a city....March 8—United States acknowledge independence of South America....Oct. 3—Treaty with Colombia.

1823.

President Monroe promulgates the doctrine that the United States ought to resist the extension of foreign dominion or influence upon the American continent.

1824.

Aug. 15—Lafayette revisits the United States.

1825.

March 4—John Quincy Adams inaugurated President. ....Corner-stone of Bunker Hill Monument laid by Lafayette....Lafayette leaves for France in frigate Brandywine....Erie canal completed....Contest between the Federal government and Georgia concerning Indian lands.

1826.

July 4—Death of ex-Presidents John Adams and Thomas Jefferson.....Morgan excitement and formation of Anti-Masonry Party.

1828.

May—Congress passes a tariff bill imposing heavy duties on British goods. Denounced by the Southern people as oppressive and unconstitutional....Title of "Democrats" adopted generally by Republican Party.

1829.

March 4—Inauguration of Gen. Andrew Jackson as President....July 4—Corner-Stone laid of U. S. Mint, Philadelphia.

1830.

Treaty with the Ottoman Porte....Workingman's Party originated in New York City.

1831.

Jan. 10—King of the Netherlands renders his decision on the boundary question between Maine and the British possessions. Rejected by both parties and question settled in 1842 by the Treaty of Washington....July 4—James Monroe dies.

1832.

Black Hawk Indian War commenced....June 27—Cholera breaks out in New York....Aug.—Indians driven beyond the Mississippi—capture of Black Hawk and end of the war....South Carolina declares the tariff acts null and void and threatens to withdraw from the Union if the Government attempts to collect the duties....Dec. 10—President Jackson issues a proclamation, denying the right of any State to nullify any act of the Federal Government....The Morse system of electro-magnetic telegraphy invented.

1833.

Tariff dispute settled by the passage of Henry Clay's bill....March 4—President Jackson inaugurated for a second term....He rmoves the public funds from the Bank of the United States ...Widespread commercial distress....Opponents of Andrew Jackson first call themselves the Whig Party....Oct. 14—Political riots in Philadelphia.

1834.

Cholera again rages in New York.

1835.

War with Seminole Indians, led by Osceola, in Florida ...Texas declared independent....Nov. 15—Great fire in New York....Democrats first called "The Locofoco Party."....July 12—Negro riots in Philadelphia.

1836.

The Creeks aid the Seminoles in their war....Arkansas admitted as a State....National debt paid off....March 29—Pennsylvania newly incorporates the Bank of the United States.

1837.

Jan. 25—Michigan admitted as a State....March 4—Martin Van Buren inaugurated President....The banks suspend specie payment; panic in business circles.... Many Americans assist the Canadian insurgents....The steamboat Caroline burnt by the British, near Schlosser, east of Niagara, on United States Territory.

1838.

Proclamation by the President against American citizens aiding the Canadians....The steamship Sirius, the first to make the Western transatlantic passage, arrives at New York from Cork, Ireland, and is followed on the same day by the Great Western from Bristol, Eng..... The Wilkes exploring expedition to South Seas sailed.

1839.

Another financial panic, and, in October, banks suspend specie payment.

1840.

July 4—Sub-Treasury bill becomes a law....Railroad riots in Philadelphia.

1841.

March 4—William H. Harrison inaugurated President; died April 4....Aug. 9—Sub-Treasury act repealed and a general bankruptcy bill passed....Alex. MacLeod, implicated in the burning of the Caroline, tried for arson and murder at Utica, N. Y., and acquitted, Oct. 12.... Feb. 4—United States Bank failed and other banks suspended specie payment.

1842.

Aug.—Treaty, defining the boundaries between the United States and the British American Possessions and for suppressing the slave trade, and for giving up fugitive criminals, signed at Washington....Aug. 1—"Abolition Riots," in Philadelphia. Churches burned.

1843.

Suppression of a threatened insurrection in Rhode Island, caused by the adoption of a new constitution, known as the Dorr Rebellion....Jan. 11—"Weaver's Riots," Philadelphia.

1844.

Treaty of commerce with China... May and July—Riots, and Catholic churches burned in Philadelphia.... May 27—Anti-rent riots in New York State....Telegraphic communication established between Washington and Baltimore.

1845.

March 1—The Republic of Texas received into the Union....3—Florida and Iowa admitted as States....4—James K Polk inaugurated President... June 8—Death of Gen. Andrew Jackson....Treaty with Great Britain fixing Northwestern boundary....Gen. Zachary Taylor ordered to defend the Texan border against a threatened invasion by Mexico.

1846.

War with Mexico....May 8—Battle of Palo Alto....9—Battle of Resaca de la Palma. Mexicans beaten in both ....July 6—Com. Sloat takes possession of Monterey.... Aug.—Gen. Kearney takes possession of New Mexico.... Col. Fremont occupies California......Aug. 19—Com. Stockton blockades Mexican ports....Dec.—Iowa admitted as a State...Oct. 25.—Com. Perry bombards Tobasco, Mexico....Nov. 14—Com. Connor occupies Tampico.

1847.

Feb. 8—Kearney proclaims the annexation of California to the United States....Col. Doniphan defeats Mexicans in Chihuahua and takes possession of that province ....Feb. 23—Battle of Buena Vista, Taylor defeats Santa Anna....March 27—Surrender of Vera Cruz and castle to Gen. Scott and Com. Perry....Battle of Cerro Gordo, April 18....Aug. 20—Battles of Contreras and Cherubusco....Sept. 8—Battle of Molino del Rey....13—Battle of Chepultepec....14—American army enters City of Mexico.

1848.

Feb. 18—Gen. Scott superseded in Mexico by Gen. Wm. O. Butler....Treaty of Guadaloupe Hidalgo which stipulated for the evacuation of Mexico by the American Army within three months; the payment of $15,000,000 by the United States to Mexico for the territory acquired by conquest; and it also fixed boundaries, etc.....Feb. 23—John Quincy Adams dies....Postal convention between United States and Great Britain....May 29—Wisconsin admitted as a State....July 4—Peace with Mexico formally proclaimed....News of the discovery of gold in California reached the States....Mormons (founded by Joseph Smith 1827) settled near Great Salt Lake, Utah....Dec. 8—First deposit of California gold in Mint.

1849.

Great exodus of gold-seekers to California....March 4—The "Wilmot Proviso" passed by Congress....March 5—Gen. Zachary Taylor inaugurated President....June 15—James K. Polk dies....The people of California vote against slavery in that territory....Cholera in New York....May 30 to Sept. 8—Philadelphia depleted by cholera....Treaty with England for a transit way across the Isthmus of Panama.

1850.

March 31—John C. Calhoun dies....May—The Grinnell expedition, in search of Sir John Franklin, leaves New York....July 9—President Taylor dies....Great fire in Philadelphia....10—Vice-President Millard Fillmore assumes the Presidency....Violent debates between the Pro-slavery and Free-soil parties in Congress over the proposed admission of California....Sept. 9—Passage of Henry Clay's "Omnibus Bill," relative to slavery....Territory of Utah organized.

1851.

Letter postage reduced to three cents....Lopez's expedition landed in Cuba....Lopez captured, and executed in Havana, Sept. 1....Minnesota purchased from the Sioux Indians....Dec.—Louis Kossuth arrives in New York....Dec. 24—Capitol at Washington partly destroyed by fire.

1852.

United States expedition to Japan, under command of Com. Perry, a brother of the hero of Lake Erie....June 29—Henry Clay dies....Oct. 24—Daniel Webster dies.

1853.

Washington Territory created out of the northern part of Oregon....4—Franklin Pierce inaugurated President....May—Four vessels, under Capt. Ringgold, leave on an exploring expedition to the North Pacific Ocean....Expeditions start to explore routes for a railway to the Pacific coast....Second expedition in search of Sir John Franklin leaves, under command of Doctor Kane....Capt. Ingraham upholds the rights of American citizenship in the affair of Martin Koszta, at Smyrna.

1854.

May—Passage of the Kansas-Nebraska Bill, which created those two Territories, and left the people of every territory, on becoming a State, free to adopt or exclude the institution of slavery....Feb. 28—Seizure of the American Steamship Black Warrior in harbor of Havana....June 7—Reciprocity treaty between Great Britain and the United States, respecting international trade, fisheries, etc.....July 13—Capt. Hollins of sloop Cyane bombards San Juan de Nicaragua....March 31—Commercial treaty with Japan concluded by Com. Perry....Oct 9—Ostend Conference.

1855.

Serious trouble in Kansas over the slavery question....William Walker takes possession of Nicaragua and establishes a government there....June 28—Railroad from Panama to Aspinwall opened....Dispute with England over enlistment of soldiers for Crimean War.....Gen. Harney chastises the Sioux Indians.

1856.

May 22—Preston S. Brooks of South Carolina, assaults Charles Sumner, in Senate.

1857.

Jan. 4—Kansas rejects the Lecompton Constitution....Disturbances in Utah....March—The Supreme Court gives judgment in the Dred Scott case....Aug. 24—Beginning of financial panic, which culminates in an almost general suspension of banks.

1858.

May—Minnesota admitted as a State.....Aug. 3—Kansas again rejects Lecompton Constitution.....Aug.—Atlantic telegraph cable laid. President's message to Queen Victoria sent 16, but cable proved a failure.

1859.

Oregon admitted as a State....June 25—Commodore Tatnall of U. S. Navy, in Chinese waters, makes his famous utterance: "Blood is thicker than water!"....July 4—A. H. Stephens of Georgia advocates the formation of a Southern Confederacy....Oct. 16—John Brown's raid on Harper's Ferry....18—Brown and his companions captured....Dec. 2—Brown hung....Nov.—Gen. Scott sent to protect American interests in San Juan.

1860.

March—John Brown's companions hung....March 27—Japanese Embassy, first to leave Japan, arrive at San Francisco. Received at Washington, D. C., by President Buchanan, and afterwards have public receptions in Baltimore, Philadelphia and New York, departing from the latter city in frigate Niagara June 29... May 17—Abraham Lincoln nominated at Chicago....Sept. 21—Prince of Wales arrives at Detroit, visiting United States, and subsequently goes to Philadelphia, New York and Boston, embarking for home Oct. 20, at Portland, Me....June 28—Steamship Great Eastern first arrives at New York....Dec. 18—U. S. Senate rejects "Crittenden Compromise."....Dec. 20—Carolina secedes from the Union....Dec 26—Gen. Anderson evacuates Fort Moultrie, Charleston, and occupies Fort Sumter...Dec. 30—President Buchanan declines to receive delegates from South Carolina.

1861.

Jan. 9—Mississippi secedes. Confederates at Charleston fire into reinforcement steamer Star of the West....10—Alabama and Florida secede....11—Major Anderson refuses to surrender Fort Sumter ...12—Confederates fortify Vicksburgh, Miss. and seize Navy Yard at Pensacola, Fla....18—Georgia secedes....Jan. 26—Louisiana secedes....29—Secretary-of-Treasury, John A. Dix, issues his thrilling order, addressed "W. Hemphill Jones, New Orleans:" "If any one attempts to haul down the American flag, shoot him on the spot!"....Feb. 5—Texas secedes by legislative act....Peace conference assembles at Washington, D. C., and first congress of the seven seceded States assembles at Montgomery, Ala....Jefferson Davis chosen President of Confederate States, and A. H. Stephens, Vice-President.......18—Davis inaugurated at Montgomery, Ala. Gen. Twiggs surrenders to the Confederates in Texas, and March 1 is dismissed from U. S. Army in disgrace....22—President-elect Lincoln, with his own hands, raises the American flag at the State House, Philadelphia....March 4—He is inaugurated at Washington....April 12—Major Anderson again refuses to surrender, and the Confederate batteries open fire on Fort Sumter. The North aroused... 14—Major Anderson evacuates Fort Sumter "with colors flying and drums beating, bringing away company and private property, and saluting his flag with fifty guns."....15—President Lincoln calls for 75,000 troops....17—President Davis issues letters of marque, and President Lincoln blockades Southern ports....Virginia passes ordinance of secession....18—U. S. Arsenal at Harper's Ferry destroyed by Federal authorities....First troops arrived at Washington, via Harrisburgh, Pa.....19—Sixth Massachusetts Regiment attacked while passing through Baltimore. Seventh Regiment of New York leaves that city for Washington....21—Norfolk (Va.) Navy Yard burnt by Federal authorities....May 6—Arkansas formally secedes....9-11—Tennessee secedes...20—North Carolina secedes....24—Col. E. E. Ellsworth murdered at Alexandria, Va.....June 3—Stephen A. Douglas dies... July 21—Battle of Bull Run....Aug. 10—Battle of Wilson's Creek, Missouri—Gen. Nathaniel Lyon killed....20—Gen. G. B. McClellan assumes command of Army of Potomac....Sept. 20—Col. Mulligan forced to surrender at Lexington, Ky....Oct. 21—Battle of Ball's Bluff, Va.—Gen. E. D. Baker killed....31—Gen. Winfield Scott resigns, and McClellan is made commander-in-chief....Nov. 8—Capt. Wilkes of the San Jacinto captures Mason and Slidell on board of the Trent. War with England imminent....30—Jefferson Davis elected President of Confederate States for six years....Dec. 2—Congress votes thanks to Capt. Wilkes....30—Banks in New York suspend specie payment....Mason and Slidell surrendered, and on Jan. 1, 1862 they sail for Europe.

1862.

Jan. 17—Ex-President John Tyler dies....Feb. 6—Gen. Grant captures Fort Henry....7-8—Gen. Burnside captures Roanoke, N. C....13-16—Assault and capture, by Gen. Grant, of Fort Donelson, Tenn....27—Government enjoins newspapers from giving publicity to important military movements....March 2—Gen. F. W. Lander dies at Camp Chase, Va....6-8—Battle of Pea Ridge, Ark.....8—Rebel ram Virginia (formerly Merrimac) sinks the Cumberland and the Congress....9—Naval battle between the Monitor and the Merrimac....11—McClellan assumes personal command of the Army of Potomac....14—Burnside captures Newburn, N. C....18—Gen. W. H. Keim dies....April 1—Slavery abolished in District of Columbia....5—McClellan begins siege of Yorktown, Va.....6-7—Battle of Shiloh or Pittsburgh Landing—death of Gen. A. S. Johnston; Gen. C. F. Smith dies 25, and Gen. W. H. L. Lawrence 10....25—New Orleans surrenders to Farragut....May 1—Gen. Butler formally takes possession of New Orleans....5—Battle of Williamsburg, Va....31-June 1—Battles of Fair Oaks and Seven Pines, Va....27-July 1—Seven Days' Fight, Va....12—President Lincoln appeals to the Border States in behalf of emancipation....14—Gen. Pope assumes command in Virginia....18-19—New York and Philadelphia begin using car tickets and postage stamps as currency....23—Halleck made General-in-chief of U. S. army....Aug.—Admiral George C. Reid dies....5—Battle of Baton Rouge, La.—Gen. Thomas Williams killed....6—Gen. Robt. L. McCook shot by guerillas... 9—Battle of Cedar Mountain, Va....16—McClellan retreats from Harrison's Landing, Va....23—Gen. Henry Bohlen killed....29—Battle of Groveton or Manassas, Va....30—Second Battle of Bull Run, Va.—Gen. George B. Taylor dies Sept. 1....Sept. 1—Battle of Chantilly, Va.—Gens. Philip Kearney and Isaac J Stevens killed....President Lincoln issues proclamation as a preliminary to emancipating slaves... McClellan placed in command of fortifications of Washington....14—Battle of South Mountain, Md.—Gen. Reno killed....13-15—Harper's Ferry, Va., surrendered... 17—Battle of Antietam, Md.—Gen. Mansfield killed; Gen. I. P. Rodman dies Sept. 29, and Gen. I. B. Richardson Nov. 4....24—President Lincoln provisionally suspends habeas corpus ....Oct. 1—Internal-revenue Stamp Law goes into effect ....3-4-6—Battle of Corinth, Miss.—Gen. P. A. Hackelman killed....8—Battle of Perryville, Ky.—Gens. R. J. Oglesby, Wm. R. Terrill and J. S. Jackson killed....10-13—Confederates, under Stuart, enter Pennsylvania....30—Gen. Rosencrans supersedes Gen. Buell at the West....Gen. O. M. Mitchell killed at Beaufort, S. C....Nov. 5—Gen. McClellan superseded by Gen. Burnside as commander of Army of Potomac....Nov. 6—Gen. C. D. Jameson dies. ....7—Com. Garrett J. Pendergast dies.....10—Rear-Admiral E. A. F. Lavalette dies....22—Gen. F. E. Patterson killed at Fairfax, Va....Dec. 10-15—Gen. Burnside attacks and retreats from Fredericksburg, Va.—Battle of Fredericksburg....Dec 13—Gens. G. D. Bayard and C. F. Jackson killed....31—Battle of Murfreesboro, Tenn., begun, and Bragg is defeated.

1863.

Jan.—Gen. E. N. Kirk, wounded at Murfreesboro, dies. ...1—President Lincoln emancipates slaves...,9—French Government offers mediation declined Feb. 6...26—Gen. Hooker supersedes Gen. Burnside....25—Congress passes the Conscription or Draft bill....March 3—Congress authorizes suspension of habeas corpus....6—Clement L. Vallandingham serenaded in Philadelphia—great excitement there....18—Bread riot of Confederate soldiers' wives, Salisbury, N. C....21—Gen. E. V. Sumner dies.... 28—Gen. James Cooper dies.... April 7—Federals attack Charleston, S. C....26—Gen. Burnside assumes command of Department of Ohio... May 1-4—Battle of Chancellorsville, Va.—Stonewall Jackson is wounded, and dies May 10; Gen. H. G Berry dies May 3; Gen. A. W. Whipple, May 5; and Gen. Ed. Kirby, June 1....May 4—Gen. Joseph B. Plummer dies....14—Grant defeats Gen. Joe Johnston at Jackson, Miss.... 16—Grant defeats Gen. Pemberton at Champion Hills, Miss....18—Grant invests Vicksburg, Miss....June 14—Battle of Winchester, Va. ..Gen. Lee invades Maryland and Pennsylvania.... 16—Mayor Henry of Philadelphia calls upon citizens to close their places of business and prepare to defend the State....27—Gen. Geo. H. Meade supersedes Gen. Hooker....28—Theatres, libraries and places of business closed in Philadelphia, and earthworks thrown up on roads leading into the city ....July 1-3—Battle of Gettysburg, Pa.—Gens. Reynold, Weed, Farnsworth and Zook killed....4—Vicksburg surrenders to Gen. Grant and Rear-Admiral Porter....7—Great rejoicing at the North over the surrender....State-house and fire-bells rung in Philadelphia....8—Port Hudson, Miss., surrenders....15—President Lincoln names Aug. 6 as a day of National Thanksgiving....13-16—Draft riots in New York City; also that week in Boston, Mass., and Portsmouth, N. H.....30—Gen. Geo. C. Strong, wounded at storming of Fort Wagner, Charleston (July 10-18 dies....Aug. 14—Gen. Benj. Walsh dies... 21—Lawrence, Kas., sacked and burned....25-30—Gen. Averill's calvary raid into Virginia....Sept. 5—Women's bread riot in Mobile, Ala. During the year there was also one in Richmond, Va., five thousand women taking part.... 6—Fort Wagner, Charleston, evacuated....8—Boat attack on Fort Sumter.... 10—Gen. Burnside occupies Knoxville, Tenn....19-20—Battle of Chickamauga, Ga.—Gen. W. H. Lytle killed....Oct. 10—Quantrell's attack on Fort Scott, Kansas....21-22—Battle of Philadelphia, Tenn....Nov. 12—Meeting held to restore Arkansas to the Union....14-17—Gen. Longstreet defeats Burnside....23-25—Grant and Sherman defeat Brag at Chattanooga, Tenn....25—Gen. Wm. P. Sanders dies....26-27—Battles of Locust Grove and Mine Run, Va....Dec 4—President Lincoln offers amnesty to all but the rebel leaders. ..16—Gen. John Buford dies ...22—Cooper's Shop Soldiers' Home, Philadelphia, dedicated....30—The Monitor founders of Cape Hatteras.

1864.

Jan. 8—Rear-Admiral George H. Storer dies....Feb. 11—Com. Wm. S. McCluney dies....20—Battle of Olustee, Fla....Feb 27-March 4—Kilpatrick and Dahlgreen repulsed at Richmond, Va....March 12—U S. Grant succeeds Halleck as commander-in-chief....April 8—Battle of Sabine Cross Roads, La....9—Battle of Pleasant Hill, La....12—Massacre at Fort Pillow, Tenn... May 1—Com. W. D. Porter dies....5-13—Battle of the Wilderness, Va.—Gen. Alex. Hays killed; Gen. James S. Wadsworth dies May 6... 9—Gen. John Sedgwick killed... 10—Gen. Thos. G. Stevenson killed. ..11—Stuart, Confederate cavalry leader, killed....18-25—Battles of Spottsylvania Court-house, Va., etc....June 1-6—Battle of Cold Harbor, Va., and vicinity....5-30—Battles of Lost Mountain, Kenesaw Mountain, and Little Kenesaw, Ga.—Gen. C. G Harker killed 27....19—Naval battle—the Kearsage sinks the Alabama....15-18—Assault on Petersburg, Va... July 1—Part of Lee's army invades Maryland, threatens Baltimore and Washington, and retreats July 12-13....6—Gen. Samuel A. Rice dies. .20-22-28—Sherman's three battles near Atlanta, Ga—"The March to the Sea."....30—Confederates again invade Maryland and Pennsylvania, and burn Chambersburg....Aug. 5—Confederate flotilla near Mobile, Ala., destroyed by Farragut....6—General Griffin A. Stedman killed....8—Fort Gaines captured....16—Gen. D. P. Woodbury dies....Sept. 1—Sherman occupies Atlanta, Ga....7—He orders its depopulation....14—Gen. J. B. Howell killed....19—Sheridan defeats Early at Winchester, Va.—Gen. D. A. Russell killed....24—Com. T. A. Conover dies....29—Gen. H. Burnham dies....Oct. 19—Rebel raid on St. Albans, Vt....19—Battle of Cedar Creek, Va.—Gen. D. D. Bidwell killed....29—Gen. T. E. G. Ransom dies....Nov. 8—McClellan resigns from U. S. army. ....13—Sherman destroys Atlanta....30—Gen. Thomas repulses Hood at Franklin, Tenn.—Rebel Maj.-Gen. P. R. Cleburne killed....Dec. 14-16—Thomas defeats Hood near Nashville, Tenn....21—Sherman enters Savannah, Ga.... 24-25—Admiral Porter and Gen. Butler assault Wilmington, N. C.

1865.

Jan. 13-15—Attack on and capture of Fort Fisher, N. C. ....16—Monitor Patapsco sinks, Charleston Harbor.... Feb. 1—Congress abolishes slavery in the United States. ... 6—Battle of Hatcher's Run, Va....17—Columbia, S. C., captured....18—Charleston, S. C., surrendered... 18—Gen. Lee assumes supreme command of Confederate armies, and recommends arming of the blacks... 22—Confederate Congress decree that the slaves shall be armed. Schofield captures Wilmington, N. C....27-March 6—General Sheridan's raid into Virginia....March 4—Second inauguration of President Lincoln....14-April 13—Stoneman's raid in Virginia and North Carolina.... March 10-11—Battle of Kinston, N. C....20—Mobile, Ala., besieged....29-April 3—Battles of Hatcher's Run and Five Forks, Va....April 2—Assault on Petersburg, Va.... 2-3—Grant occupies Richmond and Petersburg, Va....6—Battle of Deatonville, Va....9—General T. A Smyth dies. Surrender of Gen. Lee, Appomattox Court-house, Va.... 12—The Union flag hoisted at Fort Sumter. Mobile, Ala., captured....13—Drafting and recruiting stopped....14—President Lincoln assassinated by John Wilkes Booth... 15—President Lincoln dies, and Andrew Johnson becomes President.....22—Com. W. W. McKean dies.....26—J. Wilkes Booth shot....May 4-9—Surrender of Gen. Taylor and rebel fleet...,10—Capture of Jefferson Davis at Irwinsville, Ga....26—Surrender of General Kirby Smith....End of the Rebellion....22—President Johnson rescinds order requiring passports from all travelers entering the United States, and opens Southern ports....26—He proclaims a conditional amnesty....June 1—Solemn fast for death of President Lincoln....July 7—Execution of Payne, Atzeroit, Harrold and Mrs. Surratt, for complicity in Lincoln assassination....Oct. 11—Pardon of Alexander Stephens and other Southern officials....Nov. 2—National thanksgiving for peace....6—Capt. Waddell surrenders cruiser Shennandoah to British Government....10—Capt. Wirz of Andersonville prison executed....22—Com. J. H. Missroon dies....Dec. 1—Habeas corpus restored at the North.

1866.

Jan. 28—Hon. Thomas Chandler dies....Feb. 19—President vetoes Freedmen's Bureau bill....March 14—Jared Sparks, historian, dies....27—President Johnson vetoes Civil-rights bill... April 9—Civil-rights bill passed over the President's veto.. .12—Hon. Daniel S. Dickinson dies. ... May 16—President Johnson vetoes the admission of Colorado as a State...29—Gen. Winfield Scott dies...June 7—Fenians from the United States make a raid into Canada.... 17—Hon. Lewis Cass dies....July 16—Freedmens' Bureau bill become a law...27—Atlantic telegraph—the successful one—completed....30—Maj Gen. Lysander Cutler dies....Aug. 14—National Union Convention assembles in Philadelphia—wigwam....Sept. 1—Southern Unionist Convention assembles in Philadelphia....7—Matthias W. Baldwin pioneer in American locomotives dies....Oct. 13—"Prince" John Van Buren, son of Hon. Martin, dies....Dec. 13—Congress passes bill giving negroes the right to vote in District of Columbia.. 26—Maj.-Gen Samuel R. Curtis dies.

1867.

Jan. 9—Virginia rejects Fourteenth Amendment.... 10—Congress passes bill providing for "universal suffrage" in the territories... 25—President Johnson vetoes bill to admit Colorado .. 29—He vetoes bill to admit Nebraska ....Feb 6—Delaware and Louisiana reject Constitutional Amendment.....8—Nebraska admitted as a State.... March 2—President Johnson vetoes Reconstruction bill .. 25—Tenure-of office bill passed over President's veto... 23—President vetoes Supplementary Reconstruction bill ... 30—Announced at Washington that Russia cedes Alaska to the United States....April 9—Senate confirms Alaska treaty . 11—Site conveyed to United States Government for post-office in New York City... May 3—Eight-hour riots in Chicago.....9—General strike of workingmen throughout the States....13—Jefferson Davis admitted to bail at Richmond, Va....June 3—Gen. Sheridan removes Gen. Welles of Louisiana and on 6 appoints B. F Flanders Governor....July 3—Congress assembles in extraordinary session.....11—Reciprocity treaty between the United States and the Hawaiian Islands....19—President vetoes Supplementary Reconstruction bill.. 24—Riot in Knoxville, Tenn. New York State Constitutional Convention rejects woman-suffrage proposition......30—Gen. Sheridan removes Governor Throckmorton of Texas....Aug 5—Secretary Stanton is requested by the President to resign, but refuses . 12—

Stanton suspended, and Gen. Grant appointed Secretary of War *ad interim*....17—Gen. Sheridan relieved at New Orleans....19—National Labor Congress meets at Chicago....Sept. 8—President issues amnesty proclamation ... 30—Negro riots in Savannah, Ga.....Oct. 3—Whiskey riot in Philadelphia....Nov. 2—Gen. Sherman announces Indian war at an end ...8—Formal transfer of Alaska to Gen. Rosseau, at New Archangel....14—Denmark concludes treaty, ceding and selling the islands of St. Thomas, San Juan and Santa Cruz, to United States....22—Jefferson Davis returns to Richmond....Dec. 7—Resolution of Judiciary Committee to impeach President Johnson voted down in the House—108 to 57.

1868.

Jan. 6—House of Representatives passes bill making eight hours a day's work for Government laborers....13—The Senate reinstates Stanton....14—Gen. Grant vacates War office in favor of Secretary Stanton....Feb. 13—Another attempt to impeach President Johnson....20—New Jersey Legislature withdraws ratification of proposed Fourteenth Constitutional Amendment.....21—Stanton again removed, and General Thomas appointed Secrtary of War *ad interim*....22—Stanton adheres to the office....24—House votes (126 to 27) to impeach the President....25—Gov. Ward of New Jersey vetoes resolution of Legislature withdrawing ratification of Fourteenth Amendment... March 2—House adopts impeachment articles....4—They are presented to the Senate....5—New Jersey Senate passes over Gov. Ward's veto as to amendment; lower House does the same, 25....6—Senate organizes a Court of Impeachment......7—President Johnson summoned to appear before it....13—Impeachment Court sits....23—President's counsel answer impeachment articles, and Court adjourns to 30....26—Senate ratifies North German treaty....28—U. S. Grand Jury at Richmond, Va., finds new bill of indictment against Jefferson Davis....April 2—North German Parliament passes the Naturalization treaty with the United States. ....6—Michigan votes against negro suffrage....24—President nominates Gen. Schofield to be Secretary of War ....May 21—Grant and Colfax nominated at Chicago.... The Burlingame Chinese Embassy arrive at New York ....26—Impeachment Court declares the President not guilty. Secretary Stanton resigns....30—Senate confirms Gen. Schofield as Stanton's successor....June 1—Ex-President James Buchanan dies....5—Chinese Embassy received by President Johnson....22—King of Belgium reviews United States squadron under Farragut off Ostend....24—Senate passes eight-hour law....25—President vetoes "Omnibus bill...20—President vetoes Electoral College bill. Secretary Seward announces ratification of the Fourteenth Amendment....24—President orders Secretary of War to withdraw military forces from Southern States represented in Congress. Senate ratifies treaty with China....25—Senate ratifies treaty with Mexico....27—Jefferson Davis and family sail from Quebec for England....30—Gen. Meade declares civil government restored in Florida, Georgia and Alabama....Aug. 11—Hon. Thadeus Stevens dies—Washington, D. C.....22—President declares Sitka a port of entry ...26—Oregon withdraws ratification of Fourteenth Amendment....Nov. 3—Iowa and Minnesota vote in favor of negro suffrage, and Missouri against it.

1869.

Jan. 1—Gen. Grant holds a public reception in Independence Hall, Philadelphia....Feb. 20—Martial law declared in Tennessee....22-26—Congress passes Fifteenth Amendment. Kansas is the first State (Feb. 27), to ratify it, though imperfectly, and Delaware the first to reject it...March 4—Gen. Grant inaugurated as President ....25—Pennsylvania ratifies Fifteenth Amendment.... April 13—Senate rejects Alabama Treaty with Great Britain....May 13—Woman-suffrage Convention in New York City....19—President Grant proclaims that there shall be no reduction in Government Laborer's wages because of reduction of hours....June 18—Hon. Henry J. Raymond, *N. Y. Times*, dies....July 13—Completion of Atlantic cable from Brest to St. Pierre; thence to Duxbury, Mass....30—Hon. Isaac Toucey dies.....Aug. 16—National Labor Convention, Philadelphia....Sept. 1—National Temperance Convention, Chicago....8—Hon. Wm. Pitt Fessenden dies....10—Hon. John Bell dies.... 18—Hon. John Minor Botts dies....Oct. 8—Virginia ratifies Fourteenth and Fifteenth Amendments... Ex-President Franklin Pierce dies....Nov. 4—Geo. Peabody dies .....6—Admiral Charles Stuart dies......24—National Woman-suffrage Convention, Cleveland, O., and Henry Ward Beecher chosen President.....Dec. 10—National Colored Labor Convention, Washington....24—Hon. Edwin M. Stanton dies.

1870.

Jan. 26—Virginia readmitted into the Union....Feb. 9—U. S. Signal Bureau established by Act of Congress.... 17—Mississippi re-admitted into the Union....23—Hon. Anson Burlingame dies....March 28—Maj.-Gen. George H. Thomas dies....29—Texas re-admitted to representation in Congress, thus completing the work of reconstruction ....30—President Grant announces the adoption of the Fifteenth Amendment.....July 12—Admiral John A. Dahlgren dies....Aug. 14—Admiral David G. Farragut dies....15—National Labor Congress, Cincinnati....22—President Grant issues a proclamation enjoining neutrality as to war between France and Prussia....23—Irish National Congress convenes, Cincinnati......Oct. 4—Second Southern Commercial Convention, Cincinnati ....12—Death of Gen. Robert E. Lee....25—Convention in Cincinnati for purpose of removing National Capital from Washington to some point West.

1871.

Jan. 1—Cabral, the Dominican Chief, denounces President Grant, and opposes sale and annexation of St. Domingo to the United States....10-11—U. S. House and Senate appoint committee to visit St. Domingo....11—Hon. John Covode dies....29—O'Donovan Rossa and other Fenian exiles arrive in New York....30—House of Representatives pass resolution of welcome to Irish exiles....Feb. 9—New Jersey recommends Philadelphia as the place to hold Centennial celebration, 1876....18—Cabral, in a letter to Vice-President Colfax, denounces the union of Dominica and Hayti....19—Helena, Ark., almost destroyed by a tornado ...22—British members of Joint High Commission arrive in New York....27—Commission begins its sessions in Washington, D. C....March 3—Riots in Pennsylvania coal mines....5—Chinamen's riot in San Francisco Cal....27—Senator Sumner denounces Santo Domingo scheme... 30—Colored parade in New York in honor of Fifteenth Amendment....April 7—Coal riots in Scranton, Pa... 10—Celebration in New York of German Unity and end of war between Prussia and France....May 1—U. S. Supreme Court sustains constitutionality of Legal-tender act ...3—President Grant issues proclamation for suppression of Ku-Klux Klan....6—Joint High Commission concludes Washington Treaty ....15-16—German peace celebration in Philadelphia.... 24—Treaty of Washington ratified by Senate... 29—Naturalization Treaty between Austria and United States ratified by the Reichsrath.. .30—Decoration Day.... June 1—American naval force, making a survey of the coast of Corea, Asia, fired on from masked batteries. 2—Minister Low demands an apology, and is answered that "the Corean civilization of 4,000 years brooks no interference from outside barbarians." 10, 11—U. S. naval forces land on the island of Kang Noe, Corea, and destroy a fort and the Citadel....17—Hon. Clement L. Vallandingham dies...28—President Grant appoints Civil service-reform Commission....July 3—Naval forces, having attained their object, retire from coast of Corea.... 4—President Grant proclaims complete ratification of Treaty of Washington....12—Orange parade and riot in New York....19—Massachusetts' Centennial Committee arrive in Philadelphia....Sept. 24—Chief-Justice McKean of Utah decides against Mormons serving as grand jurors in Federal courts....Oct. 2—Postal money-order arrangement between United States and Great Britain goes into effect....Brigham Young arrested for Mormon proclivities....7—First great fire in Chicago breaks out ..8-9—Second and greatest fire in Chicago...10—Election riot in Philadelphia between white roughs and negroes, and attempts to destroy the office of *The Press*....26—Gen. Robert Anderson dies, Nice, France; Hon. Thomas Ewing, Lancastar, O....27—Arrest of William M. Tweed, New York City....Dec. 17—Internationalist funeral procession in New York City.

1872.

Jan. 10—National Woman-suffrage Convention, Washington....Feb. 28—Congress sets apart Yellowstone Valley as a national park....April 2—Prof. S. F. B. Morse dies—New York City....16—Prof. Morse memorial services in various cities and also in Hall of United States House of Representatives....May 10—Woman-suffrage Convention in New York nominates Mrs. Woodhull for President and Frederick Douglass for Vice-President.... 22—Congress passes Amnesty bill....June 1—James Gordon Bennett, *N. Y. Herald*, dies....5-6—Gen. Grant nominated for President at Philadelphia, and Henry Wilson for Vice-President....15—Board of Arbitration, under Treaty of Washington, meet at Geneva, Switzerland.... 17—Monster Peace Jubilee, Boston....July 9—Democratic Convention at Baltimore nominates Horace Greeley for President....Nov. 5—Grant re-elected President....9—Great fire in Boston, Mass.....29—Death of Hon. Horace Greeley.

1873.

Jan. 6—McEnery inaugurated Governor of Louisiana; also, Kellogg....Jan. 20—Sanguinary defeat of United States troops by the Modocs....27—Congress abolishes the franking privilege....Feb. 26—Alexander H. Stephens elected to Congress from Eighth District of Georgia ....March 4—Second inauguration of U. S. Grant as President....April 11—General Canby and Dr. Thomas murdered by Capt. Jack and the Modocs....26—United States troops surprised and slaughtered by the Modocs in the lava beds....May 9—Hon. James L. Orr, United States Minister to Russia, dies—St. Petersburg....7—Chief Justice Salmon P. Chase dies ...June 1—Capture of Captain Jack and the last of the Modocs....10—The American Department in the Vienna Exposition formally opened ... 27—Completion of the new Atlantic cable....July 20—Capt. Buddington and party rescued in the Artic Sea by the whaler Ravenscraig... 25—Great fire in Baltimore Md.,.. 26—Destructive fire in Norfolk, Va.....Aug. 2—Great fire in Portland, Oregon... 9—Disastrous Confla gration in Portland, Me....Sept. 18—Suspension of Ja Cooke & Co., and beginning of a financial panic....30—Grand Masonic parade in Philadelphia....Oct. 3—Capt Jack and three accomplices hanged. First session Evangelical Alliance, N. Y. City....31—Spanish gunboa Tornado seizes American steamer Virginius on the hig seas...4—Gen. Burriel of Santiago de Cuba shoots Gen. Ry an and others...7—He butchers Capt. Fry of the Virginiu and his crew....28—A protocol, arranging the difference between the United States and Spain, agreed upon... Dec. 24—Death of Prof. Louis Agassiz....16—Celebration in Boston of the centennial of the "tea-party" in th harbor of that city ...Spain formally surrenders th Virginius to the United States....26—The Virginius, i tow of United States steamer Ossipee, sinks off Frying pan Shoals.

1874.

Jan. 8—Repeal of the Salary Act, save with respect t President Grant ...9—Board of Centennial Supervisor Philadelphia, adopt plans and specifications for perma nent exhibition building....21—President Grant sign new salary bill....Feb 24—Women's movement agains liquor-selling begins in Ohio and spreads to other States ....25—Defeat in the House of the bill reviving the frank ing privilege... April 3—A cremation society formed i New York....14—Congress passes the inflatation or cur rency bill....March 8—Death of ex-President Millard Fillmore....11—Death of Hon. Charles Sumner....22—President Grant vetoes inflation ...May 13—The Brook forces surrender in Arkansas, and quiet is restored....2—Senate passes Supplementary Civil-rights bill....26—Senate passes bill inviting foreign nations to take part i the Centennial at Philadelphia ...June 8—U. S. Steame Swatara, with party of scientists, sailed from New York to observe transit of Venus ...10—Senate passes Moiety bill....13—House defeats Compromise Currency bill... 17-13—Government of District of Columbia abolished .. 20—President Grant signs the Compromise Currency bil July 4—Formal opening of the great bridge over the Mis sissippi River, at St. Louis. Ground broken at Fairmoun Park, Philadelphia, for Centennial buildings ; .7—Henr Ward Beecher demands an investigation of the charge against him....14—Great fire in Chicago....Aug. 28—H W. Beecher acquitted by the investigating committee o Plymouth Church....Sept. 14—Overthrow of the Kellogg government at New Orleans....17—The McEnery gov ernment, in obedience to a proclamation from President Grant, surrenders to the United States Army....19—Kel logg government reinstated....26—Victory of the Ameri can Rifle-team in the international match at Creedmoor, L. I.....Oct. 16—National monument to Abraham Lincoln dedicated at Springfield, Ill.

1875.

Jan. 8—Beginning of the civil suit of Theodore Tilton vs. Henry Ward Beecher....7—House of Representatives passes Sherman's Specie-resumption bill...14—President Grant signs it....Feb. 8—President Grant denounces the Garland government in Arkansas, and recognizes Brooks as Governor....18—He issues a proclamation con vening the Senate in extraordinary session March 5.... March 1—President Grant approves the Civil-rights bill ....2—Franking privilege partially restored....12—an nouncement from Rome that Archbishop McCloskey of New York, had been created a Cardinal....24—Extraor dinary session of Senate terminates. President Grant orders all available cavalry into the Black Hills coun try, to remove trespassers, etc.....April 18—Centennial of the Battles of Concord and Lexington, Mass., cele brated in those places... 21—Spain pays $45,000 of the $80,000 agreed upon as the Virginius indemnity....27—Cardinal McCloskey receives the beretta....May 11—First international Sunday-school Convention assembles in Baltimore, Md....17—Ex-Vice-president John C. Breck enridge dies......June 17—Celebration at Boston of the Bunker Hill Centennial...William M. Tweed released from Blackwell's Island, rearrested, and consigned to Ludlow-street jail on a civil suit....29—The American Team win the international rifle-match at Dollymount, Ireland...July 2—Jury in Tilton-Beecher case fail to agree ....9—Gen. Francis P. Blair dies....27—Duncan, Sherman & Co., N. Y. Bankers, suspend, and the failure is followed by others....31—Ex-President Andrew John son dies.....Nov. 22—Vice-President Henry Wilson dies ....Dec. 7—President Grant, in his annual message, recommends free and non-sectarian schools, separation of Church from State, taxation of church property, and a sound currency....8—Congress is memorialized to ap propriate $1,500,000 for the Centennial Exhibition. 4—Escape of William M. Tweed....11—Dynamite explo sion at Bremer-haven, 60 persons killed.....12—Sarah Alexander, a Jewess, brutally murdered at East New York, King's Co., N. Y....16—Explosion in a coal mine in Belgium, 110 persons killed....17—Weston, Thompson and Ellis executed in the Tombs for the murder of the pedlar Weisberg.....25—80 persons killed at Helckon, Switzerland, at a Christmas festival.....28—Destruc tive hurricane in the Philippine Islands. 250 lives lost.

1876.

Jan. 1—Centennial year ushered in with rejoicings .....6—Defeat of Herzegovinian insurgents by Turks, 600 killed....7—A second defeat of the Herzegovini ans, many lives lost....Ships Harvest Queen and Cape Comorin collided off the British Coast, all on board lost....8—68 military recruits burned to death in Russia by burning of railroad cars....11—Over 300 Soldiers frozen to death in Douza, Turkey....11—Defeat of Amnesty Bill in U. S. House of Repre sentatives.....15—Earthquake in Maine....17—Trede gar Iron Works, Richmond, Va., failed, liabilities, $1,300,000....18—Herzegovinians rout 6 battalions of Turks, 300 Turks killed....22—Two days fighting be tween Herzegovinians and Turks; 450 Turks killed ....25—E. D. Winslow, Boston Journalist, &c., fled, having committed forgeries to amount of $250,000... 25—The Centennial appropriation passed the House of Representatives....Masked burglars robbed the Northampton (Mass.) National Bank of $670,000.... 26—Postage on third-class matter reduced to one cent for two ounces...Writs served on Gen. Schenck, Am. Minister to England, on account of his connec tion with the Emma Mine Matter....29—Destructive overflow of the Ohio River....Feb. 2—Portuguese House of Peers voted the Abolition of Slavery in St. Thomas, Africa, and the Gulf of Guinea....4—Fire in a Colliery in St. Etienne, Belgium, 156 men killed ....8—Large fire in New York, $3,000,000 property destroyed; 4 firemen killed...11—Centennial appro priation passed the Senate....15—Winslow, the Bos ton forger, arrested in London....17—Gen. Schenck, U. S. Minister to England, resigned....18—Maine Legislature abolished Capital Punishment.....23—President of San Domingo resigned. Provisional Government established....27—Sinking of steamer "Mary Belle" on Mississippi River; loss, $500,000... 28—Carlist War in Spain declared ended....29—An nouncement of annexation of Khokand to Russia... March 1—Discovery that Gen. Belknap, Secretary of War, had sold Post Traderships and pocketed pro ceeds...Belknap resigns....2—800 Turks slain in Her zegovina....7—Alfonso Taft, of Ohio, appointed Sec retary of War....A Home of the Aged, in Brooklyn, N. Y., burned; 18 old people perished......8—Jury in the $6,000,000 Tweed suit found a verdict for the peo ple of $6,537,117.38.....Japan declared war against Corea.....A great battle between Egyptians and Abyssinians; 5,000 Abyssinians killed.....11—Daniel Drew failed....13—Lieut.-Gov. Davis, of Mississippi impeached and found guilty of high crimes and misdemeanors, and on the 23d removed from office ...16—Terrible inundations in France, Belgium and Germany....21—Great battle between Mexican Gov ernment troops and Revolutionists; Government defeated; 1500 killed....25—The dykes at Herzogen bosch, Holland, give way, flooding the town, hun dreds of horses swept away and 6,000 persons made homeless....28—500 Persians lost by a shipwreck in the Arabian Sea....29—Gov. Adelbert Ames, of Miss issippi, resigns, and J. M. Stone, President of Senate, succeeds him....April 4—Successful and bloodless revolution in Hayti....5—U. S. Senate organized as a High Court of Impeachment in the Belknap case ....10-12—The bill to issue silver coin in place of fractional currency passes both Houses of Congress ....13—Turks successful in a battle near Kjevals; 300 insurgents killed....15—Dom Pedro II, Emperor of Brazil, arrived in New York....17—Issue of silver currency began....27—Belknap's trial began....28—Queen Victoria assumed the additional title of "Em press of India."....May 6—20,000 charges of "rend rock powder" exploded on Jersey City Heights, do ing immense damage....8—The House of Represen tatives passed the Hawaiian Treaty Bill....9—Grand Jury of Criminal Court of District of Columbia, found a true bill against Ex-Secretary Belknap.... P. N. Rubenstein, the condemned murderer of Sarah Alexander, died in prison....12—A battle between Turks and Herzegovinians this day and another on the 25th; Turks defeated in both, losing 700 in the first and 500 in the second....16—Green Clay Smith nominated for Presidency by Prohibitionists....18—Peter Cooper nominated for Presidency by Inflation ists...20—Sir Edmund Brickley, Bart., manufacturer, declared bankrupt, liabilities $2,500,000.....22—Ed wards Pierrepont appointed Minister to England; Alfonso Taft, Attorney-General; J. Donald Cameron, Secretary of War....29—Abdul Aziz, Sultan of Tur key, deposed and Murad Effendi declared his succes sor....June—The Turks were defeated in encounters with the Herzegovinian insurgents on the 1st, 3d, 4th, 18th and 20th, losing in all 3,480 men....3—44,000 barrels of crude-petroleum oil were struck by light ning and burned at Oil City, Penn....4—Abdul Aziz committed suicide in Constantinople....A special train ran from Jersey City, N. J., to San Francisco, in 83 hours, 34 minutes....10-15—Disastrous inundations in China, many thousands of Chinese drowned......12—Destructive inundations in Switzerland, many lives lost....14-16—Republican National Convention in Cincinnati, Rutherford B. Hayes nominated for President, Wm. A. Wheeler, Vice-President 15—Turkish Ministers of War and Foreign Affairs, and other persons, killed and some others wounded by an assassin named Hassin....17—Benj. H. Bristow, Secretary of Treasury, resigned....Hassin, the assassin, hanged.....20—U. S. Treasurer New, and Solicitor of the Treasury, Bluford Wilson, resigned ....21—Lot M. Morrill, of Maine, appointed Secretary of Treasury.....23—Turkish atrocities in Bulgaria; within three months reported from 18,000 to 30,000 persons murdered, women ravished, and 27 towns and villages plundered and destroyed....25—Gen. George A. Custer, his two brothers and 250 soldiers killed in a fight with the Sioux on the Little Horn River, Montana....27-29—Democratic National Convention met at St. Louis and nominated Samuel J. Tilden for President, and Thomas A. Hendricks for Vice-President....29—Albert M. Wyman appointed U. S. Treasurer......July 1—Servia declared war against Turkey, and on the 3d, her army was defeated near Lulcar, losing 2,000 men, and again, on the 6th, experienced another severe defeat, losing 1,300 men....4—Centennial Anniversary of American Independence: a vast concourse of people at Philadelphia, and a universal observance of the day throughout the United States....Terrible tornado in Central Iowa, 60 to 80 persons killed 1'—Hon. D. D. Pratt, Commissioner of Internal Revenue, resigned...Hon. Marshall Jewell, Postmaster-General, resigned and gave place to James M. Tyner, of Ind., who was appointed on the 12th....19—At the College regatta, at Saratoga, Cornell University won all three of the races....26—The French Government's powder magazine at Toulouse exploded, with great loss of life....29—The Ex-Queen, Isabella, returned to Spain...30—The Turks were guilty of great atrocities in Bosnia, 3,000 Christians were massacred and all manner of outrages committed; their troops were defeated by the Servians and Montenegrins... Aug. 1—Colorado declared a State of the Union by President Grant....Gen. Belknap acquitted on the impeachment trial.....7—Servians defeated by the Turks, losing 5,000 men....14-15—The Turks were defeated by the Montenegrins, losing 8,000 men, and the next day by the Servians, with great slaughter..... 17—Great famine in the northern provinces of China, thousands dying daily.....Great outrages by the Turks in Bulgaria....18—On this date and the 19th and 23d, the Turks were repulsed and defeated by the Servians....22—the great Coal Combination was broken.....23—N. Y. State Republican Convention held at Saratoga, E. D. Morgan nominated for Governor, Sherman S. Rogers Lieutenant-Governor.... Severe fight between the Sioux and Gens. Terry and Crook, Indians defeated, but losses heavy....30—N. Y. State Democratic Convention nominated Horatio Seymour for Governor, but he would not accept.... Lieut.-Governor Dorsheimer renominated.....31—Murad Effendi, Sultan of Turkey, deposed, and Abdul Hamed proclaimed his successor.....Sept. 4—Servians defeated by the Turks....6—Wm. M. Tweed arrested at Vigo, Spain....Turks lost 1,800 men in a fight with the Montenegrins. .7—1,500 Egyptian troops massacred in Abyssinia.. 9—Indian village captured and destroyed by Gen. Crook's troops..... 13—N. Y. Democratic Convention reconvened and nominate Lucius Robinson for Governor....14—International Rifle Match at Creedmoor, American Team victorious....15—Yellow fever raging at Savannah .16—Gen. Crook destroys another Indian village ....17—Fight between whites and blacks at Aiken, S. C. .24—Hell Gate reef, in N. Y. harbor, successfully blown up; 50,000 pounds of dynamite and powder used....27—Statue of Seward in Madison Park, N. Y., unveiled....28-30—The Servians were twice and the Turks once defeated....30—Great hurricane in Porto Rico, many lives and much property lost ....Oct. 3—Cyclone passed over Central America; many lives lost; $5,000,000 property destroyed. .5—E. A. Woodward, one of the Tammany Ring, arrested in Chicago... 7—Montenegrins defeat the Turks; 850 Turks killed....10—State Elections held at Indiana, West Virginia and Ohio; Democrats successful in first two and Republicans in the last....12—Monument to Christopher Columbus unveiled in Philadelphia....10,000 Egyptians massacred by Abyssinians ....Montenegrins defeat Turks and kill 1,500 of them ....17—South Carolina declared in a state of insurrection. .21—Turks evacuate Montenegro. ..24—Gen. Crook captured 480 lodges of Indians. .25—Continental Life Insurance Company suspended... 28—British Arctic Expedition, Capt. Nares, returned; they had penetrated to within 400 miles of the Pole ....29—The Servian General, Tchernayeff, defeated by the Turks. 31—About 215,000 people perished during a Cyclone in India; several thousand houses demolished.....Nov. 1—Armistice signed between Turkey and Servia....5—400 Cheyenne lodges surrender to Gen. Miles.....7—Day of Presidential Election; result uncertain. .Lerdo de Tejado re-elected President of Mexico. .10—Centennial Exhibition formally closed....12—Gold discoveries in the Black Hills....16—European Powers preparing for war... Germany refuses to take part in the Paris Exposition of 1878 ....20—The Younger Brothers plead guilty to the murder of Haywood, Cashier of Northfield (Maine) Bank...22—Chief-Justice Iglesius revolts from President Lerdo, and declares himself Provisional President of Mexico....23—The Sultan abolishes Slavery in the Turkish Empire....Tweed arrives in New York from Vigo, and is imprisoned in Ludlow Street Jail....26—Russian loan of $73,000,000 subscribed...South Carolina Canvassers imprisoned for contempt....Webster Statue unveiled in New York....28—Gen. Crook captures 100 Indian lodges .....29—Great fire in Tokio, Japan; 5,000 houses destroyed; 50 lives lost....Dec. 1—Sale of the Centennial Buildings....2—Resignation of the French Ministry...4—Greeley monument unveiled in Greenwood Cemetery......5—Burning of the Brooklyn Theatre, about 300 lives lost...New Anglo-American Extradition Treaty negotiated......6—Remains of Baron de Palm cremated at Washington, Pa.....7—Lerdo flees from the Mexican Capital and General Porfiris Diaz proclaims himself Provisional President....8—Severe gale and snow storm, from the Rocky Mountains to the Atlantic....13—Ice gorge in the Mississippi, at St. Louis; many steamers crushed .....15—Centennial congratulations received from the Mikado of Japan....19—Midhat Pasha appointed Grand Vizier....25—120 vessels lost on the Coast of Scotland by a gale....26—The Isthmus Canal Commission report in favor of the Nicaragua route.... Conference of European Powers at Constantinople ....29—Terrible railroad disaster at Ashtabula, O.: Train breaks through a bridge, cars take fire, about 80 lives lost.

1877.

Jan. 1. Orders sent to U. S. troops on the Rio Grande to protect American citizens against Mexican outrages..Two Legislatures organized in Louisiana..Terrific gale and many shipwrecks on the S. coast of England..Queen Victoria proclaimed Empress of India at Delhi...Rev. Dr. W. L. Breckenridge, Presbyterian, 73, died at Raymond, Mo....2. Turks attack Negotin in Servia; are repulsed with loss of 146 soldiers....3. Centennial celebration of the battle of Princeton..Terrible hurricane in Guipuzcoa, Spain...Gen. Diaz attacks and defeats Iglesias at Guanajuata..Railroad accident near Copenhagen, Denmark; 9 killed, 37 injured....4. Cornelius Vanderbilt died, aged 83, N.Y..Extradition treaty signed between U. S. and Spain: applies to all criminal offenses except political..Spain severs relations with Chinese government....5. Active war preparations in Russia. Active German officers forbidden to enter the Russian army..Steamship George Cromwell wrecked off Cape St. Mary, N. F.; all on board lost....6. Rev. Richard Cobbold, Eng. author, died in London, 80....7. S.S. L'Amerique ashore at Seabright, N. J.; 3 of the crew lost..Duel between Bennett and May in Delaware; nobody hurt..Str. Montgomery sunk by a collision off Cape May; 13 persons drowned....Gen. Miles defeats Crazy Horse's band at Wolf Mountain..Hermann Brockhaus, German Orientalist, died at Leipsic, Ger....9. The Russian fleet, with the Grand Dukes Alexis and Constantine, arrives off Charleston.... 12. Fall of 300 feet of the glass roof of Grand Central Depot, N.Y., from the weight of the snow..Earthquake in California.....13. Ice gorge on Ohio River; great loss of life and property; $2,000,000 each at Pittsburgh and Cincinnati....14. Battle with the Indians near Elkhorn....15. The Great Powers submit their modified ultimatum to Turkey..American ship George Green lost with all on board, on the English coast....17. Rear Admiral Joseph Smith, U.S.N., 83, died at Washington, D C..Shower of serpents at Memphis, Tenn..Election riot at Montreal; sacking of Town Hall..News of dreadful famine in India; British Government estimate cost of relief at $32,500,000....18. Crazy Horse captures a wagon train and kills 20 men west of the Missouri..Turkish Porte unanimously reject the ultimatum....20. Str. George Washington, N. Y. for St. Johns, N.F., lost near Cape Race; 29 persons drowned....21. Capt. Richard R. Locke, one of the Dartmoor prisoners and a veteran of 1812, died at Rye Beach, N.H..Jno. C. Lord, D.D., Presbyterian, 71, died at Buffalo.... 23. Fire in Bolton, Eng., colliery; 15 lives lost.... 24. 300 people massacred in Cali, U.S. of Colombia, S.A.....25. Memorial statue of Robert Burns unveiled at Glasgow..Guerillas attack Gen. Welshes, of Santander, Spain, and are defeated with 400 killed and 600 wounded and prisoners....27. Memorial of

1,500 bankers and brokers, asking for repeal of all special taxes on National banks, presented to Congress....28. Moody and Sankey meetings commence in Boston...Signor Blitz, prestidigitateur, dies at Philadelphia, 67....29. First meeting of National Sunday School Congress in Chicago....31. Electoral Commission (bill signed 28th) organized with five Senators, five Representatives, and five Supreme Court Judges..First Mexican installment ($300,000) paid....Feb. 1. Keeper Custer, of Auburn State Prison, murdered by Wm. Barr, a convict..Servia and Turkey agree upon a preliminary treaty of peace....5. A Spanish vessel boarded by pirates off North Guinea..Midbat Pasha deposed from Grand Viziership of Turkey; Edhem Pasha his successor ....6. Burning of S.S. Bavaria, en route from N.O. to Limerick..Rev. W. M. Daily, D.D., LL.D., formerly President Louisiana State University, Methodist, 65, died at N. Orleans..Outbreak among Apache Indians in Arizona..Rear Admiral James Alden, U. S. N., died at San Francisco..Col. J. O'Mahoney, Fenian leader, 57, N.Y. City..British Str. Ethel ashore on Lundy Island, Wales, and ten persons drowned..The Electoral Commission by a vote of 8 to 7 decides not to go behind the returns..Crazy Horse's band defeated by Gen. Miles, near Tongue River...... 8. Henry B. Smith, D. D., LL. D., Professor Union Theological Seminary, Presbyterian, 61, died in N. Y...Rear Admiral Chas. Wilkes, U. S. N., 76, died Washington, D.C...Opening of English House of Parliament....10. Gunpowder explosion at Adhernahed, India, kills 50 and wounds 1,000 persons..R'r Admiral Theodorus Bailey, U.S.N., 74, died at Washington, D.C....11. Sir Wm. Ferguson, President of Royal College of Surgeons, 69, died in London....12. Rinderpest spreading throughout Germany..New insurrection in Bosnia....13. New Stock Exchange organized in New York....14. Receiver appointed for New Jersey Central Railroad..Aime de Pichot, French writer, died in London..Gen. Changarnier, 84, died in Paris, France....15. Attempt to assassinate Gov. Packard, in New Orleans..Col. Gordon, African explorer, appointed governor of the Province of Soudan, Africa..Coal mine explosion at Graissessoc, France, and 55 miners killed....16. L. D. Pilsbury confirmed as Supt. of N. Y. State prisons..Midhat Pasha arrives at Naples....17. Gen. Diaz elected Pres., and Ignacio Vallaste, Chief Justice of Mexico....18. Attempted assassination of the Archbishop of Mexico..Rear Admiral Chas. H. Davis, U. S.N., 70, died at Washington, D.C....19. Judge H. W. Williams, a Justice of the Supreme Court, died at Pittsburgh, Pa....20. Rear Admiral Louis Goldsborough, U. S. N., 72, died at Washington, D. C.. Rinderpest at Hull, Eng... 21. British bark Marie wrecked off west coast of Africa; 12 men lost..Boiler explosion at Middleton, Ohio, killing 4 and injuring 12 persons....22. Train thrown from railroad track near Lowell, Mass., by train wreckers..Str. Franconia wrecked off Point San Blas..Maj. Gen. Amos B. Eaton, Commissary Gen. U. S. A., died at New Haven, Conn....24. Submarine volcanic eruption at Kalakaua Bay, Hawaiian Islands....25. Furious storm on the coast of Long Island; several vessels and crews lost....26. 229 Sioux Indians surrender at the Cheyenne Agency....27. Whaling Str. Spitzbergen, with 20 persons, lost near Bergen, Norway.. Ex-Gov. Joseph Johnston, 92, died at Bridgeport, Va. ..The Electoral Commission decide all the doubtful States for Hayes and Wheeler by a vote of 8 to 7.... March 1. Formidable mob dispersed in Charleston, S C...Gov. Hayes leaves Columbus, Ohio, for Washington..The Miridites take up arms against Turkey, and besiege the Puka fortress..The British Mediterranean squadron ordered to concentrate at Malta.. ..2. The electoral count completed, and Messrs. Hayes and Wheeler declared duly elected President and Vice-President of the U. S.....3. Joel T. Hart, sculptor, 67, died at Florence, Italy..Chief Justice Waite administers the oath of office to Pres. Hayes ..Diplomatic relations between Turkey and Servia restored.....5. Bateman House at Kansas, Pa.. burned; 6 persons perish..XLIVth Congress adjourns *sine die*..President Hayes and Vice-President Wheeler publicly inaugurated..Special session of Senate opened..Marquis de Compiegne, distinguished African traveler, killed in a duel at Cairo, Egypt ..Austria concentrates troops on the frontiers of Dalmatia and Croatia..C. D. Compton,.Marquis of Northampton, 61, died in London....6. Franklin J. Moses, Sr., Ch. Jus. Supreme Court of S. Carolina, 72, died in Columbia, S. C...Destructive fire in Bond street, N. Y. (Robbins & Appleton building); loss, $1,561,000..Joe Coburn, notorious pugilist, sent to Sing Sing for ten years....7. The President nominates his cabinet..Matilda A. Heron, actress, 47, died in N. Y..Panic in the St. Francis Xavier Church, N. Y.; several persons killed...Ashtabula bridge declared by coroner's jury to have been unsafe, and Lake Shore R R. Co. censured....8. Explosion in Worcester, Eng., coal mine and death of a large number of miners....9. Montenegro and Turkey cannot agree upon a peace basis....10. Tenement house in New York burned with three inmates.. Cabinet nominations confirmed...Senator Simon Cameron resigned..Rev. E. O. Hovey, Professor of Chemistry and Geology, 76, died at Crawfordsville, Ind....11. 250 Communists (convicts) pardoned in France....13. Chas. Cowden Clark, Eng. author, 91, died at Genoa, Italy..Mme. Octavia Le Vert, authoress, 67, died at Augusta, Ga..Henry M. Stanley announced the survey of Lake Tanganyika.....14. Six Chinamen murdered in Chico, Butler Co., Cal., by a gang of white ruffians..The Khedive presents Cleopatra's needle to Great Britain..Fred. Douglass appointed United States Marshal for the District of Columbia....15. Diaz recognized as President of Mexico by U. S...Stephen S. Jones, editor, Chicago, shot dead in his office by Dr. W. C. Drake....17. U. S. Senate adjourns..Six hours fight between Bosnians and Turks near Orezgonia.....18. Str. Russland from Antwerp for New York, went ashore at Long Branch..Iglesias, late President of Mexico, but deposed by the Diaz revolution, issued a proclamation from New Orleans..England demanded a modification of the Russian protocol..Sir Edward Belcher, Rear Admiral, commander of an expedition in search of Sir John Franklin, 78, died in London .....19. Ex-Gov. Emory Washburne, of Mass., 77, died at Cambridge, Mass..J. Donald Cameron, late Secretary of Treasury, elected U. S. Senator from Penn..Saigo begins a formidable rebellion in Japan .....20. Congress appropriates $200,000 to complete the Washington Monument....21. Leipsic fixed upon as the seat of the Imperial Court of Germany..Death of Prince Charles of Hesse Darmstadt..President Hayes' cabinet decide upon a Louisiana Commission ....22. Labor crisis in Germany....23. Jno. D. Lee, one of the Mormon murderers at the Mountain Meadow massacre, was executed there; his confession implicates many leading Mormons....24. Village of Madrid, St. Lawrence Co., N. Y., almost destroyed by fire....26. Walter Bagehot, publicist, died in London..Prof. Jno. S. Hart, teacher and author, 67, died in Phila....27. Dam of the Staffordsville, Conn., reservoir gives way; two persons drowned; $1,000,000 loss..One editor kills another in Topeka, Kansas..Sir J. F. Fitzgerald Field Marshal British Army, 91, died in Tours, France...28. Prince Antoine Bonaparte, nephew of Napoleon I, died in Florence, Italy....29. Mexican authorities imprison U. S. Consul Sutton....30. Revolt in Pashalik of Diarbekir, Armenia..General Charette presents Cardinal Simeoni with an album containing the signatures of over 30,000 volunteers, who are ready to fight for the temporal power of the Pope....31. The Cabinet decides to withdraw the U. S. troops from South Carolina..Russia amended protocol, incorporating England's suggestions, accepted by the powers..... April 2. First telephone concert at Steinway Hall, N. Y. City..Bismarck tenders his resignation as Chancellor of Germany....3. Capt. Fred'k Lahrbush, formerly of British Army, 111, died in N. Y. City....4. Prospects of war in the East increasing; Russia determined to fight....5. Orville D. Jewett kills his uncle and himself by exploding a hand-grenade in his store in Front st., N. Y....6. The Louisiana Commission commences its session at New Orleans..Insurgent Gen. Trujillo defeats conservative forces in U. S of Colombia, S. A., and the State of Antioquia is surrendered to him....8. Rev. Frederick A. Muhlenberg, D.D. an eminent philanthropist and founder of St. Luke's Hospital, and St. Johnland, 80, died in New York; and John Conant, also a philanthropist, 87, died at Jaffray, N.H...... 10. U. S. troops withdrawn from the State House in Columbia, S.C.; Gov. Chamberlin gives up the contest....11. Southern Hotel in St. Louis burned, and 10 lives lost..Prof. Smith, of Rochester, discovers a new comet near Cassiopeia..Ross Winans, an eminent inventor, 80, died at Baltimore, Md....12. Joseph, chief of Nez Perces, in Oregon, declines to go on the Lapwai reservation..Russian troops move toward the Roumanian frontier.....13. S.S. Leo, Savannah to Nassau, burned at sea; 3 passengers and 18 of crew lost..Darien exploring expedition returns to Panama....14. Lorenzo Sabine, ex-M.C. and author, 75, died at Boston, Mass..1,000 Indians, Roman Nose's band, with their chief, surrender to Gen. Crook at Spotted Tail Agency..Turkey rejects the terms of the protocol of the Great Powers; panic on the Vienna Bourse....15. Grand Duke Nicholas reviews Russian army of the Pruth....17. Japanese insurgents defeated and put to flight..50,000 people in London make a demonstration in favor of Tichborne claimant..Russia and Turkey making energetic preparations for war..Tweed delivers a statement to the Attorney General....18. The Murphy temperance movement spreading throughout Pennsylvania and Ohio..An insurrection breaks out in Spain....19. The Louisiana Commission reports in favor of Nicholls for Governor, and his Legislature....20. Twelve oil wells and tanks destroyed by lightning in Butler Co., Pa...The Roman government determines to dissolve all Republican and International Associations in Italy....21. Eight lodges of Cheyennes, comprising 550 persons—85 fighting men, surrender to Gen. Crook..Brig Roanoke, Wylie, Philadelphia to Porto Cabello, lost at sea; 11 persons drowned..Emperor of Russia arrives at Kischeneff..Revolt in Paraguay; a brother of the President assassinated, but the conspirators routed....23. Russia declares war against Turkey..Jassy (in Roumania) occupied by Russian troops: the Montenegrins occupy Kistar. Russians cross the Pruth at three points.....24. Withdrawal of U. S. troops from Louisiana State House. End of the Packard government.....26. Atrocious murder of Judge Chisholm, his son and daughter and Mr. Gilmer, by a mob in De Kalb, Kemper Co., Miss...First battle of the war near Batoum, on the Black Sea; Russians lose 800....29. Str. Sidonian, Glasgow to N.Y., explodes a boiler, 7 killed..Montreal Novelty Works burned; 9 killed, 10 injured..Battle before Kars. Russians under Melikoff defeat Moukhtar Pasha..Ex-Senator and Gov. Wm. G. Brownlow (Parson Brownlow), 72, died at Knoxville, Tenn....31. Roumanians, Montenegrins and Herzegovinians join Russia against Turkey....May 1. Queen Victoria issues a proclamation of neutrality in the Eastern war..Part of the roof of the N.Y. post-office falls, killing 3 men....2. Diaz declared elected President by the Mexican Congress...Russian troops capture Bayazid in Armenia. Montenegrins hold the Duga Pass, blockading Goransko and Niesics. the Press law of 1865 suspended at Constantinople..Col. John Forsythe, editor, 66, died at Mobile....3. Great land slide in Canada on banks of river Veillett; 5 persons killed..The Porte issues a circular denouncing Roumania's treachery.....4. Rev. Mr. Miller suspended for heresy by New Jersey Synod..Turkish monitors bombard Reni..President Hayes calls an extra Congressional session for Oct. 15....5. Spanish government offer amnesty and pardon to all Cuban insurgents who will lay down their arms.....6. Crazy Horse and his band of 900 Sioux surrender..Russians bombard Kars....7. King of Abyssinia declares war against the Khedive of Egypt..Transvaal Republic, South Africa, annexed to British Empire....8. Expiration of sewing machine patents..Postal convention with Italy signed by President..Turkish monitors bombard Russian batteries at Ibrail, and with the fortress at Widin, bombard Kalafat also..Cossacks cross the Danube....9. Explosion in Wadesville mine, St. Clair, Pa., killing 7 and wounding 2..A fanatical outbreak in the Tchelohantse country, in consequence of the Turkish war, put down by the Russians; 100 killed, 250 wounded..Commodore B. S. Totten, U. S. N., 71, died at New Bedford, Mass....10. Opening of permanent exhibition at Philadelphia by President Hayes..Iquique, and 15 other towns and villages in Peru partly or wholly destroyed by an earthquake; 600 lives and 20 millions of property lost..Rev. F. X. Schenhous, founder of the Redemptionist order in America, 68, died in Baltimore....11. Prof. Taylor Lewis, LL.D., 75, died at Schenectady, N.Y..Walls of an unfinished court-house at Rockford, Ill., fell, killing 10 workmen..Turkish iron-clad sunk by Russian masked batteries near Ibrail..Russians defeated at Batoum with heavy loss, in an 8 hours battle....12. Japanese Empire admitted to Postal Union from June 1....13. Diaz recognized by Germany..L.J.E. Picard, French statesman, 56, died in Paris....14. Poisoning of miners at Streator, Ill..Burning of villages of Clinton Mills, Edinburgh and Forest in northern N. Y...Six Turkish iron-clads bombard Sukum Kaleh, but are defeated..President Hayes attends the banquet of the Chamber of Commerce....15. Unveiling of statue of Fitz Greene Hallock at Central Park, N.Y...Five-foot tidal wave in Lake Erie..The Mirdites drive the Turks from Oroschi..Mexican authorities at Acapulco apologise for imprisoning Consul Sutton, and salute his flag.....16. The Legislature of Illinois attempts to make silver coin a legal tender for all debts in the State..Commodore E. W. Carpenter, U.S.N., 70, died at Shrewsbury, N. J...Crisis in the French cabinet..Destructive forest fires in Michigan..Tornado at Fulton, Mo., destroys 10 buildings and part of railroad depot....17. Dedication of revolutionary monument on Dorchester Heights, Mass...Ex-President Grant sails for Europe in the Str. Indiana..Ardahan with 22 cannon captured by the Russians...Terrible famine in Shan-tung and Chih-li provinces, China....19. Convention at Deadwood, Dakota, to take steps for organizing the new territory of Lincoln..Prince Cassan, the Khedive's son, left for Constantinople with 6,000 Egyptians...Ex-Gov. Kent, of Maine, 75, died at Bangor, Me...Count H. de Tocqueville, life Senator, died in Paris, France....21. Roumania declares her independence and proclaims war against Turkey....22. Accident at launch of S.S. Saratoga, at Chester, Pa.; - men crushed to death and 2 injured..Sir M. D. Wyatt, architect, died in London...Ghivet burned by Russians; Adler bombarded by Turks; Forts Tahmaz and Kara Dagh, outworks of Kars, bombarded by Russians....23. W. H. Hosmer, poet, died in Avon, N.Y...Don Carlos leaves France for Linz, Austria...Russians repulsed at Batoum.....24. Religious war proclaimed in Bosnia..Ten Broeck, at Louisville races, makes the fastest one mile on record—time, 1.39¾.....26. Gen. and Mrs. Grant arrive at Queenstown..The Russians blow up a large monitor on the Danube with torpedoes....28. Lieut. Lawton leaves Red Cloud Agency for the Indian territory with 972 Cheyennes and Arapahoes...The Russians carry Sameba Heights.....29. The Turks defeat the Russians near Kutari....29. Fletcher Harper, last survivor of the original Harper Brothers, 71, died in N. Y...John Lothrop Motley, historian and diplomatist, 63, died in London.....31. Moukhtar Pasha dismissed and disgraced....June 1. Gen. Ord instructed to follow marauding parties of Mexicans across the Rio Grande...Gen. Grant given a reception by the Prince of Wales at Marlboro House, London.....2. Fire caused by lightning near Millerstown, Pa.; $85,000 worth of petroleum destroyed....3. Fiftieth anniversary of the consecration of Pius IX as a bishop observed at Rome..Sophia Frederica Matilda, Queen of Holland, 59, died at the Hague, Holland...Mrs. Elizabeth F. Ellet, authoress, 59, died in N. Y.....4. Tornado visits Mt. Carmel, Ill.; 11 persons killed and many injured...Waterspout does great damage in Iowa, N. W. of Burlington.....5. Over 15,000 million feet of standing pine timber destroyed by forest fires in Michigan and Wisconsin..A Greek patriarch, in a pastoral letter, counsels loyalty to Turkey...The Czar arrives at the front.....6. A bridge falls at Bath, Eng., and nearly 200 persons thrown into the Avon; 12 killed and 50 injured.....7. Cleopatra's needle, destined for England, exhumed.....8. A hat shop burned at Bridgeport, Conn.; 11 men killed by falling walls...Destructive fire in Galveston, Texas; $1,500,000 of property destroyed...New levy of 218,000 men ordered in Russia...The Turks try to force the Duga Pass in Montenegro and lose 4,000 men.....9. Fast passenger traffic inaugurated by the Pennsylvania and connecting Western roads...Persia applies for admission into the Postal Union.....12. Collision on Balt. & Ohio R.R. near Point of Rocks; 6 persons killed.....13. Corner stone of a Soldier's Home laid at Bath, N.Y...Mustapha Tewfic Pasha appointed commander at Kars..Suleiman Pasha, after a bloody battle, forces the Duga Pass and advances on Niesics...Ludwig III, Grand Duke of Hesse-Darmstadt, dies at Darmstadt.....14. Prince Louis of Hesse, under the title of Ludwig IV, becomes Grand Duke..Russians repulsed before Kars after three days fighting...Covered bridge over Connecticut river at Hadley, Mass., blown down...Celebration in Boston of the 100th anniversary of the adoption of our present national flag..A dam bursts near Belvidere, N. J., killing 6 persons...Gen. C. F. Henningson, 62, died at Washington, D.C...Bancroft Davis resigns as minister to Germany.....15. Rt. Hon. Sir George Mellish, Lord Justice of Appeal, died in London..Mary Carpenter, authoress, died in Bristol..Lady Maxwell (Hon. Mrs. Norton), 70, London.....16. Severe battle between Turks and Montenegrins at Rasnoglevika; Turks defeated with a loss of 2,000 dead and wounded...James Russell Lowell accepts the mission to Spain.....17. Str. Lizzie burned in the Gulf of Mexico, 3 lives lost..Rev. John S. C. Abbott, author, 71, died in New Haven, Conn.....19. Moukhtar Pasha's right wing defeated.....20. Three-fourths of St. John's, New Brunswick, destroyed by fire; 30 persons killed..Chas. F Briggs, author and journalist, 67, died in Brooklyn, N. Y...Admiral Rous, 82, died in London..C. H. Upton, U. S. Consul at Geneva, Switz., died there....21. Ten "Mollie Maguires" hung—six at Pottsville and four at Mauch Chunk..Judge Hilton excludes Jews from the Grand Union Hotel, Saratoga.....22. President Hayes issues an order prohibiting office-holders from taking an active part in politics..Iowa Republican Convention refuses to indorse the President's Southern policy..Commodore John W. Goldsborough, U. S. N., 69, died in Philadelphia, Pa.....23. The Turks march on Cettinje, capital of Montenegro, having effected a junction after six days fighting.....25. Large fire at Marblehead, Mass., 72 buildings destroyed...President McMahon pardoned 844 Communists...Queen

Victoria received Gen. Grant at Windsor Castle... Robert Dale Owen, author, died at Peerless Point, Lake George.....26. Harvard defeats Columbia in an eight-oar boat race at Springfield, Mass......28. Monument in honor of the defenders of Fort Moultrie in 1776, unveiled in Charleston, S. C ...A revolution breaks out at Puerto Plata, San Domingo... Giovanni Santini, Italian professor of Astronomy, died at Padua, Italy....July 1. The celebrated trotting mare, Lady Thorne, died..General reduction of wages on railroads; fears of strikers...Battle at Sistova. The Turks victorious.....2. Fight between Col. Whipple's command and Indians on Clearwater River, Idaho..The Pan-Presbyterian Council began its session in Edinburgh, Scotland..President MacMahon called on the army to sustain him through the crisis.....3. The British Mediterranean fleet arrived in Besika Bay..Inundations in the province of Murica, Spain; 22 persons drowned.....4. Capt. J. A. Webster, senior officer in U.S. Revenue Service, died in Baltimore, Md.....5. The Turks driven out of Montenegro...Louisiana Returning Board members tried on charge of forgery.....6. Gen. Grant arrives at Brussels..120,000 Russians cross the Danube..Russian campaign in Armenia a failure..F.W. Hacklander, traveler and author, died in Munich. .....7. U. S. troops cross the Rio Grande in pursuit of Mexican marauders...Destructive storm in Pensaukee, Wis.; almost the whole town levelled; 6 persons killed..Russians capture Tirnova, capital of Bulgaria...Khedive of Egypt offers a fleet to the Porte....8. Russians forced to withdraw from Kars, with heavy loss.....9. Hurricane at Springfield, Mass...Export of horses from Germany prohibited. ..Prof. Sanborn Tenney, of Williams College, 50, died in Buchanan, O......10. Chief Joseph's Nez Perces kill 31 Chinamen in Idaho....11. Six miners killed in a mine explosion at Wheatland, Pa...Fight between U.S. troops and Nez Perces at Cottonwood; Capt., Lieut. and 11 men killed; 13 Indians killed.. Meeting of Georgia Const. Convention... 12. Attack on Orangemen in Montreal, 1 killed, 4 wounded.... Russians routed and driven from Plevna....Gen. Grant in Germany..Gen. Sir Geo. Bell, K.C.B., died in London....13. Baron W. E. von Ketteler, Bishop of Mayence, died there.....14. Boiler explosion at Macurgy, Pa., 3 men killed....15. British Str. Eton wrecked off the coast of Chili, and over 100 lives lost ....16. Great railroad strike on Balt. & Ohio R.R. ..$68,000,000 subscribed to date of the U.S. 4 per cent. loan..The Russians capture Nikopolis on the Danube ....17. Strike continues on Balt. & Ohio R.R. The whole line blocked...Ex-Gov. Tilden and Hon. J. Bigelow, Sec. of State of N. Y., sail for Europe....18. Gov. Matthews, of W. Virginia, calls for government aid to suppress the riot; 250 regulars sent.....19. The strikes become general over all the roads managed by the Balt. & Ohio and Penn. Central ..Suleiman Pasha appointed commander of the army of Roumelia..Hon. D. A. Lapham, author and scientist, 68, died at Milwaukie, Wis.....20 to 26. The strikes become general on most of the trunk roads, though very slight on New York Central.... 21. Terrible riot and conflagration at Pittsburgh, Pa., more than $3,000,000 of property destroyed.. Collision between State troops and rioters; many killed and wounded..Pittsburgh rioters surrender on 23d..Riotous demonstrations against Chinese in San Francisco..On the 25th riots in Chicago, Louisville and St Louis; many killed and wounded.... 26. Another riot in Chicago; 21 killed and many wounded..Bloody riot in Reading, Pa....27. Affair quieting in all quarters...N. Y. militia ordered to their homes....29. All trunk roads open again, but great disorder in the coal regions....Foreign, 20 to 29. Russians attack Osman Pasha, but are repulsed with heavy loss..Suleiman Pasha is defeated by Russians at Karabunar..The Russians destroy six railroad bridges on the Danube..Montenegrins bombard Niesics..On the 29th the Czarowitch's forces defeated the Turks near Rustchuk, taking 8,000 prisoners, 31 guns and 10 standards..On the 24th Escobedo, the Mexican insurgent general, was arrested..On the 26th eight men were killed by a boiler explosion near Tunstall, Eng..30. Centennial anniversary of the adoption of the New York constitution celebrated at Kingston...The Russians were defeated near Plevna...Gen. Ghourka won a victory over the Turks at Yeni Sagra, Roumelia.... On the 25th George W. Matsell, ex-police superintendent and commissioner, died in New York....On the 28th Prof. Isaac W. Jackson, M.D., of Union College, 72, died at Schenectady, N. Y....On the 29th George Ward Hunt, 1st Lord of the Admiralty of Great Britain, died in Hamburg....On the 30th Commodore J. W. Swift, U.S.N., died at Geneva, N. Y., and same day Samuel Warren, an eminent English author, died in London....31. W. H. Vanderbilt ordered $100,000 to be distributed ratably among the employees of the N. Y. Central who had not joined in the strike......August 1. Gov. Robinson pardons young Walworth, the parricide...Riot at Scranton Pa..Schr. Florence, of Howgate's expedition, sailed for the North Pole....2. The town of Conejo, Panama, burned....3. Wm. B. Ogden, first mayor of Chicago, 71, died at Fordham Heights, N. Y...Box factory in Cincinnati burned; several girls burnt to death..Great fire at East Saginaw, Mich.; $200,000 destroyed....4. Poorhouse at Simcoe burned, 17 inmates perished..Field Marshal Von Steinmetz, 71, died at Landeck, Silesia....5. Eaton, Wis., burned; several lives lost..Russians defeated south of the Balkans....6. Centennial celebration of battle of Oriskany....7. General order prohibiting the sale of arms and ammunition to Indians..Repulse of Russians at Lovatz....8. Riots at Belfast, Ireland ..Gen. Grant in Switzerland....9. Gen. Gibbon fights the Nez Perces in Montana, a drawn battle.... A train fell through a drawbridge at Oceanport, N. J.; 60 persons injured..Dr. A. B. Crosby, professor in Bellevue Med. College, 45, died in Hanover, N H. ... 10. Political troubles increasing in France; many Republican papers there suspended.....13. Mexican outrages on the Rio Grande: Mexicans cross the river, murder Judge Cox and another man, release Mexican murderers from jail and escape across the river....Chauncey Rose, an eminent philanthropist, died in Terre Haute, Ind....15. The struggle between the Russians and Suleiman Pasha for Shipka Pass commenced..Wm. Longmuir, London publisher, 78, died in London....16. Rev. Asa D. Smith, D.D., LL.D., president of Dartmouth College, died at Hanover, N.H ..Prof. Asaph Hall discovers two satellites of Mars..Centennial celebration of the battle of Bennington attended by more than 60,000 people....18. Gayville, Dakota, almost entirely destroyed by fire, 200 buildings consumed, loss $60,000....19. Moukhtar Pasha repulses a Russian attack....20. Consolidation of Western Union and Atlantic and Pacific Telegraph Companies.. Great strike in Pennsylvania coal regions, 50,000 men out....21. Meeting of National Board of Trade at Milwaukee, Wis....22. Insurrection in Crete.. Another revolt in Bosnia....24 and 25. Sharp and continuous fighting in Shipka Pass..The Russians gain and hold some important positions..The Turks capture Kiziltope, but are defeated at Kuruk Dara ... 26. Dr. H. Draper and Prof. C. S. Holden discover a third satellite of Mars...Hon. E. P. Noyes, Minister to France, reaches Paris...27. The Knights Templars of the U. S. hold their 20th triennial conclave at Cleveland, Ohio...Strike ended in the Lehigh Valley coal regions..Senor Costello and his son, leading Cuban insurgents, surrender to the Spanish authorities....28. Conference of State Governors at Philadelphia..Ben De Bar, actor, 61, died at St. Louis, Mo....29. Railroad accident near Des Moines, 20 persons killed..Brigham Young, the Mormon prophet and chief, 76, died at Salt Lake City, Utah... 30. Monument to John Brown, of Ossawatomie, Kansas, dedicated, in presence of 10,000 people..Raphael Semmes, ex-commander of the Confederate cruiser Alabama, 68, died at Point Clear, Ala..The village of Karahassenlar captured by the Turks after a severe battle, Turkish loss 3,000 killed and wounded, Russian loss 4,000...Russians defeated on the Lom, Popkoi abandoned, and the Russian position completely turned....31. Fire at Paris, Texas, 10 business blocks destroyed, loss $250,000..Osman Pasha gains a signal victory at Plevna ....September 1. Tornado at Maysville, Ky..Meeting of Am. Association for Advancement of Science at Nashville, Tenn....Alvan Adams, founder of Adams Express Co., 73, died at Watertown, Mass.. E. L. Davenport, actor, 61, died at Canton, Pa..... 2. Insurrection in China among interior tribes.... 3. Louis Adolphe Thiers, ex-president of France, 80, died in Paris, France..Hale's piano factory, N. Y., burned and several persons killed..A house in Cincinnati undermined and falls, killing 4 women ....4. "Crazy Horse" arrested at Spotted Tail Agency for attempting to induce the Indians to go to war..Russians capture Lovatz after 12 hours fighting....5. "Crazy Horse" is killed while trying to escape from the guard house at Camp Robinson ....7. President Hayes and party leave Washington for a visit to Ohio and other States....8. Rev. Edwin Hall, D.D., professor of Theology at Auburn, died there..The Catholic Bishop, Amedeus, died at St. Albans, Vt....9. Niesics surrenders to the Montenegrins..The deaths from famine in Madras, India, reported to be about one million....11. Yellow fever appears at Fernandina, Fla....12. The British ships Avalanche and Foster collide off Portland, Eng., 104 persons drowned..Gambetta sentenced to fine and imprisonment for a political speech, but the case appealed and the sentence never carried out..The Russians again repulsed at Plevna with terrible loss..Herculano de Carvalho, Portuguese historian, 67, died at Lisbon....14. Rev. Benjamin Schneider, an eminent missionary to Turkey, died in Boston, Mass....15. The American rifle team win the international match at Creedmoor..Four persons murdered by Chinamen near Rockton, Placer county, California..Constantine Canaris, prime minister of the Kingdom of Greece, 86, died at Athens, Greece ....17. The Presidential party cordially received at Louisville, Ky..Chinese quarters at Grass Valley, Cal., burned..Soldiers' and Sailors' monument at Boston dedicated..Queen Pomare, of the Society Islands, died there.....18. Eastern bound express train on Union Pacific R.R. robbed by thirteen men at Big Springs, Neb.; $78,000 taken..H. M. Stanley, the African traveller, reaches St. Paul de Loanda (west coast of Africa), having crossed the Continent and traced the Congo or Livingstone river from its source to the sea....19. Centennial celebration of the battle of Bemis Heights... 20. Louis V. Bogy, U. S. Senator from Missouri, 64, died at St. Louis, Mo. ....21. Collision on N. Y. Central R.R. near Rome, N. Y., three killed and several wounded..Str. Olga sails from Alexandria, Egypt, towing the caisson containing the obelisk..Great battle of Biela, in which the Russians are defeated, losing 4,000 killed, 8,000 wounded....22. W. H. Fox Talbot, the father of photography, 77, died in London, Eng.... 23. The famine in India subsiding, heavy rains having fallen in many of the districts...Urbaine J. J. Leverrier, astronomer, 66, died in Paris....24. Patent Office at Washington partially burned..President Hayes in Va..Japanese insurgent leaders slain and rebellion ended..A hurricane in Curaçoa, W. I., destroying two million of property and many lives..Yellow fever raging at Vera Cruz; 140 deaths in August.... 25. The Montenegrins captu e Goransko, Pina and Fort Grivica, and Vum Belek and surrou ding villages....26. Lieut. Bullis crosses the Rio Grande in pursuit of Mexican raiders..Commodore J. M. Frailey, U. S. N., 6), died in Philadelphia, Pa ...28. Conference at Washington of Sioux Indians with the President....29. Osman Pasha again defeats the Russians at Plevna..Henry Meiggs, the great South American railroad contractor, 66, died in Peru.... 30. Village of Putnam, Conn., nearly destroyed by fire..Wm. C. Gilman, a wellknown business man in New York, detected in forgery and swindling to the extent of $236,000..Unsuccessful attempt at revolution in Hayti..Russians defeat 4,000 Daghestan insurgents......October 1. Sioux delegates at Washington consent to removal to the new reservation recommended by the President..Heavy but indecisive battle in Asia Minor between Russians and the Turks under Moukhtar Pasha....2. The Sultan confers the title of Ghazi (conqueror) upon Osman Pasha and Moukhtar Pasha..Woman suffrage proposition defeated in Colorado..Lewis Lillie, inventor and manufacturer of safes, died at Elizabeth, N. J. ....3. Car shops of New York Dry Dock R.R. Co. burned, loss $500,000..Boiler explosion at Shedder-town, Ohio, three men killed and several others fatally injured..Spanish troops defeat 2,000 insurgents on the Looloo Islands...Railroad accident between Worenseh and Norstoff on the Don; 400 Abchasian prisoners killed...J. R. Bayley, D.D., Roman Catholic Archbishop of Baltimore, 63, died in Newark, N.J...Mme. Teresa Titjiens, prima donna, 43, died in London ....4. Centennial of battle of Germantown, Pa..Severe cyclone, doing great damage, along the S. and E. Atlantic coast..Excursion train wrecked near Phœnixville, Pa.; 12 killed and a number injured....5. Col. Miles captures Chief Joseph and the Nez Perces after a three days' battle ....6. Great number of Cuban insurgents surrender ..Wm. Gale walks 1,500 miles in 1,000 consecutive hours, beginning Aug. 26....7. Senator L. O. Bordeau died in Paris, France....8. First suit under the timber depredation laws, in Minnesota, is decided for the government...Severe earthquake at Geneva, Switzerland....11. Explosion in a colliery at Pemberton, Eng., 40 killed..Spanish government pays $570,000 indemnity to Minister Lowell for losses by American citizens in Cuba....12. Wm. C. Gilman (referred to in Sept.) surrenders himself and is sent to State prison for five years....14. The "Cleopatra's needle" encounters a heavy storm en route to England, and is abandoned off Cape Finisterre; is subsequently picked up and taken to Ferrol, Spain..Republicans gain an overwhelming victory in the French elections....15. Prof. Peters, of Clinton, N.Y., discovers a new planet of the eleventh magnitude..Extra session of Congress opened at Washington; Samuel J. Randall chosen speaker of the House..Antonio Scialoja, eminent Italian lawyer and publicist, dies at Rome....16. 4,000 N. Y. cigar makers on a strike..Theodore Barriere, dramatic author, died in Paris..Geo Hadley, M.D., Prof. of Chemistry, 64, died in Buffalo....17. Centennial celebration of surrender of Burgoyne at Schuylerville, N.Y....19. Heavy fighting at Kars....20. Fire in Portland, N. B.; 250 buildings burned; 2,500 persons homeless....22. Colliery explosion at High Blantyre, Scotland; 200 lives lost...23. Commission interviewed Sitting Bull at Fort Walsh, Canada, but were unsuccessful....24. George L. Fox, pantomimist, 52, died at Cambridge, Mass..Prof. Jas. Orton, of Vassar College, scientist, 47, died in Bolivia, S. America....25. The Turks repulse the Russians at Phrygos....26. Ismail Pasha effects a junction with Moukhtar Pasha..Ku Klux outrages in Clark Co., Ohio..91 deaths from yellow fever in Fernandina to date....28. Edwin Adams, actor, 42, died in Philadelphia, Pa...Julia Kavanagh, novelist, 53, died in Nice, Italy..Joseph Durham, sculptor, died in London....29. N. B. Forrest, ex-Confederate general, 56, died in Memphis, Tenn..Meeting of National Liberal League at Rochester..E. W. Stoughton nominated as Minister to Russia....30. John Walsh nominated Minister to England..Goldsmith Maid, famous trotting mare, 21 years old, withdrawn from the turf..... November 1. Collision between freight and express trains on Philadelphia and Erie R. R.; 5 men were killed....Wm. Gale, pedestrian, London, completed 4,000 quarter miles in 4,000 consecutive periods of 10 minutes each, beginning October 20.... President McMahon gives a dinner to Gen. Grant at Elysee, Paris....Oliver P. Morton, U. S. Senator from Indiana, and former Governor, 54, died at Indianapolis....Field Marshal Frederick Von Wrangel, 93, died in Berlin, Prussia.....2—Chief Justice, W. K. Draper, C. B. 77, died in Toronto, Canada....4 Earthquake shocks throughout northern New York, New England, and the Eastern British Provinces, at 2 A.M. ....5—Bland Silver bill passed the House....6—Elections held in 12 States....Gustav Brion, French painter, died in Paris... Heavy battle near Erzerum; Russians repulsed....7.—Amelia, dowager Queen of Saxony, died in Dresden....9—Insurgents in San Domingo increasing in numbers. Alarm at the Capitol.....10—Schooner Magellan wrecked on Lake Michigan; 8 lives lost....Forty of Ex-Sultan Murad's servants strangled, for aiding in a conspiracy to reinstate him....Martin Paine, M.D., LL.D., professor, &c., 83, died in New York City.....11—Riot in El Paso County, Texas.....12—Suit commenced by Cornelius J. Vanderbilt and his sister Mrs. LaBau, to break his father's will....Prof. Watson of Michigan University discovers a planet of the 11th magnitude.... Great Storm on the British Coast; loss $1,200,000.... F. Blodgett, Ex-Governor of Georgia, died at Atlanta, Ga ....Passage of the Army appropriation bill by the House....13—Henry Peters Gray, artist, 58, died in New York City....14—Burning of Field, Leiter & Co's dry goods house, Chicago; loss, $250,000.... Billiard match for the world's championship, Saxton beats Cyrille Dion....Trans-Pacific Cable Company, organized to lay a Cable from California to Japan, *via* Honolulu, Capital stock, $10,000,000....15—Explosion of fire-damp, in Jermyn Colliery, near Scranton, Pa., a number killed and injured....Earthquake shocks in Iowa, Nebraska, and in the N. W. generally, and S. to Tennessee....Army appropriation bill amended and passed by Senate....16—Pierre Lantrey, Republican Senator of France, died at Versailles....18—Russians capture Kars by a brilliant night assault....19—Fort Edward Institute burned. ....20—Julius Kircher of New York, cremates his dead infant....21—The Roumanians after a three days battle, capture Rahova....John V. L. Pruyn, LL.D., Chancellor of Board of Regents of University of State of New York, died at Albany, N. Y.....23—Steamship Alabama, lost on Coast of South America; 70 drowned....Diaz orders Trevino with 2,500 troops to the Rio Grande, to repel invasion by U. S. troops ....Canadian Fisheries commissioners, one dissenting, deci es that the U. S. shall pay Great Britain $5,500,000 for fishing in Canadian waters....24—The revolution in Ecuador collapses....U. S. Steamer Huron wrecked at Kitty Hawk, N. C.; 100 lives lost ....26—All night session of U. S. Senate....27—Steamer C. H. Northam burned in N. Y. Harbor, three lives lost....27—Twenty colored people drowned and 30 horses swept away by a flood at Buckhannon, Va....29—Workingmen's demonstration against the Chinese in San Francisco; Kearney comes to the front....The insurrection in San Domingo spreads over the entire country....30—The Senate pass the Paris Exposition bill....Thirty mile Oil Pipe between Great Belt and Pittsburgh, Pa. completed....Commodore C. N. B. Caldwell, U. S. N., died at Waltham, Mass....December 2—Messrs. Moody & Sankey commence their labors in Providence, R. I....The leading merchants and manufacturers of Paris, appeal to President McMahon to yield to the majority, in the interests of trade and of the International Exposition....2—Steamboat Lotus burned on the Mississippi, near Waterloo, La.; 11 lives lost....Extra session in Congress closed and regular session opened....Attorney Gen. Conner of S. C., resigned ....4—Turks capture Elena....Robert Tyler, son of the late Ex-President, died in Baltimore..Consul Gen. Sturz a German philanthropist, died in Berlin, Prussia....5. Austria protests against Servia's participation in the Russo-Turkish war....6. Fire in Millerstown, N. Y. loss $200,000..French ministry tender their resignations, and McMahon accepts them..M. Dufaure granted perfect liberty in forming a new Cabinet by the President..Reports of terrible famine in Bulgaria....7. John A. Collins *alias* Thorpe hung in Auburn for the murder of a fellow convict..Erie Canal closed..Wreck of the Steamer European in the English channel, no lives lost..Rev. Dr. A. T. Bledsoe, editor and author, 69, died in Alexandria, Va. ..Active Temperance crusade in Baltimore, over 12,000 sign the pledge....9. $800,000 fire in Louisville, Ky...Plevna surrendered unconditionally to the Russians by Osman Pasha, 30,000 prisoners and 77 guns surrendered....10. Gen. John M. Harlan, takes the oath of office as Associate Justice of the U. S Supreme Court....12. The Grand Turkish Council at Constantinople resolve to carry on the war to the last extremity..The Czar visits Osman Pasha, and returns his sword....J. Cogswell Perkins, author, 68, died at Salem, Mass..13. A new French Ministry announced.. Rev. Samuel Spring, D. D., Congregationalist author, 85, died in East Hartford, Conn. 14. Town of Osceola, Mo. taken possession of by a masked mob..Servia declares war against Turkey; the Turks burn and evacuate Elena..An insurrection in the province of Amyro, Crete....15. The Porte asks the European powers to mediate..The Servians cross the Turkish frontier at Pirot, and march on Kossovo, and on the 16th fortify the heights of Topolnitza and Secanika, commanding the defence at Nitzsch....16. President Hayes nominates ex-Gov. R. C. McCormick, of Arizona, Commissioner General to the Paris Exposition....17. Ardanitzsch carried by assault by the Russians..All the powers except England refuse to interfere between Russia and Turkey..D'Aurelle de Paladines, corps commander in 1870-71, and life Senator of France, died in Paris. 18. Texas State troops surrender to the mob at San Elizario..Orders given in Russia for the immediate mobilization of 60,000 more troops....19. Jas. Ballantine, author, 69, died in Edingburgh, Scotland. ..Reports of famine in Nothern China..Six persons suffocated with coal gas at Randolph, Mass; two children burned to death at Newport, N. Y....20. Explosion in Greenfield & Son's confectionary factory in New York, 15 lives lost..Cabinet crisis in Germany..Russian loss by the war to date, officially stated at 80,412 men..Merry B. Jackson, M. D., Prof. of diseases of children, Boston University, 75, died in Boston....21. The famous racing mare Flora Temple, died near Philadelphia, aged 32 years... Prince Charles of Roumania, receives the Iron Cross from the Emperor William....22. American Museum of Natural History at New York, formally opened by President Hayes..Excise Commissioner Murphy of New York, absconds with $50,000 of the public funds....23. The Porte ineffectually attempts to depose Prince Milan of Servia..Henry M. Stanley arrives at Aden, Arabia, on his way home..Terrible snow storm in Roumania; hundreds of Russian soldiers and Turkish prisoners perish....24. Robert P. Parrott, (Parrott's rifled cannon,) inventor, died at Cold Spring, N. Y...Mrs Hatfield and three children drowned through the ice near Yarmouth, Nova Scotia....The insurgents at Crete convoke the National Assembly to establish a Provincial government. ..The Servians are repulsed at Yatic, but capture Ak-Palanka after eight hours fighting....26. Thirty thousand Servians with 120 guns invest Nitzsch.. Montenegrins defeat a Turkish force near Dulcigno. ..George A. Bailey, publisher of the Congressional Globe, died at Deering, Me....27. The Servians are repulsed at Novi Bazar and Pirot by the Turks..... 28. Explosion in the Stanton shaft near Wilkesbarre....30. The British Channel fleet and all commissioned ships under repair, ordered to be ready for sea by January 15..G. Dodge, M. D., for several years superintendent N, Y. State Inebriate Asylum, died at Binghamton, N. Y....31. Gustave Courbet, artist and communist, died in Paris... President Hayes' silver wedding celebrated in Washington.

1878.

January 1. John S. Randall, noted entomologist and numismatist, 60, died at Utica, N. Y.....2. Albania invaded by the Montenegrins..Turks defeated at Bogrov..Seven men killed by a nitro-glycerine explosion at Negaunee, Mich..Emile Lambinet, French artist, 70, died in Paris.....3. Russians capture Sophia in Central Turkey..Communication between Servians and the Russian army of the Vid..Retreat of Suleiman Pasha on Stalitza....4. Marquis Wilopolski, Polish statesman, died in London....5. Report of the massacre of 15,000 people in Kashgar by the Chinese..Stanley welcomed at the court of the Khedive..U. S. steamer Kearsarge driven ashore in Portsmouth harbor..John Orton Cole, 84, died in Albany..Gen. Alfonso de la Marmora, Italian soldier and statesman, 73, died in Florence, Italy....8. Occupation of Stalitza and Petrichero by the Russians. ..Retreat of Chakir Pasha..Don Francisco de la Guerra, Mexican statesman, died in Mexico. Count de Palikao, French statesman and Senator, 81, died in Paris....9. Russians under General Radetsky capture entire Turkish army at Shipka Pass..Resolutions introduced in the Massachusetts Legislature favoring a gold standard, and condemning the Bland Silver Bill..Victor Emanuel II, King of Italy, 57, died in Rome....11. Fernando Wood's investigation resolution passes the House..Nissa captured by the Servians after a five days' battle..Eski-Saghra and Yeni-Saghra occupied by the Russians..Demetrius Bulgaris, Greek Statesman, died in Athens....12. Great fire in London, loss over $1,000,000....13. Central Superintendency of Indian affairs discontinued by order of Secretary Schurz....14. Thirteen lives lost by the wreck of the schooner Little Kate, off Duxbury. Mass....15 Sixteen persons killed and a large number injured by a railroad accident near Tariffville, Conn..$300,000 voted for the new State Capitol at Albany..General McClellan inaugurated Governor of New Jersey....16. Lead City, Dakota, captured by border ruffians..Samuel Bowles, journalist (Springfield Republican), 51, died at Springfield, Mass....17. Four negroes killed by a mob at Lexington, Ky..Treaty of commerce and friendship between the United States and Samoa signed....18. Commodore George W. Hollins, U. S. N., 79, died at Baltimore....19. The Ohio Senate passes a joint resolution favoring remonetization of the silver dollar and passage of the Bland bill..Turks evacuate Adrianople..Banquet to Stanley at Paris..Insurrection at Thessaly and Macedonia....21. Cleopatra's needle arrives in England..Servian troops occupy Pristina and Kar Shumli..Widdin completely invested and bombardment commenced..E. K. Collins, founder of Collins' line of Steamships, 76, died in New York city....22. Russians occupy Adrianople. ....23. Marriage of Alfonso, King of Spain, to the Princess Mercedes .The Austrian Cabinet resigns.. Gen. Aug Willich, 68, died at St. Mary, Ohio....24. Earls of Derby and Carnarvon, of the British Ministry, resign....25. The U. S. Senate passes Matthews Silver resolution....26. Terrible famine reported in China; 9,000,000 people starving..William Gale completes a walk of a quarter of a mile every ten minutes for thirteen consecutive days..Dr. Jno. Doran, a noted English author, 70, died in London. ....27. Three islands in Lake Scutari, captured by Montenegrins..George P. Gordon, inventor of the Gordon printing press, 67, died in Norfolk, Va....28. Defeat of the Turkish army at Raschasink by the Servians..Revolt in Athens....29. Turks defeated by Thessalian insurgents on Mount Pelion..Sir Edward S. Creasy, English historian, 65, died in London....30. Joseph Hildebrand, German philosopher, 72, died in Germany. . 31. Sir. Metropolis, Philadelphia to Brazil, driven ashore on Currituck Beach, N.C., and wrecked, nearly 100 lives lost..Armistice signed between Russia and Turkey......February 1. Storm on the Atlantic coast, many vessels wrecked ..Panic in Constantinople..Russians occupy Kazan ..Stranding of British steamer Astarte at Castillos, and 30 lives lost...George Cruikshank, English artist and designer, 85, died in London....2. Postal convention signed between the United States and Australia....3. 800 Red Cloud Indians go upon the war-path...Gov. Wells, of Louisiana, surrenders... Chas. Thomas, brevet Maj-Gen. U. S. A., 80, dies at Washington, D.C..Erzeroum surrenders to the Russians .An asylum in Tien-Tsin, China, burned with 2,000 persons....5. Prefect of St. Petersburg shot by Vera Sassulitch....6. Russians take possession of the fortifications at Constantinople.. .7. Giovanni M. M. Ferretti, Pope Pius IX, 85, dies at Rome..Conclusion of Louisiana trial; Anderson convicted.... 8. Tornado at Augusta Ga.....9. Epirus insurgents proclaim a union with Greece..Immense tidal wave on the coast of Peru..Evacuation of Widdin, Rustchuk, Silistria, and Belgradshvik by the Turks.... 11. Ship British America and brig Carrie Winslow collide off Sandy Hook; several lives lost...Gideon Wells, ex-Sec. of Navy, 75, died in Hartford, Conn. ..Charles M. Conrad, ex-U. S. Senator and ex-Sec. of War, 73, died in New Orleans, La...Wm. Welsh, philanthropist, 76, died in Philadelphia...12 Reception by Congress of Carpenter's picture of Abraham Lincoln....13. The British fleet entered the Dardanelles..Rev. Dr. Alexander Duff, missionary, 71, died at Lidmouth, Eng...Mother Teresa (Miss Mary Hannah Sowell), founder of a religious order, 87, died in Baltimore.....14. Turkish Parliament dissolved

....15. Opening of the Spanish Cortes..Bayard Taylor nominated Minister to Germany....16. Passage of the Bland silver bill..Withdrawal of the British fleet to Madanea Bay...Rev. Wm. Goodell, pioneer abolitionist, 85, died at Janesville, Wis....17. Fourteen persons drowned by the sinking of the steamer C. R. Palmer..Disastrous fire in New York, two churches and six stores burned; loss, $1,000,000.....18. Russia persuaded not to occupy Constantinople....20. End of the ten-years' Cuban rebellion..Cardinal Pecci elected Pope, and takes the name of Leo XIII....21. Concurrence of the House in the Senate amendments to the silver bill, and the measure sent to the President... 22. National Greenback party organized at Toledo, Ohio..Prof. Albert Smi h, M.D., LL.D., 78, died at Peterboro, N.H....23. Passage of an act by the Utah legislature disfranchising Gentiles....24. Collision of a ferryboat and a schooner in the Hudson river; several killed... 25. R. W. Taylor, first Comptroller of U. S. Treasury, died in Washington..Hon. Townsend Harris, ex-U.S. Consul to Japan, died in N.Y. City..Gen. Duplessis, French soldier, died in Paris....26. Destructive floods in California, causing the loss of many lives..Father Angelo Sacchi, Italian astronomer, 60, died in Pisa, Italy....27. The Bland silver bill vetoed by the President..The Archbishop of Rennes died there....28. Passage of the Bland silver bill over the President's veto..reorganization of the New York State Military Association......March 1. Excitement in England, and preparations made for a conflict with Russia....2. Duel between M. de Cassagnac and M. Thompson, the latter wounded in the throat..Benj. F. Wade, ex-Vice-President of U. S. and ex-U. S. Senator, 77, died at Jefferson, O....3. Signing of the treaty of San Stefano between Russia and Turkey..Coronation of Pope Leo XIII..Great demonstration at Pottstown, Pa., in opposition to the Tariff bill....4. Tornado in Casey county, Ky., and several persons killed..Mr. Porter, of Indianapolis, nominated for first comptroller of the Treasury..Confirmation of Bayard Taylor as Minister to Germany....5. Hot Springs, Ark., nearly destroyed by fire....6. Judge Asa Briggs, ex-M.C. and ex-U.S. Senator from N. C., 68, died in N.Y. City....7. Opening of Italian parliament...Count Paolo F. Schlopis, one of the "Alabama" arbitrators, an Italian statesman, 79, died in Italy..The Archduke Francis, uncle of Emperor of Austria, died in Vienna...8. Colliery explosion near Glasgow, great loss of life....9. Printing of one and two dollar greenbacks resumed by the Treasury department..Terrific wind and snow storm in the west; snow 15 feet deep in the streets of Cheyenne, Wyo....10. Outbreak of cholera in Arabia..Burning of the transport steamer Sphinx near Cape E in, 7,000 Circassians perish...Overthrow of President Baez in San Domingo.....11. Disgraceful hazing affair at Dartmouth College....12. Colliery explosion near Bolton, Eng., 40 lives lost....13. Jefferson county, W. Va., swept by a terrific storm..A. Viollet le Duc, architect, landscape painter and author, died in Paris....14. Commodore Robert F. Pinkn y, U.S.N., 66, died at Baltimore, Md....15. Commodore John H. Graham, U.S.N., 84, died at Newbury, N. H...England commences a war with the Caffres in South Africa.....17. Treaty of peace ratified at St. Petersburg..Robbery of the Lechmere bank, Boston ...18. Great strike of weavers in England ...19. O'Donovan Rossa riot in Toronto, Can...Anderson released by order of Supreme Court of La...20. End of the Hayti rebellion...Prince Bismarck's ultimatum to Nicaragua...Paul Boyton swims the Strait of Gibraltar....22. Five persons killed by a boiler explosion at Richmond, Va....23. Steamer Magenta bursts a steam pipe near Sing Sing, N.Y., six persons killed..O'Leary wins the international walking match in London..4 000 houses destroyed by fire in Tokio, Japan...John Allison, Register of the Treasury and ex-M. C., died in Washington, D. C.... 24. Sinking of the British naval training ship Eurydice off the Isle of Wight, 300 lives lost.. .25. A million-dollar fire in Philadelphia....26. Fire in New York, loss $500,000....27. Forty persons killed by a colliery explosion in North Staffordshire, Eng... 28. Glenni W. Scofield confirmed as Register of the Treasury ....30. Ex-President Grant received by the Pope.... April 1. Opening of the Mexican Congress..Marquis of Salisbury becomes Secretary of State in English Cabinet... 2. Assassination of the Earl of Leitrim, clerk and driver, in Derry, Ireland....5. Mob violence in Rhode Island cotton mills, Kent county..20 persons killed and injured by an oil explosion at Mauch Chunk.....7. Burning of the Bath, N. Y., poorhouse, 15 inmates perish in the flames...Boiler explosion in a Boston factory and several persons killed....9. Thirteen buildings destroyed by fire in Galveston, Texas....11. Steenburg, the Amsterdam, N.Y., murderer, confesses to eleven murders..Prince Napoleon Lucien C. J. F. Murat died in Paris...Ex-Chief Justice T. Bigelow, 68, died in Boston, Mass... Rev. George Putnam, D.D., 71, died in Boston, Mass. ....12. Portions of Kansas swept by a tornado, great loss of life and property..Wm. F. Tweed, 55, died in New York..E. Delafield Smith, ex-U. S. District Attorney, died in New York..Dr. J. Behrendt, ethnologist, died in Guatemala, Central America..George Tyler Bigelow, LL.D., 66, died in Boston, Mass....13. Fifteen acres of Clarksville, Tenn., burned over, loss $500,000..Oxford wins the boat race with Cambridge on the Thames....14. Canton, China, devastated by a hurricane, accompanied by two water-spouts... Town of Goa, Venezuela, destroyed by an earthquake...17. Three murderers lynched at Huntsville, Ala...18. Collision between white and black miners, and a number killed, at Coal Creek, Ind....19. A general strike in the manufacturing districts of England..Riots in Montreal...Geo. W. Blunt, Pilot Commissioner and author, 76, died in New York.. Rev. P. F Lynden, Catholic Vicar-general of Boston, 66, died there....20. Rev. J. P. Dubreuil, D.D., Vicar-general of Baltimore, Md., 63, died there....21. The Azor sails from Charleston, S. C., with 250 colored emigrants for Liberia....22. Promulgation of the Pope's encyclical asserting temporal power..Nihilist troubles in Russia...Wm. Orton, President Western Union Telegraph Co., 54, died in New York....23. Destructive tornado in western Iowa...24. Prof. Malaguti, chemist, 78, died in Sevres, France....26. Geo. Grant, founder Victoria Colony, Kansas, died there....27. The Barclay street explosion, in New York City, loss $1,500,000..Delegation of distinguished Southerners entertained at Boston.....28. Gen. Todleben appointed to succeed the Grand Duke Nicholas in command of the Russian army in Turkey..Twenty persons killed by a boiler explosion at Dublin, Ireland....30. First contingent of British troops sent to Malta.....May 1. Opening of Paris Exposition..John Morrissey, gambler, State Senator and ex-M.C., 47, died at Saratoga....2. Flour mill explosion at Minneapolis, killing 17 persons..W. S. O'Brien, "Bonanza King," died at San Rafael, Cal. ....4. England transports native troops from India to operate against Russia.....5. Count Schouvaloff sets off on a mission of peace....6. Packard nominated for consul at Liverpool....7. An insurrection in Central Turkey; 21 Mohammedan villages destroyed....10. The Canadian parliament prorogued ..S.S. Sardinian burned at harbor of Londonderry, three killed and forty injured...Troubles with the Mexicans on the Texas border...The bankrupt act repeal bill passed....11. Attempted assassination of Emperor William by Hoedel.... 13. Seventeen American vessels chartered by Russia...Catharine E. Beecher, educator and author, 77, died in Elmira, N. Y.....13. Prof. Joseph B. Henry, LL.D., scientist, secretary Smithsonian Institute, 80, died in Washington, D.C...Mrs. John Bright, wife of Hon. John Bright, died at Rockdale, Eng....Maj.-Gen. Thos. S. Dakin, celebrated rifle shot, 46, died in Brooklyn, N. Y.....16. Cotton strike riots at Preston, Manchester and Burnly, Eng.....17. The Potter investigation ordered by the House of Representatives...Message from President Hayes on the fishery award....18. Meeting of the American Social Science Association in Cincinnati....19. Forty persons burned to death in a Calcutta theatre..Rev. S. M. Isaacs, journalist, 74, died in New York....22. A pleasure steamer capsized in Grand river, Canada, and nine persons drowned..Francis Peralto rode 305 miles in 14 hrs. and 31 min. at Fleetwood Park, N Y....23. An Indian outbreak in Montana....24. Great storm in Wisconsin, attended with loss of life ....25. Duchess of Argyle died at Edinburgh...John A. Bolles, naval Solicitor-general, 69, died in Washington..Jno. Scott Harrison, ex-M. C., died at North Bend, Ind.....28. Invitations to the Berlin Congress issued by Germany..Earl Russell (Lord John Russel.), formerly British Premier, 86, died in London, Eng..30. Severe drought on the Island of Jamaica...Sinking of the German naval vessel Grosser Kurfurst in the English channel, and nearly 300 lives lost..The body of the son of ex-President Harrison found in an Ohio medical college....June 1. Uprising of the Bannock Indians....2. A tornado destroys 100 houses at Richmond, Mo..Wreck of the str. Idaho on the coast of Ireland...Nobeling attempts the assassination of Emperor William.....3. Vera Sassulitch escapes from the Russian authorities...400 Russians massacred in Roumelia....6. The Pope appeals to the powers to protect Catholics in Turkey..Rev. Nath'l Bouton, D.D., historian, 77, died at Concord, N. H... John Wingate Thornton, historian, 60, died at Boston, Mass..Gen. Neville Baraguay d'Hilliers, French soldier and statesman, 83, died at Paris....7. Peace proclaimed in Cuba..Colliery explosion in Lancashire, Eng., killing 240 persons...The act repealing the bankrupt law signed by the President..Five negroes lynched at Bayou Sara, La....9. Capt. Har per's fight with the Bannock Indians...Amnesty granted to Cuban patriot prisoners...Turkey selects two Christians to attend the Berlin Congress..Bulgarians burn 19 villages and commit horrible atrocities..Earthquake in Lisbon, Portugal..John A. McGahan, journalist and war correspondent, 33, died at Constantinople..Dr. Manuel Freyro, Peruvian Minister, dies at Washington, D.C....11. Ten thousand natives killed by a tornado in China..Adjournment of the French Senate and Chamber of Deputies...Downfall of the Catholic Ministry in Belgium..Wm. Cullen Bryant, poet and journalist, 83, died in New York..Ex-King George of Hanover died....13. Meeting of the Berlin Congress..Prof. G. W. Keeley, LL.D., 73, died in Waterville, Me.....14. Messrs. Fenton, Groesbeck and Walker nominated as commissioners to the International Monetary Congress....18. Col. Wm. M. Vermilye, founder of banking house, 72, died in New York....19. Schr. Eothen sails from New York for the Arctic regions in quest of the relics of Sir John Franklin...Centennial anniversary of the evacuation of Valley Forge..Rev. Chas. Hodge, D.D., LL.D., theological professor and author, 83, died at Princeton, N.J..Thos. Winans, of Baltimore, inventor and millionaire, died at Newport, R.I....20. Hanlan defeats Morris in a sculling race at Hulton, Pa...Congress adjourns..Gen. Fitz Henry Warren, 62, died at Brimfield, Mass..800 French Communists pardoned....22. Great fire in Montreal....23. Col. Geo. P. Kane, Mayor of Baltimore, &c., died there....24. Chas. T. Matthews, comedian, 77, died in Manchester, Eng....25. Battle with the Indians at Curry Creek, Oregon....26. Russia sends troops into Servia....26. Queen Mercedes of Spain, 18, dies at Madrid, Spain....27. Austria empowered to occupy Bosnia and Herzegovina...Judge Sidney Breese, ex-U. S. Senator, 85, died in Illinois..Mrs. Sarah H. P. Whitman, poet and author, 75, died in Providence, R.I....28. Harvard defeats Yale in a boat race at New London, Conn..Centennial of the battle of Monmouth in New Jersey....29. Tunnel caves in at Schwelm, Ger., burying 25 persons....July 1. Independence of Roumania and Montenegro acknowledged.....2. Twenty five thousand men out of employment in the Schuylkill mining regions....3. Centennial anniversary of the massacre of Wyoming...Dr. J. C. Ayer, chemist and patent medicine manufacturer, died at Winchendon, Mass....4. Ten persons killed and fifteen injured by lightning at a picnic near Pittsburgh..A New London picnic party struck by lightning...Rev. John Dowling, D. D., clergyman and author, 70, died at Middletown, N.Y....5. Victory of the Columbia College crew at the Henley regatta in England....6. Indian fights in Oregon....7. Batoum ceded to Russia..Resignation of the Austrian Cabinet..4,700 houses destroyed by fire in Mandalay, Burmah...French elections for deputies, and large Republican gains..Explosion in a petroleum factory in France, and 30 lives lost....8. Battle with the Indians at Willow Springs and Beasley's Mills, Oregon...Geo. S. Appleton, book publisher, 53, died at Riverside, N.Y...9. Announcement of a secret treaty between England and Turkey....10. Gen. Howard fights a severe battle at Head Birch Creek ...12. Capt. Webb swims about 40 miles in 9 hrs. 57 min., Thames river, England....13. Berlin treaty signed by all the plenipotentiaries, and Congress adjourns...Harvey J. Eastman, educator, mayor of Poughkeepsie, died there.....14. Canadian troops fire into a mob at St. Henri Junction ...15. Removal of Arthur and Cornell from the New York custom-house...150 cases of sunstroke at St. Louis....18. A train of 22 cars fall through a bridge at a height of 90 feet near Monticello, Ind., killing several persons....20. Gen. Merritt becomes collector, and Gen. Graham surveyor of customs at New York...Geo. F. Shepley, judge of First United States District Court, Maine, 67, died in Bangor.....21. Grand Army encampment at Gettysburg....22. Lord Beaconsfield made a knight of the garter....23. The order of the garter conferred upon the Marquis of Salisbury...Meeting of the National Greenback Convention at Syracuse..Riot at East St. Louis, Mo...."Minnie Warren" (Mrs. Newell), a very beautiful dwarf, sister of Mrs. Tom Thumb, 28, died in Massachusetts.....25. British ship Loch Ard lost with 47 lives..Rev. Samuel C. Jackson, D.D., Congregationalist clergyman and author, 76, died in Mass....26. A boat capsizes near Blackwater, Ireland; 14 children and 3 teachers drowned..Riotous demonstrations in Washington, D.C....Col. Forsyth routes the Indians near Sharkie's ranche.....28. Grand banquet to Beaconsfield and Salisbury in London...Austrian army enters Bosnia...Marquis of Lorne appointed Governor-General of Canada...29. Total eclipse of the sun, observations being made at Denver and other points....Four negroes hanged by a mob at Monroe, La....30. German parliamentary election...31. Ratification of the treaty of Berlin..Hanlon defeats Ross in a boat race at Riverside, N. B.....31. Yellow fever breaks out at New Orleans.....August 1. Arrival of Chinese embassy at San Francisco...Cardinal Alessandro Franchi, 59, died at Rome....2. Michael Rees, California millionaire, died at Wallenstein, Germany... 3. Rarus trots a mile in 2:13¼ at Buffalo, N.Y., the fastest time on record...Commodore Chas. H. Jackson, U.S.N., 75, died in Philadelphia....6. Bogardus wins the international shooting match in England... 7. Beginning of the Austro-Bosnian war..Collision on the Panhandle R. R., near Steubenville, O.; 15 persons killed and 40 injured.....8. Powder magazine explodes at Fratesi, Russia, killing 45 persons.....9. Terrific storm and loss of many lives at Wallingford, Conn....10. Arrival at New York of the Columbia crew..Opening of the international monetary conference at Paris....11. A Russian embassy sent to Cabul...H. T. Montague, actor, 35, died in San Francisco.....12. Gen. Grant received with great honor at St. Petersburg..Hanlon wins the scull race at Barrie, Ont...Russian torpedo boat explodes at Nicolaieff, and 31 persons killed....13. The Sultan ratifies the Berlin treaty..Serious Orange riot in Ottawa..The cabinet approves the universal postal treaty..Yellow fever appears at Memphis, Tenn.....15. Passenger train wrecked near Chillicothe, Ohio..Austrians defeated near Tuzla..Stacy Baxter, Prof. of Elocution at Harvard University, 60, died at Cape May, N. J....J. H. Raymond, LL.D., President Vassar College, 64, died at Poughkeepsie, N. Y....16. Hoedel beheaded at Berlin....17. Rapid spread of the yellow fever in the South...Richard Upjohn, architect, 77, died in New York....18. Terrible explosion at Pottsville, Pa...Gen. Grant has an interview with the Czar....20. Austrians occupy Serajevo....21. National regatta at Newark..Ex-Queen Maria Christina de Bourbon of Spain 72, died at St. Adresse, France..Wm. Niblo, founder of Niblo's Garden, 89, died at New York....22 Powder mills explode at Negaunee, Mich., and several employees killed....27. Ex-Gov. Padelford, of R.I., 71, died at Providence, R.I....30. A pardon to the Fenians Melody and Condon granted by the English government...Miskolcz, Hungary, almost entirely destroyed by a storm, and over 500 persons drowned..A nitro-glycerine explosion at Negaunee, Mich., with great loss of life....31. A general rush into bankruptcy, owing to the expiration of the bankrupt act..Judge Thomas B. Dwight, 41, died in Andover, Mass.....September 1. J. G. Dickerson, LL.D., Judge of the Supreme Court of Maine, 65, died in San Francisco....2. Anniversary of Sedan celebrated in Germany..British Columbia wants to withdraw from the Union..Forest fires on the shore of Lake Michigan, extending over 160 miles....3. Bishop McCoskry, of Michigan, deposed from the Episcopate. Sinking of the steamer Princess Alice in the Thames, causing a loss of over 500 lives....6. Gen. J. T. Sprague, U. S. A., died in New York City....7. Albanians murder Mehemet Ali, the Turkish general, and 20 of his suite....8. Trebinje surrendered to the Austrians....9. Meeting of the German Reichstag..Maine election, and large increase of Greenback vote....11. Two hundred and eighty lives lost by a colliery explosion in Wales....13. Russians evacuate Erzeroum..Great storms in the west, causing much destruction to railroad property....14. The Porte accepts the English programme of reforms for Asia Minor....16. Defeat of the Canadian Government in the elections....17. The Butler-Democratic-Greenback Convention at Worcester..Rev. Pierre P. Irving, D. D., Episcopal, nephew of Washington Irving, and author, 72, died at New Brighton, S. I., New York......18. Ex Gov. A. Charlet, of Ill., 78, died at Dixon, Ill.....20. Arrival of the Chinese Embassy in Washington. Cheyenne raid in Kansas..Col. Thomas B. Thorpe, author, 63, died in New York....22. Whole towns swept away by a tornado in Hayti..British mission to Afghanistan refused permission to enter Cabul....23. Russians evacuate San Stefano..Eruption of Mt. Vesuvius..Tuzla surrendered to the Austrians.....24. Suicide of Ex-Congressman A. H. Laflin, at Fitchburg, Mass..Treaty between the United States and the Samoan islands ratified..Col. James A. Hamilton, eldest surviving son of Alexander Hamilton, 90, died at Irvington, N. Y..25. John Penn, an eminent mechanical engineer, died in Philadelphia..Gen. Henry Raymond, oldest survivor of the war of 1812, 90, Jersey City....Ex-Judge B. F. Thomas, Ex-M. C., died at Salem, Mass..Dr. August H. Petermann, eminent geographer, by suicide, 56, Gotha, Germany....29. Betrothal of the old King of Holland....30 Yellow fever at its height at Memphis and New Orleans; more than 300 deaths per day....October 2. Failure of the City of Glasgow Bank. Austrian ministerial crisis..Moungion,

King of Burmah, probably, died Sept. 12, but not announced till Oct. 2..Cyrille Dion, champion billiard player, 35, died at Montreal, Can....3. Hanlon defeats Courtney in a sculling race at Lachine, Can...4. Insurrection in Santa Cruz..Turks massacre Sadi Pasha, and 156 officers and men at Podgoritza ....5. Austria conquers the Bosnian insurgents.... Sir Francis Grant, President Royal Academy, 75, died in London, Eng..6. Lord Chelmsford died in England..Rev. Nehemiah Adams, D. D., 72, died in Boston..Advance of the Afghans to the Khyber pass..Disaster on the Old Colony Railroad near Boston; 21 persons killed and a large number injured....9. The Porte's circular to the powers arrests Austrian cruelties in Bosnia and Herzegovina ....10. Rt. Rev. Thomas Galbeny, D. D., R. C. Bishop of Hartford, 45, died there....11. Panic in a Liverpool theatre, 22 persons trampled to death.... Archbishop Felix Antoine Dupanloup, of Bordeaux, member of French Assembly, died at Bordeaux..... 13. The town of Edinburgh, Pa., reduced to ashes.. Five negroes lynched at Mt. Vernon....14. Mysterious murder of Policeman Smith, at Jersey City... The jury in the Billings trial disagree, and are discharged..Meeting held at Rheims in favor of the Franco-American commercial treaty..Pierre Soule, Ex-Minister to Spain, rebel Commissioner, died in New Orleans, La....15. Commodore Schufeldt's cruise to Africa..Baron Von Pretis Cognoda intrusted with the task of forming a new Austrian cabinet....16. Convention signed between the Cretans and the Turks..Nine persons killed by a panic in a colored Baptist Church, at Lynchburg, Va.... Gen. Gideon J. Pillow, Mexican war and rebel General, died at St. Helena, Ark....17. A New Bedford whaler capsized and 73 fishermen drowned......19. Passage of the German Anti-Socialist bill....Benjamin H. Latrope, Jr., eminent civil engineer, 71, died in Baltimore, Md....20. Rear Admiral Hiram Paulding, U.S.N., 81, died at Huntington, L. I....20. The German Socialists leave the Reichstag in a body... Railroad collision in Wales, and 12 persons killed and 20 injured....21. Fifteen villages inundated by the Nile..Rt. Rev. S. N. Rosecrans, R. C. Bishop of Columbus, and brother of Gen. Rosecrans, 51, died at Columbus....22. Resignation of the whole Italian cabinet....23. Pennsylvania visited by a windstorm, and many people killed and injured...Cardinal Paul Cullen, 75, died in Dublin....25. Loss of the steamer City of Houston, on the Florida coast.. Moncasi attempts the assassination of King Alfonso, of Spain....27. Robbery of the Manhattan Bank, New York....28. Strike of 30,000 Clyde iron workers..Bulgarian insurrection spreading..Arrival in Ireland of Lord Dufferin....30. Resignation of the Grecian Ministry....31. Terrible ravages of cholera in Morocco..Steamer Helvetia, from Liverpool to New York, runs down and sinks the British coastguard cruiser Fanny, and 17 lives lost....November 1. Great conflagration in Maynooth College, Ireland..Extensive strike in English cotton-spinning district..Garnier Page, French statesman and historian, died in Paris....3. Christopher R. Robert, philanthropist, founder of Robert College, Constantinople, 77, died in Europe....6. Jean Jaques Fazy, Swiss statesman, died in Switzerland......7. Robbery of A. T. Stewart's grave in New York..Appeal of Mormon women in Utah against polygamy...H. W. Bache, U. S. coast survey, died in Bristol, R. I.. Robert Howell, artist, engraver of "Audubon's Birds," died at Tarrytown, N. Y.......9. Principal part of Cape May, N. J., destroyed by an incendiary fire....11. Midhat Pasha appointed Governor of Syria.....N. B. Judd, Ex-M. C., and Ex-Minister to Berlin, 66, died in Chicago....12. Switzerland gives notice that she will withdraw from the Latin Union ..End of the yellow fever in the southwest..Total number of deaths from the scourge, 20,000..Memphis the greatest proportional sufferer; 5,000 deaths out of 12,000 people....14. Gen. Grant received with great honors in Madrid..Great flood in Italy...John S. Sleeper, "Hawser Nightingale," former proprietor of Boston *Journal*, 84, died in Boston....17. Passanante attempts the life of Humbert I., of Italy.... Publication of Lord Salisbury's reply to Secretary Evarts on the fishery question....18. Political massacre at Lemberg, Germany..Destructive inundation in Norwich, England..Assassination of Don Manuel Pardo, Ex-President of Peru..Serious loss of life by inundation of the river Save, at Pesth, Austria....20. A reward of $50,000 offered for the recovery of A. T. Stewart's body and conviction of the thieves..War begun between England and Afghanistan..Duel between M. Gambetta and M. de Fourtou; neither injured ...21. Explosion at a coal mine at Sullivan, Ind., fourteen men killed and a number injured..Payment of the fisheries award under protest by Minister Welsh in London, Russian Gen. Kauffman's extraordinary assurance to the Ameer..British success in Khyber pass......23. Arrival of the Sarmatian at Halifax with the Marquis and Marchioness of Lorne on board....24. Unveiling of the Humboldt statue at St. Louis......25. Sinking of the steamer Pommerania by a collision near the English coast, with the loss of twenty lives ..27. Khurum Fort occupied by the British..Flight of the Afghan garrison to Peiwar.....Fifty persons jump off a ferry boat at Liverpool, and are drowned, owing to a panic..Robert Heller, magician, 45, died in Philadelphia..28. Louis A. Godey, proprietor of "Godey's Lady's Book," 76, died in Philadelphia... English forces enter Khyber pass, in Afghanistan... 29. Riot in Breathitt county, Ky..Lyman Tremain, Ex-M. C. and Ex-Attorney-General of N. Y., 65, died in Albany..Col. Robert Chustre Buchanan, U.S.A., 67, died in Washington, D. C..Commodore William T. Spicer, U.S.N., 57, died in Washington....December 1. Collision on the Mississippi between the steamers Charles Morgan and Cotton Valley; sinking of the latter with the loss of 20 lives..George H. Lewis, author, husband of "George Eliot," died in London..Alfred Wigan, an actor, died in London... 2. Opening of the International Dairy Exhibition in New York city....Congress convenes..Rt. Rev. Joseph P. B. Wilmer, Professor, Bishop of New Orleans, died there....3. Evacuation of Jelallabad by the Ameer's forces; twenty villages burned and most of the inhabitants massacred by the Macedonian insurgents..4. Opening of the English Parliament..Formation of a new Turkish Ministry..General Roberts wins a victory in Peiwar pass......5 Ovation to Emperor William on his return to Berlin.....Capt. Whyte Melville, novelist, died in England..Senor Rivero, chief of the progressionists and democrats in Spain, died there....7. Arrest of an American, Romer, in Constantinople, charged with conspiracy against the Sultan....8. Failure of the West of England Bank....9. Publication of the Ameer's reply to the Viceroy of India..British Consulate at Adrianople raided by the Russians.....10. Banishment of Mahmoud Damad Pasha to Tripoli.. Heavy floods in New York and various other States ..James H. Monahan, Chief Justice of Common Pleas and privy councillor, 73, died in Dublin...... Henry Wells, founder of Wells College, and Wells & Fargo's Express, 73, died in Glasgow, Scotland..... 11. Discovery of rich silver fields at Leadville, Colorado..12. A general uprising reported against the authority of the Ameer in Afghanistan.....The commandant of Fort Ali-Musjid blown from the mouth of a cannon..The Afghans plead for peace... 14. Abdul Kerim and Redif Pasha banished to Rhodes..The Princess Alice Maud Mary, of England, Grand Duchess of Hesse Darmstadt, died at Darmstadt of diphtheria, aged 35 years.......16. Cholera and famine carrying off thousands of people in Morocco..Severe business depression in England....17. Gold at par in New York city for the first time in 17 years..John H. Almy, journalist and former army agent, 48, died in New York....18. Execution of Jack Kehoe, leader of the Molly Maguires..Steamer Byzantin sunk in the Dardanelles, and 100 lives lost ..Formation of a new Italian Cabinet.....19. Bayard Taylor, author, traveller and poet, American Minister to Germany, 53, died in Berlin...20. Jelallabad occupied by Gen. Browne....Flight of the Ameer from Cabul to Turkestan......21. Reported loss of the brig C. R. Burgess, bound from Boston to England, with all on board......Rev. Dr. McCauley, principal of King's College, Windsor, N. S., died there....24. Accident on the Lehigh Valley Railroad, and five persons killed..American steamship State of Louisiana founders upon the rocks of Lough Larne, Ireland..Rear Admiral Hoff, U.S.N., 69, died at Washington, D. C....Rev. Jos. B. O'Hagan, S. J., President of College of the Holy Cross, Worcester, Mass., died there....26. Rev. Leonard Woods, D. D., LLD., Ex-President of Bowdoin College, died in Mass......Submission of Yakoob Khan, son of the Ameer, and virtual ending of the Afghan war..The capital of Northern Brazil devastated by small-pox; 600 deaths daily.....27. Arrival of the Ameer of Afghanistan at Tashkend.....News received of the loss of the steamer Emily B. Souder, two days out of New York, on the 10th instant, with the loss of 36 lives....Gen. D. C. Collum, Superintendent of Railways and Army Transportation, during the war, and former Superintendent of Erie Railway, died in Brooklyn, N. Y..Rev. George Thacher, D.D., Ex-President of the University of Iowa, died in Hartford, Conn...Ex-Gov. Onslow Stearns, of New Hampshire, died in Concord, N. H..Nitro-glycerine explosion at Upper Preakness, N. J., killing three men....30. Harriet Grote, widow of George Grote, authoress, died in London.

POLICE STATISTICS IN VARIOUS CITIES.

NEW YORK—Number of officers 2,600; Patrolmen's pay $100 per month; Sergeants' pay $133 per month; Captains' $166 per month; latest census, 1875, 1,046,037; number of arrests 78,451; average per officer 37; square miles 41; Superintendent, G. W. Walling.

PHILADELPHIA—Number of Patrolmen 1,200; 1876, arrests 44,919; Patrolmen's pay $2.25 per diem; Captains' pay $125 per month; Sergeants pay $90.20 per month; Population 1876, 817,488; K. H. Jones, Chief of Police. Square miles $125\frac{38}{100}$; square acres 82,803; Park Police 114; number of Buildings Jan. 1st, 1876, 145,001; 4 Captains; 26 Lieutenants; 62 Sergeants.

BROOKLYN—Number of officers 567; Patrolmen's pay $100 per month; Sergeants' pay $133 per month; Captains' $166 per month; official census, 1870, 396,099; number of arrests 25,558; average per officer 45; square miles 25; Superintendent, Patrick Campbell.

ST. LOUIS—Number of officers 439; Patrolmen's pay $75 per month; Sergeants' pay $100 per month; Captains' $150 per month; official census, 1870, 310,864; number of arrests 19,082; average per officer 51; square miles 5.2; Superintendent, James McDonough.

BOSTON—Number of officers 630; Patrolmen's pay $90 per month; Sergeants' pay $100 per month; Captains' pay $150 per month; official census, 1870, 250,526; number of arrests 25,261; average per officer 51; square miles 104; Superintendent, Wm. Savage.

BALTIMORE—Number of officers 592; Patrolmen's pay $78 per month; Sergeants' pay $82 per month; Lieutenants' pay $86 per month; Captains' pay $92 per month; official census, 1870, 267,354; number of arrests 26,365; average per officer 47; square miles 16; Superintendent, John T. Gray.

NEW ORLEANS—Number of officers 585; official census, 1870, 191,418; number of arrests 21,286; average per officer 50; square miles 150; Superintendent, W. F. Loan.

CHICAGO—Number of officers 507; Patrolmen's pay $850 per year; Sergeants' pay $1,220 per year; Chief's pay $1,615 per year; population 298,977; square miles 40; Superintendent, M. C. Hickey.

CINCINNATI—Number of officers 332; Patrolmen's pay $66.67; Lieutenants' pay $75 per month; official census, 1870, 216,239; number of arrests 4,517; average per officer 26; square miles 24; Superintendent, Ira Wood.

COLUMBUS, O.—Number of officers 37; number of arrests 4,031; average per officer 109; Superintendent, Samuel Thompson.

BUFFALO—Number of officers 203; Patrolmen's pay $66.67 per month; Sergeants' pay $75 per month; Captains', $100 per month; official census, 1870, 118,000; number of arrests 8,858; average per officer 44; square miles 27; Superintendent, John Byrnes.

ALBANY—Number of officers 112; Patrolmen's pay $68 per month; Lieutenants' pay $85 per month; Captains' pay $116 per month; official census, 1870, 69,422; number of arrests 6,373; average per officer 56; square miles 22; Superintendent, John Maloy.

SAN FRANCISCO—Number of officers 150; Patrolmen's pay $125 gold, per month; Sergeants' pay $150 per month; Captains', $175 per month; official census, 1870, 149,473; number of arrests 20,108; average per officer 134; square miles 37.5; Superintendent, H. H. Ellis.

WASHINGTON—Number of officers 232; Patrolmen's pay $90 per month; Sergeants' pay $100 per month; Lieutenants' pay $150 per month; official census, 1870, 109,099; number of arrests 14,226; average per officer 62; square miles 14; Superintendent, A. C. Richards.

CLEVELAND—Number of officers 171; Patrolmen's pay $825 per year; Sergeants' pay $930 per year; Lieutenants' pay $1,020 per year; Captains' pay 1,400 per year; official census, 1870, 92,229; square miles 29; Superintendent, J. W. Schmitt.

TOLEDO—Number of officers 52; Patrolmen's pay $720 per year; Sergeants' pay $800 per year; Chief's pay $1,700 per year: official census, 1870, 31,584; square miles 16; Superintendent, J. C. Purdy.

MILWAUKIE—Number of officers 62; Patrolmen's pay $66 per month; Sergeants' pay $75 per month; Captains' pay $80 per month; official census, 1870, 71,440; square miles 13; Superintendent, Wm. Beck.

WORCESTER—Number of officers 50; Patrolmen's pay $820 per year; Captains' pay $900 per year; Chief's pay $1,600 per year; population 41,405; square miles 12; Superintendent, Ansel Washburne.

CHELSEA, MASS.—Number of officers 22; Patrolmen's pay $2.25 per day; Sergeants' pay $2.50 per day; Captains' pay $3 per day; official census, 1870, 18,547; square miles 1.8; Superintendent, Wm. P. Drury.

JERSEY CITY—Number of force 165; Four stations 2 subs.; Chief Benjamin Murphy, salary $2,000; Four Captains $1,500; Sixteen Sergeants $960; Patrolmen $840. The numerical strength of Department is considered inadequate in proportion to number of population, valuation of property and area square miles to patrol.

CHARLESTON, S. C.—Number of officers 138; official census, 1870, 48,956; number of arrests 2,705; average per officer 20; square miles 16; Superintendent, H. W. Hendricks.

NEWARK, N. J.—Number of officers 177; official census, 1870, 105,059; number of arrests 6,752; average per officer 38; Superintendent, Jno. Mills.

SALEM, MASS.—Number of officers 42; official census, 1870, 24,117; number of arrests 1,682; average per officer 40; Superintendent, —— Hill.

INDIANAPOLIS, IND.—Number of officers 62; Patrolmen's pay $900 per year; Captains' pay $1,200 per year; official census, 1870, 48,244; Superintendent, A. C. Dewey.

COVINGTON, KY.—Number of officers 20; Patrolmen's pay $720 per year; Lieutenant's pay $1,200 per year; official census, 1870, 24,502; Superintendent, P. J. Bolan.

LOWELL—Number of officers 52; Patrolmen's pay $900 per year; Captains' pay $1,200; Chief's pay $1,800 per year; population 40,928.

ALLEGHANY—Number of officers 57; Patrolmens' pay $803 per year; Captains' pay $900 per year; Chief's pay $1,000 per year; population 53,180; number of arrests 2,641.

OSWEGO—Number of officers 11; Patrolmen's pay $60 per month; Captains' pay $960 per year; population 20,910; number of arrests 1,117; Chief, Nathan Lee.

PROVIDENCE—Number of officers 191; Patrolmens' pay $1,080 per year; Captains' pay $1,300 per year; Chief's pay $1,250; number of arrests .8,964.

RICHMOND—Number of officers 84: Patrolmens' pay $900 per year; Captains' pay $1,200 per year; Chief's pay $2,000 per year; population 51,038; number of arrests 6,800.

UTICA—Number of officers 20; Patrolmens' pay $720 per year; Assistant Chief's pay $960 per year; Chief's pay $1,200 per year; population 28,804; number of arrests, 1876, 1,200; average per officer 60; square miles 8; cost Dept. $16,000; Chief, James Dwyer.

SYRACUSE—Number of officers 34; Patrolmen's pay $75 per month; Captains' pay $1,200 per year; Chief's pay $1,500 per year; population 60,000; number of arrests, 1876, 3,360; arerage per officer 33; Chief, Thomas Davis.

NORFOLK—Population, 1870, 19,256; number of force 44; Chief's pay $3 per day; Assistant Chief's pay $2.75 per day; Patrolmen's pay $2 per day; 18 hours' duty in 48; number of arrests, 1876, 1,977.

READING—Number of officers 28; pay $45 per month with uniform; Chief's pay $950 per year; population 33,000; Chief, Peter Cullin.

HARRISBURG—Population 30,000; Chief, Christian Cilley; pay $900 per year; Lieutenant's pay $780 per year; Officers' pay $600 per year; square miles 3½.

SCRANTON—Population 35,000; Chief, Jack Breese; number of officers 11; pay $75 per month.

DAYTON—Population, 1870, 30,473; number of force 35; Chief's pay $1,440 per year; Sergeants' pay $900 per year; Roundsmen's pay $850 per year; Patrolmen's pay $800 per year; 11 hours' duty every 24; Chief, Amos Clark.

London, Eng.—Number of officers 8,833; population in 1878, 3,533,-184; number of arrests 42,951; average per officer 8; square miles 122; Superintendent, J. T. Willmayer.

Liverpool, Eng.—Number of officers 1,018; population in 1878, 527,-000; number of arrests 32,243; average per officer 32; square miles 12; Superintendent, Anthony Jones.

Manchester, Eng.—Number of officers 682; population in 1878, 400,-000; number of arrests 31,158; average per officer 46; Superintendent, W. H. Palin, *Ch. Con.*

Dublin, Ireland—Number of officers 2,085; population in 1878, 314,-666; number of arrests 32,243; average per officer 16; square miles 5.

THE QUEEN AND ROYAL FAMILY OF ENGLAND.

THE QUEEN.—Victoria, of the United Kingdom of Great Britain and Ireland, Queen, Defender of the Faith. Her Majesty was born in Kensington Palace, May 24, 1819; succeeded to the throne June 20, 1837, on the death of her uncle, King William IV.; was crowned June 28, 1838; and married Feb. 10, 1840, to His Royal Highness, Prince Albert. Her Majesty is the only child of his late Royal Highness, Edward, Duke of Kent, son of King George III. The children of Her Majesty are—

Her Royal Highness Victoria Adelaide Mary Louisa, Princess Royal of England and Prussia, born Nov. 21, 1840, and married to His Royal Highness William, the Crown Prince of Germany, Jan. 5, 1858, and has had issue, four sons and four daughters. One son (the third,) died June 18, 1866. The eldest daughter, V. E. A. Charlotte, was married Feb. 18, 1878, to Hereditary Prince of Saxe Meiningen, and has one child.

His Royal Highness Albert Edward, Prince of Wales, Born Nov. 9, 1841; married, March 10, 1863, Alexandria of Denmark, (Princess of Wales), born Dec. 1, 1844, and has had issue, Prince Albert Victor, born Jan. 8, 1864, George Frederick Ernest Albert, born June 3, 1865; Louisa Victoria Alexandra Dagmar, born Feb. 20, 1867; Victoria Alexandra Olga Mary, born July 6, 1868; Maude Charlotte Mary Victoria, born Nov. 26, 1869, and Alexander J. C. A., born 6th April, died 7th April, 1871.

Her Royal Highness Alice Maud Mary, born April 25, 1843; married to H. R. H. Prince Louis Frederick of Hesse, July 1, 1862, and has issue five daughters and one son; second son killed by accident May, 1873; Youngest daughter died of diphtheria, Nov. 15, 1878, and H. R. H. died of the same disease, Dec. 14, 1878.

His Royal Highness Alfred Ernest Albert, duke of Edindurgh, born Aug. 6, 1844; married Her Imperial Highness, the Grand Dutchess Marie, of Russia, Jan. 23, 1874, and has one son and three daughters.

Her Royal Highness Helena Augusta Victoria, born May 25, 1846; married to H. R. H. Prince Frederick Christian Charles Augustus Schleswig-Holstein-Sonderburg-Augustenburg, July 5, 1866, and has had issue three sons and two daughters. The youngest son died when seven days old, May 19, 1876.

Her Royal Highness Louisa Carolina Alberta, born March 18, 1848; married to the Marquis of Lorne, eldest son of the Duke of Argyle, March, 1871. The Marquis is now Governor General of Canada.

His Royal Highness Arthur William Patrick Albert, born May 1, 1850, Duke of Connaught, married March 13, 1879, to the Princess Louisa Margaret, grand niece of the Emperor of Germany, and daughter of Prince Frederick Karl. H. R. H. has received the appointment of Lord Lieutenant of Ireland.

His Royal Highness Leopold George Duncan Albert, born April 7, 1853, H. R. H. is expected to take orders in the Anglican Church the present year, (1879).

Her Royal Highness Beatrice Mary Victoria Feodore, born April 14, 1857.

FOREIGN NATIONS.

PRESENT RULERS, POPULATION, SQUARE MILES, ETC.

STATES, &C.	CAPITALS.	RULERS, &C.	TITLES.	POPL'T'N.	SQ MILES	RELIGION.
Abyssinia	Magdala	JohannesII(Kassa	King	3,000,000	158,000	Coptic.
Afghanistan	Cabool		Shah	7,600,000	500,000	Moham'dan.
Anam (Cochin China)	Hue	Tu Duc	King	10,000,000	600,000	Buddhist.
Arabia (Muscat)	Muscat	Seyd B. Bin Said.	Imaum	1,500,000	175,000	Moham'dan.
Argentine Republic	Buenos Ayres.	Dr. N. Avellaneda	President	1,877,500	838,600	R. Catholic.
Austro-Hungary	Vienna	Francis Joseph I.	Emperor	7,700,491	240,940	R. Catholic.
Baden	Carlsruhe	Frederick I.	Grand Duke.	1,507,000	5,824	R. C. & Prot.
Barbary States	Tripoli	Dabri Pasha	Pasha	1,200,000	344,400	Moham'dan.
Bavaria	Munich	Louis II	King	5,412,231	29,292	R. Catholic.
Belgium	Brussels	Leopold II	King	5,253,821	11,372	R. Catholic.
Beloochistan	Kelat	Khodadad	Khan	1,000,000	140,000	Moham'dan.
Bolivia	Oruro	Gen. H. Daga	President	2,000,000	500,870	R. Catholic.
Borneo	Borneo	Abdul Mumeiu	Sultan	1,750,000	290,000	Pagan.
Brazil	Rio de Janeiro	Dom Pedro II	Emperor	10,196,328	3,288,000	R. Catholic.
Burmah	Mandalay	Thebo	King	3,400,000	192,000	Buddhist.
Cambodia	Panompin	Ong S'detchN'd'm	King	1,020,000	33,524	Buddhist.
Canada, Dominion of	Ottawa	Marquis of Lorne.	Gov. General	3,873,000	3,620,510	Protestant.
Cape Colony	Cape Town	Sir H. B. E. Frere	Governor	720,984	222,308	Protestant.
China	Pekin	Kuang Su	Emperor	425,000,000	4,540,000	Bud. & Pagan.
Chili	Santiago	Anabal Pinto	President	2,300,000	126,060	R. Catholic.
Colombia	Bogota	Aquileo Parra	President	2,851,858	320,750	R. Catholic.
Corea	Kingkitao	Zung-Che	King	8,000,000	90,300	Confuc & Bud.
Costa Rica	San Jose	Dr. A. Esquivel	President	200,000	26,040	R. Catholic.
Dahomey	Abomey	Adahaonzon II	King	300,000		Pagan.
Denmark	Copenhagen	Christian IX	King	1,950,400	15,218	Lutheran.
Ecuador	Quito	Gen de Veintimilla	President	1,100,000	248,380	R. Catholic.
Egypt	Cairo	Tewfik Pasha	Khedive	5,250,000	212,600	Mahom'dan.
France	Paris	J. de Grevy	President	36,905,788	204,096	R. Catholic.
Germany	Berlin	William I.	Emperor	42,727,260	208,744	Protestant.
Gt. Britain & Ireland	London	Victoria I	Queen	33,895,023	121,115	Protestant.
Greece	Athens	George I	King	1,457,894	19,353	Greek Ch'rch
Guatemala	Guatemala	J. Rufino Barrios.	President	1,180,000	40,776	R. Catholic.
Hesse	Darmstadt	Louis IV	Grand Duke	884,218	2,965	Lutheran.
Hayti	P't-au Prince.	Gen. B. Canal	President	708,500	29,828	R. Catholic.
Honduras	Comayagua	Marco A. Soto	President	350,000	47,090	R. Catholic.
Italy	Rome	Humbert I	King	27,769,475	114,406	R. Catholic.
Japan	Tokio	Mutsu Hito	Mikado	33,110,825	155,525	Buddhist.
Liberia	Monrovia	A. W. Gardner	President	820,000	60,000	Protestant.
Madagascar	Antananarivo	Ranavolo II	Queen	3,000,000	228,570	Christian.
Mecklen'g Schwerin.	Schwerin	Fred'k Francis II.	Grand Duke	553,897	5,138	Lutheran.
Mecklenberg Strelitz.	Strelitz	Fred'k William I.	Grand Duke	95,682	1,131	Lutheran.
Mexico	Mexico	Gen. Porfirio Diaz.	President	9,158,250	743,820	R. Catholic.
Montenegro	Cettigne	Nicolas	Hospodar	110,000	1,710	Greek Ch'rch
Morocco	Morocco	Muley Hassan	Sultan	3,750,000	260,000	Moham'dan.
Netherlands	Amsterdam	William III	King	3,924,792	12,680	Protestant.
Nicaragua	Managa	P. J. Chamorro	President	250,000	58,170	R. Catholic.
Oldenburg	Oldenburg	Peter I	Grand Duke	319,314	2,470	Lutheran.
Orange Free States	Bloemfontein	J. H. Brand	President	50,000	42,470	Protestant.
Paraguay	Asuncion	J. Baptista Gill	President	300,000	56,700	R. Catholic.
Persia	Teheran	Nassar-ed-Din	Shah	5,000,000	636,000	Moham'dan.
Peru	Lima		President	3,371,000	503,380	R. Catholic.
Portugal	Lisbon	Dom Luis I	King	4,367,882	35,812	R. Catholic.
Prussia	Berlin	William I.	King	25,742,404	137,566	Protestant.
Roumania	Bucharest	Karl I	Dominu	5,376,000	49,262	Greek Ch'rch
Russia	St. Petersburg	Alexander II	Emperor	85,685,945	8,325,3[illegible]3	Greek Ch'rch
Saxe Coburg & Gotha.	Gotha & C'b'rg	Ernst II	Duke	182,599	760	Lutheran.
Saxe-Meiningen	Meiningen	George II	Duke	194,494	933	Lutheran.
Saxe-Weimar	Weimar	Charles Alex'nder	Grand Duke	292,4[illegible]3	1,421	Lutheran.
Saxony	Dresden	Albert I	King	2,760,586	5,788	Luth. & R. C.
Sandwich Islands	Honolulu	David Kalakaua	King	62,000	7,628	Protestant.
San Domingo	San Domingo.	Ulysses T Espaillet	President	150,000	20,596	R. Catholic.
San Salvador	San Salvador.	Rafael Zaldivar	President	600,000	7,335	R. Catholic.
Servia	Belgrade	Mil'n Obrenovic IV	Hospodar	1,720,000	18,787	Greek Ch'rch
Siam	Bangkok	P. S. Paraminthra	First King	5,700,000	379,000	Buddhist.
Spain	Madrid	Alfonso XII	King	*23,262,000	320,975	R. Catholic.
Sweden & Norway	Stockholm	Oscar II	King	6,303,395	293,260	Lutheran.
Switzerland	Berne	Dr. K. Schenck	President	2,776,035	15,991	Prot. & R. C.
Turkey	Constantinopl	Abdul Hamid II	Sultan	28,165,000	1,742,874	Moham'dan.
United States	Washington	Ruthert'd B. Hayes	President	49,185,000	3,603,844	Christian.
Uruguay	Monte Video	L. Latorre	Dictator	440,000	73,538	R. Catholic.
Venezuela	Caracas	Gen. F. Alcantara	President	1,784,194	403,276	R. Catholic.
Wurtemburg	Stuttgart	Charles I	King	1,815,057	7,531	Lutheran.
Zanzibar	Zanzibar	Seyd B. Bin Said	Sultan	150,000	625	Moham'dan.

* With its Colonies.

COMMERCE WITH GREAT BRITAIN.

The United Kingdom of Great Britain and Ireland, and its dependencies and Colonies, has always been our largest customer for our productions, and was for many years our largest creditor also, sending us her manufactured goods and receiving in return our raw materials in such quantities as she required for home or foreign consumption, and thus having almost always a balance of trade against us, which we were obliged to pay in coin.

Of late years, the balance has been the other way, and a large portion of our bonded debt, held by foreigners, has been paid from this surplus.

It will be interesting and instructive to review this commerce for the 89 years of which we have record of it. In 1790, we imported from Great Britain, merchandise of the value of $13,563,044, and exported to her and her dependencies, merchandise valued at $6,888,478, our exports thus being almost exactly one-half of our imports. Our total imports in 1790, were $23,000,000, and our total exports $20,205,156. Our total imports in 1878, were $466,872,846, and our total exports $722,811,815. In 1878, our imports of merchandise from the British Empire, were $157,244,953, and our exports of merchandise to the countries comprising that Empire, were $152,032,886.

The imports and exports of specie and bullion, which were about equal, are excluded in both cases. In other words, our imports are about 12 times as large as they were in 1790, and our exports 65½ times as large. It will be interesting to notice some of the items which made up our early exports to Great Britain, and to compare them with the exports at the present time. In this way we can ascertain, in part, what have been our principal productions, for, as a general rule, a nation exports only those things of which it has a surplus, after supplying its own wants. In rare instances, it has not facilities for working up its raw material to advantage, and exports it, receiving back that material in a manufactured form. This was the case with our cotton, to some extent, for many years, and also with our ores of copper, zinc, &c., and the demand was so great abroad for some of our fruits, that the entire crop was exported. The following table gives our principal articles of export to Great Britain, in 1790. Some of these were goods imported and re-exported by us:

EXPORTS FROM THE UNITED STATES TO GREAT BRITAIN DURING THE FISCAL YEAR ENDED SEPT. 30, 1790.

	Quantity.	*Value.*
Tobacco, hogsheads	73,708	$2,754,493
Cotton, raw, bales	1,403	47,428
Ashes, pot and pearl, tons	7,675	747.079
Flax-seed, cakes	36,917	219,924
Wheat, bushels	292,042	355,361
Corn, bushels	98,407	56,205
Flour, barrels	104,880	676,274
Meal, barrels	1,401	5,435
Rice, tierces	36,930	773,852
Beef and pork, Barrels	154	898
Bread, barrels	201	610
Butter, firkins,	384	2,310
Honey, firkins	151	906
Tallow, pounds	156,708	17,211
Oil, whale, barrels	1,738	21,048
Oil, sperm, barrels	3,840	60,000
Tar, barrels	71,077	105,510
Turpentine, barrels	27,800	71,240
Pitch, barrels	7,000	13,920
Seeds and roots	...	1,242
Staves and heading	...	177,968

	Quantity.	Value.
Lumber	...	$35,204
Timber, scantlings, shingles, &c.	...	27,402
Leather, pounds	8,650	2,316
Snuff, pounds	4,100	1,394
Wax, pounds	87,294	21,852
Deer-skins	...	25,642
Furs	...	35,899
Ginseng, casks	529	32,424
Pig-iron, tons	3,258	78,676
Bar-iron, tons	40	2,936
Indigo, pounds	532,542	473,830
Logwood, tons	216	3,019
Lignum vitæ, tons	75	750
Mahogany	...	16,724
Wines, pipes	45	4,425
Merchandise	...	8,041
Unenumerated	...	10,330
Total		$6,888,978

The indigo, dye, and cabinet woods and wines were of foreign production, as was also, without doubt, the bar-iron and a large quantity of pig-iron. It will be observed that the great Southern staple, tobacco, soon to yield the supremacy to cotton, was of the value of $2,750,000, or 40 per cent. of the whole export.

We should notice, also, that cotton, before the invention of the cotton gins, was but a very small item, its value being only $47,428, nearly $34 per bale, though the bales at this time weighed only 150 pounds. The exports of cereals, wheat, corn, flour and meal, were about $1,092,000, a small amount as compared with our present export, but almost one-sixth of the whole export to Great Britain at that time.

The amount of provisions exported is very trifling, in marked contrast with our present immense export. There was no marked increase in the export of cotton until 1796, when 5,628,176 pounds were sent to Great Britain, valued at about $1,407,000. Seven years later, the export to that country was 27,760,574 pounds, worth $6,107,326, or almost as much as the entire exports to that country 13 years before. The same year (1803), 50,274 hogsheads of tobacco, worth $4,524,660, were exported to England. These two items making more than five-eighths of the whole export. From this time till 1860, there was a steady increase in each decade, of the cotton export. In 1860, though the price of cotton had fallen to 10 or 12 cents a pound, the export of it to Great Britain and its dependencies, amounted to $134,929,000, while the total exports to that country, amounted to $168,960,000, only $34,000,000 being for all other articles. In 1866, the price of cotton being high, our cotton exports to the British Empire amounted to $218,772,000, against $287,516,000 of our total exports to that Empire. During the 12 years since 1866, our exports of cotton to the British Empire, have aggregated $1,445,064,000, an annual average of $120,442,000, against $3,445,037,000 of exports of all kinds of merchandise to that Empire, or an annual average of $287,089,083; cotton being nearly 42 per cent. of the average exports. The following table gives the aggregate by decades, of imports and exports, and of exports of cotton to the British Empire, for 58 years·

Periods.	Imports.	Exports.	Exports of Cotton.
1821–30....	$290,831,000	$242,482,000	$185,397,000
1831–40....	475,194,000	462,146,000	378,185,000
1841–50....	464,358,000	570,651,000	378,576,000
1851–60....	1,166,322,000	1,193,350,000	840,436,000
1861–70....	1,343,702,000	1,748,307,000	799,810,000
1871–78....	1,386,576,000	2,588,377,000	1,106,846,000
Total for 58 years..	$5,126,983,000	$6,805,313,000	$3,689,250,000
Annual average...	88,396,000	117,333,000	63,608,000

Our trade with the United Kingdom during the last 58 years aggregates, in round numbers, $5,127,000,000 in imports, and 6,805,000,000 in exports, an excess of exports over imports of $1,687,000,000, which has been used in paying balances to creditor nations.

It was not, however, till 1847, that our exports to the United Kingdom, began, as a rule, to exceed our imports. Since that date there has been but six years out of

31, in which we imported more merchandise from Great Britain than we sent her; these years were 1850, 1852, 1853, 1854 and 1855, and 1864, and as we have said, the excess of our exports in the 58 years since 1820, amounts to $1,678,000,000.

Let us now give a list of our principal exports to the British Empire in 1878, by way of comparison with those of 1790, on a preceding page.

PRINCIPAL DOMESTIC EXPORTS TO THE BRITISH EMPIRE IN 1878.

	Values.
Agricultural Implements and Machines	$1,102,293
Living Animals of all kinds	4,396,453
Bread Stuffs	146,304,119
Carriages, Carts and Railroad Cars	685,022
Clocks	591,425
Coal	1,871,277
Cotton, raw	117,014,743
Cotton, manufactured	3,299,405
Drugs and Chemicals	967,488
Fur and Fur Skins	2,014,594
Hemp and manufactures of	825,135
Hides and Skins	673,615
Hops	2,122,983
Iron and manufactures of Iron	4,266,740
Steel and manufactures of Steel	681,761
Leather and manufactures of Leather	6,164,904
Musical instruments	557,562
Naval Stores	1,125,856
Oil Cake	5,076,550
Oils, mineral	10,001,528
Provisions	82,374,578
Sewing Machines	611,509
Spirits of Turpentine	1,776,216
Refined Sugar and Molasses	3,360,879
Tallow	3,240,469
Tobacco, manufactured and unmanufactured	12,317,788
Wearing apparel	270,863
Wood, Timber and manufactures of Wood	8,464,287
Total exports	$452,032,886

A comparison of these two lists will show that while the exports of most of the articles which then were staples, have increased enormously, a few have dropped out entirely. We do not export now, pot and pearl ashes, flax-seed, rice, wax, (nor till the present year, honey,) whale and sperm oils, and very small amounts of seeds and roots, ginseng, or indigo, logwood, lignum vitæ, or mahogany. We do export some wines, but they are of our own manufacture.

Tobacco, cotton, bread stuffs, provisions, tallow, furs, and naval stores have been sent to England the past year, to the amount of nearly 310 millions of dollars; while mineral oils, which were unknown in 1790; wood in manufactured forms, oil cake, living animals, leather and its manufactures, iron and steel and their manufactures, refined sugar and molasses, hops, agricultural implements, sewing machines, musical instruments, clocks, carriages and railroad cars, manufactured cotton goods, coal and hemp, are among the new articles which figure most largely in our exports, even to Great Britain, after the great staples.

A considerable portion of these new exports are the result directly and indirectly, of our Centennial Exposition here, and that of Paris in 1878; and if we are careful to encourage our agriculture and our manufactures, and to make known our products to the world, it is not too much to hope that before the dawn of the twentieth century, we shall be the leading commercial nation of the world, and New York will be, what London has been for so many years, the financial Capital of the world.

BRITISH AMERICA.

The territory claimed by Great Britian in North America, includes all that portion of the continent lying north of the northern boundary of the United States, except the territory of Alaska.

Its sub-divisions are:

THE DOMINION OF CANADA, THE ISLAND OF NEWFOUNDLAND.

NEWFOUNDLAND, though not a province of the Dominion of Canada, is partially in accord with it, and may be treated under the same general head. The LABRADOR and HUDSON'S BAY REGION are Territories, occupied at wide intervals, by trading posts or forts, and under the Government of the Dominion.

THE DOMINION OF CANADA

consists of the Provinces of Ontario and Quebec—formerly Canada East and Canada West, or Upper and Lower Canada—Nova Scotia, New Brunswick, Manitoba, British Columbia, and Prince Edward Island. The North-western Territories are controlled by the Dominion, but not represented in its Parliament. These Provinces were united under one Government, by the Act of Imperial Parliament, passed in March, 1867, and which took effect July 1, of the same year.

The seat of Government of the Dominion is at OTTAWA.

The Executive Officers of the Dominion Government are a Govornor-General and Privy Council of thirteen members, who also constitute the Cabinet of the Governor-General. The present Governor-General, who is the direct representative of the Queen, and answers to the Viceroy of India, though with somewhat more restricted powers, is most Hon. JOHN DOUGLAS CAMPBELL, MARQUIS OF LORNE, K. T. G. C. M. G., born in 1845, and married in 1871 to the PRINCESS LOUISE CAROLINE ALBERTA, fourth daughter of Queen Victoria. The Marquis was appointed Governor-General July 28, 1878, and arrived in the Dominion with the Princess, on the 23d of November, 1878.

His salary is £10,000 ($50,000) per annum, and a residence.

His civil establishment or personal Staff consists of:

Gov.-General's Secretary—Major J. De Winton, R. A.,

Military Secretary, V. C.—Col. J. C. McNeill, C. B.

Controller—Hon. R. Moreton.

Aides de Camp—Capt. V. Cater, 91st Foot; Hon. C. Harbord, Scots Fusilier Guards.

Dominion Aides de Camp—Lt.-Col. Hewitt Bernard, C. M. G.; Capt. G. R. Layton.

Commander of the Forces—Gen. Sir P. L. McDougall, K. C. M. G.

Assistant Adjutant and Q. M.-General—Lt.-Col. A. S. Cameron, V. C.

Aides de Camp—Lieut. J. C. Barker, R. E.; Capt. Hon. N. F. Elliot.

Commanding the Militia—Lieut.-Gen. Sir E. Selby Smyth, K. C. M. G.

Deputy Governor—Hon. Sir W. B. Richards, Chief Justice of Canada.

THE QUEEN'S PRIVY COUNCIL

for the Dominion, are:

Premier and Minister of the Interior—Sir John A. Macdonald, K. C. B. D. C. L. (Oxon.), Q. C.

Finance Minister—Hon. H. L. Langevin, C. B.

Minister of Public Works—Hon. C. Tupper, C. B.

Minister of Agriculture and Statistics—Hon. John H. Pope.

President of Council—Hon. John O'Connor, Q. C.

Minister of Justice—Hon. J. McDonald, Q. C.

Postmaster-General—Hon. Samuel L. Tilley, C. B.

Minister of Militia—Hon. Louis R. Masson.

Secretary of State—Hon. J. C. Aikens.

Secretary of Marine and Fisheries—Hon. J. C. Pope.

Minister of Customs—Hon. Mackenzie Bowell.

Minister of Inland Revenue—Hon. L. F. G. Baby.

Receiver-General—Hon. Alexander Campbell, Q. C.

Without Portfolio—Hon. R. D. Wilmot.

*.*The members of the Council (except the Premier) receive salaries of £1,440 ($7,200) per annum. The Premier's salary is £1,643 ($8,215).

Chief Justice of the Supreme Court and Court of Exchequer for the Dominion—Hon. Sir William Buell Richards, Kn't.

Puisne Judges—Hons. W. J. Ritchie, S. H. Strong, T. Fournier, W. A. Henry, Henri E. Tachereau.

The Chief Justice receives an annual salary of £1,646 ($8,230), and the Puisne Judges £1,440 ($7,200) each.

THE DOMINION SENATE, according to the Constitution, consists of 77 members, viz: 24 each for Ontario and Quebec, and 24 for the three Maritime Provinces; 2 for Manitoba and 3 for British Columbia. Provision is also made for the representation of Newfoundland when it shall come into the Dominion. The Northwest Territories have no representatives or delegates in the Parliament. The members of the Senate are nominated for life by summons of the Governor-General, under the Great Seal of Canada. Each Senator must be 30 years of age, a born or naturalized subject, and possessed of property, real or personal, of the value of $4,000, in the Province for which he is appointed. The Speaker of the Senate has a salary of $4,000 per annum. Each member of the Senate receives $10 a day for attendance on the sessions up to 100 days, but nothing beyond. They are also allowed 10 cents a mile for traveling expenses. There are at present but 72 Senators, whose names and residences are as follows:

Hon. John Hamilton....................Kingston
" Benjamiu Seymour............Port Hope
" Walter H. Dickson................Niagara
" James Shaw................Smith's Falls
" Alexander Campbell..............Toronto
" David Christie........................Paris
" James Cox Aikins..................Toronto
" David Reesor....................Markham
" Elijah Leonard.......................London
" William McMaster................Toronto
" John Simpson...............Bowmanville
" James Skead.........................Ottawa
" David L. Macpherson.............Toronto
" Donald McDonald.................Toronto
" Billa Flint........................Belleville
" George W, Allen....................Toronto
" Jacques O. Bureau................Montreal
" Luc Letellier De St. Just..Riviere Ouelle
" John Hamilton................Hawkesbury
" Charles Cormior...............Plessisville
" David E. Price......................Quebec
" L. Dumouchel.....................Longueuil
" Louis Lacoste.................Boucherville
" J. F. Armand.........Riviere des Prairies
" Charles Wilson....................Montreal
" William H. Chaffers............St. Cesaire
" Jean B. Guevremont....................Sorel
" James Ferrier.....................Montreal
" Thomas Ryan......................Montreal
" T. D. Archibald.....Sydney, Cape Breton
" Robert B. Dickey.................Amherst
" John Bourinot.........................Sydney
" William Miller.......................Arichat
" A. E. Botsford............Westcock, Wind
" William H. Odell..............Fredericton
" David Wark.....................Fredericton

Hon. John Ferguson, Bathurst, NewBrunswick
" B. D. Wilmot..........Belmont, Sunbury
" A. R. McClelan......Hopewell, Albion Co.
" J. C. Chapais...............St. Denis, Kam.
" James R. Benson............St. Catharines
" John Glasier................Sunbury, N. B.
" James Dever................St. John, N. B.
" A. W. McLelan..............Londonderry
" A. Macfarlane..............Wallace, N. S.
" Jeremiah Northrup..................Halifax
" Frank Smith.........................Toro to
" Robert Read.......................Belleville
" M. A. Girard......St. Boniface, Manitoba
" J. Sutherland........Keldonan, "
" R. W. W. Carrall...Barkerville, Brit. Col.
" C. F. Cornwall........Ashcroft " "
" W. J. McDonald.......Victoria " "
" H. A. N. Kaulbach.............Lunenburg
" M. H. Cochrane...................Compton
" William Muirhead ....Chatham, N. B.
" Alexander Vidal........................Sarnia
" Eugene Chinic........................Quebec
" George Alexander.............Woodstock
" J. H. Bellerose.......St. Vincent de Paul
" D. Montgomery................Park Corner
" R. P. Haythorne...........Charlottetown
" T. H. Haviland............Charlottetown
" George W. Howlan..............Alberton
" F. X. A. Trudel..................Montreal
" George A. Brown.................Toronto
" R. W. Scott......................... Ottawa
" E. G. Penny.......................Montreal
" Pierre Baillamgeon...............Quebec
" A. H. Paquet.................St. Cuthbert
" Hector Fabre ....Quebec
" Christian H. Pozer..................Beauce

Hon. David Christie is Speaker of the Senate, and Robert Lemoine, Clerk of the Parliaments.

The House of Commons, or Representative House of the Canadian Parliament, is elected by the people for five years, at the rate of one representative for every 17,000 souls. On the basis of the Census of 1871, it consists of 206 members, viz: 88 for the Province of Ontario, 65 for Quebec, 21 for Nova Scotia, 16 for New Brunswick, 4 for Manitoba, 6 for British Columbia, and 6 for Prince Edward's Island. The constituencies vary in the different Provinces. In Ontario and Quebec, a vote is given to every male subject being the owner, or occupier, or tenant, or real property of the assessed value of $300, or of the yearly value of $30, if within cities and towns, or of the assessed value of $200, or the yearly value of $20, if not in towns. In New Brunswick a vote is given to every male subject of the age of 21 years, assessed in respect of real estate to the amount of $100, or of personal property, or personal and real, amounting together to $400, or $400 annual income. In Nova Scotia, the franchise is with all subjects, of the age of 21 years, assessed in respect of real estate to the value of $150, or in respect of personal estate, or real and personal together, to the value of $400. Voting in Quebec, Ontario, Nova Scotia, Manitoba, British Columbia, and Prince Edward's Island, is open, or *viva voce*, but in New Brunswick, votes are taken by ballot. The Speaker of the House of Commons has a salary of $4,000 per annum, and each member $10 per day up to the end of 30 days, and for a session lasting longer than this period, the sum of $1,000 with, in every case, 10 cents per mile for traveling expenses. Eight dollars per day is deducted for every day's absence of a member during the session, unless the absence is caused by illness.

The Dominion Parliament answers to the Congress of the United States, and its legislation concerns solely the National or Dominion affairs. Each of the seven Provinces has its own Lieutenant-Governor and Executive Council. Ontario, Manitoba and British Columbia have only a House of Assembly in addition for legislative action; but Quebec, New Brunswick, Nova Scotia and Prince Edward's Island have each a Legislative Council and Legislative Assembly. The Executive Council and Provincial Cabinet of Ontario consists of six members, viz: An Attorney-General, Treasurer, Commissioner of Crown Lands, Commissioner of Public Works, Minister of Education, and Provincial Secretary. The House of Assembly has 82 members. Hon. D. A. Macdonald, of Toronto, is Lieutenant-Governor. The Lieutenant-Governor of the Province of Quebec was, in January, 1879, Hon. Luc. Letellier de Just, but his removal has been requested; there is an Executive Council of 7 members, viz: Premier and Minister of Agriculture and Public Works, Commissioner of Crown Lands, Treasurer, Provincial Secretary and Registrar, Speaker of Legislative Council, Attorney-General, and Solicitor-General. The Legislative Council consists of 24 members, and the Legislative Assembly of 65 members. The Seat of Government is Quebec.

Hon. E. B. Chandler, Q. C., is Lieutenant-Governor of the Province of New Brunswick. The Executive Council consists of 9 members, a President, Attorney-General, Provincial Secretary, Surveyor-General, Chief-Commissioner of Board of Works, and four members without other office. The Legislative Council consists of 17 members, and the House of Assembly of 41 members. The Seat of Government is Fredericton. The Lieutenant-Governor of the Province of Nova Scotia is Hon. Adams George Archibald. There are 9 members of the Executive Council (besides 8 retired members who may participate in its deliberations), viz: Treasurer, Attorney-General, Provincial Secretary, Commissioner of Public Works and Mines, Commissioner of Crown Lands, and four members without other office. The Legislative Council consists of 19 members, and the House of Assembly of 38. The Seat of Government is Halifax.

The Lieutenant-Governor of Prince Edward's Island is Sir Robert Hodgson, Knight. The Executive Council consists of 9 members, namely: Attorney-General, Minister of Public Works, Provincial Secretary and Treasurer, and six members without office. The Legislative Council has 13 members, and the House of Assembly 30 members. The Seat of Government is Charlottetown.

The Lieutenant-Governor of the Province of Manitoba, is Hon. Joseph Edward Cauchon. The Executive Council has 5 members, Provincial Treasurer, who is also Premier, Provincial Secretary and Attorney-General, and Minister of Public Works. The Legislative Assembly has 24 members. The Seat of Government is Fort Garry.

The Province of British Columbia has Hon. Albert N. Richards, Q. C., for its Lieutenant-Governor. Its Executive Council consists of 5 members, viz: The Attorney-General and Provincial Secretary, the Minister of Finance and Agriculture, and the Chief Commissioner of Land and Works. The Legislative Assembly has 25 members. Victoria, Vancouver's Island, is the Seat of Government.

The North-west Territories are so far organized as to have a Lieutenant-Governor, Hon. David Laird, and an Executive Council of 5 members, which includes the two Stipendiary Magistrates, and the Commissioner of Police. The Seat of Government is at Battleford.

JUDICIARY OF THE DOMINION.—The Dominion has only two Courts. The Supreme Court, or High Court of Appeal, composed of a Chief Justice and five Puisne Judges, viz: Hon. William Buell Richards, Chief Justice; Hon. William Johnston Ritchie, Hon. Samuel Henry Strong, Hon. Jean Thomas Taschereau, Hon. Telesphore Fournier, and Hon. William Alexander Henry, Puisne Judges. R. Cassells, Jr., is the Registrar of the Court—this Court has appellate, civil and criminal jurisdiction within and throughout the Dominion of Canada. It holds, annually, two sessions, in January and June, at Ottawa, at which place the Judges reside. The Exchequer Court, presided over by the same Judges, possesses concurrent original jurisdiction in the Dominion, in all cases in which it is sought to enforce any law relating to the revenue, and exclusive original jurisdiction in all cases in which demand is made, or relief sought, in respect of any matter which might, in England, be the subject of a suit or action in the Court of Exchequer, on its revenue side, against the Crown or an officer of the Crown. In each of the Provinces, there are Provincial Courts of Appeal, of Queen's Bench, of Common Pleas, Chancery, County and Division Courts, more or less numerous, according to the population and necessities of the Provinces.

AREA AND POPULATION.—The area of the seven Provinces of the Dominion, and of the outlying colony of Newfoundland, and their population, in 1871, were as follows:

PROVINCES.	AREA, ENGLISH SQ. MILES.	POPULATION, 1871 to 1877.		
		MALES.	FEMALES.	TOTAL.
Ontario	106.935	828,590	792,261	1,620,851
Quebec	193,355	596,041	595,475	1,191,516
Nova Scotia	21,731	193,792	194.008	387,800
New Brunswick	27,322	145,888	136,706	285,594
Manitoba and N. W. Territories	2,947,923	....	....	125,000
British Columbia	225,500	....	....	50,000
Prince Edward's Island	2,173	47,121	46,900	94,021
Newfoundland	40,200	75,547	70,989	161,389
Totals	3,555,149			3,916,171

The population of the Dominion has increased with considerable rapidity since 1871. About 358,000 immigrants had arrived in the Dominion, up to the close of 1876, of whom 210,000 are known to have actually settled in the Provinces—this is exclusive of the natural increase, as well as of persons who have migrated from the United States to Canada. The population of the Dominion and Newfoundland is now, 1879, probably about 4,500,000.

The finances of the Dominion of Canada have not been for some years past in a prosperous condition, though there are some indications of improvement. The public debt of the Dominion July 1, 1877, was £35,892,453 ($179,462,265); about $100,000,000 of this debt was payable in England.

In proportion to her population this debt was as great as that of the United States, and in proportion to the wealth of the two countries, considerably larger. Since 1877, however, while the aggregate amount of the Canadian debt may have slightly increased, her means for paying it have largely increased also, and her relative financial position is better than it was two or four years ago.

The public revenue of the Dominion for the year ending June 30, 1878, was £4,532,721 ($22,663,605), and its expenditures £4,832,726 ($24,163,630), showing a deficiency of $1,500,000. The extravagance and wastefulness of former Administrations is not likely to be repeated at present.

In the year ending June 30, 1878, the total imports into Canada were £19,125,084 ($95,625,420); and the total exports were £16,298,267 ($81,491,335); showing an excess of imports of $14,134,085. The imports from Great Britain into the Dominion in 1877-78 were £7,584,480 ($37,722,400), and the total exports to Great Britain, £11,186,195 ($55,930,975).

The trade with the United States was also very large, the commodities imported from the United States being of the value of $49,631,700; and the exports from the Dominion to the United States, $27,971,193.

EXPORTS AND IMPORTS.

The following table gives the exports and imports, from all countries, and those from Great Britain and the United States, for the years 1875, 1876, 1877, and 1878:

Years.	Great Britain.		United States.		Total Commerce.		Am't to Other Countr's	
	Exports.	Imports.	Exports.	Imports.	Exports.	Imports.	Exports.	Imports.
June 30, 1875.	$48,079,635	$42,070,695	$32,763,870	$50,805,820	$77,886,979	$123,070,283	$3,659,936	$6,537,898
" 1876.	51,923,525	34,513,615	30,930 607	51,188,506	88,966,435	98,210,846	6,412,303	13,513,725
" 1877.	55,930,975	37,922,400	25,033,467	51,023,461	75,875,393	94,721,180	....	4,875,319
" 1878.	....	....	27,971,193	49,631,700	81,491,335	95,625,420	....	....

TONNAGE OF THE DOMINION OF CANADA.

STATEMENT SHOWING THE NUMBER OF VESSELS AND NUMBER OF TONS ON THE REGISTRY BOOKS OF THE DOMINION OF CANADA ON DECEMBER 31, 1873, 1874, 1875, 1876, AND 1877.

Provinces.	1873.		1874.		1875.		1876.		1877.	
	Vessels.	Tons.	Vessels.	Tons.	Vessels.	Tons.	Vessels.	Tons.	Vessels.	Tons.
New Brunswick..	1,147	277,850	1,144	294,741	1,133	307,926	1,154	324,513	1,133	329,457
Nova Scotia.......	2,803	449,701	2,787	479,669	2,786	505,144	2,869	529,252	2,961	541,579
Quebec...........	1,842	214,043	1,837	218,946	1,831	222,965	1,902	238,502	1,951	248,399
Ontario..........	681	89,111	815	113,008	825	114,990	869	123,947	926	131,791
Prince Ed. Island..	280	38,918	312	48,388	325	50,677	338	50 692	342	55,547
British Columbia..	30	4,095	35	3,611	40	3,685	40	3,809	43	3,809
Manitoba.........	......	....	......	....	2	178	2	178	6	178
Total.........	6,783	1,073,718	6,930	1,158,363	6,942	1,205,565	7,194	1,260,893	7,362	1,310,760

miles more had been surveyed and concessions granted by the Government. A railway has been projected, crossing the whole Dominion, from the Atlantic to the Pacific, intended to bind British Columbia to the Eastern Provinces, and the British Government has guaranteed a loan of $12,500,000 in aid of this enterprise.

POSTAL FACILITIES AND POST-OFFICES.—There were, June 30, 1876, in the Dominion, 4,893 post-offices. The uniform rate of postage, of three cents, has been established all over the Dominion. The number of letters and postal cards sent through the post-office during the year 1875, was 34,510,000; the number of newspapers, 23,500,000. There are in all the principal cities and towns of Ontario and Quebec, Post-Office Savings Banks, in which any person may leave a deposit account, and may deposit any sum yearly, from $1 to $300, the Dominion paying interest at the rate of 4 per cent., compounded annually. Depositors may make their deposits in any P. O. Savings Bank, and on their removal, may continue at any other, and draw the entire amount of deposit from the P. O. Savings Bank nearest them, by applying to the Postmaster-General at Ottawa.

BANKS.—There were, on the 1st of Jan., 1876, 289 Banks and branches in the Dominion, and their condition was as follows:

Total Authorized Capital $68,966,666, of which $64,899,321 had been subscribed, and $61,270,220 paid up. The amount of their circulation was $20,831,009, of their deposits, $64,553,720; their total liabilities $89,271,144; of their assets, $6,276,273, or about 10 per cent. of their capital, was in specie, and $30,717,467 was immediately available, while their total assets amounted to $167,155,600 or almost twice their liabilities.

FIRE INSURANCE.—The following are the Statistics of Fire Insurance Companies doing business in Canada, January 1, 1876.

	Net Cash Prem.	Am't of Policies written within the year.	Am't at Risk, at date.	Losses paid.
Canadian Companies............	$1,646,654	$168,896,111	$190.284.543	$1,082,206
British Companies...............	1,683,715	166,953,268	154,835,931	1,299,612
American Companies...........	264,393	17,357,605	19,300,555	181,713

FISHERIES OF THE DOMINION.—The Fisheries form a very important portion of the industry and wealth of the Dominion of Canada. At the close of 1875, the following were the official statistics of their yield and value:

Nova Scotia	$5,573,851.58
New Brunswick..	$2,427,654.16
Quebec..	$1,594,259.15
Ontario..	453,194.00
British Columbia, Manitoba and North-Western Territories (estimated).	434,723.00
Newfoundland and Labrador (exports only)............................	2,983,485.00
	$13,468,166.89

This total is, doubtless, far below the truth, as many items are not recorded—such as the home consumption of Newfoundland and Labrador, the yield and value of the rivers, smaller lakes and streams of the interior, etc.

EDUCATION.—The School systems of Ontario, Quebec and New Brunswick, are quite efficient and furnish primary instruction which compares very favorably with that of many of the States of the American Union. Nova Scotia, Prince Edward's Island and Newfoundland are less complete and effective, while those of British Columbia and Manitoba are as yet in an unorganized condition.

Higher education is very liberally provided for. There are seven universities, and fifteen Colleges, (some of them affiliated with the universities) in the Dominion, and a large number of Collegiate Institutes, Female Colleges, Young Ladies' Seminaries, &c., &c. Most of the Universities have faculties of Theology, Law and Medicine, and several of them Scientific Schools also, presided over by eminent scientists. There are two Normal Schools and a model Training School in the Province of Ontario, and three Normal Schools in the Province of Quebec. There are also similar schools in New Brunswick and Nova Scotia. There are County High Schools in Ontario, and to some extent in Quebec and New Brunswick. At the close of the year 1875, there were in the Province of Ontario, 5,258 educational institutions of all kinds, with 494,065 pupils, and $4,212,360 was expended annually in their support. Of these, 4,834 were public schools, with 474,241 pupils.

RELIGIOUS DENOMINATIONS.—The Roman Catholics are the most numerous religious denomination, its adherents numbering, in 1871, 1,492,029; eighty-five per cent. of these were, however, in the Province of Quebec, and they had a plurality also in New Brunswick. In Ontario the Presbyterians were most numerous, while the Methodists and the Anglican Church were not far behind. The Baptists are next in numbers to these three denominations, and there are also some Lutherans, Congregationalists, and a small number of several minor denominations.

BROWN BROTHERS & CO.,

59 WALL STREET,

211 Chestnut St., Phila. NEW YORK. No. 66 State St., Boston.

AND

ALEXANDER BROWN & SONS,

Cor. Baltimore and Calvert Streets, Baltimore.

BUY AND SELL BILLS OF EXCHANGE

ON

GREAT BRITAIN & IRELAND, FRANCE, GERMANY, BELGIUM AND HOLLAND,

Issue Commercial and Travelers' Credits, in Sterling,

AVAILABLE IN ANY PART OF THE WORLD, AND IN FRANCS, FOR USE IN MARTINIQUE AND GUADALOUPE.

Make Telegraphic Transfers of Money,

Between this and other Countries, through London and Paris.

Make Collections of Drafts drawn abroad on all points in the United States and Canada,

And of Drafts drawn in the United States on Foreign Countries.

To Travelers.—Travelers' Credits issued either against cash deposited or satisfactory guarantee of repayment: In Dollars, for use in the United States and adjacent countries; or in Pounds Sterling, for use in any part of the world. Application for credits may be addressed to either of the above houses direct, or through any first-class Bank or Banker.

BROWN, SHIPLEY & CO.,
26 Chapel Street, Liverpool.

BROWN, SHIPLEY & CO.,
Founder's Court Lothbury London.

ATLANTIC WHITE LEAD & LINSEED OIL COMPANY

LEAD!

Pure White

The Atlantic White Lead

Is manufactured exclusively from the best Selected Refined Leads, and is ground in Refined Linseed Oil.

RED LEAD, LITHARGE, ORANGE MINERAL,

ATLANTIC WHITE LEAD PURE WARRANTED ROBERT COLGATE & Co. TRADE MARK

PURE LINSEED OIL,

Raw, Boiled, Refined.

Robert Colgate & Co.,

287 PEARL STREET,

New York.

ATLANTIC

Mutual Insurance Company,

NEW YORK.

OFFICE, 51 WALL STREET.

ORGANIZED 1842.

INSURES AGAINST MARINE AND INLAND NAVIGATION RISKS,

And will issue Policies making Loss payable in England.

Its Assets for the Security of its Policies, are more than

TEN MILLION DOLLARS.

In the course of its Business it has paid losses amounting to

$80,000,000,

and has returned to its dealers in Certificates of Profits, bearing interest,

$45,000,000,

of which amount there has been redeemed in cash

$37,000,000,

The Profits of the Company revert to the assured, and are divided annually, upon the Premiums terminated during the year, Certificates for which are issued, bearing interest until redeemed.

J. D. JONES, President.

CHAS. DENNIS, Vice-President.

W. H. H. MOORE, 2d Vice-Pres't.

A. A. RAVEN, 3d Vice-Pres't.

J. H. CHAPMAN, Secretary.

www.ingramcontent.com/pod-product-compliance
Lightning Source LLC
Chambersburg PA
CBHW030847270326
41928CB00007B/1250

* 9 7 8 3 3 3 7 1 8 4 9 4 0 *